Eng^d by A.H.Ritchie

Dan.l Baker

THE LIFE AND LABOURS OF THE REV. DANIEL BAKER, D.D.

PASTOR AND EVANGELIST.

PREPARED BY HIS SON,

REV. WILLIAM M. BAKER,

PASTOR OF THE PRESBYTERIAN CHURCH, AUSTIN, TEXAS.

And I, brethren, when I came to you, came not with excellency of speech, or of wisdom, declaring unto you the testimony of God. For I determined not to know any thing among you, save Jesus Christ, and him crucified. And my speech and my preaching was not with enticing words of man's wisdom, but in demonstration of the Spirit, and of power; that your faith should not stand in the wisdom of men, but in the power of God.—1 COR. ii. 1, 2, 4, 5.

Third Edition.

PHILADELPHIA:
PRESBYTERIAN BOARD OF PUBLICATION,
No. 821 CHESTNUT STREET.

CONTENTS.

CHAPTER I.

FROM HIS BIRTH UNTIL THE CLOSE OF HIS CLERKSHIP IN SAVANNAH.

CHAPTER II.

WHILE A STUDENT AT HAMPDEN SIDNEY COLLEGE.

CHAPTER III.

WHILE A STUDENT AT PRINCETON.

CHAPTER IV.

WINCHESTER, VIRGINIA.

CHAPTER V.

HARRISONBURG—WASHINGTON CITY.

CHAPTER VI.

PASTORATE IN SAVANNAH.

CHAPTER VII.

AS AN EVANGELIST.

CHAPTER VIII.

LABOURS IN OHIO—PASTORATE IN FRANKFORT AND TUSKALOOSA.

CHAPTER IX.

TUSKALOOSA—LABOURS AS AN EVANGELIST—MISSION TO TEXAS.

CHAPTER X.

LABOURS AS AN EVANGELIST—PASTORATE AT HOLLY SPRINGS.

CHAPTER XI.

SECOND MISSION TO TEXAS.

CHAPTER XII.

FOUNDING OF AUSTIN COLLEGE—LABOURS AS AN EVANGELIST AND AS AGENT OF THE COLLEGE.

CHAPTER XIII.

THIRD AND FOURTH TOURS AS AGENT OF AUSTIN COLLEGE.

CHAPTER XIV.

FIFTH AND SIXTH TOURS ABROAD, AND LABOURS IN TEXAS AS AGENT OF AUSTIN COLLEGE.

CHAPTER XV.

CLOSING SCENES.

PREFACE.

It would seem most natural that the preparation of this volume should have devolved upon the Rev. Daniel S. Baker, of Louisiana, an elder brother, rather than upon myself, the youngest of the family; yet, for twenty years, I have intended, should I survive my father, to prepare such a volume. With this intention secretly cherished, by urgent and long-continued entreaty, I prevailed upon my father, in the rare intervals of a life of incessant occupation, to write the narrative or autobiography which is the basis of this book—a narrative, therefore, not prepared for the purpose for which it is used, but solely for the gratification of his children. With the same object in view, I have made it a business, since I could first remember, to rescue from loss, in the frequent removals of the family, the various journals contained herein, as well as the letters of which such abundant use is made. Not only did God put this, as I trust, into my heart, but, in his providence, during the last years of my father's life, we were associated in ministerial labours in Texas. The last weeks of his life were spent with me in Austin, and upon my bosom was pillowed the venerable and beloved head of my father during his last hours on earth.

Thus has God devolved upon me the labour of love which I have endeavoured to perform in these pages. No one can wish more sincerely than myself that this duty had devolved upon one better qualified. I have derived, however, great help from the taste, judgment, and other assistance, of an elder brother, Howard M. Baker, Esq.

It was my intention to have thanked by name the many friends who have contributed toward the work, from all parts of the land. Their number, it is found, forbids this. The good which may be accomplished by the volume will be the most acceptable reward to them for their Christian kindness—a kindness not to the dead only, not to myself only, but to every reader of this book.

There are few who must not be aware of the delicacy of the task here undertaken. Hence my object has been to do little more than weave together the materials before me into a continuous and complete narrative. As much as possible I have permitted others to speak, rather than myself; but when I have spoken, it has been only upon points concerning which others were ignorant; and in these cases, I have expressed myself frankly and fully. It is believed that this volume possesses an historical value in the annals of the Church.

From the outset, I have looked to and relied upon One who is all-wise, to prompt and control and guide my pen. This volume is now sent forth along the many paths trodden by its subject, during his life-time of sixty-seven years, with fervent prayer that the Holy Spirit, which so accompanied this servant of God during his life, will also accompany and bless this endeavour at a rehearsal of his Life and Labours, pressing home upon the heart of each reader such instruction as may be contained herein.

Such as it is, I place this book humbly, yet hopefully, in the hands of the Church of God, and lay it, at least, as my choicest offering, at the feet of its Glorious Head.

W. M. B.

LIFE AND LABOURS

OF THE

Rev. DANIEL BAKER, D. D.

CHAPTER I.

FROM HIS BIRTH TILL THE CLOSE OF HIS CLERKSHIP IN SAVANNAH.

As it is one of the most precious promises of Scripture, that "the mercy of the Lord is from everlasting to everlasting upon them that fear him, and his righteousness unto children's children," it should be both a duty and a delight to acknowledge any marked fulfilment of this gracious promise. As far back as the ancestry of the subject of this Memoir can be traced, such fulfilment of the promise flowed down in winding but deepening current, generation after generation.

From the annals of the Midway church in Liberty county, Georgia, it appears, that "in the beginning of the year 1630, a Congregational church was gathered at Plymouth, in England, of persons who intended to come to America for the purpose of enjoying those religious privileges, which the measures of Archbishop Laud denied them at home." Observing a day of fasting and prayer to seek Divine assistance, they selected two ministers, who, accepting the office of spiritual guides, on the 30th of

March the church embarked. In May following they were put ashore near Boston. Here they were in "a forlorn wilderness, destitute of any habitation, and most other necessaries of life." Ascending Charles river, they finally settled at a place where they began to build a town, which they named Dorchester. An historian of that period bears witness to the character of this colony. "The first inhabitants of Dorchester," says Harris, "came chiefly from the counties of Devon, Dorset, and Somersetshire. They were a godly and religious people, and many of them persons of note and figure, being dignified with the title of *Mr.*, which but few in those days wore."

In October, 1695, a church was organized in Dorchester, "with a design to remove to Carolina, to encourage the settlement of churches, and the promotion of religion in the Southern plantations." Embarking, after solemn religious services, the church arrived, with its pastor, in Carolina, on the 20th of December, and formed a settlement upon the Ashley river, eighteen miles from Charleston, which, in memory of their former home, they called Dorchester. This settlement proving unhealthy, and the quantity of land too small, on the 11th of May, 1752, three persons were sent to Georgia, who selected a home for the church in Liberty county, as it is now known, at a place called Midway. A petition being prepared, the Council of Georgia made a grant of thirty-one thousand nine hundred and fifty acres. After many misfortunes by land and sea, the whole church was finally settled at their new home, with Rev. Mr. Osgood their pastor, in March, 1754, the Baker and Bacon families of the church preceding by two years the remainder of the colony. A log church was immediately built, and an agreement entered into among the members. It marks the character of these pious people, that, in this agreement, in order to leave their "children after them compactly settled together," no member should "sell his tract of land, or any part thereof, to any stranger or person out of the Society, without first giving the refusal of its purchase to the Society." In 1757, a larger house of worship was completed.

From the first, the people engaged heartily in the cause of their country. So obnoxious did they make themselves to the British, that, in November 1778, a special detachment of the British army from Florida attacked the settlement, "burned the church building, almost every dwelling-house, and the crops of rice then in stacks, drove off the negroes and horses, carried away the plate belonging to the planters, and outraged even the graves of the dead." A leading patriot among the members of the church was Benjamin Baker. In consequence of his zeal, his house was rifled and burned, and himself and son imprisoned. There remains a poem by this son, descriptive of the invasion, and the bitterness of its indignation is at the destruction of the church edifice. On the return of peace the settlement was re-established, but during 1788 was greatly annoyed by inroads of the Indians. In 1791, during a visit of Washington to Savannah, the church presented to him an address, which, with the answer of Washington, glows with all the fire of '76. It may be added here, that on the breaking out of the last war with England, the grave and godly members of the Midway congregation were in the front files of their country's defence. During all these years an acade my was maintained for the education of the children of the church, and an unbroken succession of pastors was kept up.

It was the privilege of the writer of these pages to visit, on one occasion, this home of his ancestors. Seated in view of the spot whereon this people of God had gathered, during so many years, for the worship of the God of their fathers; under the funereal moss which drapes the trees of the ancient grave-yard; upon a tombstone which records the name of the grandfather of the subject of this Memoir as a "worthy deacon" of the church, the writer mused upon the history and character of the multitudes slumbering around him in Christ. They were a race, the chief culture of whose heart, conscience, and understanding, was at the family altar, and in the closet; was in the Sabbath sanctuary, that central home of their souls; was in often repeated seasons of fasting and prayer, and gathered in real as well as outward brotherhood around the table of the Lord's Supper. With them religion was a matter of their brightest hopes, their warmest feelings, their deepest convictions; it was the knowledge in which their servants and children were chiefly instructed; the thing to which they instinctively and habitually subordinated every thing else. Knowing all this so well, the writer understood how, with the blessing so often and so fully promised of God in such a case, it was but in the order of things that there should have been trained up there so many holy men and women serving God in private life; so many ministers of the gospel to serve God over a vast empire, but just born when this spot was first settled; so many servants of God to go thence to preach Jesus, even beneath the palm-trees, and beside the pagodas of heathen lands. He understood, too, how it was that other churches from its bosom had grown up around it—daughters around the venerable mother; how it was that the community must be what it is still to this day; and how natural it was, under God, that from such a stock, and from under such influences, should result such a man as the one whose Life and Labours are herein portrayed.

This much by way of Introduction to "The Autobiography of Daniel Baker, prepared for the use of his Children."

Descended from Puritan parentage, I was born in Midway, Liberty county, Georgia, on the 17th of August, 1791. My father and my mother, both, were for many years reputable members of the Congregational church, which had been planted as a colony in what is known by the name of the Midway Settlement. Well do I recollect seeing the ruins of their second church edifice—a frame building on the west side of the road, and immediately south of the site of the present grave-yard. My venerated father was for many years a much esteemed deacon of the Midway church, as was his father before him, both bearing the same name—William Baker. I have no recollection of either of my grandparents, but have reason to believe both died before I was born. My father was married three times. By his first marriage, he had four sons and three daughters; by his second wife, who lived but a short time, he had no children; and by the third, only one—a son, named Joseph Stevens—who is still alive, and a distinguished preacher and editor, of the Baptist denomination.

I was the last child of my father by his first marriage; and as my mother took her flight to heaven when I was but an infant, I never knew a mother's smile. I have no recollection of my father's second wife—but the third I remember well, for she lived until I was quite a young man. My father died when I was about eight years of age, and I have some recollection of him, but my reminiscences are neither numerous nor very lively. I can well recollect, however, that he was a tall, slender man, and very erect and elastic in his gait. I can recollect the spot where stood the family stand, with the large old Bible upon it; and well do I remember that it was our practice not to kneel, but to stand during family prayer. It was usual for the whole family to spend what was called the sickly season on Colonel's Island; and this was always a very pleasant affair for me. I recollect well the room in which my father died, and that brother John and myself were playing under the shade of a large oak, when some one came and told us that my father was dying; and it put an end to all of our sports. My father when first taken sick was in some spiritual darkness; but his mind was completely relieved by having this passage of Scripture brought with great power and sweetness to his soul: "For after that in the wisdom of God the world by wisdom knew not God, it pleased God by the foolishness of preaching to save them that believe." I recollect that this was the subject of much conversation in the family after my dear father was laid in the grave.

Young as I was, I felt the death of my father very much, and very frequently would I, on the Sabbath, go into the grave-yard, and look upon the graves of my parents, who were buried side by side, near the gate on the right hand as you enter into the grave-yard. I know not how often, when I was a little boy, that I visited the hallowed spot; nor can I tell how many tears I there shed; certainly it had a melancholy but peculiar charm for me; particularly as being the resting-place of my dear mother, of whom I had heard much, but had never seen. A poor little orphan boy, I would think a great deal about my own dear mother, and wished that I was with her in heaven. Sometimes I would look around, and when I saw other children who had mothers to love them, and give them good things, it made me very sad to think that I had no dear mother on earth, to love me and give me good things. Sometimes I would take up the idea that nobody loved me; but I thought if my mother was on earth she would love me if nobody else did; but she was gone to heaven. "Well, I will meet my mother there."

One night, falling asleep probably more sorrowful than usual, I had a very sweet dream. I thought, all at once, that the room in which I slept, was filled with the angels of God. In the midst of them I thought I saw my own dear mother! I thought I knew her at first sight—my little heart leaped for joy. Pushing away the angels, I thought I rushed towards my mother, and wanted to throw my arms around her, and tell her how glad I was to see her, and that I had never seen her before. O, I was happy! I was so happy! But scarcely was I with my mother a single moment, when I thought the angels began to spread their wings and rise from the floor!—and I would not have cared if every angel had gone back to heaven, if they had only left my mother behind; but I thought my mother was an angel herself now; and she too had wings, and she too began to rise and ascend. Immediately they all began to sing very sweetly, and while I was looking on, they continued to ascend and sing, until their forms faded upon my sight, and their voices were lost in the skies. I remember the tune which they sung to this day; and so far as I can recollect, I had never heard it before; nor since, until some twelve years after. I heard it one morning at family worship at Dr. Hoge's, with whom I boarded, at Hampden Sidney, where I had gone to prepare for the ministry. This dream was indeed a very pleasant dream for a little orphan like myself; and the next morning I resolved (if I could) to meet my mother in heaven; and the idea of not meeting my mother in heaven was more than I could bear. When I heard the tune sung in Dr. Hoge's family, the very tune which I had never heard before, so far as I can recollect, except in my dream, I confess it caused the dream of my childhood to rush upon my memory with great sweetness; and even to this moment it has a charm for me which no other tune ever had or can have. My dream made a great impression upon me, and my impressions were deepened by my aunt Margaret Dunham, my mother's sister, who was very pious, and with whom I was a great favourite.

It would seem that the heart of this aunt was often moved at the sight of her little orphan nephew. On more than one occasion, touched by his forlorn appearance, she took him into her room, locked the door with a mysterious air, and then producing a bag from her chest, in which were the gains of many a long hour at the spinning-wheel and the loom, and of many a dozen of eggs and pounds of butter and cheese, she would jingle its golden contents in his ear, with the consolatory remark, "Never mind—never mind, Dan'l, this shall be yours when I am gone." But, alas, how it was is not known, the sound of the coin was all the advantage the money ever was to the nephew.

A venerable lady, still living, can remember him, when about eight years of age, passing her door every day to the school-house, two miles distant from his home, in company with his brothers William and John, and his sisters Rebecca and Sally, all older than himself. They carried their dinner with them in a pan, and, on their return, little Dan was almost invariably the bearer of the pan. She remembers pitying the little fellow, manfully trudging along, with one hand supporting the dinner-pan, a heavy one, and the other nervously grasping the waistband of his trowers, there being no suspenders in those days.

I recollect (the narrative proceeds) one day that I wrote a friend a very religious letter, and showed it to my aunt, who read it and bestowed upon it great praise; but, although my religious impressions were somewhat deep, yet they were not very evangelical, for, I recollect, that one day I went out into the corn-field and prayed; but knowing little of the hidden evils of my heart, I was very self-righteous. I recollect I did not like the prayer of the Publican at all. This thing offended me, "he would not even so much as lift up his eyes to heaven:"—thinks I, not even so much as lift up his eyes to heaven! that was very wrong! So lifting up my eyes, I began my prayer, Pharisee-like, and said, "God, I thank thee that I am not so bad as other people are;" and then left my place of retirement very much pleased with myself; sometimes serious and sometimes not. I thus went on (never once, however, I believe, omitting my evening prayer, "Now I lay me down to sleep,") until I was about twelve years of age, when, one Friday afternoon, after getting my Shorter Catechism lesson in school, I turned over towards the end of the book, and read a dialogue, in verse, between *Christ, Youth, and the Devil.* This made a very great impression upon me, and my serious impressions, if I recollect right, were very much deepened by a frightful dream which I had. I thought I died suddenly, and woke up in hell! The first overwhelming thought was, that I was actually in eternity, and my day of grace was over for ever! O, I thought I would give the world if I could only go back to the earth, and have only one hour more to seek salvation in! Waking up from this awful dream, I was much rejoiced to find myself in this world once more; but I thought my case was a peculiar one, and that there could be no hope for me. I felt sure that my brother John would go to heaven, for he was good, and every body loved him; but I was very bad, and nobody loved me. I much feared that I should never meet my mother in heaven, after all. I did wish that I was a bird, or insect, or any thing that had not to meet God in the judgment day! Before I was fourteen years of age I was taken from school, and living with my eldest brother, I was much alone, and was very fond of reading religious books.

One day I was thrown into a state of great alarm. There came up a dreadful storm—one flash of lightning came after another in such rapid succession, and such loud thunder it seemed I had never heard in all my life. I was alone, and expected every moment to be struck dead. Very much alarmed, I made a solemn vow that if God would spare my life I would serve him as long as I lived. My life was spared, and, thank God, my seriousness did not pass away. About this time my eldest brother was seen to go to a certain place of retirement every evening, about the going down of the sun. I noticed it, and suspected what it meant. This encouraged me in my good resolutions. I was anxious about my soul, but had no one, about this time, to speak to me, except a coloured man by the name of Joe, whom I occasionally saw when I went to Canoochee, to visit my sister Rebecca. After going on in darkness for many months, fearing the worst, and not knowing what to do, I took up the hymn-book one day, and read the hymn beginning with these words:

> "Come, humble sinner, in whose breast."

Coming to these lines,

> "But if I perish, I will pray,
> And perish only there,"

my mind was made up. I went out into the grove, and resolved that if I perished, I would perish at my Saviour's feet. If I did perish, I would perish praying. I went out in great distress, I returned with great joy. In prayer my mind experienced a sweet relief; I had new views of my Saviour, and saw that Christ could save even so great a sinner as I was. Frequently since then I have thought upon these words, as applicable to my case, "the darkest time is just before the dawn." I became one of the happiest creatures upon earth, and thought if I only had a little pair of wings, I could fly. Every thing around me seemed very lovely; and O, if I could only be a preacher! I recollect one evening walking in the piazza at "Cato's place," so called—I thought what a great thing it would be if I could go to College! But that was a thing far out of my reach, and far away; there was no such good thing for me.

The greatest favour I expected from my brother was that he would one day take me with him to Savannah, some thirty-five miles distant. I wondered how a city looked. My brother promised that if I would attend to a little shop he had, that he would take me to Savannah the coming winter. Time after time I was disappointed, but finally the period came; my brother set out with a bale of cotton in a cart; and whilst he rode on horseback, and a servant was walking at the side of the cart, I had the great privilege of riding upon the bale of cotton in the cart. Mounted upon my elevated seat, and going to see a great city, of which I had long heard, I was almost as happy as a young king who had just mounted his throne. I was going to Savannah! I was going to the very place where my father was wont to go, and from which place he used to bring so many good things in his saddle-bags for me, and others left behind. Reaching the city in the evening, I looked around and wondered at the number of houses which I saw; and some were so fine! I was not ashamed of the humble chariot in which I had entered this great city, and was pleased with every thing I saw. The next morning my brother, having me at his side, went round to several stores under the bluff, and tried to get me a situation as clerk, and finally, to my great joy, succeeded.

Taken into the dry-goods and grocery store of Mr. M., I was very awkward, and was so unfortunate as to misplace the key, which occasioned me immense mortification and trouble. After much searching, however, the key was found, and I was once more happy. Although awkward, I endeavoured to please, and soon found that my employer liked me very much, and had so much confidence in me, that sometime after, going to the North for goods, he left the store and all its interests in my hands. I can truly say, that without the permission of my employer, I

3

never took a cent from his drawer, for I was very conscientious. I had great simplicity of character, and my moral and religious feelings were deeply seated in my soul. Unfortunately, however, hearing one day that the body of a murdered man had been drawn out of the river, I imprudently left the store open, to see the sight, and upon my return, found, to my consternation, that nearly all the silver, amounting to some forty dollars, had been taken out of the drawer! To this day the thief has not been found, so far as I know; but in all probability, before this, he has had to answer for it at the bar of his Maker.

Mr. M. had some very excellent traits of character, but he was very profane, loose in his morals, and, perhaps, never went to church. Having no family himself, he boarded me out. At this boarding-house, so far as I can now recollect, not one had any fear of God before his eyes; and all the youths with whom I associated, I think with only one exception, were profane, and all desecrated the Sabbath. At first, I was very much shocked at these "carryings on," and even ventured to reprove them, but gradually I began to look with less horror upon their conduct; and as "attrition wears the solid rock," in process of time I began, to some extent, to copy their example. I began to neglect secret prayer, and would occasionally take a stroll into the country on the Sabbath, instead of going to church; and sometimes would go into confectionary shops and beer-gardens; but this I consented to not speedily, nor without many checks of conscience. My companions, all of them as I have said, except one, were profane, and they would laugh at me for my religious turn, and would call me "parson." This was almost too much for me; and I recollect that once I attempted to swear, but the oath died, unuttered, upon my tongue; and so sharp were the rebukes of my conscience, that I never attempted it any more.

After living with Mr. M. about three years, I was taken into the employment of Messrs. L., cotton factors, who were gentlemen of high standing, and who were doing a fine commission business. This was high promotion, but so far as religion was concerned, it brought no great advantage to me, for although the family in which I now resided was very genteel, yet there was no Bible in the house, nor any trace of religion. Being now introduced into a better circle, I must needs become a little more polished, and therefore went to the dancing-school: and now, getting to be a young man, I soon bought me a suit of uniform, and had the honour of being enrolled amongst the *Rangers*, and of course, when the Fourth of July came, we must, like the other volunteer companies, celebrate it with mirth and feasting. On one occasion, before I became a Ranger, however, I was appointed a Fourth of July orator. A copy of my oration was requested for publication. I, of course, with all due modesty, yielded, and a few days after, I saw myself in print, as large as life. Some compliments were paid, and I began to fancy that I was a person of some consequence, and began to write for the public papers.

About this time I began to enlarge the circle of my acquaintance, and attended several private balls.

To crown the matter, on one occasion, I was made one of the managers of a public ball, given by certain young men in the Exchange; and by this time, I confess, the tide of worldly feeling and worldly amusement had nearly swept me away; but as the providence of God would have it, several things occurred to hold me in check. I came very near shooting myself, accidentally, when out hunting one day; and on another occasion, I was upon the point of being drowned, in the Savannah river, when bathing on the Sabbath day! and to crown the matter, I was taken very sick, and within a few hours was brought very low, even, apparently, to the borders of the grave. But none of these things so wrought upon me as the sudden and unexpected death of a wicked companion of mine. This death was announced from the pulpit by Doctor Kollock, after preaching a very eloquent and powerful discourse. I was in church at the time, and the announcement came upon my ear as a clap of thunder from a clear sky. I had been playing cards with him a few nights before; he was then the very picture of health. And is Vanderlot dead! O, dreadful! thought I; he certainly was not prepared. And what if I had been taken! That afternoon I attended his funeral. I will never forget the occasion; I felt awful. My young companion taken away in his sins!—suddenly and without warning! What—said I to myself, over and over again—what if I had been taken! I was as a blind man whose eyes had been opened just as he had reached the brink of an awful precipice. By the grace of God, my soul was thoroughly aroused; my mind was made up, and I resolved that I would no longer neglect the salvation of my soul. I resumed private prayer. I wanted a Bible to read, particularly at night; but I had neither Bible nor Testament, nor was there one in the house. O, I would be willing to give almost any thing in the world for a Bible! What was to be done? There was a bookstore in the city, and there were Bibles and Testaments there, but a companion of mine was there as clerk, and how could I brave his ridicule. Night after night I thought I would certainly muster courage, but when the next day came, my courage failed. One night, however, I was in a kind of agony because I had no Bible or Testament; and I then firmly resolved that I would, at all hazard, purchase one the next day. The day came, and as we are told, it required uncommon resolution to pass certain forms, seated, as it is fabled, at the gate of Elysium; so it seemed almost too much for me to look Mills in the face, and from him to buy a Testament; but I had firmly resolved, and buy a Testament I would. In pursuance of this resolution, after breakfast, bracing my courage up, I boldly entered the store, and said, "Mills, have you any Testaments for sale?" but quickly added, "But I don't want it for myself." What a wonder the Spirit of God did not leave me that moment! What Bunyan in his Pilgrim's Progress has said about shame, I found to be but too true. As a *Ranger*, I could perhaps have looked an enemy in the face without flinching; but to do that which I believed would expose me to ridicule—this was more than I could well do. Having obtained the long wished for prize, I bore it off in secret triumph. In my estimation it was a prize indeed. I suppose I would not have parted with it for ten times what it cost. O, it was a precious book to me! and I think I could say with Jeremiah, "Thy words were found, and I did eat them."

About this time I recollect going to a prayer-meeting, and not having courage enough to go in, I remained without in the street, and was much impressed by what I heard; and now having made up my mind to serve the Lord as long as I lived, I thought, O how I would like to become a minister of the gospel! Not that I had much spiritual comfort, but I wished religion to be the very element in which I should live, and move, and have my being. I had enjoyed religion once; I had wandered; I did not wish to wander any more. I thought entering upon the ministry would be a new bond upon my soul. Indeed, I felt as if I could be happy in no other pursuit or calling. To be a herald of salvation, this was my chief desire; this was the height of my ambition; but I had no education, and how to obtain one I knew not; besides I was nearly nineteen years of age. I thought I was too old to enter upon a course of learning; but even if not too old, the means—where could I get the means?

Just at this time, my brother W. came to Savannah, and I recollect that one night, in the street and near the old church, he and myself had a long talk upon the subject, and he mentioned a fact which seemed very surprising. He said that just before he left home, in Liberty county, a letter had been received from the Rev. C. Gildersleeve, late pastor of Midway church, stating, that spending a night with Dr. Moses Hoge, President of Hampden Sidney College, this very worthy man asked him if he knew of any young man of piety who wished to enter the ministry in the Presbyterian Church, and had not the means; adding, that provision was made at that College for the very purpose of aiding such as needed it. The circumstance appeared very remarkable; and the providence of God had removed one grand difficulty out of the way—but there was another difficulty; the term of my service with my employers was not out; would not be for some eighteen months. What was to be done? One of the firm, and the very one who, as I learned afterwards, would never have given his consent to release me from my engagement, was absent at the North. Those at home finally, but with great reluctance, did consent. Thus was a second grand difficulty taken out of the way. There was yet another; Mr. G. F. P. and myself were to form a partnership. He had already commenced merchandizing, and I was to become a partner in trade with him, so soon as my engagement with the firm of J. L. & Co. should come to an end. Besides, Mr. L. was to do something handsome for me. This difficulty, however, was soon settled; and now for the North and a College! and never, perhaps, did any creature ever enter upon any new and brilliant career with more delight.

CHAPTER II.

WHILE A STUDENT AT HAMPDEN SIDNEY COLLEGE.

SEARCHING among the papers of his father, the writer has found the loose sheets of a Journal, yellow with age, tattered, and almost illegible; intended by him who kept it only for his own eye. This Journal is the more valuable, as it unveils the inmost springs and emotions of his soul. Extracts from it will be inserted as the course of the narrative may demand.

The narrative proceeds:

Being furnished with one hundred dollars, (a part of my patrimony,) I embarked in a schooner, early in the summer of 1811, for Baltimore; and taking a certain land route, I reached Hampden Sidney College, I think, about the 1st of July. On presenting my letters to Doctor Hoge, he received me with great kindness, and I and two or three other young men, candidates for the ministry, were taken into his house as boarders. I took up the Latin grammar for the first time, and entered upon my studies with great zeal. I recollect I studied very hard; and for a length of time I had a dark circle around my eyes. It was customary with me, for the sake of exercise, to walk three miles every day, except the Sabbath; one mile in the morning, one at noon, and one in the evening. This kind of exercise was of no service to me; for I would employ much of the time, whilst walking, in committing to memory some speech or lesson; and sometimes upon returning, I would throw myself upon the bed, completely exhausted both in body and in mind. One day after studying very hard, I caught hold of the limb of a tree, to swing; the next thing I knew, I was lying prostrate upon the ground, my head downwards on the slope of a hill. How long I remained unconscious I know not. This seemed a serious affair, but it did not abate my ardour in study. I was now turned of nineteen years, and I had no time to lose.

I recollect that near this time I was for about two or three weeks in a state of great despondency. I found it hard to commit the Latin grammar to memory; and by reason of several things, I thought I never could be made a preacher—never would be able to preach to any white congregation in any place. One day, being greatly discouraged, when in a state of the deepest despondency, all at once—and I recollect it well—all at once the idea flashed across my mind, that there are many negroes in the land, and perhaps I might be able to preach to the negroes! This was a new and happy thought. It cheered me greatly, and in one moment my despondency left me, and I resumed my studies with new life and pleasure. At this time I formed an acquaintance with several interesting young men, who, equally with myself, had the ministry in view. Amongst these was one of uncommon loveliness and piety, W. C. W., who became my bosom friend. Our natural dispositions were widely different, and yet our friendship was very much like that of David and Jonathan. Our correspondence, when absent, was unreserved and of long continuance; our letters would make a large volume.

I had not made any public profession of religion before leaving Savannah, and after reaching Hampden Sidney College, I was for a length of time in great spiritual darkness, even on the borders of despair. I remembered my broken vows, and all my wanderings in Savannah, and seriously feared that I had sinned away my day of grace. The unpardonable sin! The unpardonable sin! I was very much afraid I had committed that; but one day, reading a book called "Russel's Seven Sermons," I met with a sentence in the last sermon which gave me great comfort. It was to this effect, that if a man has any serious concern about the salvation of his soul, and has any tender thoughts in relation to the Redeemer, that was proof positive that he had not committed the unpardonable sin. Immediately my burden was gone, every cloud was scattered, and my feelings became most delightful. It was like the beauty of spring after a long and dreary winter. I had new views of my Saviour, felt that I could rest upon him, and was enabled to rejoice with joy unspeakable and full of glory. The question has since been often started in my mind, When was I converted? At what particular place and time? Was it in Midway, or Prince Edward? Was it when I was about fourteen, or when I was about nineteen? The conclusion to which I have come, after much thought, is, that it was when I was in Midway, about fourteen years of age. I am strongly inclined to think that in early youth I was converted, and having wandered, was, in early manhood, happily, through abounding grace, brought back to the Shepherd and Bishop of my soul.

Breaking off from the narrative, we turn to his journal, commencing as follows:

Sunday, *August*, 1811. I purpose committing to paper the most remarkable incidents of my life, my reflections thereon, and those resolutions the several occasions may suggest, in order that I may, with greater advantage, frequently review my life and renew my resolutions; that I may, by the assistance of divine grace, be stimulated to the active exercise of every Christian virtue, and with unwearied diligence aspire to greater attainments in piety and usefulness. And may the God of grace, who strengthens the weak by the invigorating influences of his Holy Spirit, on which alone I would rest, enable me to benefit by these feeble means, and strengthen me to a faithful compliance with such resolutions as he may dispose me occasionally to make.

1. *Resolved*, That I am too prone to indulge in improper levity in conversation; that in future I will endeavour to avoid every wicked sally of mirth or pleasantry, particularly on the Lord's day.

2. *Resolved*, That I much too highly estimate my oratorical attainments; that I am too fond of, and too apt to court, vulgar applause; that I will endeavour to think meanly of myself, and make it my supreme object to obtain the approbating smiles of my God, and that of my own conscience.

3. *Resolved*, That I will frequently pray to Almighty God to point out all my vices and follies,

and supplicate his grace to dispose me to turn from them.

Sunday, September 7th, 1811. This day Dr. Hoge preached a sermon eminently calculated to arouse saints to a clear evidence of their interest in the covenant of grace. After divine service I retired to pour out my warm desires before my prayer-hearing God.

Sunday Evening, November 17th, 1811. This day being deprived of the outward church ordinances, the second meeting of a praying society was held at Dr. Hoge's, attended by the teachers and six or eight students; a solemn attention was given by all, and there were some who appeared peculiarly affected in the several exercises of praying and singing; in fine, it seemed manifest that our gracious Saviour had condescended to be in the midst of us. * * * * Satan, begone! I am now your inveterate foe, and, by the grace of God, I trust I ever will continue irreconcilable to you. "Get thee behind me, Satan!" I have made an unreserved, a cheerful surrender of myself and all that I possess to my lawful Prince, and I cannot recall my words. Assail me now no more with your insidious darts, for Jesus, in whom alone I trust, has already vanquished you, and will, I humbly hope, give me strength to overcome all your efforts to destroy my soul. Yes, adorable Jesus! I am thine—soul and body—all thine. I would again renew the solemn covenant I made with thee; keep through thine own name what I have committed unto thee until the decisive day. I am of myself weak and helpless, and would become an easy victim to the subtle enemy, but do thou arm me with thy grace, and I shall triumph over all his machinations, over all his efforts to subjugate my soul to base captivity. O, gracious Lord! I pray thee, leave me not one moment to myself, but let "thy rod and thy staff" comfort and protect me, while I pass through "the howling wilderness of life," and finally bring me to that happy state where my soul shall no longer be harassed and distressed by the assaults of the evil one, but where I shall unite my voice with thy saints above in for ever celebrating the praises of redeeming love.

Sunday, December 22d, 1811. Alas! how cold, how insensible my heart. I read and meditate, but no sweet emotion warms my soul. With what strange indifference do I view the compassions of the Redeemer; how slightly do I estimate his love; how languid my spiritual graces; how joyless do I pass the moments of this sweet day of rest; how unlike the calm and sweet delight I have frequently enjoyed in humble converse with God on his holy Sabbath. Alas! this hard, this sinful, this stubborn, rebellious heart of mine, that has caused the Holy Spirit to withdraw his influences; that has provoked the blessed God, and caused him to hide his face from me. My once sweet and consolatory evidences, where are they? All have disappeared, and thick, gloomy darkness hovers over my soul. O, when will the Sun of Righteousness again rise to dispel these thick mists, and shine resplendent upon my benighted mind; again to animate and enliven my languishing spirit by his cheering influences! O, hasten, bright morning, when I may again view the sweet smiles of a reconciled Redeemer! Dear Lord! I would humble myself before thee, and patiently wait thine appointed time; but in the mean time, O stir me up to renewed diligence; may I be more devout in thy worship; may I not faint nor be cast down, though I go mourning without thy presence. O may this lead me to deeper humility, deeper repentance for sin; may it lead me to see my absolute dependence on thee for all my comforts and enjoyments, as well as strength and support; and O, blessed God! in thy good time, lift upon me the light of thy countenance, pardon my many and aggravated sins, and cause my soul to "rejoice with joy unspeakable and full of glory," through the riches of grace that are treasured up in Christ Jesus.

4. *Resolved*, That I am but too much subject to sinful passions, inconsistent with that meekness and gentleness positively enjoined by the meek and lowly Jesus; that I will endeavour to get the better of them, and keep them all under proper subjection.

5. *Resolved*, That I am too prone to envy others more eminently pious, or in more favourable situations; that this is wicked and must not be indulged, but that I will endeavour, as much as may be in me, to imitate their good qualities.

6. *Resolved*, That I am not sufficiently zealous in the cause of Christ; on that account it shall be my indispensable duty frequently to pray that I may feel a more lively interest in the prosperity of Zion, that I may be inspired with a pure, ardent, and unabating zeal in so glorious a cause.

Sunday Evening, January 19th, 1812. This day,

after much coldness and insensibility of heart, it pleased God to revive my spirits, and grant me sweet comfort and refreshment in attending upon our praying society. I would desire to return the Great Fountain of all mercies my humble and sincere thanks for the establishment of this society, inasmuch as he has made it so beneficial to my soul, and that of my fellow-members, and has permitted sweet delight and comfort frequently to flow from it, to water and refresh our thirsty souls.

Sunday, P. M., February 2d, 1812. This day Dr. Hoge preached in College Hall, from Micah vi. 9, last clause—"Hear ye the rod, and who hath appointed it;" designed chiefly to improve the late calamitous conflagration of the Richmond theatre, in which perished about an hundred souls. Although this affliction was so recent, and of so awful a nature; although the discourse was so pathetic and applicable; although the transitory and uncertain nature of all sublunary, and the reality and importance of eternal things were exhibited so clearly and impressively, yet all could not move my flinty heart—cold, dull, languid, and insensible, I retired from the house of worship. O for the animating and invigorating influence of the blessed Spirit, without which I find all my precious privileges will be of no avail, will but increase the load of my already accumulated guilt. O Lord! let not thy wrath consume me as a cumberer of the ground, but O! do thou touch my heart as with a coal from off thy altar; quicken my drowsy powers, and make my heart to be easily impressed with thy word, thy providences, and thy Spirit.

Saturday Evening, February 15th, 1812. It has always been my decided opinion that I should be ever active and vigilant to discover and embrace every opportunity to benefit my fellow-men, however trifling in appearance, however faint might be the hope of success; for as God's ways are above our ways, and his thoughts above our thoughts, who knows but he might cause the feeblest effort to be powerful, to be of resistless energy, and to be productive of the most happy consequences. Thus impressed, and having learned a few days since that my friend and fellow-student, Mr. T. C., was unhappily infected with the principles of infidelity, I borrowed from him that pernicious, and infectious, and impious book, entitled "Thomas Paine's Age of Reason," intending to peruse it throughout, and then return it, accompanied with suitable remarks, reflections, and friendly admonitions. It came to hand—I commenced reading it; but disgust and horror deterred me from proceeding very far. O, Paine! Paine! unhappy wretch! what could have induced you thus to have prostituted your shining talents? If you were infected with such odious principles, why not keep them to yourself? Why disseminate them to corrupt youth, embitter old age, and fill the vaults of despair with thy infatuated votaries? Thanks to God for the commentary of thy death on thy works; may it please Him to unnerve the strength of thy subtle reasonings, and avert the fatal consequences to which they lead! I closed the book and returned it with a letter, the "*Christian Panoply*," and my fervent prayers.

Sunday, March 8th, 1812. Dr. Hoge in a lecture

delivered this evening, took occasion to introduce the present state of Christianity in the East Indies, when, to my inexpressible surprise and satisfaction, he mentioned a glorious discovery that has very recently been made, of nearly half a million of true Christians in that land which, hitherto, I considered as almost wholly enveloped in the darkness of heathenish ignorance. These Christians, it appears, have never participated in the corruptions of the church of Rome, but have, happily, preserved their faith inviolate, as delivered by the Apostle Paul and primitive Christians. O my soul! rejoice in the Lord, and sing praises to his name for his marvellous loving-kindness in preserving a chosen remnant to himself undefiled, whilst the great mass had degenerated into superstition and abominable idolatries. How pleasing must this discovery have been to the faithful missionaries zealously labouring in the vineyard of Christ! How must it rejoice the hearts of all who love the prosperity of Zion! Methinks this should cheer up and inspire with lively hopes the humble believer weeping for the desolations of the Church. This bears a flattering appearance; methinks I behold the dawn of a glorious day brightening in the East. O arise, Sun of Righteousness! speedily arise, and usher in the splendours of that day when pure and undefiled religion shall prevail throughout the world, and God shall dwell on earth again.

Sunday. This day I finished the perusal of *Witherspoon on Regeneration*, a work which has afforded me peculiar delight and satisfaction. I think I have derived much advantage from it; let it be my care to recommend it to others, and may God always accompany it with his blessing by whomsoever it may be read. In considering the characteristics of a regenerate person, as there and in other works laid down, and in carefully examining my heart, I think I have experienced some saving change, have had some sweet evidences of an interest in my Saviour's love. O rapturous thought! how vain, empty, and insignificant are all earthly enjoyments when compared with the enjoyments of a reconciled God and Saviour. Poor wretches, who feed on the vile husks of this world, when there are such riches treasured up in Christ Jesus! O how wonderful is it that God should have called upon me—me, so vile and ungrateful a rebel, to feed on the rich dainties of his love, while so many others have been passed by! O it was free, sovereign, discriminating grace! What shall I render to God for his marvellous love in making me to be a monument of the riches of his grace, when I deserved to have been a monument of his wrath! Bless the Lord, O my soul! and never cease to magnify and adore his holy name. Lord, may I henceforth live devoted to thee—live unreservedly to him who hath loved me and given himself for me. O Lord, I think I sincerely hate all sin, enable me for the future to resist more vigorously its assaults. I think I love thee unfeignedly; O enable me to increase more and more. O Lord, I long to praise thee in more noble strains. O teach my heart and my lips unceasingly to praise, magnify, and adore thy name, so long as I have any being. O Lord, my heart is very deceitful—preserve me from deceiving myself. "Search me, and try me, and see if there be any wicked way in me, and lead me into the way everlasting." Let me not rest with any attainments, but may I continually press forward in the divine life; may I daily become more and more assimilated to thine own glorious image, and more and more ripe for thy enjoyment hereafter.

Sunday, April 12th, 1812. This day cold and languid in my exercises; how unlike a short time since, when the candle of the Lord shone upon me; when I had those comforting evidences of an interest in the love of Christ; when I took such delight in the worship of my God; when I thought my heart was fixed. Ah, then I was too confident. I said in my heart, my mountain stands strong, I shall never be moved; but God has humbled me, and shown me that if he hide his face I must be cast down; if he withdraw the influences of his blessed Spirit, my heart must become callous, my prayers and meditations must be insincere and unprofitable. O, Lord, for the Redeemer's sake, remember not my provocations against thee, but be pleased again to lift upon me the light of thy reconciled countenance; again shed abroad in my heart thy blessed Spirit; and cause me for the future to have my life and conversation more holy, heavenly, and conformed to thy will.

The narrative proceeds:

Having obtained peace in believing, the next thing was to "join the church," but what church? My eldest brother and my only sister had become Baptists, and for some time my mind was not at rest in relation both to the proper mode and subjects of baptism. Dr. John Mason's Essays on "The Church of God," poured much light upon my mind, and being now at rest in this matter, I made application to Dr. Hoge, who was at that time pastor of the "College Church," and was received by him. I, for for the first time, on Sabbath, the 19th of April, 1812, sat down at the sacramental board. It proved a memorable season to me, and I believe to many others.

Journal.—Well, at length I have dismissed my scruples; I am the Lord's. Next Sabbath I hope to celebrate the dying love of my dear Redeemer. I have applied for admission, and I am now to seal my covenant with the Lord by that solemn ordinance—why not? I have long ago made a surrender of myself to him; I think he possesses my supreme affections, why should I delay to make this public confession of my love to him who died for me? Jesus invites me to his table, to feed on the rich dainties of his love, although I am unworthy of the least crumb; in the strength of the Lord, I will humbly approach his table, that my soul may be refreshed, that it may rejoice as with "marrow and fatness." O, what sweet, what unspeakable delight do I hope to enjoy at that banquet of love. O for a heavenly frame of mind. O that I may be clothed with the resplendent robes of Christ's righteousness, that when the King shall come to view his guests, I may not be found wanting a wedding-garment. O, my soul! I charge thee, diligently prepare for solemnizing thine espousals to Christ, thy Redeemer; avoid every thing that may cool thy affections, or unfit thee for so solemn an approach to him. I charge thee, O my tongue! to keep silent before the wicked, to restrain thy frowardness; to exercise thyself alone to the glory of God; this week especially let "holiness to the Lord" be inscribed on every sentence thou dost utter; and, especially, O thou wicked and corrupt heart, I charge thee, to leave off thy vain and sinful practices; to spurn the wicked suggestions of Satan; to invite in and cherish profitable thoughts and reflections; that thou grieve not God's Holy Spirit to withdraw. And now, O Lord, I am weak and helpless—I would implore strength of thee to carry into execution my resolutions. O dear Jesus! prepare me for celebrating thy dying love; may this week be a week of humiliation, self-examination, and fervent devotion. O enable me to live nearer thee than I have ever yet done. O give me some suitable sense of my sinfulness and unworthiness, and of thy matchless love!

Sunday, April 19th, 1812. This day arose somewhat earlier than usual, in order better to prepare for the exercises of the day; worldly cares happily banished, and tranquillity of mind reinstated, my soul looked up to God with longing desires for sweet communion with him; experienced considerable enlargement of soul in my morning devotions, although I had not as bright views of the excellencies of Christ as I wished, yet he was graciously pleased to discover himself unto me as the "chief among ten thousand, and altogether lovely;" altogether worthy my supreme affections, my implicit confidence; in fine, just such a Saviour as I and all perishing sinners stood in need of. O! how precious a Redeemer has God provided for his rebel enemies; "bless the Lord, O my soul!" An excellent sermon was delivered by the Rev. C.

Read, after which the sacrament of the Lord's Supper was administered. The courts of God's sanctuary were on this occasion crowded with "the excellent of the earth;" many, very many of God's dear children surrounded his board. O, what a happy sight! what a glorious company! O, what amazing grace and condescension in God, that he should have invited me to share the rich dainties of his children; that he should have permitted me to come to his table, and to taste and feel how precious Jesus is. Surely "his banner over me was love." O, how I love thee, dear Saviour! but how cold is the warmest emotion of my heart, when compared with thy love to me, who only merit thy hatred and detestation. Surely thy love is unprecedented, unparalleled. O, that thy love may be shed abroad in my heart; that it might kindle mine, and cause it to burn with all the ardours of heavenly affection. On a similar occasion I do not recollect ever having seen communicants more deeply impressed, more affected; all seemed to feel deeply a sense of their unworthiness, and the love and compassion of Christ, and gave vent to their feelings by tears and sobs; and even my heart was melted. O what a sweet frame to be in, with genuine repentance to mourn over sin; to have the soul drawn out in love to Jesus; to weep at the foot of the cross; surely it is an enjoyment worthy an immortal soul; surely it is the gate of heaven. Thanks be to God for the rich provisions of this day. Another sermon was preached by Mr. Rice, which, with a short exhortation by Dr. Hoge, closed the public exercises of the day.

And now, my soul, remember thou hast again

solemnly renewed thy covenant to be the Lord's; recollect thou hast made an entire surrender of thyself to Him who hath redeemed thee from hell—no clause of reservation; thou hast devoted thyself wholly and unreservedly to Him who hath bought thee with a price, an inestimable price, even with the precious blood of the Son of God; then let it be thy care, thy business, thy ardent desire to glorify Him with all thy powers. O, my soul, he is not a hard master thou hast now to serve; O no! "His yoke is easy, and his burden light." His service is delightful; recollect the sweet, the inexpressible satisfaction thou hast sometimes heretofore experienced in waiting upon Him, and let that animate thee; let the love, and the kindness and condescension of thy Master quicken thy diligence. And, O my soul! recollect that soon thou wilt become a disembodied spirit; and if thou shalt have acted thy part faithfully here, then, O then, what joys await thee! Thou shalt then behold the unveiled glories of the Lamb; him who died for thee, and whom thou dost so dearly love, and dost so ardently pant for the enjoyment of—even he shall sweetly smile on thee, and welcome thee to those happy seats of never ending joys, and will introduce thee to his Father, and then thou shalt be completely happy. O then, my soul, be not discouraged nor cast down; manfully endure afflictions, trials, and hardships, for the love of Christ; cast thy cares upon him; he cares for thee, is willing to undertake for thee, to be thy surety for good. O, then, give thyself up wholly to his mercy, guidance, and direction; be careful not to grieve his blessed Spirit, but ever pray for strength to live nearer him, and to obey all his commandments, which are surely all holy, just, and good; then may you confidently hope that he will keep you from falling, and finally "present you faultless before the presence of his glory with exceeding joy."

Narrative resumed:

After this most solemn ana memorable occasion, for a considerable length of time, (with some interruption,) I seemed to bathe in the love of God, as in the sunlight of heaven. Frequently would I go out into the woods to meditate and to pray, and not unfrequently, my soul being as the chariots of Amminadib, I would in my solitary walks break out into expressions of delight, and would for some considerable time go humming these and similar words, "Victory! Glory! Alleluia!" Filled with zeal and love, I had my heart greatly drawn out towards my fellow-students. I conversed with some, I wrote to others, and invited many to come to the prayer-meetings, weekly held in the house of the President; and I believe that my efforts to do good, in various ways, were not in vain.

The following extracts from his journal will disclose the exercises of his mind at this period:

Sunday, May 10th. Last week cruelly harassed and tossed about with temptations. Satan, as a roaring lion, sought to devour me. I was cast into despondency; God hid his face; my soul was troubled and shrouded in gloomy darkness. I was powerfully tempted to doubt the providence, nay, the very existence of God; my heart too boiled up with impure thoughts; I was "in much heaviness through manifold temptations." O the tyranny, the cruel tyranny of sin! Then I knew what it was to cry out in anguish, "O wretched man that I am! who shall deliver me from the body of this death?" Rom. vii. 24. Blessed be God, through Jesus Christ our Lord, who has this morning in some measure scattered the thick darkness that brooded over my soul. This day I have enjoyed much sweet consolation in the courts of his sanctuary; my thirsty, parched soul was refreshed from on high. O my soul, look back and bear in grateful remembrance how often God hath timely visited thee with gracious smiles, when thou wast faint, languid, and almost overpowered by the assaults of the wicked one. Be encouraged, for he is a shield and buckler to all that put their trust in him. Trust him then, O my soul; he will never leave thee nor forsake thee, if thou wilt always affectionately cleave to him, and never apostatize from him. Blessed be God for his many precious promises to his poor, weak creatures. Bless the Lord, O my soul!

I have been, and am now, sorely exercised in the furnace of affliction; the hand of God lays heavy upon me; I would wish to be resigned; I would wish to kiss the rod that smites me; but, alas! how rebellious is my heart; how prone am I to murmur and repine. O! what sweet and consolatory comforts are administered to the afflicted in the twelfth chapter to the Hebrews. There I learn that afflictions are sent by a kind and compassionate Being, to subserve some important purpose. "Whom the Lord loveth he chasteneth." Yes, my soul, thou art chastened for thy profit; then be comforted, be tranquil and submissive. Great God, grant me resignation!

O bring all my powers into sweet subjection to thy divine will; let me only glorify thy name in my afflictions, and I am content.

Sunday, June 28th. In the review of last week, I discover many things for which I have cause to be deeply penitent and humbled. One thing I would now record, is, that I permitted my passions to get too great an ascendency over me on Friday evening in the polemic society; my expressions to Mr. W. were unbecoming the relations we sustain to each other. His frank, forgiving disposition, raised him much in my estimation. Let it be my diligent care to imitate him in all those mild Christian virtues which appear so excellent and amiable in him, and which so well adorn the character of a Christian.

Mr. L. preached this day, from Isaiah xxvi. 20, 21, a sermon admirably adapted to the existing state of our national affairs, war having been been so recently declared against Great Britain. Now we are especially called upon to obey the injunction of the text, to flee to Christ, our only hiding place against the wrath of God and the fury of man. O that God would overrule the present perils and afflictions of America to his honour and glory, and the advancement of the Redeemer's kingdom.

This day too cold and lifeless in the worship of God; not sufficiently humble nor importunate in prayer; made but a poor improvement of the privileges of the day. O, if the heart-searching God should strictly mark my shortcomings, I must be condemned; but there is an all-sufficient Saviour; Jesus alone is my hope, my righteousness, and the

Rock of my salvation. O that I might praise him more highly, and love him more sincerely!

Sunday, August 2d, 1812. How languid and heartless in my devotions! How few affectionate thoughts do I have of my Saviour and my God! Hosannas languish on my tongue. In the distress of my soul I cry unto the Rock of my salvation, but I find no comfort; my soul longs and pants for sweet communion with God; but, alas! my flinty heart remains callous and unimpressed in reading, in meditation, and prayer. I do not feel the melting and enlivening influences of a Saviour's love beaming on my soul. I am as a wretched outcast—my sins—my accumulated sins have separated between my God and my soul. O where shall I find him against whom I have sinned, but whom I would still love. Dear Jesus! it is thy blood—thy peace-speaking blood alone that can bring me near to God; that will cause him to smile upon me. O lead me to thy Father, for I am poor and ignorant, blind and naked! How dim my views of spiritual things! How little do I know of God, my Maker and Redeemer. O, Spirit of light and love, descend; give me understanding, illumine my benighted mind; unveil to my adoring view the lovely, the transcendent beauties of Emmanuel, that my soul may be drawn out in love, supreme love to him.

BIRTHDAY. *Monday, August 17th*, 1812. Another year has now rolled away, and I still continue in the land of the living, a monument of God's great mercy; and now, my soul, where art thou? What advances hast thou made in the divine life? What new conformity to the image of thy Redeemer?

In the review of the last year I find many things to weep and lament over; many follies, many sins and backslidings to lay me low in repentance and humility, and I likewise find many things for adoring love and augmented gratitude to God. After a careful examination, I think I can discover that I have (through Christ strengthening me) made some progress in my heavenly course. I find that impetuous, imperious, and malignant passions do not exercise that tyranny over me which they did; by divine influences they have been in a measure restrained, and brought into sweet captivity to the obedience of Christ.

I find I have been led to discover more and more the excellence and necessity of humility, and that I have been enabled to practise it, although in a very imperfect degree.

I find I have become somewhat more resigned under afflictive dispensations, but, alas! I am still too prone to murmurings and repinings.

I find that my love to God has increased a little, O that it might be more intense! and that my knowledge in spiritual things has been somewhat augmented, and my faith in Christ and belief in revelation strengthened; but I must even now say, and mourn for it, that I know but little of the character and perfections of God, that I have but dim views of the beauties of Emmanuel; this I would bewail, and pray to have clearer views of God my Saviour, clearer views of the plan of redemption.

I think I have had better apprehensions of the nature, excellence, extent, and spirituality of the divine law; I think I have been convinced that the commandment is holy, just, and good, perfectly reasonable, and admirably conducive to the highest interests of man.

I think I have discovered that it is an evil and a bitter thing to sin against God, and that sin is inconceivably hateful and malignant, as committed against the best, the most beneficent, the most compassionate, as well as the greatest of beings; and that I, as a vile, guilty wretch, deserve his heavy, everlasting, and righteous displeasure.

I think I have had better views of my absolute need of a Saviour, of the suitableness of Christ, and have had more affecting views of his amazing love and compassion to poor, helpless, condemned sinners. O what a precious, precious Redeemer, God has provided for man! O my soul, praise, magnify, and adore the name of God, who made and redeemed thee!

I think I have been much more heavenly-minded, enjoy greater delight in meditating on God and on divine things; for all these things I do now humbly acknowledge God as the only author, to whom be all the praise and glory. I feel a conviction, which I need not disguise, that of myself I am prone to evil; that I cannot change my heart nor disposition; that I cannot do a single good action; while at the same time I would acknowledge the good hand of God, if I have been enabled to make any real advances in the divine life. I would desire to be deeply humbled for the slowness of my progress, my great shortcomings, and the misimprovement of many precious privileges.

I have experienced many vicissitudes of heavenly

affections during the last year; sometimes the light of God's countenance beamed upon me, which let in sweet comfort and joy into my soul; at other times, under the hidings of God's countenance, under the heavy pressure of temptations and afflictions, my enjoyments were dried up, and I went sorrowful. Sometimes, but especially about the first of Spring, I had clear manifestations of the love of God, brighter hopes of a joyful immortality. At one time in particular, I would gladly have breathed out my soul in the arms of my Redeemer; for about a month at a time, I thought "to depart and to be with Christ would be far better," yet I felt sweetly resigned to await my appointed season. At other times, heavy clouds hung over my soul, and shed a dismal gloom on all things. I began to imagine all my former experiences to be mere delusions; that I had never cordially closed in with the terms of the gospel; never truly repented; never sincerely loved my God; my views were low, my hopes almost extinguished; but, blessed be God, even in these seasons of darkness and distress, God did not utterly forsake me; some glimmerings from above would, now and then, cast a bright though transient gleam into my soul, and I was enabled to persevere. Always wait upon the Lord, O my soul, for though in anger he may hide his face for a short season, yet his loving-kindness will he not utterly take from thee.

And now as I am entering on another year, O Lord, I would enter on it only in thy strength; I would commit to thee my way. Be pleased to order it in mercy; guide me by thy counsels; secure me by thy grace. O give me nearness of access to thee.

O may I make greater attainments in holiness, and every Christian grace; may I live more devoted to thee the ensuing year than I have ever yet done, for Christ's sake. Amen.

Sunday, August 23d. I have this day seen the table of the Lord spread; with a longing appetite I approached it. I hope the Lord prepared my heart for that solemn ordinance. I had some views of the glories of Christ; of his amazing love to guilty, perishing men; and I think I had some sweet evidences of cancelled guilt, of an interest in his love. O that the impressions then made upon my mind might be permanent; that the resolutions I then made might be strictly attended to; and that at the celebration of each ordinance I might find myself always advancing from one degree of holiness to another in the Lord.

Friday, September 26th, 1812. Our summer session terminates this day; this morning I shall accompany my friends, the M's, to their rural seat; probably I shall spend the chief portion of this vacation abroad. My chief object for laying aside my studies at this time, is that I may recreate my body, relax my mind, and invigorate my strength, in order better to prepare me for resuming my studies in the winter session. Tc this purpose may the Lord sanctify my recreations.

This session closes in sweet tranquillity; students all united in harmony and affection. I love and respect all my fellow-students, but feel a peculiar attachment to Mr. Bolling. How many pleasing hours have I passed with him lately! Not long since he was as wild, thoughtless, and profane, probably, as any student at the Seminary; but, blessed be God, for a fortnight passed there has been a great and visible change in him for the better. He no longer, as formerly, glories in his wickedness, but at the foot of the cross, as a repentant prodigal, he mourns over his past follies. By frequent conversation with him, I find his impressions are strong and rational, such as I have abundant reason to believe have been made by the Holy Spirit; and such as, I trust, have already or shortly will issue in a saving and happy conversion. O may he be more and more enlightened, strengthened, and animated; may he be cheered with some sweet evidence of cancelled guilt; of an interest in the blood of atonement. His first impressions were made at our praying society; what encouragement to persevere in prayer and supplication! From his lately being much in my company, some of the students have taken occasion to call him "*Baker's disciple;*" if I thought this was really the case, I fear I should be puffed up with pride. O what joy must it afford a pious minister to be the means of the conversion of one precious soul! The students have endeavoured to laugh Mr. Bolling out of his religious notions, but he has been supported. He appears daily to acquire new strength and firmness. Blessed be God, for this trophy of redeeming grace! I hope it may have a happy influence on others. I hope many more may taste and see that the Lord is gracious.

A letter I wrote to Mr. A. some time ago, I have some reason to believe was not altogether unserviceable to him. He appears somewhat impressed; may God carry home conviction to his heart, and that of many others, and raise up a seed at this Seminary to serve him, and to show forth the praises of redeeming love. O that I knew how I might best promote the eternal interests of my fellow-students, who are likewise my fellow-immortals!

Sunday, December 14th, 1812. A goodly number of the pious students of this Seminary have united, (prompted, I hope, by a pure and fervent zeal,) and have formed a praying society, to be held every Sunday afternoon, in this neighbourhood, for the benefit of the poor, ignorant, and too much neglected negroes. O may God command his blessing to rest on this little organization, and grant that it may be a nursery of piety and vital religion. Our first meeting was held last Sabbath; the audience was quite small, and I am grieved to say, but too careless and inattentive; the number was increased this day; a few white people likewise attended. Mr. D. H. exhorted last Sunday and this, tolerably appropriate. O for fervent, prudent, unremitting zeal, that each of us may discharge our several duties with fidelity, earnestness, and affection! O that God would bless these our labours of love to our own edification, and the happy conversion of some one precious soul; how amply, how bountifully would our toils and hardships be recompensed. O for more love to God, more and more zeal, more and more heavenly-mindedness.

Sunday, December 22d, 1812. O what a painful void do I feel in my soul! Cheerless and disquieted, I read, and meditate, and breathe out my broken petitions; my heart is hard, insensible, and but too far estranged from my God. I do not experience that sweet calmness, serenity, and elevation of mind, which I recollect sometimes to have felt. Few are the joys which spring up in my soul. I have not that nearness of access to God, nor do I now have that sweet communion with him, which have, at some favoured seasons, shed abroad in my soul a joy, a peace, which the stranger intermeddles not with. Ah! how bitter is it to live under the hidings of God's face; how dreary and comfortless to the soul to feel no warm, cheering, and enlivening beam of the Sun of Righteousness; and now, O my soul, whose fault is it that thou dost now mourn, art disquieted and disconsolate, and art not rather drinking in those pleasures which Christ has promised to every thirsty soul? Let God be cleared, and thou brought to lie low in the dust of humiliation and repentance. It is but too true thou hast been but too careless, formal, and negligent, in the pursuit of the one thing needful; thou hast been but too remiss in the grand duty of self-examination; humble thyself before thy God; look to the cross of Christ; plead for forgiveness; plead for a return of the manifestation of his favour and loving-kindness: and O, be diligent and circumspect in thy conduct for the future, that wherein thou hast done iniquity thou mayest do so no more. And now, O most gracious and compassionate God, here I lie, at this awful distance from thee, a guilty, helpless, forlorn sinner. I cannot extenuate my guilt, before thee; I plead nothing but the merits of thy dear, well-beloved Son. O, my God, I am unhappy! I cannot live at this distance from thee, deprived of communion with thee; denied the communications of thy good Spirit, and the sweet smiles of thy countenance; my eyes must flow down with tears, and my soul must go mourning, weighed down with grief and sorrow. O my Maker! my Redeemer! it is indeed an evil and a bitter thing to sin against God, the Supreme, the gracious, the ever blessed God! O, guard, fortify, and secure me from every alluring temptation, every unhallowed affection, every wicked thought which may offend my God and pierce my soul with many sorrows. O give me that fervency of zeal, that devotedness of heart, that heavenly-mindedness which should characterize all thy true and acceptable worshippers.

Friday, January 1*st*, 1813. This morning I have been almost overwhelmed with a sense of the infinite majesty of Almighty God, and my own insignificancy and unworthiness. O how astonishing is the grandeur, love, and condescension of Jehovah! He who created and sustains universal nature; who keeps in quiet and unceasing motion the countless and stupendous systems of planetary worlds; who causes them all to roll along and revolve with inconceivable velocity, and most exact order and harmony. This great and glorious Being has been and is still mindful of man; man that is a worm, and the son of man that is a worm; nay, has devised a plan for his redemption; a plan, O how wonderful and astonishing! a plan for the execution of which the Lord of glory bowed the heavens, came down upon earth, was clothed in human flesh, and suffered a cruel and ignominious death; and all this, that guilty, apostate man might be redeemed from his pollutions, and introduced into the blissful presence of his Maker and his God. Be astonished, O heavens! be amazed, O earth! at this wonder of wonders; and thou, my soul, admire, and adore, and magnify thy Creator, Preserver, and Redeemer, and let the mystery of godliness be for ever the sweet, the delightful, the enrapturing theme of thy meditations. O that I might be more abstracted from the world; that I might worship my God with more devotedness of heart! O that I might feel the influence of a Saviour's love shed abroad in my soul; that I might be more zealous in his cause; that I might feel a more lively and affectionate solicitude for the eternal welfare of my fellow-men; that I might devote myself more unreservedly, more heartily and diligently to the service of the greatest and the best of Beings. My God! to thee I commit my way—bring it to pass.

Sunday Morning, June 13th, 1813. Last Sabbath the Lord's Supper was administered at C. On the whole it was a pleasant season to me. During the intermission for the purpose of spreading the table, I was happily enabled to indulge myself in appropriate meditations. I had some tolerably humbling sense of my unworthiness, sinfulness, and ingratitude. I was enabled to look with the eye of faith upon the Lamb of God, who taketh away the sin of the world. I thought I could really call him my dear Saviour, my Lord and my God; my heart was quite melted, and fearing lest I should attract notice, I found it necessary in some measure to restrain my feelings. When at the table, I was in a more calm and composed frame of mind, and I employed the most of those precious moments in reflecting that I was no longer my own, but Christ's, being bought with a price, and I thought that from that time I would certainly endeavour, in the strength of divine grace, to live more devoted to God, and keep a stricter guard on my future conduct. After rising from the solemn and beloved ordinance, I was much encouraged, roused, and animated, by an uncommonly excellent sermon, delivered by Dr. Hoge, from Rev. vii. 9; but, alas! what a changeable, frail, wretched creature I am! A little trifling occurrence after worship showed that I did not possess that meekness and sweetness of temper which I ought; I felt unusually irritable, peevish, and fretful, and felt too great a disposition to censure little improprieties in others. This last week, I have fallen far short of the good resolutions I formed at the Lord's table and elsewhere; I have been cold and languid in religious exercises, and shamefully remiss in the duty of self-examination. My miscarriages and shortcomings are continually before me;—if thou shouldest be strict to mark iniquities, O God! who could stand?

Saturday, July 31st. Dry, logical sermons, with rounded periods, delivered in a cold, formal, and heartless manner, I can never relish, however beautified by the superficial elegances of composition; and I question if the good effects which flow from such preaching will be sufficient to compensate the minister for all his care, labour, and refinement. I love warm, animating, lively, *evanggelominos* preaching, full of fire, breathing love and compassion. O may I never become a cold, lifeless, sentimental preacher, but may I imitate the zeal of a Whitefield, the tenderness of a Hervey, the affection of a Baxter, and blend all with the pure, sound, evangelical principles of a Doddridge.

Sunday, August 1st. Bless the Lord, O my soul, for the entertainment of his sanctuary this day; for the sweet refreshments of his table. I was at first dull, but the Lord was pleased to enliven me. O what a precious Saviour Jesus is, who died for the salvation of those who put their trust in him. O for more faith, more love, more humility, more zeal, and more of every thing which is calculated to adorn the doctrines of God, my Saviour. O shall I ever be honoured as the ambassador of the living God—shall I ever be called to preach the unsearchable riches of this, my crucified, my risen, my dear, my glorious Redeemer? I humbly hope so. O if I should, may I go forth in the fulness of the blessings of the gospel of Christ, with burning love, flaming zeal, tender compassion, and a melting heart. O God, grant this for Christ's sake, for to thee belongs the power, the glory, the dominion, for ever and ever, Amen and amen!

Narrative resumed.

Praying societies, as they were called, were held by Mr. W., Mr. B., Mr. H., and myself, in the vicinity of the College, for the special benefit of the blacks; although several white persons attended. At these meetings we exhorted; and although not very many persons attended, we did hope that by the blessing of Heaven, some good was done.

At this time there was war with England, and students in Virginia not being exempted from military duty, a draft was made for the army, I think one in ten. Having, on that occasion, my spirit stirred within me, (if I recollect aright,) I was very willing to be drafted. My friend, Mr. W., dreaded it, and, strange to tell, he was drafted and I was not. His friends, however, procured a substitute, and not very long after, he and myself both left Hampden Sidney for Princeton, New Jersey. Before we left, however, an alarm being given that Richmond was in danger, a call was made for volunteers. Roused by martial music, and the speeches which were made by Mr. John Randolph and others, Mr. B. and myself offered ourselves as volunteers; but the alarm proved a false one, and my friend Mr. B. and myself won our laurels very cheaply; but for years after, Mrs. Hoge, wife of the President of the College, was wont to tell a tale upon me to this effect, that in my eagerness to have a company made up, I almost rode a horse to death. The case was only this: I rode with great speed to Captain P., to prevail upon him to be our captain.

As the state of things in Virginia interfered with our studies, it was determined by our friends that Mr. W. and myself should go to Princeton, as I have already said; and getting a horse and gig, we set out for Winchester, intending to take that place in our route. When perhaps half way to Winchester, as Mr. W. was driving, and I was walking down a hill, the horse took fright and ran. The vehicle was soon upset, and my companion was thrown with violence upon the ground. Considerably injured, Mr. W. was unable to go with me any further, and I went alone; and here I would remark, that many times, before and since, have I been most providentially protected.

CHAPTER III.

WHILE A STUDENT AT PRINCETON.

HAVING reached Princeton, I offered myself, on the opening of the winter session of 1813, as a candidate for the Junior Class, and after examination was admitted. I was located in room 39, and had for my room-mate a most estimable and pious young man named Biggs. At this time religion was at a very low ebb in the College. There were about one hundred and forty-five students, and of these, only six, so far as I knew, made any profession of religion, and even two of these six seemed to care very little about the matter; for, although four of us, Price, Allen, Biggs, and myself, agreed to meet every evening for what was called family prayer, they kept entirely aloof. Feeling it my duty to do what I could for my fellow-students in Princeton, as at Hampden Sidney College, I selected certain individuals to be made the subjects of special prayer and effort, one named M. and the other V. The first, during the revival which subsequently took place in College, professed conversion, and in after years became a Presbyterian preacher. The other was an uncommonly lovely young man, and at one time bid fair for heaven; but sad to relate, even when comparatively young, he came down to the drunkard's grave. He was very amiable, very yielding, and could never say, No. During the whole of this session, religion was at a very low ebb indeed; it was deemed a matter of reproach to be professor; and by way of contempt, those who did make a profession of religion, particularly those who composed the praying band, were termed the "*Religiosi.*" Grieved to see the abounding of iniquity in College, I proposed to my three associates, Price Allen, and Biggs, that we should establish a weekly prayer-meeting for the especial purpose of praying for a revival of religion in College. This proposition was made some time during the second session, and was immediately and cordially acceded to. Accordingly, this prayer-meeting was held regularly until the close of the session, and none attended but the four already named, and one non-professor, S. C. Henry, who subsequently became, for many years, pastor of Cranberry church, New Jersey. At the commencement of the third session, as our prayers seemed not to have been heard, I was somewhat doubtful about continuing our weekly prayer-meeting, but, very happily, my associates were clear for continuing it, and it was well; for although we knew it not, the blessing was nigh, even at the doors.

At this time the war was still raging with Great Britain; and by the President of the United States, James Madison, a day was set apart for fasting, humiliation, and prayer. I recollect that day well. My feelings were much excited; and, after engaging in private devotions, I proposed to my room-mate that we should spend the whole day, as far as practicable, in visiting from room to room, and converse with our fellow-students on religious subjects: and I recollect distinctly saying to my room-mate, "Brother B., what does the Bible say?—'Is not this the fast that I have chosen, to loose the bands of wickedness?' Come," added I, "and let us do what we can to break the bands of wickedness this day." The proposition was also made to P. and A., who occupied the room just under ours; they cordially concurred, and we had four warm-hearted missionaries in College that day. We went from room to room, conversing on the subject of religion only.

In a report made by Dr. Green to the Trustees of the College, and extensively published, referring to the causes, humanly speaking, of the revival, he remarks:

"The few pious youth who were members of College before the revival, were happily instrumental in promoting it. They had, for more than a year, been earnestly engaged in prayer for this event. When they perceived the general and increasing seriousness, several of them made an agreement to speak privately and tenderly to their particular friends and acquaintance, on the subject of religion. And what they said was, in almost every instance, not only well received, but those with whom they conversed became immediately and earnestly engaged in those exercises which it is hoped have issued in genuine piety."

The narrative proceeds:

Some of the students seemed to be taken by surprise. They knew not what to make of it. At length some of them began to assume a very serious look, and even the tear began to trickle down the cheek. This sight, this novel sight, electrified our souls, and gave us new zeal. The services in the chapel were that day uncommonly solemn; and that evening we saw six or eight new faces at our "family prayer."

The next day an event occurred which produced a considerable excitement amongst the students, and served to increase the religious interest greatly. One of the students, W. J., a very profane young man, but of a warm heart, and great oratorical powers, had been out at a tavern the night before, with some others, gambling. Returning to College at a late hour, he was arrested in the campus by an officer of College, who, laying his hand upon him, said, "Ah, my young man! have I got you?" The moment this was said, W. J. (as he told me afterwards) was struck under conviction of sin. He felt that he had violated the laws of his Maker, as well as the laws of College. He was suspended by the faculty; but it being known that he was under conviction, he was permitted to remain on the College grounds for some two or three days. Much of this time was spent by the "young orator" in telling his fellow-students what a great sinner he had been, and urging them all to attend to the salvation of their souls, as the one thing needful. That night the room in which we held our family worship was crowded. A little after we changed our place of meeting to the largest room in College, and that was nearly full; some seventy or eighty students being present.

It became common now for A., P., B., and myself, when our turn came round, after reading a portion of Scripture, to make some remarks by way of exhortation, seated in our chair. The interest in the College continued to increase, and in about a week from the day of the national fast, I made this record in my diary, "Thank God! we can now say, there is a revival of religion in Nassau Hall College." Yes, our prayers had been answered at last, and the Lord had done for us far more than we ever dared to hope for. When it was known that the work was a genuine and powerful one, our worthy President, the Rev. Dr. Green, rejoiced greatly. He would every now and then send for A., P., B., and myself, to inquire about the religious excitement in College, and would occasionally hold special meetings for the young converts and serious inquirers. Some of these "Counsels and Cautions" were subsequently given to the public in the form of a tract. Dr. A. Alexander would also, every now and then, come in, and favour us with some very appropriate remarks. I recollect once he said, "The promises were like so many steps in a ladder, by which we might ascend to heaven." O, it was a beautiful sight to see some seventy or eighty young men under the influence of deep religious feeling, about forty-five of whom were rejoicing in Christ. It was worth an angel's visit from the skies, to see them walking, so lovingly, arm in arm, or in groups, talking about the great things the Lord had done for them.

The revival continued up to the very close of the session; and very touching were the scenes presented when they bid each other farewell. The room which brother B. and myself occupied was the place of chief resort, and was the birth-place of many a happy soul. All varieties of character came to converse with us, even some who were not much wrought upon, but who knew not what to make of the state of things in College. One, a very rich young man, finding that the suppers which he had been in the habit of giving late at night were not attended as usual, came one night into our room, and sitting down at my side, asked me "what all this meant?" and added, "Why, a man here looks like a fool if he has not religion now!" After telling him that religion was, indeed, the

"Chief concern of mortals here below,"

and urging him to secure for himself the "pearl of great price," "Well," said he, "I will try for one week, and if I do not get it, you see, sir, my character is gone!" With what sincerity he tried, I will not say, but I fear he never gained the prize: and although many others besides, were only almost persuaded to be Christians, some forty-five or fifty were, in the judgment of charity, soundly converted. About twenty or thirty, I should think, became ministers of the gospel, several of whom became pillars of the Church; two at the present time are distinguished bishops of the Episcopal Church; one has been, and perhaps still is, president of a College, another, according to a British print, is "the greatest divine now living," whilst another has become famous as a missionary to the Sandwich Islands; and I must not forget the Rev. Amzi Armstrong, whose death, a few years since, excited such painful and universal interest. O it was a glorious work of grace, and verily its blessed consequences will not only run along down the whole stream of time, but will not lose their traces throughout the wide ocean of eternity!

One who was at this time in the Seminary thus speaks, after the death of Dr. Baker, of those days:

"There are some men concerning whose developments of character and usefulness you are never disappointed. And such an one, in an eminent degree, we think, was the late Daniel Baker. I knew him first when he was yet a member of Nassau Hall College. There was prevailing at that time (1815,) in that institution, that remarkable revival of religion, of which Dr. Green has given so interesting a narrative. Being a student of the Theological Seminary, I had naturally something to do with this wonderful movement; and there commenced my acquaintance with our deceased friend.

"There were, according to my recollections, but a few professors of religion in College, and this rendered the more prominent the position of such an one as Mr. Baker. He was already of mature years, and being known as a man of great singleness and steadfastness of aim, he was universally respected, and much sought unto by those who were seriously concerned.

"In matters relating to religion, he seemed to have their unbounded confidence; and what with the peculiar elevation and sanctity of his mind, it is not wonderful they regarded him as a sort of superior being. Such indeed was the impression, to some extent, which he made upon my own mind, especially on one occasion. After attending to the usual duties of the day, he was found at the twilight hour, sitting in his room, with his head thrown back upon his chair, in a state of trance-like and holy abstraction. I cannot render this as an incident, or convey it as I would, as a description of character; but it seems to me now, that if ever mortal man could appropriate the language of seraphic adoration, our friend might have been saying,

> 'Into the heaven of heavens, I have presumed,
> An earthly guest, and drawn empyreal air.'

Besides the usual promise of fair talents, untiring industry, and great steadfastness of purpose in doing good, there was about this man a singular sweetness of disposition and loving character of his piety, (loving, we mean in spirit like that of Rutherford's letters and Solomon's Songs, not, of course, in language,) and these marked the man, and continued, I believe, more or less through life. None were ever disappointed in him, and it need not be said now that his usefulness, both in the ordinary and higher departments of religious labour, was such as few men of our day have reached."

The narrative proceeds:

A little incident may here be mentioned, showing what power religion has to warm and expand the heart. Early in the summer session of 1815, a Mr. Harned came from Philadelphia. Sabbath-schools had then lately been introduced in that city, and were becoming very popular. He came to Princeton, and proposed that the religious students in College should establish Sabbath-schools in Princeton and its vicinity. This was cordially seconded by a Mr. N., a young man of uncommon popularity in

College. The plan was, with the approbation of the faculty, submitted to the students, and it went like fire in the prairies. All were pleased with the idea of doing good in this way. A subscription was circulated, and in a short time more than three hundred dollars were subscribed.

At the close of this session I graduated. There were five "honours," and seven "distinctions." One of the honours was given to me, which was beyond my expectation, as I had entered the junior class when I was not well prepared for it, and during the revival I had many things to interrupt my studies. It will be seen, that as I first took hold of my grammar in July, 1811, and the senior vacation took place in 1815, my whole course occupied only four years, which was certainly too short a period for me to be thorough in any of my studies. A speech was assigned me for the "commencement;" but, having obtained permission, I left Princeton for Virginia, expecting to return in due time, and enter the Theological Seminary.

A distinguished minister, who was an intimate friend in College, speaking of him at this period, says: "He was a fine scribe, wrote many letters to pious friends and relatives; delighted in composing, and composed well. He was very fond of speaking, and would, in the early part of his education, compose and exhibit original pieces. No student in the College took such delight in their exercises. He was fonder of them than Latin or Greek. He did not like the long and tedious course of academic and collegiate life. I roomed with him one session, and say he was a man given to prayer. I think I prospered from my intercourse with him. I have never been intimate with any youth who was more consecrated to the Lord, and devout in his service. For me to write, that it was his meat and his drink to do the will of his Father in heaven, and to serve him in the gospel of his Son, would be no more than what all know, who are acquainted with his zeal and diligence in untiring and persevering efforts to save immortal souls. He was instant in season and out of season, in the work of his Master."

At this time, not yet twenty-four years of age, and in all the flush of ardent youth, religion, nevertheless, was the one thought of his mind, the one emotion of his heart. "My dear friend," says he, in one of many letters to a young lady in New England, dated Princeton, January 21st, 1815, "My dear friend, I am sorry that you should for a moment have supposed that your letters are displeasing to me. Believe me, they are really very interesting; more so on account of the tender and lively interest I take in your temporal and eternal happiness. And I will now request, that if at any time you should not receive letters from me as soon as you expect, you will attribute it to any thing rather than a diminution of my esteem for you, and an indifference to our epistolary correspondence. Your last letter gave me much satisfaction, yet it was of a mingled kind. I was pleased to find that your religious impressions are not less deep, nor your desires less fervent; but I lamented that you had not yet obtained peace and pardon. I had hoped that you would have had a new song put into your mouth, even praise unto our

God. I am, however, glad that you are not discouraged, and that you are earnestly endeavouring to secure to yourself that good part which will never be taken from you. O may you soon be brought to share the pardoning love of God! But, what do I say—perhaps you are even now a dear child of God, and are enabled to rejoice in the Lord, having no confidence in the flesh. If so, I rejoice with you, and would most tenderly urge you to renew your diligence, and press on toward the celestial city.

"In this world you will meet with many things to distract your attention and cool the fervour of your affection; but if you keep up a close walk with God, you will have strength sufficient unto your day. But probably my dear friend is still in heaviness on account of manifold temptations. If this is indeed your case, I sincerely desire to say something which may encourage and animate you. I think if I were present with you, I could speak more suitably and appropriately, because I should then have a better knowledge of the feelings and exercises of your mind; but this satisfaction is at present denied me.

"You are, my dear friend, engaged in seeking the salvation of your soul. It is a happy thing that you have been brought seriously to reflect upon eternal concerns. This is the first step in that path which leads to the heavenly world. You have also been brought to see your sinfulness, and your exposure to the curse of a violated law. You feel that you are in a lost and perishing condition, and that you need a Saviour. It is well that you feel these things But perhaps you have no distinct views of the

Saviour; your ideas are obscure, and you long to have clearer discoveries of the character of the dear Redeemer. Well, my friend, it is really important that you should be well acquainted with Him who loved you, and gave himself for you. For this you are permitted fervently to pray. O then, pray for the enlightening and invigorating influences of the Holy Spirit; for it is his province to irradiate the mind, open the eyes, soften the heart, and take of the things of Christ and show them unto us. Faith in the Lord Jesus is indispensably necessary, and we need expect no safe and durable peace until we feel our entire weakness, and rest upon him alone as the Lord our righteousness and strength.

"Perhaps you think your convictions of sin are not as deep as they ought to be, and this distresses you. But, Miss Betsy, you must not rest entirely upon your feelings; the question is not so much, if you have deep convictions of guilt and bitter repentance for sin, as whether they have been such as to lead you to the Saviour. There is a diversity of operations; and whatever means are made use of, whether love or terror, the event is equally happy; therefore, if you have any satisfactory evidence of being vitally united to the Lord Jesus, enjoy the comfort which it is calculated to inspire. Bless the Lord for what he has done for your soul, and pray that you may grow in grace, and have clearer discoveries of divine things. Press on, my dear friend, and O, may you be enabled to live to the praise of His grace, who hath called you out of darkness into his marvellous light.

"I am happy to inform you that the Lord has

visited us in mercy, and that there is now a revival of religion in Nassau Hall College. The inquiry has become quite general, What must I do to be saved? and a goodly number have already crowded around the standard of the cross. O, my friend, it would fill your heart with sacred joy to view those scenes which are now daily presented to my eyes. Many of the students who last week were gay and thoughtless, now hang down their heads like bulrushes, and go mourning after the Saviour. Some of them have already found Jesus precious to their souls, and are now joying in the God of their salvation, whilst others are in bitterness of soul on account of their sins and the hardness of their heart. This glorious work commenced last Thursday week, the day appointed by the supreme magistrate of our country as a day of fasting, humiliation, and prayer. It has been progressing ever since, and now I suppose there are about thirty or forty of the students more or less impressed. The College has become a Bethel, a house of prayer; and prayer is now set up in those rooms which have not resounded with the voice of supplication for forty years past. I hope we are all revived, and are enabled to take the cup of salvation, and call upon the name of the Lord. Join with me, my dear friend, in adoring the unsearchable riches of Jesus Christ.

"Blessed be God, there are many new-born heirs of glory here, who will ere long swell the triumph of the Saviour, and who will be everlasting monuments of redeeming love. O, my friend, I long to hear from you. I want to know whether you have yet entirely given your heart to God, and whether you have yet tasted that the Lord is gracious. If you have not yet, I most earnestly entreat you to renew your exertions. O do not let the world ensnare you; do not let its blandishments charm you; do not let any thing keep you from the dear Redeemer. Come to him, rest upon him, and receive him as the Lord, our righteousness and strength; then will the peace of God, which passeth understanding, keep your heart and mind in Christ Jesus; then will you love to meditate on divine things; then will you rejoice in the hope of the glory hereafter to be revealed.

"I am much pleased with the account you give of your Reading Society. May the blessing of God descend upon it as rain upon the mown grass, and as showers that water the earth. Have you introduced prayer as an exercise? I think it would be very proper, especially as you have so many of the followers of the Lamb. O, faint not, press on; strengthen your heart, and look unto Jesus as the great author and finisher of your faith. The time is short; it remaineth that those who weep be as those who weep not; although weeping may endure for a night, yet joy cometh in the morning. Our sorrows, trials, and temptations are but of short continuance, and although they cause us heaviness, yet,

"They will sooner waft us o'er
This life's tempestuous sea;
Soon we shall reach the peaceful share,
Of blessed eternity."

Yours, sincerely,

DANIEL BAKER.

CHAPTER IV.

WHILE AT WINCHESTER, VIRGINIA.

After consulting with my friends, it was finally thought best that I should study theology under the direction of Mr. Hill, pastor of the church at Winchester, and spend a part of my time in assisting Mr. Nichols in the Female Academy. This arrangement was made with my very free consent, as an important part of the plan was, that I should be married early in the next Spring.

A lady who knew him at this time thus writes in regard to him after his death:

"Well do I remember the first time I saw him; then I was but eleven years old. I was in the boarding-school. The house I lived in had been broken into one night, and Mrs. Nichols, my aunt, said she would call on Mr. Hill, and ask him to let one of the students board with us for our protection. Your dear, dear father came. He was my day and Sabbath-school teacher for, I think, two years. At one time I had displeased him, and he did not notice me with a smile as usual. He passed through the room where I sat with my book. I could not run and tell him how sad I was, but he saw it. I thought he had gone and not spoken to me. I threw my little apron over my face, and sobbed as if my heart would break. He came back and spoke so kindly I wept the more. He told me how wrong

I did to neglect my lessons, how I grieved him. He told me God would not love me; spoke sweetly, as he ever did, of the blessed Jesus. With new life I went to my task. On one occasion one of the servants came in and said they heard a great noise in the school-house, that was at a little distance from the house we lived in. It was night. One of the older girls, bolder than the rest of us, went to see what it was. Your dear father was there praying for us all."

Immediately on taking up my residence in Winchester, Mr. Hill set me to exhorting at his Wednesday evening meetings; and in the course of a month or two he went over the Blue Ridge on a long visit to his friends, in Charlotte county, and left me in charge of his two congregations, in Winchester, and Smithfield, fifteen miles distant. This was rolling a great burden upon me, raw and inexperienced as I was; but although deeply sensible of my unfitness for so great a work, I determined to do the best I could. I did not read much, but spent most of the time which I could command in the writing and committing of addresses for Wednesday evenings, and exhortations for the Sabbaths.

My first exhortation in the church was based upon these words, "Arise ye and depart, for this is not your rest." My second from 2 Kings v. 1; and my third from the 12th verse of the same chapter. On the first occasion I had a pretty full house; on the second, crowded, and the meetings continued to be well attended, until the return of the pastor, which, if I recollect aright, did not take place for about four months.

Finding that religion was at a low ebb, I tried to do something in the way of visiting, and determined to make one special effort to wake up the slumbering people of God. I prepared with great care an address to professors of religion, pointing out some of the duties which lukewarm Christians are apt to neglect: coming down to life and manners, I spoke in a very plain and pointed manner. When I finished I was scared, and much feared that I had given mortal offence. How was I surprised the next day to learn that my address had been extremely well received. Several of the members of the church remarked that it was just what they all deserved, and what they all needed. Encouraged, I went on and proposed establishing a prayer-meeting, to be held in the house in which I resided, every Friday evening. This also was well received. We appointed our first meeting, I think, about the last of October; it was well attended, and Mr. W. (already the Rev. Mr. W.) being in Winchester, on a visit, I got him to make the opening address. The Friday evening prayer-meeting was continued up to the return of the pastor, and I suppose even up to this time. Those meetings proved to be deeply interesting, and the room in which they were held was no doubt the birthplace of many a soul.

About this time, in connection with Mr. W. and some lay members of different communions, we started a Sabbath-school, to be held every Sabbath afternoon, at three o'clock; and I was made superintendent. We had a noble set of teachers, and the first day the school opened with one hundred and thirty scholars; which afterwards, I think, increased to two hundred. In this school I took a very great delight; and, I think, it contributed towards the pleasing work of grace which soon followed. For several months, indeed, during nearly the whole of the winter, we had a measure of religious excitement, not powerful, but very pleasing, in which something like twenty-five individuals professed to find peace in believing.

Upon the close of the session in the Female Academy, I paid another visit to my betrothed, and on the 28th of March, 1816, we were married, at noonday, by Dr. Moses Hoge.

In the earlier days of Virginia, there emigrated from Scotland to that province, the Rev. Archibald McRobert, an Episcopal clergyman, the certificate of whose ordination by certain English bishops still remains. This minister became incumbent of the living of St. Patrick, embracing what is now known as Prince Edward Court House. Abandoning the Established Church, from conscientious scruples in regard to the test-oath, he became a Presbyterian minister, and, warmly espousing the cause of this country at the Revolution, his estate was invaded by Tarleton, and his house rifled and fired. The family portraits, all sliced by dragoon sabres, are still preserved. His son Theodoric rose to distinction at the bar; and it was to Elizabeth, a daughter of this son, that Dr. Baker became united in marriage. Of rare intellectual attainments and unfeigned piety, she often expressed that deep and fervent piety in strains of poetry which were counted—at least by those who loved her so well—of surpassing sweetness. For so many years a beloved companion of her husband, the messenger that bore him away, soon returned again for her also. It was the priceless privilege of the compiler of this volume to attend the dying couch of his mother, as he had that of his father; in his arms, and upon his bosom, to bear her like a babe, in her great physical weakness, for weeks, about the house. Often, while preparing these pages, has he laid aside his pen from this task of love, to enjoy the greater privilege of ministering to her who bore him; and as this task approached its completion, he laid it altogether aside, to stand with other of her children by her side, to receive her last assurances of a love for them, less only than her love for him who has gone before, and for her Saviour. In the sixty-fourth year of her age, in the forty-second year of her married life, after being separated from her husband a much shorter period than she had often been during his life, she rejoined him in heaven, and there sings with him now the song of Moses and the Lamb.

The autobiography proceeds:

Returning to Winchester, I resumed my duties in the Academy; and although Mr. Hill had returned, he made me oftentimes officiate on Wednesday and Friday evenings; and an arrangement was made for me to go out and hold religious meetings on the Sabbath, at Berryville, Newtown, and Jarratt's Town. These meetings were generally much crowded, and I hope that a goodly number will bless God for them to all eternity. During the summer several cases of hopeful conversion occurred in the Female Academy in Winchester; and in relation to Jarratt's Town, I will state a circumstance as recorded in one of my letters to Mr. Walton, and written about this time: "You know I went to Jarratt's Town last winter, and delivered four discourses, or exhortations. Well, as I was on my way there, Saturday before last, I met an old black man on the road, who asked me if my name was not Mr. Baker. On my answering in the affirmative, he must needs shake hands and chat awhile. 'Why, Massa,' said he, 'you *russelled* de people when you was here before.' '*Russelled the people!*' replied I—'what is that?' 'Yes, Massa, you russelled de people—you come too close on 'em—you say, de best way to try if de tree is sound, is to take a stick and knock 'em.' So saying, a tree being fortunately at hand, suiting the action to the word, he gave me a practical illustration of his meaning. But I hadn't *russelled* him, it seems—O no; *he* liked plain, close preaching. I began to fear that I had offended the people here, as in some other places, and that my usefulness in Jarratt's Town was at an end; but I was soon very agreeably undeceived, for, on reaching the town, I heard that although some did not like my singing

'When I can read my title clear'

to a Methodist tune, yet the people generally were much pleased; and it appeared that the Lord had blessed my labours, and awakened an unusual attention in the place to religious concerns. The next day, although I had a dreadful headache, I spoke, perhaps, for one full hour with great freedom and earnestness; and from the church I went to the house of a friend, and immediately called in a physician, and went to bed. As the case threatened to be of a very serious character, I sent for my beloved wife, who came in all haste. With good nursing, I soon began to get better, and in a few days I was able to return to Winchester."

It may be remarked here, that up to this time, and for years after, Dr. Baker, having been reared in the swamps of Georgia, was of a sallow, slender, sickly appearance, giving no promise of the health and vigour he afterwards possessed. It would be well for those brethren who bewail their spiritual darkness; their fearful apprehensions in regard to things of earth and heaven; their manifold prayers, fastings, and efforts for God, without result, to see if the cause of their unhappiness and inefficiency does not lie in their want of bodily health. By anxiety, over study, too little exercise and recreation, or some other violation of the ordinance of God, multitudes of good men, in weakening their body, greatly diminish both their happiness and usefulness, debilitate intellect and soul, as well as physical frame; make themselves, in fact, of that outward appearance—tall, lean, sour in face, repelling in manner, gloomy in bearing—which scoffers so often picture as the very ideal of the Puritan, and especially the Calvinistic divine. We have only to observe the instinctive aversion and shrinking of the young, and of children especially, from such, to know that there is a painful lack herein.

Though "a man of sorrows, and acquainted with grief," there must have been every thing the reverse of this in Jesus, every thing genial and attractive in his very bearing and countenance. Around his knees children joyfully clustered, sitting in his arms, and receiving his blessing.

The man who stands in the pulpit, broad-chested, in evident possession of health and happiness, exerts a living force upon an audience, even apart from what he has to say. Full health is our natural condition. He who, by any act of commission or omission, impoverishes himself in this, is guilty of breaking the law of God—is guilty of so much suicide, of so much sin, in fact—a sin which, like all other sin, is punished directly, indirectly, and invariably, by the Almighty.

As to Dr. Baker, his incessant travels and preaching developed and strengthened his constitution to a remarkable degree. Avoiding all stimulants, with a healthful appetite for food, careless of its quality—all that he required was a certain amount of sleep. His capacity for labour was almost unlimited—bounded by consideration for his hearers, not for himself. At a Synod upon which he attended, a resolution was unanimously passed, at the very opening, requesting and directing him to "do all the preaching during Synod." Though it was a very large Synod, and this seemed unreasonable, on many accounts, yet he obeyed. As to his untiring energy, it was remarked of him, by a business man, himself by no means lacking in this quality, "Dr. Baker's energy would be worth to me ten thousand dollars a year." Owing to his health, his cheerfulness also was never impaired; in fact, amounted, all the year around, to steady joyousness. No one, in or out of his family, can remember even a momentary cloud of depression on his sunny brow, or a breath of petulance on his smiling lips. He may have been angry at times, but never for an instant cross. Into the fun of children he entered as cordially as themselves, never losing his dignity thereby; and this, with his sincere love for them, was one cause of his singular success in interesting and impressing them. And when defeated in one plan, he turned instantly, without a murmur, and but a transient emotion even, to another; and to him every step in life opened new and captivating vistas of usefulness—he was never at a loss. Of all "croaking," as he termed it, he had a cordial dislike. Whatever else may be said of him, since Adam left Paradise a happier man never walked the earth.

There is a joy which lends a deeper glow to the cheek, and a brighter sparkle to the eye, and a sweeter song to the lips, even of the angels in the presence of God—the joy over a repenting sinner. Of this celestial joy, the subject of this memoir had a full share—a larger share, perhaps, than generally falls to those on this side the gates of heaven. It need scarce be said, his energy, cheerfulness, buoyancy, had their fountain-head in his faith in God, manifested in Christ; but their deep, wide, unobstructed channels were in his healthfulness of body. He undoubtedly was somewhat impatient of invalid men; yet it was not so when such were really prisoners in chamber and bed; then no one could be more sympathizing.

Here we give some extracts from his journal of this period.

October 30*th*, 1815. This evening I have had some very humbling views of myself; my sins in Savannah, and the long-suffering goodness of God was the subject of my meditation; my feelings were indescribable. I could do little else than confess my exceeding unworthiness, and praise the Lord for his rich and unmerited mercy shown toward me. It seems to me I shall never repine or murmur at any of the afflictive dispensations of Heaven toward me; for O, I deserve not a crumb; I deserve now to be in hell, lifting up my eyes in torment. Blessed, for ever blessed be the Lord for his great goodness manifested toward me. "Bless the Lord, O my soul, and all that is within me bless his holy name."

November 4*th*. This evening, Selina, a sweet little girl, of about ten years of age, came to me with a very serious countenance, and said she "wanted me to talk good to her. I asked her, about what? "About God," said she. I told her something of God, of Christ, of our natural state by nature, and the way of salvation through a Mediator. She appeared much impressed. O, may the Lord work a saving change in her dear little heart. This seems to be some of the first fruits of the Sunday-school, for she goes to it. * * * This evening our praying society was remarkably well attended—much seriousness and devotion was manifested, and those who prayed were enabled to pour out their souls before God with great freedom. O that it would please God to revive his work in this place Dear Lord, will it not be for thy glory? Will it not magnify the riches of thy grace?

November 5th—Sunday. This day I spoke for the first time in the church in this place. The Lord graciously assisted me, and, I believe, blessed the word in some measure. Many seemed touched, even to tears. This encouraged me much, for I was afraid they were almost perfectly insensible. I believe these dry bones can live, if the Lord only breathe upon them—Lord, our help can only come from thee. In the afternoon I attended the second meeting of the Sunday-school; a great many persons attended, besides about one hundred and fifty children. All are charmed, yet I know nothing good will come of it unless the Lord bless the institution. Gracious God, do thou deign to smile, and how many of these dear children shall be made happy in thy love. Found much sweetness in devotional exercises this evening, and was enabled to pray in much faith and earnestness for the dear children of this town; and not for them only, but for the people of Winchester generally. O for times of refreshing. I feel my own weakness very sensibly; I feel, unless I am supported by divine grace, I shall certainly soon fall into sin. O, Jesus, I lean upon thee; thou canst bear me up and make me strong against temptation.

November 9th. Last evening and this morning I felt remarkably dull—no freedom in any religious exercises. Without divine grace I see I can do nothing. What a poor creature I am. May I feel my weakness still more sensibly; and O, may it induce me to lean more unreservedly upon my adorable Saviour.

Saturday, November 18th, 1815. Situated as I am in Winchester, having the temporary charge of two congregations, I feel it proper for me, this day, to draw near to God by fasting and humiliation, that I may, in an especial manner, obtain mercy and find grace to help in this time of need. In reviewing my feelings and exercises of mind since I began publicly to exhort in this town, I find I have the most abundant cause for humiliation. I have to lament: 1. my lukewarmness; 2. a want of a devoted heart; 3. want of a suitable sense of the value of souls, and the importance of eternal concerns; 4. my want of proper fervour in my private devotional exercises; 5. want of conduct and deportment sufficiently exemplary. Whilst I would, in the sincerity of my heart, mourn over these things, I would desire also to lament the desolations of Zion in this place; that many make void the law of God, and that even real Christians, in this town, are apparently in a state of sad and awful declension. O for the spirit of a weeping Jeremiah! God grant that I may this day know something of the feelings of the pious Psalmist when he said, "Rivers of waters run down my eyes because they keep not thy law."

Evening. I think I have been enabled this day, in some humble measure, to mourn over my past shortcomings, and to wrestle with God for grace to help in time to come. I have had some enlargement of heart in prayer and meditation, and have been enabled to mourn not only over my heart, but the desolations of Zion. Help me, gracious God, henceforth, to be more humble and exemplary in my walk and deportment, and more useful in thy Church.

1816—*Spring.* The last winter has been a memorable winter in Winchester. The north and south winds have been in some measure felt in this valley of vision, and many dry bones have been shaken. The praying society has been much blessed; it has been uniformly well attended; oftentimes the meetings were remarkably solemn, much feeling was manifested under the short exhortations that were made, and frequently the power of God was felt throughout the whole society. O what sweet and precious seasons have we been favoured with during the latter part of the winter. The recollection of them still fills my soul with joy and gratitude. At our communion season, this spring, thirteen were added to the church; the most, if not all of them, it is believed, were awakened in our praying society. Bless the Lord, O my soul, who has been pleased to bless and crown with visible success my poor weak labours of love. Several persons who have not as yet joined the church, seem to be, at this time, sincerely and earnestly inquiring the way to Zion; the Lord in mercy lead them to Jesus, the sinner's friend.

September 26th. The summer session in the Female Academy has this day terminated. In reviewing my conduct during the session, I find I have the most abundant cause for the deepest humiliation and abasement of soul; and I desire now to take some low place at the foot of my Jesus, and fling my arms around his blood-stained cross. O, my dying Christ, thou art my hope, my joy, my only Saviour. The past session has been an eventful one to the females belonging to the Academy; my weekly exhortations to them have been blessed, and a number have been awakened. Scenes truly interesting have been presented; about fifteen have been seriously impressed, five or six of whom give a pleasing evidence of a saving work of grace upon their hearts. O, my Lord, deal gently with these precious little lambs, and keep them by Almighty power through faith unto salvation. The awakening in the Academy has excited mnch interest in town, and while some have rejoiced in it, others have disapproved of the work, and have endeavoured to bring it into disrepute. Many slanderous reports have been circulated, and I have been caught up in a tempest of persecution; but I committed all to the Lord, and endeavoured to endure my trials patiently, and continue steadfast, unmovable, always abounding in the work of the Lord; and I bless God I have not been put to shame. Every thing has been cleared up; and I have had the unutterable pleasure of seeing several of the young ladies, as I believe, made savingly acquainted with the Lord Jesus. O, how richly am I recompensed for the persecutions I have been called to endure for the sake of Christ. O, my God, may I rejoice in tribulations, if so be thy glory may thereby be promoted.

October 12th. In the prospect of my being licensed in the coming week, I have set apart this day, by fasting and prayer, to draw near unto the Lord. I am now about to go forth to preach the everlasting gospel to poor, perishing sinners; to proclaim liberty to the captive, and the opening of the prison to those that are bound; tc proclaim the acceptable year of the Lord. O, may I go forth in the strength of the mighty One of Jacob, and lift my banner in the name of the Captain of my salvation! I know that my duties will be arduous, and I am sensible that I am not sufficient for these things; but I know in whom I trust; it is not in myself, it is not in any arm of flesh—it is in the living God, the merciful and covenant-keeping God, who has been pleased to say, "My grace is sufficient for thee; my strength shall be made perfect in weakness." To thee, O my God, do I commit myself, and again would I solemnly renew the dedication of myself and my all to thy service. O condescend to accept the unworthy offering, and lay me out for thy glory. I ask not to be rich in silver and gold, and to be admired and caressed; I ask to be rich in faith and good works, and to be blessed and owned in my labours of love. I ask not to be exempted from grievous trials and persecutions, but I ask grace to glorify thee in the hour of trial; grace to be useful, grace to be triumphant in death, and grace to reach, at length, the Mount Zion above, where I may for ever sing the triumphs of my dearest Lord. To thee, O my God, do I now commit my way; be pleased to direct my paths, for the Redeemer's sake. Amen.

Narrative resumed:

At the fall meeting of the Presbytery of Winchester, which held its sessions in Leesburg, I was licensed to preach the gospel; but I must confess I was by no means prepared. Mr. Hill had strangely neglected my theological studies, and, so far as I can now recollect, had put no book in my hand save

Butler's Analogy. I however made great use of the Shorter Catechism; I was told it was an admirable "summary," and I studied that and my Bible. The Presbytery debated the matter two days, whether I should be licensed or not. Mr. G. opposed it with all his might. Mr. W. and a few others advocated it, and endeavoured to show that my case was a peculiar one, and provided for by the constitution. Much was said about my labours and success in Winchester and other places; and whilst Mr. G. affirmed that I was "born to trouble the church," my friend, Mr. W., was pleased to say that "the Lord had licensed me." My other parts of trial having been sustained, I was required to deliver my *popular discourse* from the pulpit. The text assigned me was Eph. ii. 8. I went into the pulpit; there was a great crowd; I was dashed, and began my sermon without announcing my text! In a few moments I thought of it, and became a little more embarrassed; but in a short time, recovering my self-possession, I managed to introduce my text, and then went on without any more difficulty to the end. I spoke with great earnestness; tears were shed; and I have since heard of one man, and he a rich man, who was awakened under the discourse. The Sabbath after I was licensed I spent in a town not far from Leesburg—the name I cannot now recollect. I had a very great crowd, and I hope that some good impressions were made. I then hurried on to Alexandria, District of Columbia, whither I had been invited by Mrs. S., one of the jewels of Dr. Muir's church. On reaching Alexandria, Dr. Muir very courteously invited me to preach for him, which I did on Friday night, Saturday night, and three times on the Sabbath. Awakening influences went abroad in a most remarkable manner. An inquiry or prayer-meeting was held in Dr. Muir's parlour, on Monday afternoon, for young ladies. The room was crowded to excess; there was much weeping; some six or eight persons, I think, had obtained a hope, and perhaps at least twenty more were inquiring what they must do to be saved. I was astonished, and marvelled that my few sermons should be so remarkably blessed. On Monday night I attended the monthly concert meeting, held in the Methodist church; after the services closed, I suppose one hundred persons came up, without invitation, and lingered around the altar. In a familiar and affectionate manner I continued my remarks for perhaps some thirty minutes, urging them all, with full purpose of heart, to serve the Lord. Many, many tears were shed. The next morning I left for Prince Edward, where my wife had gone. Dr. Muir and many others were exceedingly urgent that I should remain and preach a few days longer; but my arrangements were made, and I must go. Shortly after reaching Prince Edward, I received many affectionate letters.

In compliance with letters of invitation, I returned to Alexandria; but in consequence of some domestic matters, did not get there until some weeks after the period fixed upon. I was received very cordially by Dr. Muir, and the people generally. I preached usually to large congregations, and after two months I left for Prince Edward. Upon my leaving Alexandria there was a meeting of the congregation, and I was duly elected collegiate pastor. Dr. Muir gave me a statement of the matter. I then wrote him a very brief, but very respectful letter, declining the call. Three elders out of five, with about one-half of the congregation, or more, broke off; and the church edifice occupied by the Episcopalians being bought, I was invited to become pastor of the second church. This affair grieved me much. After much thought and prayer, I declined; and having, at the same time, a call to the united congregations of Harrisonburg and New Erection, Rockingham county, Virginia, I accepted that, recommending Mr. Wells Andrews to the second church, Alexandria. This brother was accordingly duly elected, and officiated with great acceptance as their pastor for many years.

About this time, with my brother John, (leaving my wife with her mother in Prince Edward,) I paid a visit to my friends and relatives in Liberty county, Georgia. When in Savannah, I called upon Dr. Kollock; told him who I was; that I formerly attended upon his ministry; had been much benefitted by it; and that I was now a licensed preacher. The doctor was much pleased; his eyes filled with tears; and, it being Wednesday, he invited me to preach for him that night, which was his stated evening for preaching. I complied, and preached from these words: "For there shall be no night there." The next day my brother and myself reached the place of our nativity, and received a very cordial reception. Remaining in the county, I think about two weeks, I preached in various places, but chiefly in Midway church and at Riceboro'. On every occasion, almost without exception, I had a great crowd. There was a very considerable religious excitement, and, I think, some ten or twelve persons professed conversion; some, however, who were much wrought upon, I fear, fell short of the mark. I will state a case or two which excited much interest. One Mr. M., a merchant in Riceboro', a very profane and wicked man, was invited to hear me preach in the court-house on a certain evening. "Go to hear Mr. Baker preach!" said he, "why I would not go across the street to hear him." Well, I went to the court-house to preach, and he went to bed. As his chamber was not very far from the court-house, as the sashes were up, and my voice was loud, Mr. F. in his bed, listened to me, and in his bed was awakened. Powerfully wrought upon, the next morning he came down out of his chamber, having a very serious look, and did not swear at all as he was wont to do. His servant noticed it, and remarked, that he did not know what was the matter with his master, for he had stopped swearing. The next night he was at preaching, and seemed to be very much interested. The day following, he went to see a sick friend at a distance, and of him and his impressions I could hear nothing further. Another case which may be mentioned is this. Mr. M. M., a very irreligious man, and the keeper of a billiard-room, was powerfully wrought upon—did not profess conversion, but was so much interested in the preaching, that when I was coming away he gave me fifty dollars. On my second visit to Georgia, some three or four years after, I was called to see him in his dying chamber. Alas! I fear he died without hope.

Leaving Liberty county, still in company with my brother John, I called again upon Dr. Kollock in Savannah, and preached for him a second time—my text, Isaiah liv. 10. This sermon, I have reason to believe, pleased Dr. Kollock very much; and I am not sure but, subsequently, it had an influence in procuring for me a call to become pastor, upon the death of that great and good man. Receiving a very handsome "purse," as a free-will offering from my friends in Midway, and also having received my patrimony, I returned to Prince Edward, and with my first-born child, Howard, I hurried on to Harrisonburg, to which place I had received a call. During my absence in Georgia, a letter had been sent to me at Prince Edward, inviting me to become seamen's preacher in the city of New York; but under existing circumstances, I could not, of course, accept.

CHAPTER V.

HARRISONBURG—WASHINGTON CITY.

Settled in Harrisonburg, I was ordained and installed as pastor of the united congregations of Harrisonburg and New Erection, at a meeting of Presbytery held in Harrisonburg, March 5th, 1818. I preached alternately at each place. Having bought a house and lot in town, I taught school for some two or three years. Amongst those taught by me were Gessner Harrison and Henry Tutwiler, both subsequently distinguished Professors; the first, in the University of Virginia, the other in Lagrange College, Alabama.

Prof. Harrison, in a note penned after the decease of his old teacher, says:

"For some years of my boyhood I was a pupil of the late Rev. Daniel Baker, D. D., and have always regarded him as having displayed, in a very eminent degree, some of the best qualities of a teacher of youth. To say that he was diligent and faithful; that he showed a warm solicitude for the moral as well as mental improvement of his pupils, and that his heart was in the work of training them in useful knowledge and virtue, would hardly convey an adequate idea of the enthusiastic zeal with which he laboured in his school. He carried into it the same warm-hearted energy that distinguished his efforts as a preacher. It was not strange, considering his character as a teacher, and that in maintaining discipline he happily mingled firmness with kindness, that his pupils so universally and so greatly loved and respected him."

The narrative proceeds:

Besides preaching regularly in my two churches on the Sabbath, it was common for me to preach on Saturdays in various places around. It pleased God to bless my labours, and there were considerable additions to both churches. Having taken a missionary tour in the western part of Virginia, the tour proved to be so interesting and successful, that, by request, my journal was published; and I began to have a hankering after a missionary life—and in the year 1820 or '21, I cannot recollect which, I resigned my charge, to the great regret of the people, who gave me very touching proofs of their most affectionate regard. I recollect the remark of Mr. J. B., one of the elders: "Mr. Baker, you have endeared yourself to the hearts of the people." Appointed by the Lexington Presbytery, I went to the General Assembly in Philadelphia, intending to make that my starting point. Upon the dissolving of that Assembly, I set out, not knowing precisely what ground I should occupy. Visiting the city of Washington, I preached several sermons in various churches, and was invited to remain some months and preach in the Navy Building to a congregation which was about being formed into a new church; the church edifice near the President's House being nearly finished. After preaching several weeks, I hope with some success, I received a letter from my wife in Prince Edward, communicating the melancholy intelligence of the death of my second son. Leaving Washington suddenly, I hurried on to my afflicted companion, and together we mingled our tears over the grave of as lovely and promising a child, we thought, as ever lived. Although only about a year old, there was something uncommonly noble in his looks. After leaving Washington, I was duly elected pastor. This call was sent to me to Liberty county, whither I had gone with my wife and two small children. While in the place of my nativity, I preached several sermons in the church at Midway, and the borough. There was some religious excitement, and a few, but not many, cases of conversion. One case may be mentioned, of a Mr. Way, an uncommonly fine man, who soon became a very prominent and useful member of the church, but who was suddenly snatched away by death, I think in less than one year after his conversion, and in a remarkable manner. It was winter—there came up a thundergust—Mr. Way stepped to the sash to let it down, there came a flash of lightning, and he fell dead!—only one flash of lightning, and that was made, as Elijah's chariot, to take him to heaven.

Leaving Midway, upon my return to Virginia, I was requested to spend two Sabbaths in Savannah, and preach in the pulpit recently vacated by the death of that eloquent man, Dr. Henry Kollock. I consented. I preached three times the first Sabbath, and held some meetings during the week following. On the next Sabbath I had four appointments; in the morning at half-past ten, in the church; at noon, to the seamen; at half-past three P. M. in the church, and at night in the church again. Having arranged my subjects, and made all needful preparation for these four services, on Saturday, about ten o'clock at night, I was called upon by a gentleman, and informed that Mrs. Clay, a lady of great note, and a mother in Israel, had died, and he came to request that I would preach her funeral sermon in the church the next day, in the afternoon. I was alarmed. I had prepared four discourses, but not one would suit! I had no time, that night, to prepare an appropriate discourse, nor could I have time on the morrow. I had reason to believe that there would be a very great crowd in that large and splendid church, and that, from the very high standing of the deceased, something extraordinary would be expected. I could not refuse to preach; but what shall be done?—and to crown the matter, on Monday I was to be brought forward by certain friends as a candidate for pastor. I never felt so frightfully situated, scarcely, in all my life. When the gentleman retired, I took up my manuscripts, and found that I had one sermon from this text, "To me, to die is gain." O, that sermon! I was so glad to see it; and I was familiar with it, and on one occasion particularly, I had preached it, and the whole congregation was so melted down, that there was not, I suppose, a dry eye in the house! I seized the manuscript with great eagerness and joy; I would not have taken one hundred dollars for it. The next day we had a full house in the morning, in the afternoon a great crowd—I suppose there were some twelve or fifteen hundred persons present. I preached; and if I ever received assistance from on high, it was on that occasion. The orphan children, to whom Mrs. Clay had been as a mother, were all in their neat dresses, seated before me. I had great liberty in preaching. There was much feeling and deep solemnity. The character of the deceased was so excellent, I could scarcely say too much; and every individual in that great congregation fully believed with me, that to this mother in Israel "to die was gain." All believed that she was that moment with her Saviour in heaven, radiant in glory. The next day I was elected by an overwhelming majority.

I had now two calls in my hand: one, to become pastor of the Second Presbyterian Church, Washington; the other, to become pastor of the Independent Presbyterian Church in Savannah. The salary offered in the one case was comparatively small, the other large. After much reflection and prayer, I decided in favour of Washington City and a small salary. In a day or two I embarked, with my little family, for Philadelphia. Upon reaching Washington City, I was cordially welcomed by my little church, consisting of only thirty-nine members. My salary was only six hundred dollars; but the Commissioner of the Land Office, Mr. Jonathan Meigs, soon gave me a clerkship with a salary of eight hundred dollars. As one of the clerks in the Land Office, I was required to write six days in the week, from nine o'clock in the morning until three, P. M. This was a great drawback to me. I entered upon my pastoral labours with much zeal; I preached usually three times in the church on the Sabbath, and also on Wednesday evening: besides this, I attended a prayer-meeting, in some private house, on Friday evenings. Our meetings were usually well attended; and although we never had what is called a revival, we had what may be called heavenly dew. Nearly all the time that I resided in the city, at every communion, I believe without a single exception, we had some added on profession; so that when I resigned my charge, in the spring of 1828, the number of communicants had increased to one hundred and forty-two; and this not including those who had died, or had been been dismissed.

During one season, besides preaching three times in the church on the Sabbath, I preached in the afternoon in the market-house on Pennsylvania

Avenue, to a mixed multitude of loafers, loungers, the sons of the bottle and the sons of Ham. I hope much good was done by this act of obedience to the command, "Go out into the streets and lanes of the city and compel them to come in." One person, who subsequently became a member of my church, ascribed his conversion, under God, to the preaching in the market-house; and I may mention another case, in some respects very remarkable. Colonel D., a negro trader, being in the city and wandering about, was attracted by the crowd to the market-house and heard me preach. He was awakened: the next Sabbath afternoon he came again, and his impressions were deepened. Resolving on a reformation, he laid aside the intoxicating bowl, and began to read some religious tracts which were given to him. On the Saturday evening preceding the third Sabbath, he came into Mr. Wailes' shop and asked him if he knew in what church the man preached who was wont to preach in the market-house. "He is my pastor," said Mr. Wailes, "and I will be happy to give you a seat in my pew to-morrow morning." Colonel D. politely accepted the invitation. The next morning Mr. W. called for the Colonel to take him to church, when lo! he was dead! O, how uncertain is life, and how important to be always ready!

The following incident is related as connected with this period:

There was a man residing in Washington at this time, named S., proprietor of one of the principal hotels. He was a man of notorious character, very loose in his morals, and no respecter of the house of God. Probably he had not visited a place of worship for more than fifteen years. Some of Dr. Baker's friends were speaking one day of their pastor, and his excellent sermons, in presence of S., and suggested that as the church was not far distant, he ought to go and hear so eminent a minister. S., half in earnest and half in jest, replied to Mr. W., (the gentleman conversing with him,) "Tell Mr. Baker that I will go and hear him preach with great pleasure, if he will take for his text, "*Let every man mind his own business.*" Mr. W. reported the conversation to Dr. Baker, who determined at once to catch him, and sent word that he would make that the subject of his sermon next Sabbath morning. S., according to his promise, appeared in the house of God, and Dr. Baker, announcing his text in the following words, "And that ye study—to do your own business," 1 Thess. iv. 2, proceeded in a sermon so impressive and spiritual in its application, that the hotel-keeper was completely overcome. The result was, that S. immediately took a pew in the church, and was ever after a regular attendant upon the means of grace.

About this period Dr. Baker, at the request of his church, visited New York city for the purpose of obtaining pecuniary aid therefor. It seems, however, that only some five hundred dollars was obtained by him during the tour. He had not as yet learned, as he afterward most certainly did, the one secret of success in begging. In June, 1824, he paid a rapid visit to Virginia, during which he wrote the following letter to Mr. J. H. Handy. This gentleman was an elder of the Washington church, and, when Dr. Baker was elected pastor, was opposed to his settlement. Acquiescing, however, in the call, Mr. Handy soon became, and remained ever after, one of his warmest friends. Perhaps no two men were ever more alike in spirit, and the attachment between them was as that of Jonathan and David, as will appear from the correspondence. To the day of his death, Dr. Baker often spoke of Mr. Handy as a model elder. A son of this excellent man is now pastor of the Presbyterian church in Portsmouth, Virginia.

"HARRISONBURG, *25th June*, 1824.

"MY DEAR FRIEND—Amidst the greetings of my friends here, I can find scarcely a leisure moment; yet I have retired to drop you a line. I reached Prince Edward, with my family, on Wednesday after leaving Washington. Owing to a kind Providence, nothing disastrous occurred on our journey. On our arrival, there was no little joy, I assure you. On Saturday, and on Sabbath last, I preached at the College. It being a sacramental occasion, there was a very large congregation. It was a solemn and interesting season, but nothing very remarkable took place.

"On Tuesday I left Prince Edward for this place, and had the pleasure last evening of saluting my old friends here. The expressions of their affection for me have affected me very sensibly. I never knew before the full strength of their affection. It pleased God to bless my labours amongst this people in times past; on this account, I suppose, they bear me in such affectionate remembrance. The God of heaven bless them yet more and more.

"I have thought about you all in Washington very frequently and affectionately. They share in my daily prayers. I hope our excellent elders have been doing a great deal of good during my absence; the Lord encourage them to engage earnestly and actively in his service, and grant a rich blessing. You have had no difficulty, I hope, in getting the pulpit supplied; I wonder if I ought not formally to have requested from the Session leave of absence. The thing never occurred to me until I had set out on my journey; but I have quieted my conscience in this way—The visit was long in contemplation; I had spoken of it repeatedly to yourself and others; no objections had been made; but still, I do think it was proper to have stated it to the Session. This plan, I think, ought to be observed in all our churches; it is the plan I shall observe in time to come.

"Can you read this scrawl?—it is really shameful; but as my stay here is so short, I am pressed for time; besides, I have this very afternoon to preach a funeral sermon. Having many things to write unto you, I would not write with paper and ink, but I trust I shall shortly see thee, and speak face to face. Peace be to thee. Greet the friends by name. My particular respects to your family.

Yours, very sincerely,

DANIEL BAKER."

But the pastor hastens back to the charge he loved

so well. After his death, a Baptist brother thus speaks of this period of Dr. Baker's history:

"I remember him well. During a residence of five years in and near Washington, District of Columbia, I frequently attended at his place of worship. I preferred his ministry, not because it was the most intellectual, but because it was spiritual, fervent, and enforced by a consistent life. He was a man of prayer; he preached to save souls; he walked with God. For more than thirty years I have not seen him; but I have often been gratified by hearing of his evangelical labours, and his abundant success. *Twenty thousand converts!* What a host of gems for one servant to collect out of the rubbish of a depraved world for his Master's crown! Knowing the man as he was from 1822 to 1827, I can easily understand the secret of his usefulness. He sought the appointed end; he laboured upon the appointed plan; he used the appointed means. He was sincere, earnest, simple-minded. He did one thing, and did it well. Surely his rest was glorious."

The autobiography proceeds:

It was usual for me to write one sermon with care, and commit it to memory for Sabbath morning; for other occasions I had only brief notes, and sometimes no written notes at all; and here I will mention an incident which turned out better than I feared. One Sabbath afternoon, just as I had announced my text, which was this—"Ephraim is a cake not turned"—John Quincy Adams, the Secretary of State, stepped in, and walking up the aisle, took his seat near the pulpit. The reverence which I had for this great man, the singularity of the text, and my want of due preparation, all united to disconcert me; I was thrown off my balance, and preached, as I then thought, and still think, a very indifferent discourse. It had, however, one excellence, not found in most of my sermons—it was very short; not more than twenty or twenty-five minutes long. When I finished, I was excessively mortified, and thought I would never see the Secretary of State in that church again; but, to my astonishment, the next week I was told he had rented one of the best pews in the church. Whether the exceeding brevity of my sermon pleased him, or the freedom with which I pointed out the inconsistencies of professing Christians, or whether he had previously resolved to take a pew at any rate, I know not; but one thing I soon had the pleasure of hearing—that Mr. Adams had taken a pew; and that was not all—soon after, the Secretary of State became one of the most efficient trustees of my church, and one of the best friends I ever had. As a proof of this, on a certain emergency he loaned the church twelve hundred dollars; and, on another occasion, having bought a house for twelve hundred dollars, to be paid in four instalments, I called upon Mr. Adams, at that time President of the United States, and asked him to lend me two hundred and fifty dollars, which I promised to pay in a short time. He listened with much interest, inquired all about the matter, and, when informed that the gentleman from whom I bought the house resided in Ohio, he said, "I think, Mr. Baker, I had better advance the whole amount, and you can pay me." This was most generous and most unexpected. I expressed my gratitude, and observed, "If I pay the full amount down, the gentleman would, no doubt, allow some considerable discount." "That," replied he, "will be your advantage." Thus saying, he took up his pen and gave me a check on the bank for twelve hundred dollars. This was certainly doing a handsome thing very handsomely; but not more so than another thing a few years after. Wishing to sell my house, on going to Savannah, I requested a friend to call upon the President, and ask him if he would not like to purchase my house, and if so, what he would give. Mr. Adams told him that he had no particular wish to purchase the house, but he would give me fifteen hundred dollars cash, and would be willing I should have six months to look around and see if I could not do better. This was another noble act. I need scarcely say that I sold the house to him, and was promptly paid.

Mr. Adams never failed to be in his pew on Sabbath afternoon, whatever might be the weather, and was a most attentive hearer. After he took a pew in my church, and became a trustee, it seemed to come more into notice. Mr. Crawford, the Secretary of the Treasury, and Judge Southard, the Secretary of the Navy, each took a pew, and so did General Jackson, then a Senator. Here I may mention an incident, of which I am reminded by mentioning the name of Judge Southard. A certain debt pressing heavily upon the church, one of the elders, Mr. James Handy, and myself, were sent out on a "begging expedition," and succeeded in getting all that we needed, except seven hundred dollars. At the suggestion of a friend, I procured a letter of introduction from the Secretary of the Navy, Judge Southard, to Captain Downs, of the "Delaware," a seventy-four gun ship, at that time lying of Annapolis. I went—presented the letter to the commander of the "man-of-war." He received me very courteously, permitted me to preach to the officers and seamen, and take up a collection. I did so, and came away completely successful, having obtained the full amount which I told them we needed, viz. seven hundred dollars.

Shortly after this, my friend, the Commissioner of the General Land Office, having died, and a new Commissioner having been appointed, "who knew not Joseph," I, with some five or six other clerks, were put out of office. As the number of clerks was to be reduced, a lottery was resorted to. I refused to put my hand into the wheel, and said, if the Commissioner wished to dismiss me, I was ready to go out, but I would have nothing to do with the lottery. One of my elders was appointed to act in my place; he put his hand into the wheel, and drew out a blank, and I had to go. This proved a kind providence to me, and although it was a serious matter—suddenly reduced from fourteen hundred to six hundred dollars—I did not much regret it, even at the time, for I had often had some scruples of conscience about the propriety of my employing so much of my time in a business which had no bearing upon my ministerial office. Upon being suddenly cut off from this source of income, I confess I felt very badly, and did not know what to do. My people expressed great sympathy, raised my salary to eight hundred dollars, and expressed a willingness to do more; but I could not bear the thought of being a burden to them, and resolved to do what I could to support myself. I got some writing to do from the Land Office, and for a short time I assisted Mr. B. in his school. But all this was not enough, the indications of reduced circumstances soon began to appear in my furniture, wardrobe, and table-fare.

Just at this time, when my prospects for temporal support were very dark and discouraging—yes, just at this time, I received a second call to the Independent Presbyterian Church in Savannah. Sending my family, consisting of my wife, three sons and one daughter, to spend the summer in Prince Edward, I left Washington amid the deep regrets of my people; and the trustees had the kindness to vote me a beautiful Bible, as a token of their affectionate regard. I reached Savannah, and under very propitious auspices I entered upon my pastoral labours. In the fall of that year I had the pleasure of having all my family with me.

During Dr. Baker's pastorate in Washington he published *A Scriptural View of Baptism*, which was extensively circulated, with the happiest effects at the time, as facts abundantly testify. Many years after, the same tract, revised and enlarged, was published by the Board of Publication. The same treatise, added to, and yet condensed, was afterwards published under the somewhat quaint title of *Baptism in a Nutshell*. This last little book contains a clear summary of the whole argument, both in regard to the subject and mode of baptism, and has decided many a doubting mind. In all the range of Scripture doctrine, there was not one in regard to which Dr. Baker was more thoroughly convinced and ardently interested than this. Those who have witnessed his administration of this holy ordinance to adult, or to infant in the arms of its parents, will remember his deep sincerity and solemnity. He took peculiar pleasure in administering the ordinance to an adult, and none the less to the infant offspring of believing parents. Though never indulging in a controversial spirit, in or out of the pulpit, on this or any other point of difference among evangelical Christians, he regarded with unconcealed dislike an exaltation of a mere sign above the essential and all-important thing signified; regarded, with even horror, the violent and unwarranted, as he thought, exclusion of the lambs of the flock from the fold of the Shepherd of the sheep; of the children of believing members from that membership in the Church of God, which he was persuaded they held from the very origin thereof; a membership, as he believed, attested by all history, sacred and profane; based upon all principles, human and divine; decreed by ordinances never abrogated, and wrought into the very texture of revelation, as they are into the very heartstrings of connubial and filial relationship.

It is interesting to know in what light Dr. Baker was regarded by those who were most intimate with him at this time. Looking back over the many years which have elapsed since then, Dr. S. Collins, of Baltimore, thus speaks:

"In the autumn of 1823, I settled in Washington,

District of Columbia, as a practitioner of medicine, and became a member of the church of which Dr. Baker was pastor. In a short time I was elected an elder; so that, by membership and eldership, I had opportunities for intimate knowledge of his character from that time to the period of his removal from Washington.

"The incipiency of the enterprise which resulted in the organization of that church, was conducted by Dr. Baker with indomitable energy and signal success; but the salary he received not being sufficient for the support of his family, he was constrained to accept a clerkship in one of the public departments. He greatly regretted this diversion of so much valuable time from what he considered to be the great work of his life; and, if my memory be accurate, this consideration was a prominent inducement in seeking another field of labour.

"Dr. Baker secured, in a very eminent degree, the devoted affection of his people. This he attained by the faithful discharge of pastoral duties, public and private; by the guilelessness of his transparent character; by the warmth and sincerity of his friendships. Whenever he appeared in the pulpit, the audience saw that he was not preaching himself, but Jesus Christ. His delivery was very earnest, and generally his discourses were practical in their character. His power of endurance was very remarkable, and he was always ready to preach whenever and wherever opportunity offered. He was deeply impressed with a conviction of the importance of meetings for prayer to the spiriual prosperity of a church; and on such occasions he was most earnest in his addresses, and devout in his supplications. After thirty years have passed I retain a most pleasing recollection of a union prayer-meeting, held at six o'clock on mornings of the Sabbath, and attended by male members of different denominational associations. I have often heard him on such occasions, when the holy man, in subdued tones of voice, with choked utterance and flowing tears, poured out his whole soul in supplication to the God whom he adored. It was impossible to fail in discovering that the Holy Spirit was dwelling in and communing with him.

"During the latter period of his ministry in Washington, there was increased attention to religious interests in all the churches. Ministers from abroad laboured there with great zeal; perhaps not always with entire discretion. In the church of Dr. Baker the means employed were frequent meetings for prayer, private visitation, and personal conversation. We excluded all 'machinery,' in the popular acceptation of the word. The result was a deep and quiet religious impression among the people, and a large accession to the membership of the church. This season was not succeeded by any of those distressing cases of apostasy which too often follow merely animal excitements, and hasty admissions. If, on application for admission, the case was doubtful, or too recent, the Session held it for further consideration. In all revivals, as in all cases of individual conviction, the chief business of the sinner is between God and his own soul.

"I met Dr. Baker only once after his departure from Washington. I believe he made several visits to that place; but as I removed to Baltimore in 1832, I did not meet him. The occasion to which I refer was a few years before his death, when he called on me as he was passing through Baltimore on his way home, after a visit to the North. The interview was short; but, short as it was, he took occasion to ask me if I was as much engaged in the service of God as in former years. And this little incident revealed the man in his true character—always seeking after opportunities to serve his Master.

"His ingenuousness, the guileless, artless simplicity of his character, was very attractive. His character was patent, revealed by every look, word, and deed. Meaning no harm, and thinking none, he indulged no suspicions of others. We do not often find, in eminent combination, the wisdom of the serpent with the harmlessness of the dove. Memory is often employed with associations in connection with this good man, and recalls scenes when we mingled together in the communion of the Holy Ghost—places which might have been named Jehovah-Shammah, "The Lord is there." (Ezek. xlviii. 35.)

"Dr. Baker possessed, in an eminent degree, the spirit of a missionary. Gentle as he was in spirit, he was a stranger to the emotion of fear, and no 'lions in the way' would have turned him aside from unblenching progress in the path to which duty led. He would have been, like Paul, faithful in perils, in weariness and painfulness, in watchings, in hunger and thirst, in fastings, in cold and nakedness. The spirit of love made him desire that all might partake of the only true riches. Hence he rejoiced in labours as an evangelist; and in this field he employed portions of his useful life. The Holy Spirit was pleased to accompany his labours with that influence, without which the talents of an angel would not avail.

"Like Enoch, he 'walked with God;' like Abraham, 'by faith he looked for a city which hath foundations, whose builder and maker is God;' like Stephen, he was 'a man full of faith and of the Holy Ghost;' like Nathanael, he was 'an Israelite indeed, in whom is no guile."

CHAPTER VI.

PASTORATE IN SAVANNAH.

THE following letters, addressed to the church in Washington, and to Mr. Handy, will illustrate this period.

"SAVANNAH, *May* 13*th*, 1828.

"To the members of the Second Presbyterian Church,
Washington City.

"BELOVED BRETHREN—Affectionately attached to you all, it was my design to write to you at some very early period after my arrival here; but my engagements have been such that I have put off this little work of love until this late hour. You will, I hope, excuse this apparent neglect—my heart is the same—it is not estranged from you; I trust it never will be till I die.

"After labouring in your midst a little more than

six years, with much comfort to myself, and, I hope, some usefulness to you, I have withdrawn. I am now far away; another city is the place of my residence; another people the people of my charge. Was this of my own seeking? It was the providence of God—most remarkably the providence of God. There is a train of circumstances connected with the whole matter truly wonderful; some are known to you, some are not. Suffice it to say, about those things presumed not to be known to you, because referring particularly to the church here, that certain events of a peculiar character have convinced the people of my present charge that I was sent in answer to their prayers. I was happy with you; I was willing with you to live, to labour, and to die. But, brought here by the providence of God, I am also happy here; and now I am willing, if such be the Divine pleasure, with this people to live, to labour, and to die. The field of usefulness opened to me in this place is very extensive, and very promising. My congregation is decidedly the largest in Savannah, and embraces a great portion of the wealth and intelligence of the city. I am happy to add, it embraces much piety too, far more than I had any idea of. We have many of the excellent of the earth in our midst; our prayer-meetings are crowded; I have a very flourishing Female Bible-class—the present number is forty-six. I am free to say, my prospects of doing good were never more encouraging than they now are. I am contented, I am happy; but still my thoughts will recur to scenes past and gone. I remember the dear people whom I left behind; I remember their kindness; I remember our Christian and friendly intercourse, our social and other meetings. These recollections awaken peculiar feelings—pleasant, yet mournful to the soul. I cease not, my dear brethren, to remember you in my prayers; most sincerely do I desire, in your behalf, a large share of Heaven's richest and best blessings.

"I trust by this time you have a man of God sent amongst you—one that will love you as I have done, and one that will be abundantly more useful than I ever was. Love your minister; consider him as the Lord's messenger; receive his instructions in meekness, his rebukes in love; pray for him, and give him good encouragement of every kind. I hope you still remain united among yourselves; that you continue to love each other, as you were wont to do, with a pure heart, fervently: 'Behold, how good and how pleasant it is for brethren to dwell together in unity.' Christians are a peculiar people; they should walk in love, and not, as other gentiles, which know not God. There are many tender considerations which may well bind their hearts together. They have one warfare, one banner, one Captain of salvation. They are all children of the same heavenly King; they have one elder brother, one inheritance, and one hope; they are all going up through the same wilderness, refreshed by the same streams, leaning upon the same arm. They are 'all passing through one beauteous gate to one eternal home.' Dear brethren, let me beseech you once more, as I have often done before, to walk worthy of the Lord unto all pleasing; to live blamelessly and harmlessly as the children of God, without rebuke. O, it is a great matter to be a consistent and examplary Christian! It pleases God, brings credit to religion, and peace and comfort to our own soul. The time is gone by for me, in any official capacity, to press these things upon you, for I am no longer your pastor; but, as an absent friend and Christian brother, I would call to remembrance the things which ye have heard.

"There are two things which now, in review, afford me satisfaction—a consciousness that I endeavoured to be faithful whilst I was over you in the Lord, and a conviction that my labours in your midst were not in vain in the Lord. I know I came far short of my duty; and I have reason to mourn over my too great barrenness, and would desire now to humble myself before God, and take shame and confusion of face unto myself for all that was amiss; yet, through grace, I think I can say, if I did not make full proof of my ministry, I did, in some measure, do the work of an evangelist amongst you, and I thank God, I have left behind me some seals of my ministry. O, that the number were a thousand times greater! My dear friends, the idea of meeting you in glory is very delightful to my soul. Precious lambs of the flock! may the good Shepherd lead you into green pastures, and beside the still waters; and what time you are feeble and amidst enemies, may He gather you in his arms, and carry you in his bosom. O, keep near your blessed Redeemer; follow him fully in the regeneration, and soon you will be with him in a world of glory. Shall we see each other no more in the flesh? This is now quite probable; but in our Father's house there are many mansions. There, if never before—there, I trust in God, we shall meet, salute each other as brethren redeemed, and part no more.

"But what shade is that which comes over my soul? What pang was that which even now I feel? O, it is the recollection of something past—that some, that many, and those of my young friends, too, heard me preach, heard me invite, heard me warn, heard me, even with tears, entreat them to attend to the great concern, and all without profit; whilst my soul was yearning over them, their hearts were cased in adamant; I never saw them weep at the feet of Jesus; I never heard them cry, What must I do to be saved? My preaching with them is now over; my warnings are now ended, my work is done; the volume of my pastoral labours is closed, is sealed, is laid up by the throne of God against the judgment-day. And what! O my soul, must I bear witness against them in the judgment-day? The idea is too distressing; I cannot dwell upon it. O, my friend, whoever thou art, that shall read this letter in the prayer-meeting, I entreat thee tell those, especially the young who have heard my voice but have not regarded it—O, tell them that they have sinned against much light and much love; tell them that their souls are more precious than a thousand worlds, and when lost, are lost for ever! God have mercy upon them, and save them from the death that never dies. I have done. Beloved brethren, one and all, farewell.

"Your late loving pastor, and still affectionate friend,

DANIEL BAKER."

(TO MR. HANDY.)

"SAVANNAH, *May 28th*, 1829.

"MY VERY DEAR FRIEND.—I wrote to you by mail some three or four weeks since, but a fine opportunity now offering, I thought I would embrace it, although I have very little to say, and very little time to say that very little in. I have not to this day ceased regretting the miscarriage of the long letter I wrote to you; not merely because it was a dead loss, but because I think if it had reached you, your last letter would have been both more bland and lengthy. Did you know it?—your letter had a drop or two of vinegar in it; but towards the last you diluted it pretty well. You seem to have forgotten my taken-for-granted neglect, and you resumed your pleasant and most agreeable mode of expressing yourself. Now, my dear good sir, as the matter of neglect is all cleared up, I hope you will favour me with some more of your 'old fashioned,' but much valued letters. I greatly desire to know how you are all coming on; so many changes lately.

"We are about opening an infant school in this city, under the most encouraging auspices. To secure adequate funds our plan is this: eighteen gentlemen to assume the responsibility of fifty dollars each, to be reimbursed by procuring scholars to that amount; terms of tuition to be ten dollars a year, to be paid semi-annually in advance. We obtained a proper person—sent her on to Philadelphia to be trained up and qualified for opening an infant school in this city. She has just returned, and appears eminently qualified for the enterprise. It is an experiment in a southern latitude; much will depend upon our success. We trust the blessing of Heaven will be upon the institution. * * * I am coming on in the usual way; my health good, that of my family, in general, good also; some little seriousness among us, but not much; expect only a few at our next communion; one who has applied is a man of fine talents, a lately appointed judge of the Superior Court; he has been under serious impressions for a considerable time; was once, I believe, something of a deist, and about two years ago challenged a man; but I have reason to hope for better things of him now—even things that accompany salvation. Two ladies also, who have all their lives long moved in the very highest circles in this city, have lately given proof of having been brought under the blessed influences of the divine Spirit; they seem willing to give up the world and all for Christ; God grant them grace so to do. * * * If there be any thing encouraging with you, tell me; and if not, tell me. I feel a continued and lively interest in the affairs of your church. Do be full in your communications; enter into details; any thing and every thing will be interesting to me. I should like to know something also of the operations of the 'Hickory broom,' (so called); it sweeps clean, does it? Has it looked as if it would come along your way? I saw the name of 'Handy,' as one likely to be placed on the list; were you the person meant? Do tell me about my old friend and room-mate, Mr. Collins; methinks I see him full of alarm, trembling in every joint. * * * Please to remember me affectionately to all my old friends.

"Your very sincere friend,

DANIEL BAKER."

(TO THE SAME.)

"SAVANNAH, 12*th August*, 1830.

"MY VERY DEAR FRIEND—I feel much indebted to you for your kindness in writing so many interesting letters, and especially for your forbearance in not taking offence at my long-continued silence. I know not how often I have taken up my pen to write to you, and then laid it down again, not knowing exactly what to say; and, indeed, I have now before me a half-written letter to you, dated the 11th ultimo.

"Yours of the 5th inst. was received this morning; you wish a prompt reply, and I must give it. I feel sincerely thankful to my old and much esteemed friends for their kind remembrance of me, and for the desire which they have expressed that I should return to Washington, and resume my former charge. I am more than thankful—my heart has been much affected—and this moment I have feelings which I cannot express. If it were clearly the will of God, there would be no difficulty; but I must frankly say, it is not—at least, it does not appear so to me under existing circumstances.

"With regard to pecuniary matters, you know, my dear sir, that I do not suffer such things to have much influence with me; I think I proved it, when, about nine years ago, I willingly gave up (because it was my Master's will) a salary of $2500 here for $1400 in Washington. My opinion decidedly is, that those who preach the gospel should live of the gospel, but should not be enriched by it; and I think I can adopt the sentiment embraced in those oft repeated lines,

> 'Man wants but little here below,
> Nor wants that little long.'

Indeed, to tell you the truth, you were not far from the mark when you supposed that large and small salaries were much the same with me. It is singular, but so it is. My income at different periods has varied as follows, $600, $1100, $1400, $800, $2200; and yet at no time have I been flush, nor at any time have I starved. Nor is this a new case; for we are told that when God rained manna upon the camp of Israel, he that gathered much had nothing over, and he that gathered little had no lack. The matter of salary, therefore, is by no means the principal thing. * * * I feel a great interest in the continued harmony and prosperity of your church, once called mine; and rest assured, my dear friend, I shall not cease to pray that the God of heaven may have you all in his holy keeping, and may send you, and that speedily, a man that shall unite your church and be a blessing to you all.

"You have heard, it seems, that I have left Savannah. This is a mistake; I am still here, and am sincerely attached to the people of my charge. As a church and congregation they have been very kind to me. The call was not entirely unanimous; and this, with some of its consequences, has made me more inclined than ever to adopt the resolution already mentioned, to accept of no call henceforward that is not unanimous. And now I am free to say, my present purpose is, if I do not succeed in uniting the church of which I am now pastor, I will, if the Master grant permission, become a missionary, and, after a reasonable time, make my final settlement in some obscure village in the West, where I may have, what I have long desired, a church perfectly united; where I may be as a father in the midst of his children: for 'better is a dinner of herbs where love is, than a stalled ox and hatred therewith.' We have had a season of great spiritual deadness among us for some time past; but at length the prospects, I think, are beginning to brighten a little. For about five weeks past I have been preaching almost exclusively to professors. I have had my spirit strongly stirred within me, and completely delivered, as I hope, from a man-fearing spirit. I have spoken the words of truth and soberness with all boldness; and the Lord has evidently carried it home to the hearts of many, although I have been most unsparing. I find the elders, and many of the members, are getting much of a tender, self-condemning spirit, and their language seems to be that of the Psalmist, 'Let the righteous smite me—it shall be a kindness; and let him reprove me—it shall be an excellent oil that shall not break my head; for yet shall my prayer also be in his calamity.' There is no use in denying it, after all, there is something very beautiful in the Christian spirit. The Christian may be chafed for a time, but by-and-by grace gets the victory, and all is calm and sweet again. Let my lot be with the child of God.

"Last Tuesday evening we had a meeting exclusively for communicants; it was a precious time. The excommunication of an unworthy member was pronounced; this added much to the solemnity of the occasion. The evening after, we had our usual lecture; the room was unusually full; and such were the appearances, that one of the elders said he thought, if anxious persons had been requested to do so, many would have kneeled down at their seats, to be prayed for. Yesterday I learned, to my very agreeable surprise, that about four weeks ago, several of the members, with two of the elders, united in observing a day of fasting, to pray for a blessing upon my labours. I have made an appointment for an anxious-meeting, to be held to-morrow afternoon. Whether any will attend, I cannot say; I bless the Lord, however, for any thing encouraging. Should sinners be converted, and certain individuals be softened down, I suspect, after all, my dusty bed will be laid in the same city of silence where sleeps the lamented Kollock.

"Please to remember me affectionately to all my friends in Washington, especially the communicants. Tell them I love them still; have not forgotten our prayer-meetings and sacramental seasons; and hope that if I never see their faces in the flesh any more, we may greet each other in glory, even in that happy world 'where saints immortal reign.'

"Your much obliged and very sincere friend,

DANIEL BAKER."

(TO THE SAME.)

"SAVANNAH, *Sept. 30th*, 1829.

"MY VERY DEAR FRIEND—Your last long and very interesting letter has been lying by me, unanswered, for some time. You are not to think strangely of this, for I have had occasion to write so many letters of introduction to you, that I thought they might answer very well as a substitute; especially as my manner has been to slip in something besides the introductory paragraph. I hope by this time you have seen some of my Savannah friends, particularly Mr. S. and Mr. C. * * * I am anxious to hear something about my room-mate, Mr. C.; you know he was a decided Adams man. Is he still permitted to drive the quill in the service of Uncle Sam, or not? I think you must have a very gloomy time in Washington, so many excellent persons thrown out of employment. Are these almost innumerable removals right? These appointments of senators and editors, are they right? If you 'shut the door when you begin to think,' you may be afraid to trust anything to the post-office department; but what comes to me shall, if you desire it, be kept as close as the grave.

"I have been tempted to publish some of your amusing remarks, but I thought perhaps I had better not. I would not, for a pretty thing, have your name on the list of the proscribed. Does Mr. M. (chief clerk, Land-office) stand fast and firm? Do write me another long letter, and let at least one page be devoted to the subject of 'Removals, Washington table-talk,' &c. You may well suppose I take a deep interest in such things, for they concern many that are well known and much esteemed by me. As for church matters in Washington, this, you know, is a standing subject; I shall consider no letter a finished one which has not something or other about it. May the Lord prosper all of your churches, and add daily unto them of such as shall be saved. Mr. G. requested me some time ago to do something for the Fourth Church, in Savannah; I made no attempt, for I knew it would be in vain, but subscribed myself twenty dollars.

"You have an Infant School, I find. Does it flourish? We have one also in Savannah—not for the poor, but for the rich. By this I mean, it is not a charity school, but designed for those who can afford to pay ten dollars a year, payable semi-annually, in advance. It met with strong opposition at first, but is now one of the most popular institutions of the city. We expect to open another before spring, for the poorer classes. I think these infant schools are grand things—will do much good.

"Savannah has been most remarkably healthy ever since my arrival. This is called the sickly season, but doctors (as the saying is) are starving. A great many of our rich folks, as usual, went off in pursuit of health. They would, in all probability, have done much better to have remained at home. This going to the north every summer is a sad thing for Savannah; it makes the city so dull. Besides, it tends to impoverish the city, draining it of about half a million of dollars annually. My congregation, at present, is comparatively small—about four hundred hearers; in the winter we have something like seven or eight hundred. Our evening meetings, held in our Sabbath-school room, have for a time been crowded and solemn. Some are under awakenings, but not many. We occasionally have inquiry-meetings, at which we have had ten or twelve present. We much need a season of refreshing. How much pleased should I be to have you pay us a visit; a little jaunt of this kind might be for your health. I would introduce you to a goodly number of the excellent of the earth, for I think we have as good Christians here as you would find in any part of the world.

"Yours, very sincerely,

DANIEL BAKER."

(TO THE SAME.)

"SAVANNAH, *Oct.* 30*th*, 1830.

"MY DEAR FRIEND—I wrote yesterday, and now write again to-day. This is strange, is it not? I will tell you my business in few words. In your last letter you mentioned that your health was not good; immediately it occurred to me that this would be a good time to insist upon your paying me a visit this fall or winter. And now, my dear sir, you recollect that you had half a mind to visit this seat of health last winter—only get another half, and you will have a whole one this season; and that, you know, is all that is required. So it appears very feasible, indeed. How pleased would Mrs. B. and myself be to see you, and entertain you in our own house. I promise you a hearty welcome, and your lady too. I am almost sure it would be a great thing for the health of you both. Besides, don't you wish to see Savannah? and don't you wish to see your old friend once more? and see his church too—and his people? Well, if you come, you may see them all; and some of them are worth seeing, I tell you. The church—the building, I mean—is perhaps not surpassed in elegance and grandeur by any in these United States; and, indeed, it ought to be something, for it cost, as I believe I have already told you, about one hundred and twenty thousand dollars—a good round sum, truly. It was reared, I am told, with some reference to millennial times, and I myself have no doubt but in that very building the thrilling sound will be heard, 'The kingdoms of this world are become the kingdoms of our Lord and of his Christ;' whilst, at the same time, great voices shall be heard in heaven, saying, 'Behold, the tabernacle of God is with men, and He will dwell with them, and they shall be His people, and God himself shall be with them, and be their God.' O, glorious scenes of a coming day! O, sweet bursting visions of millennial bliss! Roll on! The heralds of the cross, looking forward with joyous anticipations, cry, Roll on! The sacramental host of God's elect, listening with intense eagerness to hear the sounding of the chariot wheels of the great Captain of Salvation, cry, Roll on! The souls under the altar, too, of them that have been slain for the word of God, and for the testimony which they held, methinks are ready to swell the cry, and even in glory shout—Roll on! But whither am I carried. Excuse this rhapsody. The theme is so pleasant, the bare mention of it is enough to kindle the heart into rapture.

"But my time is short again, and I must wind up this letter, which I intended to be a short one—a little *nota bene*, as it were—yet I must not absolutely put a period to it until I have mentioned one thing more. * * * * O, when will men learn to preach the gospel in all its sweet simplicity! When will they consent to give up their unscriptural and bewildering metaphysical subtleties, or when will they cease to 'dote about questions and strifes of words,' whereof cometh envy, strife, railings, evil surmisings, perverse disputings of men of corrupt minds and destitute of the truth. Some persons have a most wonderful disposition to wish to appear deep and great—but, stop!—I must bring a railing accusation against no man, lest I deservedly incur the reproach of those who are 'fierce for moderation;' or, what is worse still, the displeasure of Him who has said, 'Judge not, that ye be not judged.' I leave them with Him whose province it is to search the hearts. To their own Master they must stand or fall.—Well, did you ever see the like; it seems I will give you a long letter in spite of all resolutions. My pen seems strongly inclined to course it over this remaining beautiful white space, but I am determined to hold it in check; so with cordial and affectionate salutations for Mr. M's family and your own, I bid you farewell.

Yours, as ever,

DANIEL BAKER."

"I promised that my pen should have no more liberties in the little area on the other side; but you see how it has leaped the fence, and got upon this side. Only one word more: Savannah is quite healthy, and you may come as soon as you please. My situation here is very pleasant in many respects. One elder tells me that I have gained upon the people; another elder says that for the last five months I have preached better than I ever did before, and, adds he, your people think so too; but the best of it is, my labours have been very encouragingly blessed."

Narrative resumed.

Amid lights and shadows, joys and sorrows, hope and fear, I laboured on, without much apparent success, until the 10th of August, 1830, when, not satisfied either with myself or the state of things in the church, I took *Payson's Memoirs* in my hand, and going out early that morning, I spent nearly the whole day in a distant graveyard, engaged in reading, and fasting, and prayer. That day marks a memorable era in the history of my life. Returning to my dwelling that evening, about the setting of the sun, I resolved, by the grace of God, to turn over a new leaf, and in preaching and pastoral visitations to be more faithful and diligent than I had ever been.

We copy from his journal at this time.

Savannah, Tuesday, August 10th, 1830. Have been reading the memoirs of Dr. Payson, late of Portland, Maine; found the account given of his piety and zeal, through grace, quickening to my soul. O, what a dead state have I been in for a length of time, and how unblessed my labours! I know not that a single individual has been awakened under my preaching for six months past. It will not do to live on at this poor dying rate. Lord, revive me, all my help must come from thee! As we are to have a communicants' meeting this evening, I determined to set apart this as a day of fasting, humiliation, and prayer—a day of special devotion. Had my heart somewhat drawn out in my morning devotions; afterwards took with me the Life of Payson, and thought that I would retire into the woods that I might enjoy more perfect retirement; thought the burial ground for the coloured people would be a good place; went in and found a brick tomb under a shade; every thing very favourable for religious reading and meditation. After prayer, commenced reading; whilst I read and mused the fire burned; my heart was greatly enlarged; the place proved a Bethel, indeed; I know not when I ever had my feelings more wrought upon; compared myself with Payson, and was deeply humbled in the comparison; longed to follow him even as he followed Christ. Finding in his life an account of a prayer-meeting for the special purpose of praying for those for whom prayer might be specially desired, was much pleased with the idea, and immediately concluded to have one of the same kind. In the evening the communicants' meeting was well attended, and very solemn; many tears were shed; proposed that we should have a day of fasting some time before our next communion.

August 15*th*, *Sabbath*. This day had something of the spirit of devotion; had liberty in praying for assistance and a blessing in preaching; preached in the morning from Ez. iii. 17—19; had more liberty than I have had for a long time; wept myself, and had the satisfaction of seeing others weep. In the afternoon preached from Isa. lv. 12, 13; at night had a solemn meeting in the Sabbath-school room; gave notice then that there would be a special prayer-meeting on Tuesday evening next; and after stating the special object, invited all who felt disposed, to send in notes; told them that a box would be placed on the table, and the room opened on Monday evening to receive the notes which might be sent in.

August 17*th.* Had a great many at the meeting; forty-six notes were sent in and read; some were from parents, entreating that prayers might be made for their dear unconverted children, and some from members praying for the conversion of their brothers and sisters; one was from a husband who longed for the conversion of his wife; and one from "A sinner who desires the prayers of God's people for the conversion of his soul;" another was from a sinful and unconverted wife, who requests that the people of God would pray for the conversion of herself and husband. Some were from professors who seemed to fear that they were not on a good foundation, and some from members who felt that they were in a cold, dead state, and longed for quickening influences. I put in a note myself, requesting the prayers of my people for me; that the Lord would give me a more intense love for souls; would give signal success to my labours, and would cause me to have a richer and sweeter experience of the grace of God in my own heart. The meeting was a delightful one, and one long to be remembered. At a little inquiry-meeting, which I attended in the afternoon, four were present; two professed to have obtained a hope, the other two were evidently under very serious impressions. One of the two who obtained a hope, told me that she was so much exercised under my sermon, last Sabbath morning, that on going home she resolved that she would neither eat nor sleep until she had obtained rest to her soul. Accordingly, before the time for the commencement of the afternoon service, she obtained a hope, and was enabled to rejoice in the God of her salvation.

August 18*th*. Visited a number of families; found the members in general very tender. All spoke in high terms of the meeting last evening; one said she was so happy after she got home, that she did not retire to rest until very late at night; another said she did not go to sleep until near daybreak, she had not felt so much for a long time. Blessed be God, if any mercy drops have fallen upon any soul. Lord, revive us! All our help must come from thee.

We resume the course of the narrative.

About this time, having a case of discipline to be communicated to the church, I appointed a meeting to be held in the lecture-room on the morning of a day which, I think, had been appointed by the Session as a day of fasting, humiliation, and prayer. This meeting was appointed exclusively for the members of the church. It proved to be one of deep solemnity. A lady, who moved in the first circle of society, was so much wrought upon that she wept aloud. When this was known, it became the subject of much conversation, and excited great interest. Calling to see a lady of some note, who was very lively and pleasant in her manners, but no Christian, she affected to be quite angry with me for the partiality which I had shown to my "dear members," as she called them. "You think a great deal of your dear members," said she, "but you don't care any thing for us poor sinners." "O, madam," replied I, "how you talk; I do care for you too." "No," said she, "there you had your meeting for your dear members, and you shut us poor sinners out; you don't care any thing at all about us." "O yes, madam, I do; and to prove it, suppose we have a meeting for those who are not members, and shut out all my 'dear members,' will you come?" "That I will," replied she. "Well, madam," I rejoined, "it is fixed." Perhaps the very next Sabbath, making a statement of some interest, I made the appointment, and respectfully invited all who had the candour to admit that they were not converted, to be present, and none but such. Having, as well as I can now recollect, spent the day in fasting and prayer, I went to the lecture-room at the time appointed, and the room was crowded. What an opportunity, and how great the vantage-ground which I occupied! From the Scriptures I pointed out the necessity of a sound conversion. It was a solemn time, a melting time. Many were much wrought upon—six or eight, at least—who shortly after gave good evidence of a real change of heart; amongst others, the very lady with whom I had conversed.

About this time Mr. Baker thus writes to Mr. Handy.

"SAVANNAH, *March 16th*, 1831.

"MY VERY DEAR FRIEND—I am perfectly astonished at your long silence. Only think how long it has been! What is the matter? Have you been sick all this time? or, has the image of Daniel Baker never passed before your mind since January last? Well, if you forget me, I am determined that I will not forget you—I cannot do it, for with me friendship is a very precious thing; and, besides, you have been too kind to me for me ever to cease remembering you with sincere affection.

"I suppose you would like to know how we are coming on here. Pretty much in the old way. The temporalities of the church are in a prosperous state; and during the last year twenty or thirty souls have, as I trust, passed out of darkness into marvellous light. At this time there is no special excitement, at least nothing very great. There are a few anxious inquirers, and I think Christians are somewhat moved; but really it seems a very hard thing for religion to flourish here. I think I can truly say, that I never laboured more faithfully in my life than I have done since I came to Savannah; and yet my labours have not been very much blessed. I desire, however, to be sincerely thankful that my labours have not been altogether in vain in the Lord. We are at this time seriously thinking of the propriety of having a four days' meeting in my church. It will certainly be a new thing here; and some may think it carrying the matter rather too far; but I hope we shall have it, nevertheless, and what is more, I do hope that God will abundantly bless it. Why do you not have one in your city? Only think of what is going on in New York; and you know how the work originated. I do think that Washington is the very place for such a meeting; and right glad would I be to hear that you had appointed one. If we succeed in having one in Savannah, I think it would be about the middle or last of April next. Cannot you be with us? Congress has adjourned, and I know that you have been kept very busy. Come to Savannah, and stretch your limbs a little, and breathe a little fresh air. The beauties of spring are now opening upon us, and every thing is getting bland and pleasant.

DANIEL BAKER."

Autobiography continued.

At this time my preaching became so plain and pointed that some persons took offence. One elder remarked, that certain things which I had said from this text, "Gray hairs are here and there, and he knoweth it not," were unwarrantable; and another elder said to my face, "Mr. Baker, if you continue to preach in this way, none of the young people will join our church." "I do not wish them to join," said I, "unless they are converted." "But," said he, "the pew-holders will give up their pews." "My mind is made up," said I, "and if my preaching is not liked, I am willing to retire and give place to another." A few weeks after, endeavouring to pave the way, I proposed to the Session that we should hold a four days' meeting. There were five elders present; three were in favour; two did not relish the matter much, but were willing that the pastor and the other elders should do as they pleased. There was yet another elder, and he a man of very high standing, who, aware of the business that would be brought before the Session, would not be present, but sent in a written protest. Although I had a majority of the Session with me, and moreover, knew that I had a great majority of the church on my side, I stated to the members of Session present, that as perfect unanimity was exceedingly desirable, I thought it would be best to postpone the consideration of the matter for a season; perhaps the respected elder who had sent in his protest might withdraw it. Accordingly, the very next day, the elder, conquered by the respect which had been shown to him, wrote me another note, withdrawing his protest and yielding all opposition to the contemplated movement.

The way was now open, and we must get the very best preachers, and as many as possible. The church was a splendid one, the congregation large, and every thing must be done on a grand scale. Accordingly, at a meeting of the Session, we fixed upon the names of *fourteen ministers!* But there was one much more desired than all others, the Rev. Mr. Joyce, a great favourite with the people of the "better sort;" but where he was we knew not. The elders, to a man, would, I suppose, have been willing to have brought him all the way from New York, or Liverpool, and paid his passage. I wrote the letters of invitation, as directed, and endeavoured to wake up a spirit of prayer and expectation. When the time fixed for the meeting drew near, I began to receive replies, one after another in this strain, "Dear brother Baker, I would be glad to comply with your invitation, but"—O, this *but*, this oft-repeated BUT, it was a tremendous blow to my feelings; it prostrated all my hopes; for I had such a poor understanding of things at that time, that I thought a great array of ministers was absolutely necessary to success; and a failure would to me have been worse than death, for I knew that many would rejoice in it. I had a dream that encouraged me, but only whilst the dream lasted. I dreamed that Dr. W. McDowell, who was very popular in Savannah, had promised to come; but I awoke, and, behold, it was only a dream! That morning—I remember it well—it was raining hard, and my spirits were much depressed; the time was near at hand, and only two or three ministers had promised to come. I did not wish to live any longer! I wanted to die!—and I was ready to say with Elijah, in the wilderness, when fleeing from the face of Jezebel, "It is enough; now, O Lord! take away my life, for I am not better than my fathers."

Whilst I was thus depressed, beyond measure, and bowed down, who should come into my study, in the midst of the rain, dripping wet, but Mr. C., one of my most valued elders. With a smiling countenance, he said, "Did you know that Mr. Joyce is in town?" "What!" replied I, the Rev. Mr. Joyce?" "The same—the very same!" I was electrified. In a moment, so to speak, I rose from the "cellar to the attic." "Brother Joyce come!" exclaimed I, "surely the Lord is on our side; I don't care now if no other minister comes!" Getting my hat and umbrella in a hurry, I hastened through the rain to the lodgings of this beloved man; and most cordially did I greet him; and how greatly was I rejoiced to hear him say that he had just come from attending a protracted meeting in the city of New York, which had been greatly blessed; and when told that we had appointed a protracted meeting to be held in our church, to commence within a few days, he expressed great pleasure in hearing it. I put that day down on the list of the happiest days of my life. I said, "Surely the Lord is with us, and our meeting will be blessed." This proved true, every word true, gloriously true.

The meeting commenced. We had prayer-meeting in the morning at sun-rise, and preaching in the church three times a day. At the expiration of the fourth day, besides many more under serious impressions, there were perhaps twenty persons who professed conversion. The meeting was continued one day longer, and as the interest continued, we continued our religious exercises, in various forms and ways, for a considerable length of time; our principal extra meetings being what was called "neighbourhood meetings," which were usually held in the afternoon, in private houses, once or twice every week for some months. In conducting these and the ordinary prayer-meetings, Mr. C. H., a very interesting young man, and a candidate for the sacred office, rendered me much important aid. This religious interest continued, without much abatement, for about one year, during which period one hundred persons were added to the communion of my church, and the blessed work of grace extended to other churches; the whole number brought in, if I mistake not, was about two hundred and fifty. Behold, how great a matter a little fire kindleth! This was not an April shower; it was "a whole day's set rain!" A great many persons of the first respectability were were brought in; amongst others, Judge L., who not long after was made a ruling elder; and Miss C. E., who subsequently perished in the Pulaski, as did also some twelve or fourteen others of my former charge, including Dr. C., the elder who had sent in his "protest," and his lady."

(LETTER TO MR. HANDY.)

"SAVANNAH, *June 6th*, 1831.

"MY DEAR FRIEND—I forget whether I informed you of our four-days' meeting. It was a blessed season. Its influence upon the church was truly happy. There was a waking up of the members, such as I suspect was never known here before. But this is not all: I think something like forty or fifty persons were awakened. Yesterday we had twenty added to our church on examination; and there were four or five others who applied, but were put off. Besides these, there are several others asking what they must do be saved; and I must not forget to mention that our sister churches have gathered in some of the fruits of the meeting also. But all this, it seems, is not to be compared with the result of similar meetings held recently in your city. How pleasing to me was the intelligence which you communicated. It was, indeed, like cold water to a thirsty soul; but there was one sad drawback, the Second Church, it seems, had but little part or lot in the matter. There is to be another four-days' meeting, and you wish me to be present. Most certainly a visit, and especially on such an occasion, would give me much pleasure; but, my dear sir, it is no small step. Now, if I had Tom Thumb's boots, or to be more classical, if I had Fortunatus's cap, the case might be altered—I mean if it were in my power, but it is not. I have been invited to attend a number of such meetings nearer home, but find it no easy matter to leave my people, even for a single Sabbath. I expect, however, God willing, to attend one at Robertsville, South Carolina, which is to commence on Thursday next. O, that the Master may be present, and that all his servants may have a fresh anointing from on high! Truly, we live in a wonderful day! May still richer blessings come down from Him who is able to exceed our thoughts and our prayers.

"When you receive payment from Mr. Adams, please appropriate ten dollars to the Colonization Society—it is a favourite institution with me. I wish I could give full ten times the sum. My family are in the enjoyment of their usual health; indeed, in this respect, we have been very much blessed. O for a thankful heart!

"Tell my much esteemed friend, Miss Mary M., that her very excellent letter to Mrs. B. has been received, and it afforded us much pleasure. She might reasonably have expected an answer long before this; but Mrs. B., as a correspondent, is very little better than myself. I have reminded her of her deficiencies, however, and if I have any influence with Mrs. B., our mutual friend may expect soon to receive a very choice letter. Tell her, in the mean time, that we both love her very sincerely; and that whether there be many or few letters, our affection for her is now the same. She has had, as well as yourself, very great and peculiar afflictions: but how pleasant are the words of our Lord, 'Are not two sparrows sold for one farthing, and not one of them shall fall on the ground without your Father; fear not, therefore, ye are of more value than many sparrows. O, my dear friend, the idea that the hand of God is in all the good and ill that checker life, affords sweet consolation; and O, how delightful is the assurance that all things work together for good to them that love God, and that the time is coming when he shall wipe away tears from off all faces. Love to all.

"Yours, very sincerely,

DANIEL BAKER."

It was about this time that the Washington Church gave a pressing call to Mr. Baker to resume his pastorate among them. The following letters from Presidents J. Q. Adams and Andrew Jackson, written in connection with the making out of this call, are of interest.

"QUINCY, *October 16th*, 1830.

"James H. Handy, Esq., Washington, D. C.

"DEAR SIR—I have received your letter of the 27th ultimo, communicating to me the proceedings of the Second Presbyterian Church at Washington, consequent upon the departure of their late pastor, the Rev. Mr. C.

"I very readily comply with your request, in the assurance of my cordial approbation of the re-election of their former pastor, Rev. Daniel Baker; for whom, if I had been present, my vote would have been cheerfully given.

"Accept the assurance of my best respects and fervent good wishes for the prosperity of the church.

"From your assured friend,

J. Q. ADAMS."

"WASHINGTON, *Sept.* 30*th*, 1830.

"James H. Handy, Esq., Washington City.

"SIR—I take pleasure in acknowledging the receipt of your letter of yesterday, as it affords me an opportunity of expressing my concurrence with the result of the election in the Second Presbyterian Church, to supply the place of Mr. C. I have great confidence in the piety and zeal of Mr. Baker; and had I been present when he was put in nomination, would have voted for him.

"I am, very respectfully, your obedient servant,

ANDREW JACKSON."

Dr. Baker did not see his way clear to accept the call to the Washington Church. To the end of his life, however, he regarded the members of that church with peculiar affection, ever speaking of the Washington Church as his "first love."

CHAPTER VII.

AS AN EVANGELIST.

THE revival in my church having been noised abroad (the narrative proceeds,) and this having originated in a protracted meeting, meetings of this kind were held in various places. One was appointed in Gillisonville, South Carolina, to which I was invited, and which led to very important results. Something like sixty persons were hopefully converted; two or three of whom subsequently became preachers of the gospel; one, Mr. W. Barnwell, is still pastor of a flourishing Episcopal church in Charleston. Shortly after this, I attended a protracted meeting in Grahamsville, South Carolina, and also in a certain church on May River, both of which were also greatly blessed; but a meeting held about this time in Beaufort, South Carolina, was, of all others, the most remarkable. By the influence of Mr. W. Barnwell, who resided in Beaufort, but was converted in Gillisonville, I received a pressing invitation to visit Beaufort. I went; and there being no Presbyterian church in the place, I preached alternately in the Baptist and Episcopal churches. The Episcopal minister, the Rev. Mr. Walker, was very cordial, and offered me the use of his pulpit. Knowing the peculiar views of our Episcopal brethren, I proposed standing below; but he insisted upon it that I should go into his pulpit. (This I would do after the reading of the Episcopal service.) O what blessed meetings we had! Three times every day did I preach, and night and day to full houses. Besides, it was usual to have what was called a "concert of prayer," at the going down of the sun. A few would meet in the house of a neighbour, and after singing

"Blow ye the trumpet," &c.,

would unite in a short prayer. Those who could not meet, would hold family worship in their own houses, or retire at the same hour for private prayer. The meeting continued to increase in interest until the period fixed upon for its close.

At this time I fully intended to return to Savannah, but was finally prevailed on to continue a few days longer—even until the whole time was ten days. The crowds which attended were very great. The whole number of persons hopefully converted amounted to about eighty, embracing many heads of families, and individuals of almost every age, from fourteen to eighty-six. Towards the close of the meeting, I invited those who had lately obtained a hope, to occupy certain seats, to be addressed as a distinct class; and very interesting was the sight, to see amongst the young converts, Colonel D. S., a most venerable, patriarchal man, of four-score and six. He had, in his youth, followed the celebrated Whitefield, and heard him preach many sermons, without any saving effect. Subsequently he had been, at several times, Intendant of the city of Charleston, and was, all his life-long, if I mistake not, a confirmed Unitarian, until the period of his conversion. Here was one emphatically called in at the eleventh hour.

Many of the converts were young men; eight of whom, as I have since been informed, devoted themselves to the service of God, in the sacred office. One of them, a talented lawyer, upon his conversion, grasped my hand with strong emotion, and exclaimed, "O, Mr. Baker, I have an ocean of joy!"—adding, "what would have become of me, if you had not come here?" Another, seeing me pass by the door of his house, rushed out, and seizing me by the hand, observed, "Only to think, that that name which I used to blaspheme, is now my only hope! And now," said he, "I think I can forgive a person every thing in the world except one thing." "You must forgive your bitterest enemy," said I. "But what," said he, "if any person should attempt to take away my Saviour?" Another of the young men, devoted to the ministry, has, for many years, been the Episcopal Bishop of Georgia. Mr. R. Barnwell, subsequently President of South Carolina College, was also brought in at this meeting; and so was Mr. Grayson, who has since been a distinguished member of Congress.

At that time Mr. Grayson, a highly talented man, was editor of the Beaufort Gazette, and upon the close of the meeting, published in his paper the following well-written account of the revival.

"We had frequently heard of religious revivals with no concern, we regret to say, when our little town became the scene of these striking and interesting events. The Rev. Daniel Baker, of Savannah, has been with us for some time, and never, surely, since the days of the Apostles, has more fervid zeal, or ardent piety, or untiring labour been devoted by a Christian minister to his cause. For ten unwearied days, from morning until nine at night, have we heard the strongest and most impassioned appeals to the heads and hearts of his hearers. All that is terrible or beautiful; all that is winning or appalling; all that could steal, and charm, and soothe the heart, or shake its careless security, and command its attention to the truths of religion, we have seen pressed upon our community with an earnestness, energy, and affectionate persuasiveness almost irresistible.

"The effect no one can conceive, who was not present. Politics were forgotten; business stood still; the shops and stores were shut; the schools closed; one subject only appeared to occupy all minds, and engross all hearts. The church was filled to overflowing; seats, galleries, aisles, exhibited a dense mass of human beings, from hoary age to childhood. In this multitude of all ages and conditions, there were occasional pauses, when a pin dropping might have been distinctly heard. When the solemn stillness was broken by the voice of the preacher, citing the impenitent to appear before the judgment-seat of heaven; reproving, persuading, imploring, by the most thrilling appeals to every principle of his nature; and when crowds moved forward and fell prostrate at the foot of the altar, and the rich music of hundreds of voices, and the solemn accents of prayer rose over the kneeling multitude, it was not in human hearts to resist the influence that awoke its sympathies, and spoke its purest and most elevated feeling.

'There stood the messenger of Truth; there stood
The legate of the skies. His theme divine,
His office sacred, and his credentials clear.
By him the violated law spoke out
Its thunders; and by him, in strains as sweet
As angels use, the gospel whispered peace.'

"The union of sects produced on the occasion was not the least striking feature of the event. Distinctions were laid aside. Christians of all denominations met and worshipped together, indiscriminately, in either church, and the cordiality of their mutual attachment was a living commentary on the great precept of their Teacher, "Love one another." Animosities, long continued, were sacrificed; coldness and formality were forgotten. Our community seemed like one great family, and it was impossible not to exclaim, 'What a beautiful thing is this religion! How it cheers, and warms, and elevates! How successfully it inculcates peace on earth, and good will among men!' The cordial co-operation of our pastors was another interesting circumstance; there was no petty jealousy, no distrust, no hanging back. They regarded themselves as labourers in one vineyard, and the minor interests of a part were merged for the time in the larger and more comprehensive concerns of the whole Christian Church, of which they are all equally members. We are not surprised that these revivals are hailed with enthusiastic delight by professors of religion. They are triumphs indeed of the faith to which they adhere; and the accounts of them must fall upon their ears like glad tidings of great joy. Even to the most careless observer, however disposed to be sceptical or speculative, or occupying, as he may, the cold and cheerless region of a self-dependent philosophy, such a scene as we have lately witnessed must possess no small interest. He sees religion in a new aspect, arrayed in beauty that he never dreamed of:

> 'Not harsh or crabbed—
> But musical as is Apollo's lute;
> And a perpetual feast of nectared sweets,
> Where no crude surfeit reigns.'

"'What,' he may say, 'if the Christian is wrong? His joys are nevertheless pure, elevated, and intellectual; and he is animated through life with the cheering hope of an immortality of happiness. If his be a delusion, it is one to be envied, not avoided; but what if he should be right?'"

In regard to this remarkable revival, an Episcopal minister, well acquainted with the circumstances, thus writes:

"The Rev. Daniel Baker, a Presbyterian minister, visited Grahamville, and preached with remarkable success. Many of the young and the old, the lawyers and planters, 'turned to the Lord.' The duellist threw away his pistols, the infidel believed in Christ, political feuds were forgotten, and the power of the gospel confessed.

"A desire to participate in these benefits induced some pious citizens of Beaufort to invite Mr. Baker to visit them. The notice of his visit, and of the proposed religious services, was sent from house to house. In one instance, it was received at a whist club, during their weekly meeting, and read aloud by one of the party amidst shouts of merriment. The intended meeting, its originators, objects, and agents, all afforded ample scope for ridicule. Some advised abstaining from the services by way of frowning down such folly. But, confident of their ability to withstand all the preacher's snares, they determined to attend, and prove the strength of their own armour. But a stronger than they was about 'to come upon them,' and strip them of the armour wherein they trusted.

"Not many days after, eight of this party of eleven were found 'sitting at the feet of Jesus,' and testifying to the power of his grace. One of the number is now a bishop, and another an esteemed presbyter of the Episcopal Church.

"The services were held twice or thrice a day, alternately in the Episcopal and Baptist churches, the only two places of worship in the town; the use of the Episcopal church being tendered by the Vestry for that purpose. The congregations increased daily; the whole community, laying aside their avocations, gave themselves up to the religious services. The word was 'with power,' whenever and by whomsoever preached. The consciences of sinners were aroused. The hearts of God's people were moved to earnest, prevailing intercession. Every day brought accessions to the ranks of those who 'mourned for sin.' Every day witnessed the joy of those who exchanged tears of sorrow for smiles of happiness in attaining a hope of salvation. The voice of praise and thanksgiving burst forth from lips unused to the worship of God. The scoffer knelt down in the church to pray. The proud formalist wept over his sins, and sought the intercessions of his friends. The gambler left his cards, and the convivialist his bottle, and 'went with the multitude to the house of God.' The interval between the public services was spent in prayer in private houses, in conference with the ministers, and in religious conversation. The consciousness of eternity seemed impressed upon every individual. 'The Spirit of God moved upon the face of the' community. A holy atmosphere pervaded the town, and affected the entire population to a degree unparalleled, save in the revival described by President Edwards, at Northampton, in 1735.

"It is difficult to convey an idea of the feeling which characterized the religious assemblies. It was not noisy, like the brawling brook; but deep, still, solemn, like the mighty river. Once, at the close of an evening service, when the congregation seemed to drink in the preached gospel, the minister invited those who desired the prayers of their brethren to kneel around the chancel. There was a momentary pause in the church, when, simultaneously, every pew door appeared to fly open; and not the chancel only, but the aisles also, were thronged with a kneeling multitude, in solemn silence, 'waiting for the moving of the waters.' God was manifestly present 'in the assemblies of his saints.' The truths of the gospel were realized as they never had been before, and the 'people believed in the Lord,' and gave glory to his name.

"But what were the effects of this deep feeling? Most of our readers have probably seen enough of the transient influence of 'revivals,' so called, to distrust the results of religious excitement. But the 'fruits' of this movement remain, and are obvious at the present day. As the whole population felt the divine impulse, some, doubtless, did not obey; but the great majority became consistent and useful Christans, filling many stations of honour and influence in the church and in the world.

"The results of this revival upon the congregations in Beaufort, are as follows: The number of communicants was increased manifold. At the first visitation of Bishop Bowen, after this meeting, seventy, chiefly of the young, the refined, and the wealthy, presented themselves for confirmation, sincerely offering their hearts to God. About the same number of whites, and very many blacks, also joined the Baptists. It is a singular fact, attesting the disinterestedness of the preacher, that out of two or three hundred conversions in Beaufort, under Mr.

Baker's ministry, not one became a Presbyterian. The Episcopalians and Baptists reaped the fruit of his labours. He seemed intent upon the conversion of souls; and the Lord wonderfully blessed his preaching to the saving of many. Others came in more slowly to the Episcopal church, making the addition of communicants, during the year, one hundred. Of this number, but two have drawn back from their profession; one of whom had been intemperate for many years. Six months after the events described, the writer was present at their communion, and saw, what he has never seen elsewhere, the entire congregation, with two exceptions, remain for the sacrament. When the children retired, two adults arose and left the church. The rest of the congregation partook of the ordinance.

"The parish church has been increased to twice its original capacity, and is better filled now than it was before, though the population of the town has not advanced in fifty years.

"The effects of the revival were as visible upon the community as upon the church. It seasoned with its holy savour all the intercourse of society. The truths of God's word, the glories of his gospel, the power of his grace, were frequent themes of conversation. 'They that feared the Lord spake often one to another,' and were not ashamed. The stranger within their gates felt the influence of the holy atmosphere, and was drawn by the power of sympathy towards Jesus, and often believed unto salvation. Family prayer was established in almost every house, and as you walked along the streets, in the stillness of a summer morning, you might hear the united voice of each household ascending in well-known hymns of praise, to the honour of their great Redeemer. The singing of hymns constituted the chief recreation of the young, in all their social intercourse; and we doubt whether more true joy was ever derived by the votary of pleasure from the brilliant assembly, than by the Christian from this religious exercise.

"Such was the pervading influence of the religious principle upon the whole aspect of society, that it cast it into the gospel mould, and stamped it with its own holy features. The world was in the minority; the gospel had a strong majority, and asserted its power over the hearts and morals of the community. For twenty years past there has been a higher moral and religious tone, and a more intelligent and consistent profession of Christianity maintained in that little town than in any other which the writer has visited in Europe or America.

"What were the effects upon the ministry of our church? Within a few months, and from the impulse received from this meeting, eight men went forth from this our congregation to preach the gospel of Christ. If you include the influence of this meeting upon neighbouring congregations, and chiefly under the same ministry, three more labourers were called into the Lord's vineyard. Those who are still in the field are the bishop of Georgia, and the missionary bishop to China, Rev. W. H. Barnwell, Rev. S. Elliott, Rev. C. C. Pinckney, Rev. B. C. Webb, of this diocese; the Rev. R. Johnson, and the Rev. W. Johnson, of Georgia. The distinguished Baptist preacher, Rev. R. Fuller, of Baltimore, was also a subject of this revival, and is the sixth of this list who exchanged the profession of the law for the ministry of the gospel.

"What were the effects upon the diocese? You must calculate the influence of the ministry of these labourers, directly and indirectly, upon the cause of Christ, ere you can fully answer the question. The leaven of that revival has already penetrated the mass of our church in this diocese. It has infused a new life into Episcopacy, and awakened a more earnest and evangelical spirit in the hearts of clergy and laity. It has moulded much of the doctrinal and ecclesiastical sentiment now prevailing among us, and stimulated that missionary feeling which has given our diocese a high place among the warmest friends of missions."

The narrative proceeds:

About the same time there was also high political excitement in South Carolina. Parties were arrayed against each other, and many persons went armed. I recollect well the cases of three gentlemen, who lived not very far from each other, and who were brought to bow at the feet of the Redeemer about the same time. Two were lawyers, and the third a rich planter. In giving an account of what the Lord had done for them, one remarked, "I had a quarrel with a certain gentleman, and had made up my mind, that the first time I should see him, I would spit in his face! but O, sir, as soon as it pleased God to reveal his love in my heart, the first thing I did was to pray for that man; and meeting him a few days afterwards, I went up to him and gave him *both hands*, in token of cordial reconciliation." Another said, "I was about sending to Charleston for a brace of pistols—I thought I should have occasion for them; but now," added he, "I would be willing to kiss the dust upon the feet of the Union-men, if they would only come to Christ. The third gentleman remarked, "Sir, you do not know the state of political excitement amongst us here. Why, sir, I felt myself as if I could just seize my gun and go out to the road and shoot down my own brother if he belonged to the other party. Now I can take them *all* in my arms and say, God bless every one of them!" What a blessed religion ours is!

Upon closing the meeting, I received something life fifty notes, from persons of every class, expressive of their feelings, and tendering to me their thanks for the great good which I had been instrumental in doing them. One, I recollect, began in this way: "Joy, joy, joy in heaven! and joy on earth! and joy to you, Sir!" and then followed an account of the occasion of this joy. Upon leaving Beaufort, Mr. Means, by whom I had been most hospitably entertained, had the kindness to send me and my little daughter, Theodora, in a row-boat all the way to Savannah; adding this mark of respect, to accompany me himself part of the way. A few days after reaching Savannah, I was overwhelmed with astonishment on receiving, through the medium of the post office, a most courteous and beautiful letter, containing, amongst other complimentary things, these words: "The citizens of Beaufort have deposited to your credit, in the Bank of the United States, the sum of nine hundred and sixty-one dollars and fifty cents." This extraordinary act of munificence overwhelmed me, and was particularly gratifying, as I received it as a remarkable providence.

Hankering after a missionary life, I had pretty much made up my mind to resign my charge, and engage in the service of a missionary society in Georgia; but to be cut down from two thousand dollars to six hundred dollars, was a serious affair; and I confess that I anticipated some hardships to be endured by myself and family, and behold, here a large provision was made in advance. Was not the hand of God in this? It seemed to speak in tones from heaven, loud and distinct, "Go forth as a missionary, and preach the gospel." Accordingly, not long after this, I resigned my charge, and, I must say, a noble one it was; for I never knew a church which embraced more intelligence and piety; nor did I ever know a people more kind and generous. Great efforts were made to induce me to reconsider my determination; but when it was seen that my mind was fully made up, there was a public meeting of the congregation; a series of resolutions passed, certainly honourable to the people, and no less gratifying to myself. Amongst other complimentary resolutions was this: that the sum of five hundred dollars should be presented to me as an expression of the respect and affection of the people for me. O, how good has the Lord been to me, in raising me up so many friends in so many places! Administering the sacrament of the Lord's Supper for the last time in Savannah, on Sabbath morning, —— 1831, that evening I preached my farewell sermon to a full house, although the weather was very unfavourable. The next week I entered upon my labours as a missionary, or, as was called, an "Evangelist." I expected these labours to continue about six months, when, by reason of most unexpected success, and some very remarkable providences, they were continued for about three years. The original idea was, that I should serve in the employment of a missionary society, located, I think, in Augusta, who were willing to allow me six hundred dollars per annum; but a great desire having been expressed by Dr. W. McDowell, of Charleston, and others, that I should labour in South Carolina, I wished to labour in that State also. In regard to this, the difficulty was, that if I extended my labours beyond the limits of the State of Georgia, I could receive no support from the missionary society of that State. In these circumstances, it was suggested that I should act as a missionary under the Synod of South Carolina and Georgia. But the Synod had no missionary fund. What was to be done? I stated that if the Synod thought proper, they might adopt me as their missionary, and recommend me to the churches in their bounds, and I would trust to Providence for my support. The Synod, accordingly, acted upon this suggestion, passed appropriate resolutions, and, locating my family first in one place, and then in another, I entered upon a course of missionary labours, and especially upon a series of protracted meetings, which, if I do not greatly mistake, will mark the best period of my life; my labours were more abundant, and my success far beyond my most sanguine anticipations. My field was extensive. During the first two years, I held protracted meetings in Midway, Darien, St. Marys, Augusta, Athens, and Macon, in Georgia; in St. Augustine, Tallahassee, Monticello, Quincy, and Mariana, in Florida.

The following statement in regard to the meeting in Tallahassee, is by one who is well qualified to speak. After the death of Dr. Baker, speaking of him, he says:

"We have had few men in this country whose labours have been so greatly blessed, and it will be profitable for us to inquire, why was *he* so highly favoured? I was one of the early settlers in Tallahassee, and one of the original members of the Presbyterian church organized there in 1832. Our numbers were small, and our prospects discouraging, when, near the close of 1832, we heard of the great revivals which followed the labours of Mr. Baker. We felt deeply our need of such a work, and after consulting together on the subject, I was requested to invite Mr. Baker to visit us. He accepted the invitation, and about the last of February, or early in March, 1833, I had the pleasure of receiving him and his son W. under my roof, where they continued during the whole of their stay in the city.

"Notice of his arrival was immediately given, and a good audience was gathered in the evening to hear him. The citizens of Tallahassee and its vicinity, embracing at that time representatives of many of the most distinguished families, particularly of the Southern States, were not surpassed, and probably not equalled in intelligence and refinement by the people of any other city of its size in the United

States. I watched with much anxiety the first impression he made on such an audience. That impression was every thing his friends could desire; and it was at once evident, that so far as human instrumentality was concerned, we had nothing to fear. On my way home from the meeting, I asked a gentleman, who has since occupied the highest place in our national legislature, what he thought of the sermon. 'Excellent, excellent,' said he. 'Then, of course, you will hear him again?' 'No,' he replied, 'I am bound to occupy a seat in the Senate of the United States, and if I go to hear him, he'll spoil it all.' This gentleman was, however, persuaded to hear him again, and, on conversing with him next day, he said, 'I can stand your fire and brimstone preachers very well, but this man makes me cry, and I must keep out of his way, or he will make a saint of me.' Every one who ever heard one of Mr. Baker's sermons on the love of God, or the ingratitude of the sinner, can understand the force of the honourable senator's remark.

"There were few men hardened enough to resist these appeals. His own soul was filled with gratitude and love, and he was intensely anxious to persuade all who heard him, to be, in this respect, 'almost and altogether such as he was.' His appeals were so kind, so earnest, so evidently sincere, that, whatever other effects they produced, his impenitent hearers could not resist the impression that the speaker was their friend. And this was one secret, so far as human agency was concerned, of his great power over his audience. But there was something more in his discourses than sincerity and earnestness. They were prepared with great labour and care, and the manner of uttering every sentence thoroughly studied. They were not exactly committed to memory, but every thought was so well fixed and arranged in his mind, that it was never omitted nor introduced out of its proper place. His sermons had consequently all the order and compactness of written discourses, with the ease and freedom of extemporary appeals. This series of sermons embraced all the great topics which are usually most effectual in their influence on the human heart; and they were so carefully prepared, that it was almost impossible to change, without injuring them; once heard, they were so deeply fixed in the mind that they were never forgotten. There is scarcely a sermon which he preached during the nearly three weeks he was with us, of which I cannot now recall, not only the matter, but even his gestures and tones of voice.

"Another secret of Mr. Baker's power, was his uniform habit of earnest communion with God, in his closet, before he delivered his message to the people from the desk. That communion was at times so near, and his face was so lighted up with heavenly love and zeal, that you could easily imagine it shone like that of Moses, when he descended from the Mount. Mr. Baker visited but little from house to house; his other labours did not allow him to do so; he never, I believe, took a meal but once out of my house while he was with us, and that was with one of the most desperately wicked men in the city, who had expressed a wish to converse with him. To all invitations his reply was in the words of Matt.

x. 11; and to that he adhered. But though he did not visit himself, he strongly urged the duty on the brethren. He availed himself of the means then in common use, of church fast days, anxious seats, relations of experience, meetings of the anxious in one room, which he always attended, and meetings of the church for prayer at the same time in another room, and the agreement by two or more members of the church to visit, labour with, and pray together for one or more impenitent friends, whom they had selected for that purpose.

"In the family he was one of the most delightfully companionable men I ever knew; he loved children dearly, and they were never so much delighted as when they found him at leisure to romp and play with them. He was, for the time, as much their companion as their most favourite playmates; but in their wildest sports he never forgot his own high calling, nor lost an opportunity to do them good; and there was nothing they loved better than to gather around him, as they did every day, and listen to his instructions.

"It was in a great measure owing to this exceedingly amiable and child-like simplicity, and his strict regard to all the courtesies of social life, that he was able to present those great truths which are most repulsive to the natural heart, with the utmost faithfulness and directness, without ever giving offence. Wicked men often quarrelled with his message, but never with him. His labours in Tallahassee were greatly blessed, and the church was strengthened by the addition of more than forty members, among whom were some of the most intelligent and influential men in the city."

There is one circumstance which illustrates the feelings with which this meeting was regarded by the two classes into which the community was divided. During one of the night services, some of the opposers fired off a quantity of fire-crackers near the church. Next morning, before breakfast, one hundred dollars had been subscribed, to be offered as a reward for the apprehension of the persons guilty of the outrage.

Here may be mentioned another incident connected with this period.

Party spirit ran high in Florida. Near a certain small town, not a hundred miles from Tallahassee, lived a lawyer, a warm political partizan, a fighting character. During a protracted meeting in his neighbourhood, he was awakened, and numbered amongst the converts. A few days after, at table in the house of a friend, he was asked by a clergyman present, to give some account of his conversion. He replied: "Last Saturday morning I put a dagger into my bosom, and went to ——, fully resolved that if any man insulted me, I would stab him to the heart. On returning home, I attended preaching. It pleased God that night to show me what a sinner I was; at such a time I found peace in believing, and now I indulge an humble hope that I am a child of God." "Mr. M.," said the clergyman, looking him in the face, "Mr. M., what have you done with the dagger of which you spoke? Have you given it away yet?" "No," replied he, "I am waiting until I come to deep water; I shall drop it there, and my pistol shall go along with it." Blessed be God for that religion which can thus soften down the rough points of the human character; which can thus convert the lion into a lamb, the vulture into a dove!

The autobiography proceeds.

I held a protracted meeting also in Montgomery, Alabama.

A gentleman, writing under date of July 4th, 1833, says of the meeting in Montgomery:

"You will be gratified to learn, that during the last spring our town was visited with a shower of divine influence. In the month of April a protracted meeting was commenced and carried forward through eighteen successive days, which resulted in the hopeful conversion of more than thirty souls. Brother Daniel Baker was with us, and to him, under God, are these blessed results to be ascribed. Never have I seen more deep and general interest on any occasion. All secular business seemed for the time to be laid aside and forgotten. Religion appeared the all-engrossing subject of thought and conversation; all denominations, laying aside their sectarian prejudices and peculiarities, were united as the heart of one man, in prayer and in pointing anxious sinners to the Saviour. We felt that the Spirit of God was present, of a truth. While Christians were rejoicing with a joy unspeakable and full of glory, weeping sinners, by scores, were seen crowding to the anxious seats and inquiry meeting, with the pentecostal cry, 'What must we do?' It was a season that gave birth to joy on earth, and, I believe there were rejoicings in heaven.

"I had often heard of the indefatigable labours of brother Baker, that highly-favoured herald of the cross; but my conceptions were very inadequate, until the great Head of the Church sent him to us. It is but just to say, I have never seen more untiring labour and apostolic zeal. During the meeting, his speaking in the church would have amounted to seven hours a day; and such was his eloquence, his power to interest, affect, and charm, that all eyes were rivetted, and all hearts were by turns melted, charmed, and captivated. Although he has left us, and perhaps for ever, yet his name and his labours of love will live embalmed in the affectionate remembrance of the people of our town. His labours were also greatly blessed to the surrounding churches which he visited. But while we thus speak of our worthy brother, we do not forget that from God cometh the increase, and to his name be all the glory."

The autobiography proceeds.

I held also a few protracted meetings in North Carolina; but South Carolina was the principal scene of my labours as an "Evangelist," so called. It was common with me to locate my family in some desirable and convenient place, and go out upon a missionary tour of two or three months, and return to them and rest a while. The most remarkable tour embraced twelve protracted meetings in twelve consecutive weeks; those hopefully converted averaging forty-five for each meeting. Some of the most important places were Walterborough, Columbia,

Camden, Cheraw, Winnsboro', Laurens Court House, Newberry, Pendleton, and several churches in Abbeville and Union Districts.

"I was a student," says one, in regard to the period above mentioned, "in the Theological Seminary at Columbia, South Carolina, when, on Tuesday evening, the 8th of May, 1832, a series of religious meetings was commenced, in which Presbyterians, Methodists and Baptists united. The meetings were conducted by the Rev. Daniel Baker, since D. D., who was soon instrumental in awakening much religious interest in that capital city of the State.

"From my journal of that period, I find that the first inquiry meeting was held on the fourth day of these special services, when about fifteen persons attended, to ask what they must do to be saved. And on the 15th of May, from fifty to sixty were at the inquiry meeting, including eight or ten persons, who, by that time, were reckoned converts, and were ready to tell what the Lord had done for their souls. The 18th of May was observed as a day of fasting, humiliation, and prayer, by the churches in Columbia, and revival influences evidently increased among believers and inquiring sinners.

"This series of religious services, which were held mostly in the evening, was concluded by a regular three-days' meeting, which finally closed on the evening of May 27th; when about twenty-five were found to be rejoicing in new hopes of eternal life, and more than fifty were still inquiring the way to Zion.

"The Baptist brethren next held a protracted meeting by themselves; which was blessed with the gracious influences of the Spirit. I think Mr. Baker had then left the city. But the good work, begun under his instrumentality, went on till about one hundred were reckoned as converts, some forty of whom united with the Presbyterian Church on the first of July. How many joined subsequently, or united with other churches, as the fruits of that revival, I am unable to state; but it was a glorious season in that dark period.

"Mr. Baker having returned to Columbia, where his family then resided, at his particular invitation, on the 20th of August, I started with him to attend a protracted meeting at Nazareth Church, in Spartanburg District, about one hundred miles northwest from Columbia. We reached our destination on the 23d of August, and that day Mr. Baker preached twice to a congregation of one hundred and fifty to one hundred and seventy-five people. The next day the audience was much larger, and a number gave evidence of deep anxiety on the subject of religion. On the 25th of the month, the congregation had increased to six hundred or seven hundred persons, and that day about forty-five attended the inquiry meeting, nearly half of whom had just begun to rejoice in the Saviour; and on the 29th of August, when we left Nazareth, about eighty were numbered as converts, while fifty or sixty were still inquiring the way of eternal life.

"From Nazareth we proceeded to Winnsboro', a large and flourishing village, about thirty miles northwesterly from Columbia. We arrived on the afternoon of Friday, the last day of August, and though unexpected at the time, Mr. Baker commenced a protracted meeting by preaching in the evening. The next morning there was a meeting of professors of religion, and in the course of the day some sinners were found in an anxious state of mind. On Sabbath, the 2d of September, there were about fifty at the inquiry meeting; and at a special meeting in the afternoon, for the unconverted, about one hundred and twenty were present; and in the evening of that interesting day, some ten or twelve were found rejoicing in hope. On Tuesday, September 4th, the inquiry meeting seemed to partake of pentecostal influences, for about fifteen souls believed it to be their hour of grace. On the next day, the whole number were young, or in the fresh prime of life. About thirty were still inquiring for salvation. On Friday morning, September 7th, a week after our arrival, the protracted services closed with an inquiry meeting at sunrise.

"During that precious week, Mr. Baker preached sixteen sermons. At Nazareth and at Columbia he had abounded in the ministration of the word, though I have no memoranda of the exact amount. Other ministers shared in the preaching, especially at the two last-named places.

"He often looked over his manuscript before preaching, but he frequently dispensed with notes in the pulpit. His voice was clear and strong, his utterance easy and fluent, his manner very earnest and animated; and when in the full flow of his subject, amid revival scenes, he was strikingly eloquent and impressive.

"Few forms and faces, daguerreotyped so long ago on my mind, remain as distinct as his at this day. In person he was about the medium height, of moderately full habit, with a fair complexion, very clear, intelligent blue eyes, and black hair. In disposition, he was remarkably sociable and amiable.

"As far as I had opportunity to observe, and now recall his method in revivals, his first aim was to arouse Christians, and elicit much fervent and persevering prayer. I personally knew a circle that, during the revival at Columbia, on more than one occasion, spent the whole night in prayer. His application of truth was very plain and pungent, without being harsh and repulsive. Every where he won many friends, but I have no recollection of his having enemies. He was well aware that in revivals some would mistake sympathy and excitement for conversion; and he warned his hearers that experience had led him to expect that about such a portion, I think it was a tenth, of professed converts, would finally turn back from following Jesus.

"I have never forgotten him, and shall know him again in a better world, where I doubt not he has received a crown of righteousness gemmed with many stars."

In regard to the meeting in Walterborough, a gentleman resident there thus wrote under date of October 12th, 1832.

"On last Thursday, a religious meeting was commenced in this place by ministers of various denominations, and closed this day. You may recollect that last fall many individuals here were brought to a profession of religion in consequence of a meeting held by Presbyterian ministers. But these were comparatively few. They were enough, however, to embolden another effort, and to encourage our ministers in the belief that more hearing would produce more religion. Nor have they been disappointed. The result has exceeded the most ardent hopes of the most pious, and has carried amazement and wonder to the irreligious. On each day the interest in the meeting increased, and every argument and appeal fell upon the attentive audience with deeper and deeper solemnity. The business of the town ceased; conversation on common topics ceased; and the mind seemed to be driven in upon itself, in the business of strict and solemn self-examination. Monday and Tuesday were the days of the general election; yet the polls were either not attended, or the voters dropped their votes into the ballot-box and went away. At the close of the services the result is, that between sixty and seventy individuals, nearly half of whom are male adults, have determined to pursue the walk of a Christian life, and several others appear deeply anxious as to their religious situation. In fact, almost the whole mass of the population are now pious, as far as human discernment can extend, rejoicing in the hope of salvation. A complete revolution must be produced in the whole frame of this society, and the pure religion of Christ be its grand characteristic.

"I know the world will say—nay, some professors will say, that this is all 'animal excitement.' Without stopping to animadvert upon the phrase 'animal excitement,' I would state that the sermons and addresses, to say the least of them, are far stronger than any I ever heard in the city of Charleston, excepting in two instances. Nor was the audience of such a character that words of mere 'sound and fury' would affect them. The ministers were undoubtedly earnest, as if they really did believe the doctrines they inculcated, that the soul of man is immortal; but they did not exhibit more earnestness than is common every day at the Bar. The truth appears to me to be this: those who are brought to a sense of the importance of religion at these meetings are no more excited than those who are changed by the ordinary course of preaching. Nor are they changed upon less reflection, though in a shorter space of time. The attention is arrested for days together, and this is the whole secret, humanly speaking, of the success of these continued meetings. Attention, consideration, is all that true religion wants; and these being withheld, is, in fact, the great difficulty which impedes its progress to our hearts. Under ordinary circumstances, what is heard once or twice a week is forgotten or drowned in the cares of life before the voice is heard again; but when the whole scheme of our pure and sublime religion is laid out in some twenty or thirty sermons, and pressed home upon the mind day after day, in succession, with great faithfulness and ability, the effect is almost inevitable. The camp-meetings of the Methodists accomplish this object, and their success as a denomination, I am satisfied, is greatly attributable to this instrument. Every denomination should now adopt these protracted meetings. Their efficacy is beyond doubt or cavil.

The seal of experience and of God's approbation is put upon them, in the blaze of success which accompanies them; and if any one denomination, whilst others adopt, shall set its face against them, it will cease to exist as a Christian Church, or will exist, a very good place for decent morality, but no abode for the gospel of Christ. I shall join the Church of my forefathers, the —— Church; but if that Church throws itself in opposition to these meetings, which are now bringing thousands and thousands into the pale of Christianity, I shall, without hesitation, renounce it.

"By-the-by, why do not you Christians in Charleston raise an Evangelical Society for the purpose of supporting Mr. Baker as a mere Evangelist. All denominations should unite in such a society, for he has, indeed, like his great prototype, known nothing amongst us save 'Jesus Christ, and him crucified.' His labours benefit all denominations equally, and why should not the whole Church take upon themselves the duty of his support. Cannot every pew and bench in the State pay one dollar to his support, whilst he is going abroad carrying the light and liberty of the gospel over the land. We here, of all denominations, will freely support any scheme which will afford him a certain and ample competency. We must not let him leave the State. I mean not to undervalue other societies for the promotion of Christianity, but I do say, that to any one who has witnessed the effect of his preaching, the utility of all your other societies put together will scarcely equal the labours of this single man."

A gentleman, at that time a lawyer, resident in Walterboro', after speaking of the revival in Beaufort, thus proceeds, under date of Feb. 12th, 1858. His remarks illustrate the indirect influence of the labours of Mr. Baker, as well as the direct. So much is introduced in regard to this period, because it is all explanatory and illustrative of his labours both before and after.

"At this time, Rev. Edward Palmer, pastor to the Presbyterian church, returning from one of Mr. Baker's meetings in Beaufort District, gave to his congregation a detailed account of what he had seen, and, with his heart burning with zeal, appointed a protracted meeting to be held in his church a few days thereafter. He had caught new fire at the altars where he had been labouring with Mr. Baker, and imparted some of it to a portion of his own little flock, and, when the protracted meeting took place, although Mr. Baker was not present, God's Spirit was there; and, as the result of this meeting, a considerable number was received into both the Presbyterian and Episcopal churches, giving to both a vitality and strength never known before to them. This, I repeat, so far as human agency was concerned, was the indirect result of Mr. Baker's labours.

"The pastor of the Episcopal church at that time, although he had received into his communion as the result of that protracted meeting, if not larger numbers, more active and efficient piety than it before possessed, was, nevertheless opposed to these meetings. Not so, however, were those who had recently joined his communion. They laboured hard to bring him to their views, and great was their surprise, when, in the summer of 1833, the Presbyterians were on the eve of holding another protracted meeting, he announced his willingness to have a union meeting, provided the services should be one-half of the time in his own church. All parties cheerfully consented to this arrangement. The recent Episcopal converts promptly sent for Mr. Walker and Mr. Young, of Beaufort District, Episcopal clergymen, who had there zealously co-operated with Mr. Baker, who, surprised and rejoiced that 'Saul was among the prophets,' laid aside every thing else, and repaired to Walterboro' to take part in this union meeting.

"The meeting commenced under favourable auspices and continued for ten days. On the evening of the second or third day, one of the Episcopal ministers, at the close of the sermon in the Presbyterian church, when the house was filled to overflowing, announced his former opposition to what he was about to do, his conviction that he had been in error, and closed with a solemn invitation to all who felt an interest in their soul's salvation to kneel before the pulpit, when the people of God would unite in prayer on their behalf. No appeals were made, no effort to operate on their fears or their sympathies; but almost the entire impenitent portion of the large audience came forward. Among these was a large portion of the leading men of the place. It was a scene seldom witnessed in this heedless world; one over which angels in heaven as well as saints on earth rejoiced. The day after this scene, Mr. Baker arrived. All had heard of him, and all went out to see and hear him. For several successive days he preached, sometimes twice a day For the most part, his sermons were those known as his REVIVAL SERMONS, which have since been published. They were delivered with great simplicity and power, but with an unction that seemed to impress his hearers with the conviction that really he was an ambassador from heaven, and spoke 'the words of truth and soberness.' I saw the aged sinner, who in his worldliness and licentiousness had scarcely ever thought of God but to blaspheme his name, tremble under the power of his voice, and look as though his future doom was shadowed before him. I have heard many of the most eloquent men of our country in the pulpit, but I have never heard one who, to the same extent, could rivet the attention of the sinner, draw him insensibly to the conclusion that he was 'a fool—a consummate fool;' harrow up his soul, force him to think, and lead him to pray. It was not the power of eloquence in Mr. Baker that accomplished these results, for he was not what the world terms an eloquent man, but it was, as I believe, that unction from on high, which, reflected from his heart on his countenance and manner, fastened on the hearer the conviction that he was in truth God's ambassador. In illustration of what I mean, I will state a fact. At one of his meetings in Beaufort District, when the whole community was in a high state of excitement, a friend of mine, in middle life, an irreligious man, determined, near the close of one of his services, to go to the door of the church to see this wonderful man. Taking with him some others, influenced by similar curiosity, he went; and when they reached the door of the church, Mr.

Baker was praying. My friend told me, that for a few moments he listened, and whispered to his associates, 'That man prays as though he were really talking with God.' The more he listened, the more the conviction was fastened on his mind. He went to scoff, but remained, as did some of his associates, to pray. That prayer led to his conviction, and, as he trusted to his conversion.

"Many incidents of similar character might be told, going to show that for his power he was largely indebted to the unction of the Holy Ghost. Another incident I remember. When at Walterboro', there was a little band of sceptics or infidels residing there, who, seeing their friends passing into the kingdom, were more perturbed than they were willing to admit. One of them, a gentleman of intelligence and high respectability, remarked to me, that Mr. Baker, in his preaching had begun at the wrong end; that he ought first to have proved the Bible true; and requested me to ask him to preach on that subject. I told him I would, and advised him to bring to the church that night all who thought as he did. In the course of the day I stated the case to Mr. Baker. He hesitated—gave no answer other than to say, 'The Lord direct.' At night the 'little band' were at the church. The text was given out, and it was manifest the sceptics would not get their portion; but after he had proceeded in his discourse for a few minutes, he was interrupted by the fainting of a lady. The confusion having ceased, he announced that perhaps he was not in the line of his duty; stated the request made of him; gave out a new text, and preached a sermon on the evidences of Christianity.

The discourse did not equal in manner or argument his usual efforts; there was nothing said that his sceptical hearers had not often read; yet my sceptical friend told me the next day, 'Mr. Baker is a wonderful man—had removed all his doubts;' and added, 'If you had asked me, I would have gone up to be prayed for.' What but the unction to which I have referred, under God, accomplished this result?

"Mr. Baker was a man of great simplicity of character, as well as of unwavering faith and ardent zeal. At the time to which I refer, he acted as though he felt, in the inmost recesses of his heart, that he was an evangelist, an apostle, sent forth with the commission of his Master; and that the injunctions resting on the early disciples were the only rules of his conduct. When he first reached Walterboro' he took up his abode with the pastor. I urged him to change his residence—his prompt reply was, and expressed as though he meant literally what he said, The Master says, 'Whatsoever house ye enter into, there abide, and thence depart.'

"But what I regard as the crowning glory of Mr. Baker's life, is the new phase which some of the churches of South Carolina, (and I may say Georgia too,) through his instrumentality, were made to present. At the time he was labouring in Beaufort, with the exception of the church at that place, these churches were nearly all, in the language of one of their eminent laymen, 'little better than masonic lodges.' They had the form of godliness, but were destitute of its power. The frequenters of the race-course and the theatre found their places at the communion-table. The duellist was not excluded.

Through the instrumentality of Mr. Baker's preaching, W. B., two of the E's, and some others, abandoned the bar and other pursuits, and entered upon the ministry in the Episcopal Church, carrying with them into it the views and feelings they had received under their religious instructors at Beaufort. Through the same instrumentality, R. B. R. had united with the Episcopal church at Walterboro'; and removing shortly after to Charleston, he endeavoured there, among his Episcopal brethren, to rally together those whose views and feelings coincided with his own and those he had left behind him. He tried, as he told me, to get up a weekly prayer-meeting, such as he left at Walterboro', composed of male members of the Episcopal church; but the project failed. In his zeal, and his untiring perseverance in whatever he undertakes, he persuaded his cousin, W. B., then inducted into the sacred office, to remove to Charleston. He, with some others, principally ladies, secured a chapel, in which Mr. B. should preach; and the young, but gifted and lamented Cobia, a man of kindred spirit, coming to his aid, in that little and retired chapel they laboured until the large church of St. Peter's was built for Mr. B., and these faithful ministers of the cross had the satisfaction of seeing, in nearly all the churches of the city, assistant ministers employed, whose spirit and sentiments corresponded with their own. That party, the evangelical party, has now the ascendency in the diocese of South Carolina. The same party has the ascendency in the diocese of Georgia, its chosen leader, Bishop Elliott, acknowledging Mr. Baker as his spiritual father."

Narrative continued.

My preaching for the first two years after leaving Savannah, may, I think, be put down at two sermons a day for every day in the year. The number of those hopefully converted under my preaching, I suppose may be about two thousand five hundred. To God be all the glory! It was usual with me, during protracted meetings, to preach three times a day. Besides this, it was common to deliver addresses to various classes of persons, such as professors of religion, mothers, young men, young ladies, children, &c. In doing this, my usual plan was to come down out of the pulpit, and have the particular class of persons to be addressed gathered together immediately before me. Sometimes I would have one meeting, during the occasion, exclusively for the unconverted; Christians being in some other place at the same time, engaged in special prayer for those at the meeting for the unconverted. Sunrise prayer-meetings were also sometimes held. Occasionally, when deemed prudent, I would invite the awakened forward to certain seats, to be particularly addressed and prayed for; but inquiry meetings were with me much more common.

During this two years' term of missionary labour, my health was uniformly good; my voice also was strong, but generally somewhat hoarse. On one occasion my voice suddenly failed; from being pretty loud, though hoarse, just as I was closing a sermon in the afternoon, in one moment of time it fell to a whisper. I confess I was alarmed, and did not wish to preach, or even attempt it; but the thing could not very well be avoided. I did preach, and no evil consequences ensued. It is true, my friends were wont, frequently and kindly, to warn me of preaching so incessantly; but as frequently the converts averaged one or more for every sermon, I determined to go on as long as my Master was with me, blessing and sustaining me.

The failure of voice spoken of, was the only case of the kind he ever experienced. How often is it the case that ministers, especially those of an ardent temperament, or preaching during a revival, preach in an unnatural key, and with an unnecessary force of voice. This greatly lessens the effect of what they say on an audience, and exhausts, and permanently affects the organs of speech. Those who have heard Dr. Baker, will remember that he always spoke on a perfectly natural key and easy pitch of voice. In consequence, speaking was no weariness to him whatever. He knew nothing of throat disease, though preaching incessantly, and often in the open air. In fact, his preaching was an exercise which developed and confirmed his constitution—in it was his highest physical enjoyment. In his perfectly natural manner of speaking, too, lay a great part of his power over his audience. There was no measured cadence, no pulpit tone. His manner in the pulpit was as natural and easy as in the parlour. He stood in the pulpit as one who had something important to say; but he saw no reason why his manner in speaking to two or three thousand persons at once, should differ from his manner in speaking to two or three persons, or even to a single person, so that he made himself heard. He was too much in earnest to declaim. His effort was to present divine truth with transparent clearness, and let that truth work its own results. In a discourse, his voice and manner ran through a wide range—statement of subject, reasoning, solemn denunciation, tearful entreaty—but in all he was natural, perfectly so; it was only a man conversing with his friends most earnestly in regard to their soul's salvation.

Take the following, the first illustration that comes to mind, of the simple mode by which he would impress an important truth on his hearers. He is warning against putting off the salvation of the soul from day to day. Imagine the words, delivered from the speaker's lips in the pulpit, according to the manner just mentioned.

"One day the minister heard that his neighbour was sick, very sick. What if he dies in his present state? thought the minister. He is an amiable man, a generous man, in many points of character a most excellent man; but, by his own confession, he is no Christian, has never felt the power of God's converting grace upon his soul. Suppose he should die in his present condition! I must go and see him. Accordingly, taking his hat and cane, he calls to see him. He knocks at the door; a servant opens it.

"'How is Mr. K.?'

"'Very sick, sir; please to walk in.'

"The minister, led by the servant, enters the chamber. The curtains are down. The room is darkened, and on the bed there lies his neighbour, scorched by a raging fever. Taking him kindly by the hand—'How do you feel yourself this morning?' says the minister.

"'Very sick, sir,' replied the neighbour.

"After a while, the minister, in a subdued tone of voice, says, 'Do you think, my dear sir, that you have made your peace with God? Should God see proper *now* to take you away, are you ready to go?'

"'O, sir,' says the sick man, interrupting him, 'I am in agony. Please to excuse me. O, my head, my head! I cannot talk to you now. Please to call again.'

"'When shall I call?'

"'*To-morrow*,' says the sick man.

"The faithful man of God bursts into tears, and retires. The next day he calls again. The knocker is muffled—a bad sign. Knocking gently at the door, the servant opens it.

"'How is Mr. K.?'

"'No better, sir. Please to walk in.'

"The minister enters the chamber, and there is his neighbour, still upon a bed of sickness. 'My dear neighbour,' says the minister, 'how do you do this morning?' There is no response. The man is delirious now, and speaks in broken sentences, incoherently. The minister, leaning upon the top of his cane, looks at his neighbour, and the silent tear trickles down his cheek. He is about to rise up and go away, but the wife of the sick man exclaims,

"'O, my dear pastor, won't you pray for my husband?'

"The prayer is offered, and the minister, taking the hand of his neighbour, says, 'My dear friend, good-bye.' Still there is no response. Alas! the sick man knows not that his wife is weeping at his bedside, and that his pastor has been praying for him. As the man of God is retiring, the affectionate wife follows him to the door, and, in parting, says,

"'My dear pastor, I am in great affliction; will you not be so kind as to call again?'

"'Madam,' says he, 'when do you think I had better come?' and she says, '*To-morrow.*'

"The associations are more than he can bear, and the man of God goes weeping all the way, returning home. The next morning he calls again. The knocker is still muffled. He taps gently at the door. The servant opens it.

"'How is Mr. K.?'

"'He is said to be worse, sir.'

"'I would like to see him.'

"'You can't, sir. The doctor has just left, and he has given the strictest orders that nobody should enter the room except those who are waiting upon him. But here is Mrs. K.'

"'Madam, how is your husband?'

"'O, my dear pastor,' replies she, 'he is worse, I fear much worse!'

"'I would like to see your husband, madam, a few moments.'

"'I would be glad to have you see him, too,' replies the afflicted woman; 'but our physician says that the crisis has come, and that the slightest excitement may prove fatal; but he said that if his patient revived, he might be able to see you *to-morrow.*'

"Having received a message, about the going

down of the sun, that his neighbour was still in a critical state, and too weak to be seen, the minister can scarcely sleep that night, so anxious is he about the salvation of his neighbour. The next morning, taking his hat and cane, he goes early, at least to make some inquiry. Tapping again gently at the door, the servant opens it.

"'How is Mr. K.?' is the anxious inquiry.

"'O, sir,' replies the servant, 'he is dead!'

"'Dead!' exclaims the minister—'Dead!'

"'Yes, sir; he died this morning, at four o'clock.'

"'God have mercy—' the minister was about to say; but it flashed upon him, it is too late now.

"Dear, procrastinating sinner, it is enough. I beseech you do not say, To-morrow, any more. To-morrow! It may be too late for ever. To-morrow's sun may shine upon your grave! Once lost, you are lost for ever! Be wise to-day, 'tis madness to defer."

Being colloquial, and thus entirely at his ease in the pulpit, there was little danger of becoming embarrassed by any untoward circumstance. Only on one occasion in his life was he thrown out. In the midst of a certain discourse, a lady of immense size entered the church, and advanced down the aisle. He paused, endeavoured to resume the thread of his sermon, requested a certain hymn to be sung, then rose again from the seat he had taken, and went on as if nothing had happened. He never hesitated, in the midst of a sermon, to rebuke any disorder. If any outcry, the result of religious emotion, was made, he would pause, and say in a solemn manner, "The Lord is in his holy temple, let all the earth keep silence before him:" a course which never failed to still even the most excited. He could bear a babe crying in the congregation, but misconduct on the part of one old enough to know better, he would never permit. On one occasion, after once or twice rebuking a rude boy, he said at last, "Little boy, go home, and tell your mother you deserve a good whipping;" and, as the boy went out with his singular message, the speaker continued his discourse. When preaching in a certain college, which had been under infidel influence, the students in the gallery purposely disturbed him by audible conversation. Pausing, and addressing himself to them, he said, with the utmost solemnity, "Young men, at the bar of God, in judgment, you will answer for your conduct this day." He then resumed his discourse, without further interruption. On another occasion, in the midst of his sermon, he spoke of the infidel. A gentleman in the congregation suddenly spoke out, "And pray, sir, what is an infidel?" Without a moment's hesitation, the speaker replied, "I will tell you, sir, first, what an infidel is, and secondly, what is the doom of the infidel, unless he repent, and accept Christ"—and abandoning the previous sermon altogether, he preached upon this impromptu subject most effectively. At the close of the discourse, the gentleman came forward, explained that he had spoken out impulsively and unintentionally, and thanked him heartily for the extempore sermon which had resulted.

His style may be described in one word—it was colloquial. Although avoiding every thing unbecoming so sacred a place, he used anecdote and illustration very freely; at times causing even a smile, which would soon give way, however, to tears. He was thus colloquial in preaching, because he was too much occupied with his message to think for an instant of the manner in which he was delivering it.

The narrative continues:

With regard to pecuniary matters, I was in the employment of no society; of course, I had no fixed income. My rule was, to say nothing about the matter, but to trust Providence. In some places, I did not receive a single cent, even when my labours were greatly blessed; in other places, more was given to me than I could conscientiously accept. On one occasion I returned about thirty dollars; on another, I returned one hundred dollars. Sometimes my friends, in making up a purse for me, would greatly add to the value of the gift by the happy manner in which it was done. I may here mention a case. Upon closing a protracted meeting in St. Mary's, a gentleman, (not a professor,) told me that his house was on my road to Tallahassee, whither I was going, and very politely invited me to spend the first night with him. I did so. The next morning he said he would accompany me a few miles to show me the way. I was in my gig, with my youngest son, W., and my kind friend riding on horseback at my side. After accompanying me on the way some four or five miles, he remarked, "I believe the way is plain, and you will have no difficulty now." Saying this, he handed me a sealed letter, politely requesting me to take charge of it, and bidding me good-by, he turned his face homeward; and, putting his horse into a gallop, away he went, and in a moment was out of sight. Looking at the letter with which I was charged, to my surprise I found that it was addressed to myself. On opening it, I found inclosed, in current back notes, one hundred and twenty-five dollars! The whole amount of free-will offerings which I received during these two years, amounted very nearly to what I would have received had I continued pastor of the Independent Presbyterian Church in Savannah—say, two thousand dollars per annum. O, how bountifully did the Lord provide for me!

It may be remarked here, that Dr. Baker's ideas in regard to money matters were characteristic of the man. He never incurred a debt when he could avoid it, and was prompt in settling his accounts to an instant and to a cent. Or if this was out of his power, when he did receive money, he would distribute it among his creditors as far as it went, reserving nothing. In fact, a debt burned upon him like a fever, and he was never at ease until it was paid, esteeming the paying of his debts the greatest luxury that his money could obtain. In his travels he was careful to reward servants liberally for their little attentions; and he took a special pleasure in making presents to children. It was usual, in the earlier days of his ministry, for ministers to receive fees for burial and baptismal services; but these he invariably refused to accept. He never hesitated to return part of a wedding fee, if he thought it more than the bridegroom could afford to pay. Only once he attempted a speculation—it was in western lands—and the result of that disgusted him for ever with such things. In purchasing a horse, the writer has known him to remonstrate with the seller—"But really, sir, do you not think I ought to give you more?" Having sold a horse to an elder, the animal died several months after, when he could hardly be dissuaded by the elder from refunding the money.

When the Cherokee lands in Georgia were distributed among the citizens of the State, gold mines were supposed to exist in some of them; believing the Indians to be defrauded out of their property, he refused to partake in the matter. In the case of two of his pastoral charges, thinking his salary to be too large, he declined receiving more than a certain part of it. It may be that he ran to an extreme in such matters. Apart from any duty binding upon one to lay up of his income for old age, there are many benevolent causes upon which any superfluous revenue can very usefully be spent. It need scarce be added, that he contributed to all deserving objects, up to, and even beyond his means. A widow applied to him in her distress for ten dollars; he hesitated for a moment, and then enclosed twenty in a note to her, knowing her great necessity. It was ten dollars more than he could afford; and he considered it a marked providence when, on going to the office to mail the note, he took from his box an anonymous letter to himself, containing just ten dollars, as a donation. The prayer of Agur was his prayer, and it was answered—to the day of his death he knew "neither poverty nor riches."

The autobiography proceeds:

When I resigned my charge in Savannah, I expected to ride as a missionary about six months, and then go to Ohio, and there seek a permanent settlement; and, lo! the time had been extended to two years.

CHAPTER VIII.

LABOURS IN OHIO—PASTORATE IN FRANKFORT AND TUSCALOOSA.

THERE lies before the compiler of this volume a mass of information in regard to the many meetings in various parts of the Union at which the subject of this Memoir was present; but it would swell the volume beyond all compass to insert all the particulars of each meeting, nor is it necessary. The course of Mr. Baker, in every case, was very much the same. He never preached where there was a pastor settled, except on invitation of that pastor, and then scrupulously under the pastor's wishes, advice, and co-operation. He would arrive in a place, say on Saturday evening. On Sabbath morning he would accompany the pastor to the Sabbath-school, and, if invited, would address the children. He would then preach, if invited, morning, afternoon, and night. If the interest manifested seemed to justify it, he would permit the pastor to give notice of other meetings on Monday; and would endeavour not to outrun, but to follow, in this way, the indications of the Spirit of God. At the outset of a protracted meeting, he would endeavour, by clear, convincing presentation of divine truth, to interest and arouse both saint and sinner. He would then endeavour to engage the officers and other members of the church in special prayer, and active effort for the conversion of their sons and daughters, brothers and sisters, husbands and wives, relatives outside of their families, and other friends. If there was any special sin prevailing in the church, or if there were dissensions, he would aim, although in a very delicate and prudent manner, to remove these obstacles in the way of the desired blessing. The reader of his published *Revival Sermons*, with the Appendix contained in each volume, can judge somewhat both of the manner, and of some of the more marked results of his preachig. But the commanding form; the eye, now penetrating, now tearful; the expressive gesture; the tone of voice; the earnestness, sincerity, and manifest anointing of the Holy Ghost—these are absent from the volumes, and live only in the memory of the multitudes of those who heard him.

An eminent minister, on hearing of the death of Dr. Baker, writes:

"No man of our day was perhaps more extensively known than Dr. Baker; no minister of our denomination, certainly, has preached the gospel so often, and in so many different places, or has been instrumental in adding an equal number of persons to the church. Beyond any man we have ever known, he had the capacity for enduring labour without weariness or respite, and his devotion to his work was intense and unremitted. He loved to preach the gospel of Christ; and no matter where or under what circumstances—in the great congregation or the small; in the magnificent church of the city; in the log school-house, or under the brush arbour of the frontier; in the court-house, the tavern, or the private dwelling. If the opportunity was given, or could be made, he preached that gospel with the same fervour, the same conviction of its value, and the same confidence in its success. It was a rare thing in the history of his labours, for nearly thirty years past, that he visited any place, although the greater part of that period has been spent in what may be called the missionary work, where he was not permitted to witness the immediate fruits of his preaching in the professed conversion of sinners. He preached for results of this character—he expected them, and he saw them. His faith was strong. It did honour to the gospel, and God honoured it."

Mr. Baker continues his narrative as follows:

At the expiration of this period, I gathered up my family, and set out in good earnest for Ohio. I think it was in May. One gig, and a barouche, contained my family and baggage; my two sons, D. and W., riding, in turn, a little pony. Without any serious accident, we travelled in this way (stopping, of course, on the way every Sabbath) until we came, on one Friday afternoon, within about three or four miles of Charlotte Court House, Virginia, when one of my horses stumbled, and in falling down, broke the shaft of my gig. Stopping to have the injury repaired, I was invited to preach at the Court House on Saturday and the Sabbath. I did so; and before the Sabbath was past, the appearances were so encouraging I was invited to remain and preach a little longer. I consented. It pleased God here to bless my labours beyond my expectations. This being noised abroad, persons came in from a distance, and nothing would do but I must hold a meeting at a church called Briery, where in a few days twenty-seven persons professed conversion, of whom only two were females. At this meeting was Judge Bolling, who, some years after, dropped dead in the hall of the House of Representatives, in the city of Washington. After the meeting closed at Briery, I went by special invitation to Prince Edward, where it pleased God to do, as I hope, a blessed work. From Prince Edward I went to Rough Creek, and there entered upon an unbroken series of protracted meetings in Virginia, which lasted for one whole year. Thus, the apparently accidental breaking of a shaft led me to hold a series of protracted meetings, in which, I suppose, something like one thousand persons were, in the judgment of charity, soundly converted. Surely, there is no such thing as chance; for here, it seems, that great effects proceeded from a little cause. No, no; the Lord has prepared his throne in the heavens, and his kingdom ruleth over all. As immensity cannot confound, even so minuteness cannot escape him. As one day is with the Lord as a thousand years, and a thousand years as one day, even so an atom is with God as a world, and a world as an atom. Well, then, may we say with the Psalmist, "O Lord, my God, thou art very great!"

During his labours, the family of Mr. Baker resided at Prince Edward, and under date of Oxford, North

Carolina, 3d of April, 1834, he thus writes to his daughter:

"My beloved Daughter—It was my intention to be in Prince Edward about this time, but I find that I have got into a kind of enchanted circle, and it will yet be three or four weeks before I shall be with you. * * * I hope, my dear child, that you are doing well, and that you are making rapid improvement. Remember, your time is precious, your opportunities golden. You must be sure to be a comfort to your parents in every thing.

"I have been in a great many very interesting meetings since I saw you. I have had the satisfaction of seeing young converts in every place. The meeting at Clarkesville closed on Tuesday last. It was a blessed meeting; great crowds attended, and about twenty-two persons were hopefully converted, besides, a great many who were left under deep impressions. There was a certain pious man present who had brought two daughters and a son to the meeting, expressly that they might be converted; on Thursday they knelt for prayer; and on Friday, by the going down of the sun, all three were rejoicing in hope. Happy father! O, when shall *I* have a satisfaction like this! My daughter, remember your father and mother are going to heaven; where are *you* going, my dear child? Are you willing to be separated from your parents in that eternity which is hastening on? Take care of your soul, for if you lose that, what have you got beside? I would write you a long letter, but my time is exceedingly occupied. * * * I hope that your instructors are pleased with you, and also that you so conduct yourself as to deserve the goodwill of all around. My dear child, may God bless you.

"Your affectionate father,

DANIEL BAKER."

After closing my missionary labours in Virginia, I resumed my journey; and inquiring for the "garden spot" in Ohio, I came first to Lancaster, and located my family. It was somewhat remarkable, that the very night after reaching my journey's end, my largest horse died. Had he died a day before, it would have put me to much inconvenience and some expense. And here I must say, that in the course of my life I have met with many things indicating both a kind and watchful Providence. Leaving my family in this town, I went on to Springfield, where I was very kindly received by the Rev. J. Galloway, for whom I preached about ten days. The result was a precious season of reviving, in which about twenty-eight persons professed conversion.

"Last week," writes an editor of that date, "we enjoyed the pleasure of a visit from our esteemed brother and former pastor, the Rev. Daniel Baker. We were gratified to learn, that notwithstanding his immense labours for the last three years—perhaps not surpassed in this country since the days of Whitefield—his voice is still firm and powerful and his general health decidedly good.

"Brother Baker has enjoyed the pleasure of aiding in revivals of religion in a number of places in Ohio. At Springfield, Ohio, a short time since, during a protracted meeting, about thirty were added to the church, most of them heads of families. He related to us an interesting incident connected with this work of grace. During the progress of the meeting, a very respectable gentleman of the place was in great apparent distress of mind, and could obtain no relief. He continued so for about two weeks, only growing more and more unhappy. One day, before the meeting closed, he came to his pastor's house with joy beaming in his countenance, and his mouth filled with praise to God, informing him that he had gained a peace and satisfaction of mind to which he had ever before been a stranger. It appeared from his statement, that in a pecuniary transaction a number of years before, he had defrauded an individual of about a hundred and thirty dollars. The person was then living at the distance of several hundred miles, and was utterly ignorant of the fact that he had ever been defrauded. 'When the commandment came, sin revived,' in the heart of him who had committed the fraud; the pungent application of divine truth by the Holy Spirit furnished his conscience with a scorpion lash, in view of this great enormity, in connection with his other offences, and his soul refused to be comforted. 'But,' said he to his pastor, 'I have yielded up the wages of unrighteousness, in order to make as full and ample restitution as lay in my power. I have sent a letter to my grossly injured friend, acquainting him with the whole transaction, and enclosing two hundred dollars; and now the blessed Saviour has visited me in mercy, and I am at peace with God and man.'"

The narrative continues:

Pleased with Springfield, I contracted with a carpenter to build me a house, intending to make the State of Ohio my field, and Springfield my radiating point. Having received many invitations, I held protracted meetings in various towns and villages, all of which were, as I trust, divinely blessed.

From a journal kept by him at this time, there is an entry made which deserves insertion. So far as is known, the only absolutely insurmountable obstacle in the way of a decided blessing at any place in which a meeting was held, was of the nature here spoken of. There were other cases of this same kind; this is the only one to which allusion is made in this volume.

Friday, July 25th, 1834. Commenced meeting in Circleville. Preached at night on Saturday, and Sabbath. Prospects encouraging. In the early part of the week, strove hard to bring about a reconciliation with certain professors, who, for some time, had been at variance with each other. All in vain. The Spirit's influence seemed gradually to be withdrawn; and, at the close of the meeting on Wednesday, whilst we rejoiced over three or four hopefully converted, we had to lament that the sins of the professed people of God had prevented richer blessings.

Finding myself in the midst of rabid Abolitionists, who poured almost unmeasured abuse upon my southern friends, I felt myself, as it were, in a nest of hornets. Although I was myself no slave-holder, yet I was no Abolitionist. I verily believed that the relation of master and slave was recognized in the Bible, and that ecclesiastical bodies have no right to legislate upon the subject. Pained by the

17*

harsh remarks which poured into my ear from day to day, I became very restless, and wished to return to the South again. Providentially, I received at this time an invitation to labour, as a missionary, in Kentucky. Accordingly, leaving Ohio, I went to Kentucky, my first point being Danville, where I had the pleasure of being present at the meeting of the Synod, which procured me many invitations to labour in the churches as an Evangelist. Amongst the places where I laboured with some success, may be mentioned Lexington, Shelbyville, and Frankfort; at the last mentioned place, I preached with such acceptance, that upon closing a protracted meeting, in which, I think, about twenty persons professed conversion, I received a unanimous call to become pastor of the Presbyterian church, recently vacated by Mr. Edgar, who had gone to Nashville, Tennessee. Here I remained and laboured, with much pleasure and with some success, for about three years.

A brother in the ministry, who visited him at this period, thus remarks of him:

"I met him once in Frankfort, Kentucky, in the year 1835, and received the hospitality of his family, as well as his efficient aid in an agency for our Education Board. Here, too, I had opportunity to observe him in his favourite employment, as a preacher. There was being held at the time a series of meetings for promoting a revival of religion. Mr. Baker was the principal preacher, and evidently in his element. I heard one sermon on the divinity of our Saviour, which brought out prominently his peculiar tastes. It was truly seraphic; some would have said too much so: but those who knew the preacher best, knew it was not affected; and the sermon seemed to be blessed of God."

From his narrative:

For a considerable portion of this time, it was my practice to preach in the morning, at nine o'clock, to the convicts in the penitentiary; at eleven o'clock in the church; in the afternoon, at three o'clock, in the country, about four miles distant; and at night, in the church in town again.

In regard to the place of preaching spoken of, in the country, an elder of the Frankfort church thus speaks, after the death of Dr. Baker:

"There had existed in the vicinity of Frankfort some years before he settled here, a church known as the Lower Benson Church; but, from deaths, removals, &c., it had become so much weakened, that the house of worship was closed and converted into a barn, and there had been no Presbyterian preaching in the neighbourhood for many years. The few members remaining were sought out by him, and induced to open and repair their old church; and he commenced preaching for them every Sabbath afternoon at half-past two o'clock. The Spirit was poured out upon them; their numbers were greatly increased; a new house of worship was erected; and, since that time, they have enjoyed the regular ministrations of God's word, with the exception of some short intervals, and, I believe, mostly without aid from our missionary funds."

From the narrative:

Whilst settled in Frankfort, the Presbytery requested me to spend two or three months in visiting the churches in their bounds for the purpose of holding protracted meetings. I consented, if brother T., pastor of the church at Nicholasville, would accompany me, and if my people would give their consent. The matter being arranged, we went out, and acted as missionaries for some two or three months; and the result was, that at the next meeting of the Presbytery, it appeared from sessional reports that more than one-half of those added to the churches in the bounds of the Presbytery were brought in by our joint labours. But it must be confessed that the people of my charge grumbled not a little that their pastor was absent so long; and that, too, although a substitute had been provided.

At this time he writes as follows to Rev. R. Davidson, then pastor of the church at Lexington.

"FRANKFORT, 13*th Oct.*, 1835.

"DEAR BROTHER DAVIDSON—I have laid the matter before my people, and they have complied with the wishes of Presbytery. Brother T., of Nicholasville, is much pleased with the plan, and will accompany me. I expect to spend the first two weeks labouring within his bounds; where we shall labour next, I cannot tell; I hope the Master will direct. My congregation would by no means consent to my being absent more than eight weeks. Indeed, although both brothers L. and T. were present to advocate the measure, it had well nigh been voted down; and the congregation consented, at last, only on the condition that I might be recalled by the Session, in case the circumstances of the church should at any time seem to require it. I like the idea of being associated with a brother in these evangelical labours. The Master, you know, sent out his disciples, two and two, into every place whither he himself should come. May the great Head of the Church bless this effort to do good. Brother T. and myself are only as the lad that had two barley loaves and a few small fishes. No matter; we go forth in the name of Him who can turn water into wine, and can make one chase a thousand, and two put ten thousand to flight. I hope we shall have the prayers of all our pious friends; of all who wish well to our Zion. Brother W. W. Hall will supply my place.

"With Christian salutations, yours sincerely,

DANIEL BAKER."

From the narrative.

I have already stated, that while I was pastor of the Presbyterian church in Frankfort, I officiated for a considerable length of time as chaplain in the penitentiary, preaching every Sabbath morning at nine o'clock; some Methodist or Baptist brethren frequently preaching to the convicts in the afternoon. It pleased God to bless our labours to the awakening of many, and even to the hopeful conversion of some twelve or fourteen. With the cordial approbation of Mr. Theobalds, the keeper, a day was appointed for their making a public profession of their faith in Christ. After the administration of baptism, according to the forms of the Presbyterian Church, the sacrament of the Lord's Supper was celebrated. It was a rare sight, and proved a solemn occasion. Some of these convicts may have mistaken conviction for conversion, natural feelings for evangelical exercises; but most of them gave what was deemed good evidence of a sound conversion: it was a matter of astonishment to many. And here I may mention an incident. Wishing to press the claims of religion upon a very irreligious man, whose wife was a member of my church, I began thus: "Why, sir, there has been a pleasing work of grace even in the penitentiary; some twelve or fifteen of the convicts have professed conversion." "O, yes," said he; "and I tell you, Mr. Baker, the penitentiary is the honestest part of Frankfort!" This he said to excite laughter, and prevent any further remarks to him on the subject of religion—and he succeeded—for I never resumed the subject any more; and sad to tell, some two years after he died as he had lived, a miserable sinner. Alas! he went down to the drunkard's grave. He made an attempt to reform by *tapering off*, but, as I was told, "he tapered off with a quart of brandy a day, and a pint at night."

For some two years my situation in Frankfort was very pleasant. I loved the people of my charge, and I believe they were much attached to me. My labours, both in town and country, were blessed. Moreover, we had a very flourishing Sabbath-school; but my salary was not promptly paid, and I began to be cramped in pecuniary matters. Bills were presented, which, by reason of the non-payment of my salary, I was unable to meet. I wrote a letter to the deacons of the church, but it availed nothing. Mr. C., the principal one, offered to lend me money once or twice; I accepted his kind offer, but told him that I did not like to borrow, when, if my salary was only promptly paid, I would have money enough to meet all demands. Perhaps a month or two after this, I was called upon—it was a rainy day—to pay rent for the house which I occupied, (for which, too, I had been led to believe I should have no rent to pay.) Getting my umbrella, I went to Mr. C., and asked if any collections had yet been made. "No," said he, "but I can lend you the money." I felt hurt, and instantly rising up, "No, sir," said I, "the money is due me; I will accept no loan." At that moment a tie was cut that bound me to Frankfort. I believed it was not the fault of the subscribers, for they had not been called upon; but I was in the hands of those who seemed not to have any thought about my wants. Under these circumstances, I came to a secret but settled determination to leave Frankfort, resigning my charge whenever another field of usefulness opened to me.

About this time the Rev. B. Crawford's wife, and some other of my wife's relations, were with us on a visit; and returning shortly after to Marion, Green county, Alabama, the place of their residence, made it known that I had some desire to leave Frankfort, and was willing that my wife should be near to her relatives in Alabama. The result was, that in a little while I received a pressing invitation, both to Greensboro' and Tuskaloosa. Accordingly, making arrangements for having the pastoral relation dissolved, I left Frankfort, after preaching my farewell sermon to a crowded house. I spoke affectionately, and made no mention of my grievances touching the non-payment of my salary; but I have since thought that in this matter I may have erred. Had the people known the true state of the case, the result might have been very different. And here I will mention a little matter that somewhat troubled me. Besides having to preach my farewell sermon in Frankfort, I had made an appointment to preach a farewell sermon to my country congregation in the afternoon. Just at this time, Mrs. E., the mother of Mrs. C., died. She was a lady of high respectability, and I was invited to attend her funeral in the country at the same hour. As the request came from Mrs. C., a much esteemed member of my church, and as funeral claims were high claims, at first I knew not what to do; but thinking how large a congregation I should have, and how great would be the disappointment if I did not preach the expected sermon, I finally concluded to decline attending the funeral, and wrote a respectful note to Mrs. C., stating the circumstances of the case; but I understood she was displeased that I did not attend the funeral of her mother. This for a time troubled me, but I had the consolation to believe that I had done right.

A strong attachment existed between pastor and people here, as in every church of which Mr. Baker had charge. On hearing of his death, so many years after, the church met and passed a series of resolutions, expressing, in the highest terms, their pleasing remembrances of him as a man and a minister.

The narrative proceeds:

Disposing of my furniture at auction, I left Frankfort with my family and came to Tuskaloosa, Alabama. This was in the year 1836. I preached to crowded houses both in Tuskaloosa and Greensboro'. I was offered a salary, I think, of two thousand dollars at the latter place, but preferred the former, although the salary there was only fifteen hundred dollars, and a house rent free. Under my ministry the church was much blessed. In a short time the membership increased considerably; moreover, as was usual with me, when invited, I visited other churches, and aided pastors in holding protracted meetings, being required, however, to do most of the preaching myself. Amongst the places thus visited were Marion, Gainesville, and a country church not far from Selma. Each and every meeting was crowned with a blessing; but the richest displays of grace were seen in Gainesville, the Presbyterian church there being under the pastoral care of the Rev. John Leyburn, a young man of talent and great promise. If I recollect right, the hopeful converts there numbered some thirty-five, among whom were several men of considerable note. Some months after this meeting in Gainesville, brother Leyburn, at my request, came to Tuskaloosa and preached for me some eight or ten days in succession, preaching in all seventeen sermons. It pleased God to bless his labours greatly. Besides a goodly number of others brought in, there were some five or six students of the University, and a tutor named B.; his brother, one of the professors, having been previously brought in under my ministry.

About this time began the troubles in our Church between what were termed the New and Old-school party. Their wranglings grieved me much. I was wont to say, "I have no horns; I know not how to fight; I am one of the *working ants.*" On account of my not coming out strongly on either side, I was called a "fence-man;" and upon the fence I remained until, so to speak, every rail was taken down. What finally determined me was this: the rejection of Dr. Miller's resolution to restore Mr. Barnes, but censure certain expressions in his book. The New school party, with the "moderates," having the majority, shielded the book as well as the man. As certain sentences in the book were very exceptionable, this was more than I could stand; so in one moment I took my stand on the Old-school side. Parties were formed in my own church; some of the members were fiercely in favour of the New-school, but it so happened that all the members of the Session agreed with me. All were firm; but it must be confessed, one was as fierce for the Old-school as certain private members alluded to were for the New-school. It required much prudence and much effort, on my part, to keep them from separating, and splitting the church in two; but with God's blessing, peace and quietness were finally restored; and when two General Assemblies were formed, the church of which I was pastor gave in its adhesion to the Old-school General Assembly.

Appointed a Commissioner to attend the first meeting of our Assembly, after the separation, I went on; and on reaching Louisville, I understood that the Appellate Court in Pennsylvania had affirmed the decision previously given by Judge R. against us. Whilst under this impression, going on board of a steamboat bound for Wheeling, I fell in with some brethren on their way as Commissioners to the other Assembly. With a sad countenance, I told them what I had heard. They were wonderfully elated, and were very merry. Whilst they were indulging in all the feelings of exultation and triumph, I remarked playfully, "Well, brethren, but don't you know what a certain old book says, 'The triumphing of the wicked is short;' and, sure enough, in a few hours after, it was ascertained that the decision of the lower court had been reversed. I may mention one circumstance more: Whilst the impression was still with me and others that the New-school side had carried the day, Dr. B. said to me, "And what will you Old-school brethren now do?" "Well," said I, "if our goodly temple is taken from us, we will put up a shanty and get along as well as we can."

This Dr. B. is now perhaps one of the most distinguished ministers among the Congregational clergy. The compiler of this volume remembers him well when a guest in the family of Mr. Baker at Frankfort. Being then a boy, when tea was ready on Sabbath evening, the writer was sent into his father's study to call the distinguished guest down to the table. With astonishment he beheld the visitor lying at full length on the rug before the fire, slowly rolling himself from side to side, as he prepared his mind for the services of the night. A novel way of studying.

The narrative continues:

When in Philadelphia, as a member of the Old-school Assembly, I met with several of my old acquaintances on the other side, who expressed their astonishment to find me where I was. One remarked, "Ah, brother Baker, you are fat, and have become lazy, and therefore you are on the Old-school side." Having some curiosity to step in a moment, and see who were in the New-school Assembly, I was hurrying on to the First Church, where the Assembly was convened. Near the entrance I met a brother with whom I had been on terms of great intimacy. Reaching out my hand to him in a playful way, and smiling, I said, "Why, brother H., what are you doing here?" To my astonishment he fiercely replied, "We have come here to resist high-handed oppression." Not perceiving any cause why church difficulties should break private friendship, I made another pleasant remark. To this he replied in the same strain as before. "O," said I, "brother H., if you have such feelings, we must take different sides of the street—so, good morning." Saying this, I turned away, and went not in. And here, my children may wish to know my opinion in relation to what has been called the "Exscinding Act." My opinion is this: It was a strong measure, like General Jackson's removal of the deposites. I did not like it much, but I knew of no other that would meet the exigency. And now, after many years have passed away, I believe it was, so to speak, the very salvation of our Church; for certain forms of heresy and wild measures were coming in like a flood, which, if not checked in time, and effectually, would have led to most disastrous results.

CHAPTER IX.

TUSKALOOSA—LABOURS AS AN EVANGELIST—MISSION TO TEXAS.

THE present pastor of the church in Tuskaloosa, Rev. R. B. White, D. D., in the course of a letter to the compiler of this volume, thus speaks of the period of Dr. Baker's sojourn there:

"Your father was most highly esteemed here as a minister of Christ, as he has been every where that his character and labours have been known. His eloquent and powerful sermons were duly appreciated; his pulpit efforts were well sustained to the close of his ministry among this people. None of his sermons were indifferent; many of them were regarded, in view of the true end of preaching, as of the most superior kind. Dr. Baker's frank, affable, and guileless manners, endeared him to many here, as a man. The purity of his aims seems to have been acknowledged by all. His indifference to worldly things, his ignorance of them, as some regarded it, seemed to win him respect. Your father was remarkable, while here, for his interest in children, and his power of interesting them; he won at once their attention, their affection, and their confidence. He formed and sustained Bible-classes, which embraced the whole congregation, and proved greatly interesting and instructive. The prayer-meetings which he held were especially profitable.

"At one time, finding the prayer-meeting languishing and neglected, he adopted an ingenious mode of drawing the people to the place of prayer. He told them on the Sabbath, that if they would all meet him on Thursday evening at the appointed place of prayer, he would show them a strange sight. On Thursday evening, accordingly, there was a large attendance. He arose, and said: 'My friends, I told you that if you would come here, I would show you a strange sight. See here, is this not a strange sight—so many people at the prayer-meeting in Tuskaloosa?' The rebuke, so wisely and so wittily given, was salutary. He did much good in establishing prayer-meetings in different parts of the town. His labours among the blacks were indefatigable, and attended with great good to them. They still speak of him with a degree of admiration and love, such as they cherish for no other minister whom they have known. He has been distinguished chiefly as an Evangelist; but his labours and his success here—eighty-one being added to the church during the period of his stay in Tuskaloosa, from March 6th, 1837, to July 10th, 1839—give evidence that he possessed high qualifications for the pastoral office. He lives in the affections of this people."

Among his many correspondents, there was one, the Rev. John S. Galloway, pastor of the church in Springfield, Ohio, to whom he was greatly attached. Many letters passed between them at this period. The compiler of this volume is well aware that letters are interesting chiefly to those to whom they are originally addressed; yet the letters of Dr. Baker are so descriptive of passing events, and so illustrative of the man, as to have an interest to more than those to whom they were written. Above all, his letters, to whomsoever addressed, dwell mainly upon a theme which invariably interests the children of God—a theme for ever new, even though the paper which bears the writing be yellow with age, though the circumstances of the writing have passed away in the rush of new events, and though the person writing and the person written to, have long since realized in heaven that which they together communed about on earth. As may be supposed, Dr. Baker conducted during all his life a very large correspondence with all manner of persons. In lingering over such of his letters as are before him, the compiler of this work has found difficulty, not in determining what letters to include in the volume, but what to exclude. Such as are published in this and other chapters, are mere specimens of the many letters which have gone from his hand to every quarter of the land—radiating every where the same spiritual light and heat from the fervent spirit dwelling within him. The readers of these letters can best appreciate the degree of influence they exerted—meagre specimens as these are of tens of thousands of like pages scattered so widely abroad.

"ALABAMA, *May 22d*, 1838.

"DEAR BROTHER GALLOWAY—Your very kind letter came to hand. The remarkably friendly manner in which you write, has endeared you more than ever to my heart; and I am free to say, that I rejoice that I ever became acquainted with you. May our mutual friendship continue till merged in the purer, sweeter, and more elevated friendship of the heavenly world.

"I am happy to state that my situation here is a very pleasant one, and my prospects of usefulness still quite encouraging. Every pew in the church is rented, and, within little more than a year past, we have received, on examination and certificate, forty-four to the communion of our church. The last adult baptized was Professor B., of the University of Alabama. About the middle of March last, I attended a protracted meeting in New Orleans. It was exceedingly interesting. Christians were wonderfully revived, and perhaps twenty sinners converted unto God. Amongst the hopeful converts was a gentleman of great impiety, and some considerable standing, who, it seems, some two or three years ago, had, in connection with others, published a paper called "*The Anxious Seat.*" He and three of his sons were brought in. This was considered a glorious triumph of grace, and, I assure you, occasioned much joy. Since my return from New Orleans, I have also had the pleasure of attending a meeting in Gainesville, a new and flourishing little town, about fifty miles from this. The meeting lasted eleven days, and was truly a blessed one. I preached twenty sermons, and, of course, gave numerous exhortations. When I left, the converts were thirty-seven, amongst whom were two infidels, five young ladies, who had been very gay, one eminent physician, one old hardened sinner, two "doggery" keepers, and fourteen heads of families. Was not this a precious little harvest? A few days since, I received a letter from the pastor, brother Leyburn, a dear, charming man, who says that the work is still going on; that the last night before he closed his letter, eight new persons remained to be conversed with; and that the number of hopeful converts had increased to fifty. Bless the Lord! Anxious seats were not used, either in New Orleans or Gainesville. I greatly prefer inquiry meetings. The General Assembly of our Church is now, I suppose, in session. I feel awful. The Lord reigns! This is my comfort, and right glad am I to know that "Zion still enjoys her Monarch's love." I do not meddle with matters too high for me. If any man has a call to fight, let him go ahead, I say; as for myself, I am called to work, and I am willing to be an humble day-labourer until my work is done. Yesterday I preached from these words, "By whom shall Jacob arise? for he is small." In pointing out the instrumentalities, I mentioned, I. The ministry of the word; II. The benevolent institutions of the day; III. Maternal influence; and IV. Prayer. The subject is a noble one; suppose you take it. When I enlarged upon the third head, there was manifestly a very deep impression. The subject admits of fine inferences. Do tell me some of your choice themes.

DANIEL BAKER."

"OCTOBER 23*d*, 1838.

"DEAR BROTHER GALLOWAY—We have recently had a protracted meeting in my church, which has proved an exceedingly delightful one. Our meetings have been crowded. There has been very deep feeling, and no disorder. Fifty-seven persons have professed a hope, and many more are asking what they must do to be saved. Bless the Lord, O my soul! Mr. Leyburn, brother of the missionary in Greece, laboured with us, to great acceptance. He is a young man of fine talents, of a most excellent spirit, and, altogether, of great promise. Would that we had a thousand more of his stamp. With brother Leyburn was associated brother McMullen, whom we all greatly esteem and love; but being, like myself, pretty much at home in this place, did not take so prominent a part as brother Leyburn, who had never preached in this place before. Of the converts, so called, twenty-eight are young ladies, eleven married women, seventeen young men, and one coloured man. Christians, too, were much stirred up, and I am free to say, take it all in all, the meeting was a most blessed one. Our regular communion season takes place next Sabbath week. I hope we shall have a large addition to our church, although some of the converts are nominally of other communions.

"In haste, yours very sincerely,

DANIEL BAKER."

"NOVEMBER 28*th*, 1838.

"DEAR BROTHER GALLOWAY—Every letter I receive from you strengthens my attachment to you. You are certainly very kind in all that you do, and in all that you say. You seem at all times to be just exactly under the influence of the true Christian spirit, and there is nothing more beautiful upon earth. O, if every one who names the name of Christ would only manifest, in all circumstances, and on all occasions, the same spirit, it does appear to me that the church would indeed look forth as the morning, beautiful as Tirzah, comely as Jerusalem, and terrible as an army with banners. Give me the genuine, the consistent Christian as my companion for ever and ever. Our Zion is in trouble, but the Lord reigns! I am glad that the question is not "Approve or not approve," but "Adhere or not adhere." I have cast in my lot with the "Old-school party," and I suppose you and myself have pretty much the same views.

"The protracted meeting in my church has been productive of very important results. The excitement has extended to other churches, and I think the number hopefully converted in our city may now be put down at nearly one hundred. Bless the Lord, O my soul! Two of the officers of the University have joined my church, and ten of the students have also professed conversion, and have connected themselves with different churches, joining the communions to which their parents belong.

"We had a very pleasant synodical meeting. The preaching on the occasion, also, was much blessed. Hopeful converts, twenty-four. One of them, a gentleman of high respectability, has written me an exceedingly interesting letter, closing with these words: 'In the hour of death I think I shall see you, sir, as your finger ran over the precious promises in the third chapter of John.' The portion of Scripture referred to is found in John's Gospel, third chapter, from 14th to 19th verse, which I consider to be the gospel in miniature. I rejoice that the Lord has continued to bless the people of your charge. May your stars be as the dew-drops of the morning.

"Last week I left Columbus, Mississippi. A meeting was still going on which promised very important results. I wished to stay longer, but duty called me home. During the recent religious excitement in Tuskaloosa, I think our Governor was not left untouched; unless I am much mistaken, both he and his lady are under very serious impressions. They have a pew in my church, and I have observed several things about them very encouraging. They seem to be very willing to be conversed with on the subject of religion. Yesterday his Excellency requested me to go with him to a certain place where he was to give an unfavourable answer to a woman who came to plead for the life of her husband, under sentence of death for murder. I scarcely ever felt so awful in all my life, as when the poor woman entered the room to hear from the lips of the Governor that word which was to give life to her husband, or quench every ray of hope. When the Governor told her that he could not pardon her husband, she plead hard; but, touched as the Governor certainly was, a stern sense of duty made him firm. Poor woman!—she said her heart would break; but all availed nothing. To make matters worse, she was unconverted, and of course a stranger to the consolations of religion. After his Excellency had retired, I conversed with her and prayed; and then could do nothing more than leave her to her sorrows and her God.

"You have, it seems, another olive-plant added to those already round about your table. May the dew of heaven rest upon them all. My kindest regards to your companion, and all the members of your dear family.

"Your brother in the bonds of the gospel,

DANIEL BAKER."

"FEBRUARY 25*th*, 1839.

"DEAR BROTHER GALLOWAY—I told you of the revival with which we were favoured last fall. Well, one of the converts died a few days since, furnishing a new proof of the great importance of at once securing the salvation of the soul. This young convert, a very interesting and talented young man, was accidently shot while hunting, and died in about six hours. On hearing the sad intelligence that he had received a mortal wound, I stepped into a carriage and went to the place, about two miles from the city, where I found him lying upon the ground, weltering in his gore. He was in great agony of body; he groaned and cried aloud, so that his voice re-echoed through the grove. 'My dear brother,' said I, 'Is Christ precious?' 'He is,' replied he. 'Are you willing to die?' 'Yes.' 'Are you happy?' 'Yes.' 'Well, I trust you will soon be in heaven; and there is no pain there.' As soon as I mentioned this, he seemed to be wonderfully calmed, and, as well as I can recollect, he cried aloud no more. Observing his apparent composure, I thought his pain was really gone; but on putting the question, he said, 'Great pain.' He was brought in a furniture carriage to town. I thought he would have died on the road; but he was carried to the house of a friend, and, in about two hours after, he peacefully fell asleep in Jesus. O, what a blessed thing it is to be a Christian! As our Master says, 'Blessed is that servant whom our Lord, when he cometh, shall find watching.' Had he not been prepared, when shot, how could he have been when he died? O, how do poor sinners place in peril the salvation of their souls! My dear brother, your business and mine is to do what we can to awaken them. May the Lord make us more earnest and more faithful in our great work.

"With Christian salutations, your brother in Christ,

"DANIEL BAKER."

JULY 15*th*, 1839.

"DEAR BROTHER GALLOWAY—The meeting in Wilkesbarre, Pennsylvania, proved to be an exceedingly interesting one. Christians were wonderfully enlivened, and the number of hopeful converts amounted to about sixty; amongst whom was a lawyer of distinguished talents, at the very head of his profession. As he is a fine speaker, and only about thirty years of age, hopes are entertained that he will become a herald of the cross. Bless the Lord!

"At our last meeting for inquirers, there were something like one hundred and thirty present, and the interest seemed to be spreading and deepening every day. Brother D., the pastor, is truly an interesting brother. He is a beloved man of God, and rejoiced much to see his garden look so fresh and green.

"In an interview with Dr. John Breckinridge, some time since, he expressed a great desire that I should go to Texas. He was pleased to say he thought I could do much good there; that I might organize a hundred churches, &c. What do you think of the scheme? My brother, I am in many respects pleasantly situated here, but my field of usefulness is not as large as I could wish it, and I am kept in a very unpleasant state on account of my salary not being promptly paid. We do not preach for money, and yet without it we cannot support our families, nor pay our debts.

"We have had several sudden deaths in this place lately, and yet the living seemed not inclined to lay it to heart. O for awakening influences, fresh from the throne of God!

"*Ut olim, ut semper tuus amicus et frater,*

DANIEL BAKER."

The autobiography proceeds:

I think it was in the year 1838 that my attention was first drawn to Texas. The Rev. John Breckinridge had just visited this new republic, and upon his return, was anxious that Presbyterians should make some special efforts to send missionaries, and plant churches of our faith and order in that new field. At his special request, several members of the Tuskaloosa Presbytery met him at Mesopotamia. He gave a glowing account of Texas as an unusually promising field for missionary enterprise; and, as he closed, he turned to me and said, "Brother Baker, you are the man for Texas." A few months after, I heard him deliver a discourse on Texas, in which he spoke most favourably of its soil and climate, and especially held up the Republic of the "lone star" as a magnificent field for missionary operations. When the congregation was dismissed, meeting me at the door, he again urged me to go to Texas. I told him that perhaps I would take the subject into prayerful consideration.

Upon reaching home my mind became more and more impressed with the idea that it might indeed be my duty to go there. I finally concluded that if the Presbytery thought it advisable, and would make provision for my support, I would go. To bring the matter to a point, I announced my intention to resign my pastoral charge, and desired the church to unite with me in a request to the Presbytery to dissolve the pastoral connection. This was strongly opposed, and various measures were adopted to induce me to relinquish the idea of going to Texas. But, if I must go, why not simply make a visit? I was told that my people were willing that I should be allowed full time to visit Texas, and still retain my pastoral relation to them; and when I finally remarked that I would leave the decision of the case to Presbytery, a commissioner, Professor B., was appointed to oppose the dissolution of the pastoral connection. When the matter was brought up before Presbytery, much was said pro and con, but it was carried by an almost unanimous vote, that I should be released from my charge in order that I might go as a missionary to Texas. Moreover, the Presbytery pledged itself to give me a salary at the rate of fifteen hundred dollars per annum. This seemed a large amount, but was not more than I was receiving in Tuskaloosa; indeed, not as much, for there my salary was fifteen hundred dollars and a house, the rent of which was two hundred and seventy-five dollars per annum. Shortly after I preached my farewell sermon to a crowded house, and took my leave of a people who had uniformly shown me much kindness, and to whom I had ever been most affectionately attached.

Leaving my family as boarders with Mr. C., and my two sons as students at the school of which he had charge, I assumed the character of a missionary; but having received pressing invitations first to visit Florence, Tuscumbia, Memphis and Courtland—with the cordial approbation of the Committee appointed by Presbytery to superintend and direct my movements, I went to the places above named, and preached in each place some eight or ten days. In each place there was a very pleasing work of grace; the hopeful converts averaging perhaps some twenty-five for each meeting. Some cases of conversion were very remarkable, particularly that of Mr. L., who has since become a useful minister of our faith and order; Mr. H., who subsequently became an elder of the church in the same place, and Mr. ——, of Memphis, who, from being a very wicked man, became a very zealous member of the Methodist Church. This latter gentleman requested a copy of my sermon that had been the means of his conversion, and as a compliment, paid my passage, twenty-five dollars, to New Orleans.

In going to Texas, Dr. Baker bore with him a letter of introduction to General Sam. Houston, from Andrew Jackson, with whom he had been so cordially associated in Washington city. This letter now lies before the compiler of this volume, every rugged line breathing the wonted fire of the old hero in its expression of esteem and affection toward the bearer.

It was about this time that he addressed the following letters home:

"FLORENCE, *November 25th*, 1839.

"MY DEAR ELIZA—Remember what is written in God's blessed book, 'Be careful for nothing,' &c. I am always happy. You know my plan is to commit every thing to the Lord, and always look upon the bright side. You may rest assured this is the best way. Our meeting here has proved a blessed one; perhaps about thirty hopefully converted; most of them are young men and women. Last night I preached my last sermon, thirty-three in all. Thank the Lord, he prospers me, and makes me a happy man."

"TUSCUMBIA, *December 4th*, 1839.

"Last Sabbath we had pretty good weather, and walking a little better. There was great stillness and solemnity. The Lord, I trust, has commenced a good work in this place. Five persons have already professed conversion."

"COURTLAND, *December 15th*, 1839.

"MY BELOVED DAUGHTER—I have only a few moments to write. We have had a blessed meeting in Tuscumbia; about eighteen or twenty hopefully converted, and amongst them some of the most noted persons in the place. Dr. H., for example, one of my old pupils, and Mr. M., a lawyer of distinction. Some think that half the community are more or less impressed. We have also had a blessed meeting in this place; converts here perhaps ten or twelve; very interesting persons, indeed, and a great many more very anxious. You will observe the churches in both places are small and feeble, and therefore the revivals considered very great. Brother W. says he has not witnessed such an interesting meeting for three years. Every sermon seems to be blessed. To God be all the glory! It is now Sunday night, past ten o'clock. To-morrow I am to preach again in this place in the morning, and at Tuscumbia to-morrow night. The next night I am to preach in Florence, and the next morning I am to set off about two o'clock in the stage for Memphis, where I expect to be on Friday, and thence I am to go in a steamboat to New Orleans. I hope to reach Galveston about the 28th instant. I hope, my dear child, you will always be very attentive to your mother, and I wish you to charge your brothers to do the same. I hope they will distinguish themselves as amiable and affectionate sons.

"I am in great haste. May God bless you. Farewell. Love to all.

"Your affectionate father,

DANIEL BAKER."

"*Monday Morning.* The bell will ring in a few minutes. I have had the satisfaction of seeing Captain S., who commanded a company under the ill-fated Fannin, in Texas. You may recollect, that after fighting bravely, being overpowered by numbers, they capitulated, and then were led forth, and cruelly massacred in cold blood. Captain S. escaped as it were by a miracle. His account of the matter possesses thrilling interest. In the battle he had the blood of three men who were killed sprinkled upon him, and he received a ball in his cheek; the scar is still visible. He has given me a world of information about Texas. I think I shall probably be pleased with the country; at any rate, I am very glad that I am going there as a missionary agent. I can assure you I have been very impatient to be there, and nothing but an imperious sense of duty could have detained me in this region of country so long. I expect to reach Texas just in time to secure the land, and that is all. I know I run some risk of losing it, but circumstances were such I was willing to run the risk.* God's name has been glorified in the conversion of many precious souls in this region by my instrumentality, and that will comfort me. Once more, adieu.

DANIEL BAKER."

MEMPHIS, *December 21st*, 1839.

"MY DEAR ELIZA—I received your peculiarly interesting letter of the 5th inst. I am glad to find that you are so cheerful. You know my disposition. I cannot away with complainings and a disposition to look upon the dark side of things. If you wish to please me, and make your husband happy, be always cheerful. Indulge in no corroding cares. You recollect the passage of Scripture which I have so often quoted, 'Be careful for nothing,' &c. If at any time you have any difficulties or burdens, cast them upon the Lord; as it is said, 'In every

* The State of Texas had promised six hundred and forty acres of land to every head of a family settling in the State before January 1st, 1840.

thing, by prayer and supplication, with thanksgivings, let your request be made known unto God.' This is my plan, and I find it a good one. What is the use of having our energies crippled, and our usefulness impaired by indulging in anxieties which are of no use to soul or body, and benefit no one. Let this be your motto—Be cheerful and devout. These things are by no means inconsistent.

"On passing through Tuscumbia and Florence, in coming to this place, I was received almost as an angel of God. Every body seemed to be glad to see me, and hear me preach once more. Their complimentary remarks and demonstrations of kindness were almost more than I could bear. Amongst other expressions of love and friendship, I received the following lines, written by Mrs. Caroline Lee Hentz, a lady of high literary fame, whose husband, hitherto quite a sceptic, was numbered amongst the Florentine converts.

'Wilt thou take our parting blessing,
Servant of the God we love:
Purest bliss, the soul possessing,
Image here, the bliss above.

Round the household altar bending,
On our hearts thy name we bear;
With our holiest memories blending,
Hallowed and embalmed in prayer.

When, in God's own temple meeting,
Zion's children bow the knee,
Echo still, thy words repeating,
Turns our grateful thoughts to thee.

Thou to other climes art going,
Jesus' dying love to tell;
May salvation round thee flowing,
Like the waves of ocean swell.

Fare thee well, beloved stranger,
  Since from us thy steps must roam;
Angels guard thy life from danger,
  Till their wings shall bear thee home.'

"The converts, it seems, are all very clear and very happy, and the impression upon the community in general most delightful. Bless the Lord, O my soul! * * * This was certainly kind, and I could not help admiring their ingenuity in endeavouring to have the amount secured to the benefit of my family; but I must report it to the Committee, notwithstanding, as also a twenty dollar bill, received in a private letter from an individual, a rich man, who, with a son, was hopefully converted. Besides all this, my Courtland friends made me a present of sixty-seven dollars, and brother S. handed over to me one hundred and twenty-four dollars and fifty cents, which he said had been raised expressly for my individual benefit. I left Florence on Wednesday morning last, very early, and reached this place last evening. I made an effort to get off, but at last found it necessary (in order not to travel on the Sabbath) to spend the Sabbath in this place. It is now very doubtful whether I can get into Texas in time to secure the land; but I must remember the Sabbath-day, to keep it holy, cost what it may. If I lose the land, the Lord, if he sees proper, can make it up to me in a thousand different ways.

"*Monday Morning*, *23d.* I preached for brother H., an old acquaintance, three times yesterday, and such was the impression produced, that a very great desire has been expressed that I should remain during the week, and I have consented. So, farewell Texas land; well, let it go; if the Lord will give me souls for my hire in this place, that will do. Tell dear Agnes to be sure pa loves her, and she shall have the ring. Love to all.

"Yours ever, DANIEL BAKER."

(TO HIS SONS.)

"MEMPHIS, *Jan.* 2*d*, 1840.

"Strange as it may seem, I am not in Texas yet. I have, by earnest solicitation, been detained here preaching the gospel for the last ten days. We have had much unfavourable weather, and the streets terribly muddy; but the people have turned out wonderfully every night, chiefly men; and there has been, it seems, a very general and deep impression made upon the community, and the converts are now multiplying, I hope, every day. May the Lord grant us a pentecostal time indeed. I think I am one of the happiest men on earth. I have a good Master, and his service is perfect freedom, is delightful. I do hope, my sons, that when I go the way of all the earth, one or both of you will take my place in the gospel ministry.

"Gen. Jackson is here, on his way to New Orleans. I saw him yesterday. He seemed glad to see me. While the room was full of gentlemen, who crowded in to see him, he held my hand a long time, and then invited me to sit down by him, and said, in a tremulous way, 'If Mrs. Jackson was alive, she would be very glad to see you, sir.' General Jackson is in pretty good health, but is much withered. He has, however, an exceedingly venerable appearance. I have preached perhaps eighty times since I set out for Florence. I am just as fresh as if I had not preached a sermon. Bless the Lord!"

From the narrative.

On reaching New Orleans, it was my intention to go on immediately to Galveston, Texas; but before an opportunity was afforded, a pressing invitation came from the Rev. W. Hamilton, to come to aid him in Mobile, where a precious work of grace was in progress. I thought I had already delayed too long my intended mission into Texas, but Dr. John Breckinridge, who was at that time pastor of the Presbyterian church in New Orleans, advised me by all means to go to Mobile. I accordingly went, and have reason to hope that my labours there were not in vain in the Lord. But now I am reminded of the fact, that some two years before this, by invitation, I assisted the Rev. Joel Parker in holding a protracted meeting in the Presbyterian church in New Orleans, of which at that time he was pastor. This meeting was much blessed, and some of the substantial fruits remain even to the present time; one a converted infidel; one a merchant; one who has since became a minister of the gospel; and one a gentleman of some considerable note in the Episcopal Church.

After preaching about one week for Dr. H. in Mobile, with some considerable success, I hope, I returned to New Orleans, and thence by the first steamer to Galveston; the boat, I think was named the New York. Coming in view of Galveston Island, February 26th, 1840, I was surprised to see the island so low and flat, like a chip floating on the surface of the water; and on landing, the first thing that particularly attracted my attention was a group of tippling houses on the strand or wharf, neat McKinney's pier. My first business was to find out the "excellent of the earth." Christians here were very few; emphatically like "angels' visits, few and far between." By invitation, I went to the home of Dr. Roberts, who, in his beautiful house, for several days treated me with great kindness and hospitality. The first effort to do good was to distribute tracts, a goodly number of which I had brought with me; and, as soon as arrangements could be made, I preached daily during the week, and three times on the Sabbath, being careful also to visit and address the Sabbath-school, which I was happy to find already established, and in a comparatively flourishing state. I believe I was instrumental in increasing the number of attendants on the Sabbath-school in this way.

Walking along the streets of Galveston on a Sabbath day, I came up to a large group of boys who were playing marbles. "Heigh! boys," said I, "playing marbles on Sunday!" "O, we are in Texas," several of them replied. "Well, but boys," replied I, "don't you know that God can see you in Texas, as well as in the States?" Putting my hand in my pocket, I pulled out a good many little books, and, whilst giving, I talked very kindly to the boys; and winding up, I pleasantly remarked, "Boys, it is not right to play marbles on Sunday; you had better go to Sunday-school—didn't you know it?—there is one yonder"—pointing to the place. I then left them, bidding them good-by; but I had gone only a few steps when several of them called to me aloud, and said, "We won't play marbles any more on Sunday;

we will go to Sunday-school, sir." "Heaven bless the boys of Texas," thinks I to myself, "they only need to be taught what is right."

One day I took a stroll out of town, and whilst walking on the beach on the south side of the island, I unexpectedly came up to a military station, where some thirty soldiers were on the look-out for Mexicans, who were expected to invade Texas about this time. On conversing with them I found that no one had ever preached to them, or given them a Bible, or tract, or anything of the kind. Each could, with but too much truth, say, No man cared for my soul. Having obtained permission from the commander, who was very polite, I distributed tracts amongst them, and preached to them near the strand, in the open air. As there were no seats for their accommodation, they stood before me in military order. In the midst of my discourse, a new thought occurred, and leaving my theme, I addressed them to this effect: "Soldiers, here you are, in this new and wild country, far away from the means of grace. I think it likely that you are all quite careless and unconcerned about your soul's salvation. And yet, after all, I wonder if some of you have not pious mothers in the old States, who love you, and pray for you, and weep over you." Passing my eyes rapidly over the faces of the soldiers, I noticed one particularly who was prodigiously wrought upon. His lips quivered; every muscle was in motion; tears ran down his cheeks. Much excited myself, said I, "Soldier, come here, I want to talk to you." Leaving the ranks, he came to me, and we two retiring a short distance, I said to him, "Soldier, have you not a pious mother in the States?" Bursting into tears, he replied, "Yes, sir, a very pious mother, a member of the Methodist Church in Pennsylvania." As I spoke to him about the blessed Saviour, and the way of salvation through him, he wept aloud—so loud that his voice might have been heard for several hundred yards. After giving such instruction and encouragement as I thought the case called for, and after finishing the discourse which I had commenced, I returned to my lodgings in Galveston. Two days after, I visited the same military station again, and had the happiness to find that soldier rejoicing in Christ. His mother's prayers, it would seem, have been answered, and I, as a missionary, was sent into this frontier land to call home a wandering son. To God be all the praise! This, it seems, was the first person who ever professed conversion on Galveston Island.

The following letters were written at this period.

GALVESTON, *Texas*, *Feb.* 9*th*, 1840.

"DEAR BROTHER GALLOWAY—Here I am in Texas! Appointed by the Assembly's Board, and adopted by the Presbytery of Tuskaloosa as their missionary, I arrived at this place a few days ago. It is something like ten weeks since I set out for this land of promise, but I have taken a very circuitous route; besides, on my way, I have attended no less than five protracted meetings, all of which, I am happy to say, it pleased God to bless. In one place there were about fourteen hopeful converts; in another seventeen; in a third, fourteen; in a fourth, thirty; and in the last place (Mobile) about forty. Since my arrival in Galveston I have preached four sermons; and I am free to say, I never saw a people who seemed to set a higher value upon a preached gospel. The school-room in which preaching is held is not large, to be sure, but it is crowded every time. A Presbyterian church was recently formed here, consisting of about twenty members, having two elders; and they have given an invitation to brother McCullough to preach to them for six months. Some five months ago the citizens of Galveston had a meeting, and offered fifty dollars (Texas money) a Sabbath to any evangelical minister who would preach to them; the money, however, is not worth more than about twenty-five cents in the dollar.

"Galveston is a very flourishing town. Two years ago there were not more than perhaps three houses; there are now, it may be, three hundred. There are as many, I suppose, as ten or fifteen square-rigged vessels in port, besides small craft. Indeed, Galveston is, no doubt, destined to be a very important commercial seaport. The island is about twenty-eight miles in length, by two in breadth. It is low and level. I am told that there are three clusters of trees on the island, but I have not yet seen a single one—not even a bush or shrub; not even a switch, to switch little urchins with. The climate, however, is said to be delightful; and a continued fresh sea-breeze, I am told, makes it very pleasant in summer. Last fall there were many deaths in Galveston by yellow fever. Strangers are coming into Texas in great crowds, so that the population, it is supposed, already exceeds one hundred thousand souls. There is no apprehension now in relation to Mexico.

Indeed, the Texans, in case of conflict, would in all probability push their conquest to the very city of Mexico. Every thing now is extravagantly high.

"I expect soon to visit the interior, and in the course of a few months shall be better able to form an idea of the country. I do not think, however, I shall like this country as a permanent residence. I am now acting only as a sort of missionary agent; I am to preach wherever I can get any persons to preach to, and organize churches, and form temperance societies, Sabbath-schools, &c., &c. There are, I think, about six Presbyterian ministers in Texas, and a much larger number of the Methodist communion; how many Baptists I cannot say; and, so far as I know, not a single Episcopalian yet. Congress has just adjourned, after having adopted some very wise regulations, which, it is thought, will give a new spring to the prosperity of the country.

"Yours, as ever, DANIEL BAKER."

(TO HIS WIFE.)

"GALVESTON, *February 21st*, 1840.

"MY DEAREST E.—Well, you see I am in Texas at last! And you wish to know my opinion of Galveston, Texas, &c. My opinion is this; some have overrated, and some have underrated this land of promise. Some have looked at it with 'jaundiced eyes,' and some through 'glorification spectacles.' Having neither jaundiced eyes nor glorification spectacles, I think, therefore, I can and do take a very sober and correct view of matters.

We have, from the house in which I lodge, a very extensive view of the ocean or gulf, and the roaring of the surf seems everlasting. I took a long stroll upon the beach shortly after my arrival. I suppose I walked four miles upon the hard white sand, and would occasionally put my foot in the foam of the salt wave; and sometimes for my amusement, would assume the authority of Canute of England, and with the same success. Moreover, I would, with my walking cane, attempt to pin down the wave, rolling upward on the smooth sloping beach, but in its recoil, it seemed to laugh at the attempt; and I thought this was very much like the attempt to fasten conviction upon sinful hearts; they slide away! Galveston is a new and very flourishing town on the eastern end of the Island. It has already a population of about three thousand, and is increasing every day. A prodigious number of houses have gone up within a few months past. They are generally frame buildings, one and two stories, painted white, and some of them are very neat. They are built in such numbers, and in so short a space of time, that it appears almost as if it were done by a company of fairies, working at night.

"There are a goodly number of merchant vessels in port; one iron ship just from England, and nearly the whole of the Texan navy. I preached on board of the Commodore's vessel last Sabbath, to about one hundred and fifty, officers and men. There is no church yet erected, but preaching is held sometimes in a school-room, and sometimes in the court-house. I have preached some fifteen or twenty sermons already, to houses generally crowded, and we should probably have twice as many out, if we could accommodate them. Two or three persons have, I trust, been this week soundly converted under my preaching. They are, I believe, the very first cases of conversion that ever took place on the island. Thank the Lord for this great honour conferred upon me, a poor, unworthy instrument! One of the persons spoken of, is a lady of high respectability, who had been on the island about three years, and had never heard a single sermon before she heard me, except one from a Catholic priest some time ago. And strange to tell, this first sermon she heard me preach was blessed to her awakening. She has since obtained a hope, and is one of the most interesting and satisfactory cases of conversion I ever knew in all my life.

"*Tuesday*, *25th*. Last Sabbath we had a very interesting communion occasion. Four were added to the church on profession, two of whom were publicly baptized. This was the first communion season of the Presbyterian church on the island. I had the pleasure of seeing brother Allen from Houston this morning. To-morrow I expect to set out for that place. I shall preach in the most populous towns of this Republic, until the roads become good, and then expect to labour in the country. My health, as usual, is very good, and I pass my time very agreeably; only I cannot help thinking, at times, about the loved ones left behind. You know my disposition, however, to turn away from all needless anxieties, and to look upon the path of duty, wherever it may lead, as a pleasant one, strewed with flowers. In this way I have more vigour, and am better able to serve my God. When absent, I take pleasure in preaching; when

I return, I anticipate double pleasure in meeting 'wife, children, and friends.' Come what will, God helping me, I am resolved to be happy.

"That Roman Catholic lady, in her expressions of gratitude, has given me a rich reward for my labours here; and so has an interesting young man from Switzerland, who came up to me in the streets the other day, and with much feeling told me how greatly the Lord had blessed my preaching to his soul. And there is the case of a Texan soldier, a poor wanderer, brought back by my instrumentality, that has touched my heart, insomuch that I thought it well I had come all the way to Texas, if it were only for the sake of that poor wandering sheep. Bless the Lord!

"Yours, as ever,

DANIEL BAKER."

The narrative continues.

I remained in the city of Galveston, I think, about three or four weeks, preaching as I had opportunity. On the last Sabbath we had a communion season, at which time some six or seven professed conversion, and were admitted to the table of the Lord; two of whom were publicly baptized according to the forms of our Church; and these were the first who had ever been baptized on that island by any Protestant denomination. In the matter of the administration of the Lord's Supper, our Baptist brethren had the honour of preceding us two weeks, Rev. Mr. Huckins officiating on the occasion. When I first went to Galveston, I found there the Rev. John McCullough, who, under great disadvantages, had been preaching as he had opportunity. There were a few old members of the Presbyterian church, but brother McCullough had not been able at that time to establish or organize a Presbyterian church. This, however, was done shortly after my departure.

A few days before I reached Galveston, the Rev. W. L. McCalla also arrived, and not choosing, it would seem, to go into any public house or private family, pitched his tent out of town, and near the strand. After living in this way for some time, he was finally found out by Dr. R., who so kindly entertained me, and under his hospitable roof Mr. McCalla remained for several days. Mr. McCalla did not, I believe, visit Texas as a missionary, but to see the country, and do what he could to promote the cause of education. By his efforts a public meeting of the friends of education was held in Galveston. I was present, but said little or nothing. Mr. McCalla delivered an elaborate address, and wound up with a resolution to memorialize the Congress of the Republic to establish a University in Galveston. The motion prevailed, but came to nought, as might have been expected, for Galveston was certainly not a proper location for such an institution.

On leaving Galveston, I went in the steamboat to Houston. After passing over the bay, we came to the junction of Buffalo Bayou and the San Jacinto, made memorable by the battle-field, near at hand, where the decisive battle was fought which secured independence to the Republic. In going up the bayou I was struck unfavourably, I confess, with the sluggishness of the water, the narrowness of the bayou, and the diminutiveness of the forest trees upon its borders.

On reaching Houston, I found the place not handsome, and the streets very muddy. It was like treading mortar. I was, however, very hospitably entertained by Dr. C. and his excellent lady. They had four small children, two sons and two daughters, who appeared to me the best behaved children I had ever seen in all my life. On asking Mrs. C., at a subsequent period, how it came to pass, and expressing my conviction that there must be some secret about the matter, she replied, "No secret, sir, except I control myself." Ah, thinks I to myself, that is the secret; for if parents do not govern themselves, they never can govern their children. I remained in Houston, preaching and distributing tracts, for about ten days. The place of preaching was the old capitol. The people turned out extremely well, and I think some five or six persons professed conversion. Amongst those much wrought upon, was General Mosely Baker, whose residence was on the bay, but was on a visit to Houston. He did not at that time profess conversion, but did some time after, and became a preacher in the Methodist connection. I found in Houston the Rev. W. Y. Allen, who had for some time been labouring very faithfully, and had organized a Presbyterian church on March 31st, 1839, with ten members; but without receiving scarcely any support either from the Board of Missions or the people to whom he preached. This good man drew upon his own resources until they were almost entirely exhausted. Just as I was about leaving the place, the Rev. Mr. F., a Methodist preacher, came and took charge of the few members of the Methodist church, organizing them into a congregation, with the intention of ministering to them for one year. I heard him preach his first sermon in Houston, with which I was much pleased. Here I think I first met with the Rev. B. Chase, of whom I shall have something more to say in a subsequent part of this my autobiography.

(TO HIS LITTLE DAUGHTER.)

"HOUSTON, Texas, *March 9th*, 1840.

"MY DEAR LITTLE DAUGHTER—Your father is far away in Texas, and yet he has not forgotten his beloved Agnes, left with her mother. I have now been in Houston about ten days, and have preached a good many times; and I hope several persons here will be for ever glad, and thankful to their Maker, that they ever saw my face or heard my voice. I am staying at the house of Dr. C., who knew me in Georgia. He and his wife are very kind to me. They have four children. They are very lovely children; not only pretty, but what is much better, they are very good. They are so amiable, they are very kind to each other, and they make their parents so happy. They have not quarrelled once, nor grieved their parents a single time since I have been here. They are very fond of singing, and I have taught them several Infant-school songs, such as, 'O, what a naughty dog is that,' 'I like little pussy, her coat is so warm,' and 'Poor little dog is very good.' Henry and Joseph have a very lively little dog named Prince, and he wags his tail and runs about with them, and seems to love his little masters very much. They have made a little wagon, and Prince, properly harnessed, draws it very prettily; and what is more, if they leave him in the road, and say, 'Prince, don't go away till I come back,' he will stand still; and if any other person should call him away, and say, 'Prince, here is some meat for you,' he won't budge a peg until his little masters come back. This I think is very wonderful for such a lively little curtail, who is so fond of frisking and running about. I should like you to see these children at their sports; and they are so fond of going to Sunday-school, and reading some books which I have given them.

"I talked to the children the day before yesterday May be we had twenty-five present; they all seemed to be much pleased, and some of them wept a good deal. H's mother thinks that she is very serious, and almost hopes that she is a true Christian. O, what a lovely and blessed thing it is for a dear little child to be a Christian. When they are in trouble, they can have their Heavenly Father to comfort them, and when they die, can have angels to take them to heaven, where they will see their blessed Jesus, and be happy for ever. O, I should be so glad to have my dear Agnes a Christian too. Your father and mother, my child, are going to heaven, and it would make us very happy to have you and your sister, and all your brothers to go with us, and be with us in heaven for ever.

"I have just come from seeing a melancholy sight; a mother dead, and three children weeping most piteously. There was one little boy; he did not cry with the rest, for he is too young to know what a loss he has met with. These children are all poor little orphans now—father and mother both dead.

O, my daughter, how thankful you should be to God that your parents are still alive; but you don't know when God may take them away, and you be made an orphan too. But God does all things well; and we must at all times be pleased with all things he does. The mother that died this morning was a very poor woman; she had scarcely anything to live on, and she died suddenly; and what is worse, it seems she had no religion. O, dreadful! I looked at her, and she was almost black in the face. I believe that to ease some pain, she took too much opium or laudanum. Poor woman! poor woman!—she had a sorrowful time on earth, and I fear it will even be worse with her in the other world. Now, if she had been a Christian, O how different! If she had sorrow on earth, she would have had joy in heaven. O, my daughter, be sure that you be a Christian; be sure you love your blessed Saviour, and give him your heart while you are yet young and tender. Tell your dear mother that I am in fine health and spirits, doing some good, I hope; but many of the people here are very wicked; they swear dreadfully, and they don't care much about the holy Sabbath; but God can make them good. Be sure to write to your papa, and tell mother she must fill up every nook and corner.

"I can't tell whether I like Texas yet or not. I came from Galveston to this place by water, and have scarcely seen anything of the country yet. I expect in a few days to buy a horse, and ride about in all directions.

"Your affectionate father,

DANIEL BAKER."

Narrative continued.

Purchasing a horse, saddle, and bridle, for one hundred dollars, in the promissory notes of Texas, (worth at that time only thirty dollars,) I set off for Columbia. The first night I staid at the house of Major B., an avowed infidel, and one who was in the habit, as I was informed, of cursing preachers and lawyers, and who was moreover in the habit of charging them more than others. Being aware of his peculiar hatred of religion, I resolved to be as discreet in my behaviour as possible. At first, I would not say one word on the subject of religion, but spent the whole evening in talking about the affairs of Texas, and getting him to tell me all about its early history, and Austin, the great Texas pioneer. As Major B. had been one of Austin's colonists, no theme was more acceptable; and being much pleased with the stranger, who, from a letter which I handed, he had ascertained to be a preacher, he refrained from swearing; and in a good-humoured way at last said, "Mr. Baker, won't you take a drink?" Here I felt that we had come to "the narrows," but respectfully declining in as pleasant and polite a way as I knew how, the old theme was renewed, and at the proper hour we retired for the night, both in fine spirits.

On the next morning the same theme was brought up again, and whilst we were in the midst of a very pleasant and animated conversation we were summoned to breakfast. Reaching the chair assigned to me, just at the right time, I remarked, "Major B., with your permission I will ask a blessing"—and not allowing him time to say, No, it was all over before he was aware that a thing had been done at his table which probably had never been done before. A couple of ladies who sat opposite to me smiled, and seemed as if they would say, "The Major has been out-generaled this time!" He took it, however, all in good part; and as we rose from the table, and were going into another room by ourselves, he remarked, "I don't believe in the Bible, sir; it will do for women and children. But may be I am wrong." "Ah! Major B., said I, "May be you are wrong! My dear sir, if so, that would be a very serious matter." I then went on for some fifteen or twenty minutes with all the force and power of language which I could command, showing him the fearful consequences of a mistake being made in a matter of such immense importance; especially as no mistakes could be rectified after death. He listened to me in silence, and was as a child subdued; and when I closed, he shook me by the hand most cordially, and, inviting me to call upon him whenever I passed that way, he bade me farewell. For my fare he charged nothing. This case convinced me that any man, however wicked, may be approached, if it be done in the right way.

After leaving the house of Major B., I resumed my journey, having first Brazoria in view. Just as I was leaving the prairie, and getting into the timber bottom of the Brazos River, the sun went down, the the light of day departed, and the deep shades of a dark night gathered around me. There had been much rain, and the road was excessively boggy. Unable to see the road or guide the horse when on walked in mud and water nearly half-leg deep. Occasionally I would miss the road, and get entangled among the bushes. Supposing that the ferry could not be very far off, I struggled on, hallooing as I went; but for some time there was no response. I do confess I felt very awful at the idea of my being obliged to spend the whole night in such a place. There was, as far as I could perceive, not even a log to rest upon. My horse, too, became almost entirely unmanageable, being unwilling to go one step further when he found there was a deep mud-hole before him. This was sorrow upon sorrow, trouble upon trouble, almost more than I could stand. Although a man, I could scarcely refrain from weeping. At length I saw a torchlight. O how beautiful was that light! And I heard a voice—it was the voice of the ferryman; how sweet was that voice! With great joy I reached the ferry, was carried over safely, and came to the town. It was court time, the house was crowded—and what a vast amount of swearing! To me it seemed that every man was profane. As soon as I could get some refreshment, I retired; but not to sleep. How could I—for in the next room, separated only by a thin partition wall, were several men engaged in playing cards. Their loud laughter and profane swearing kept me awake until the clock struck twelve. They then broke up, and one of them coming into the room where I slept, threw himself upon a bed, and immediately fell asleep; but that availed me nothing, for every now and then he would utter some horrid oath in his sleep! This was cruel; after spending so many hours in the swamp, to be kept awake for hours by men swearing when awake, and then for hours more to have sleep, much needed sleep, driven from my eyes by a man in my own room swearing while asleep. That man was a judge. On a certain occasion, when on the bench, a lawyer, who did not wish the court to be held, made a flaming speech to brow-beat the judge, and make him adjourn the court. Perceiving that the judge was not inclined to yield, he drew out a bowie-knife, and laying it down on the table, said, "May it please your Honour, this is my argument." Upon this the judge as promptly drew out his pistol, and laying it also down, replied, "And this is my decision!" So the court was not adjourned. In the States, this lawyer would probably have been arrested for "contempt of court," but new countries and old countries are not the same.

As the court-house was occupied, and there was no other place for preaching, the next morning I went on to Columbia, about twelve miles, to the house of Mrs. Bell, a lady of uncommon excellence, who received me very kindly. I remained, and preached several sermons in a private house. The preaching was not without effect; several persons were awakened, and amongst the converts was Mrs. B's daughter and a Miss P., who subsequently became valuable members of the Presbyterian church. Upon leaving Mrs. B., she insisted on my making use of one of her horses, one much better than my own; saying that she would keep my "mustang" until my return. From Columbia I went to Washington, on the Brazos. This was considered a very wicked place; but I preached several nights in succession to some twenty-five or thirty persons, who seemed to listen with much interest to what I said. On Sunday morning I expected that the room in which I preached would be crowded; when, lo! the number was very small, less than on any of the preceding days. Upon expressing my surprise to "mine host," he remarked that the alcalde had been in the habit of holding his court on Sunday morning. In the afternoon and at night, however, the room was well filled. If I recollect right, there was not a professor of religion in the whole town. Mr. Alexander, a Methodist preacher, and a most excellent man, had been in the habit of preaching there occasionally, but it was with some opposition. The people generally were not at all religiously inclined, and some were very wicked, heaven-daring scoffers. In proof of this, I was told that "mock prayer-meetings" were held every Friday night; and the very week before I reached Washington, an incident of an awful kind took place, which ought to have struck terror into every heart, but did not. Whilst the "mock-meeting" was going on—whilst one, half drunk, was mimicking a certain preacher, and all present were laughing immoderately, a pistol in the hand of one accidentally went off, and one of the number, pierced in the heart, fell dead upon the floor! So sudden was the death, the features not having time to relax, that the body, when shrouded, presented the unnatural and fearful spectacle of a laughing corpse. This was enough, one would think, to put a stop to such exhibitions of horrid impiety, but it did not; for another "mock meeting" was held one night after I had preached; at least, a noise was heard, which the friend with whom I lodged pronounced, as he believed, "another mock meeting affair."

From Washington I hurried on to Independence, and had the pleasure of becoming acquainted with the Rev. Hugh Wilson, who formerly had been labouring amongst the Chickasaw Indians. At his request, I preached several days, both at Independence and in a neighbourhood some six or eight miles distant, called the "Chrisman settlement." In the former place, the meeting proved a very solemn and interesting one; but at the latter we had what might be termed a little revival. Some ten or twelve persons, if I recollect aright, professed conversion, some of whom are living and valuable members of the church at this time; and some have fallen asleep in Jesus. One of the most remarkable cases of conversion was that of Captain C., an old Texan, one of Austin's colony, and a man who had no respect for religion, and who, moreover, was awfully profane. As evidence of the first assertion, I will state an incident. On a certain day, a gentleman riding over the settlement, noticed a beautiful spot, and remarked, "Captain C., that is a beautiful place for a church." "Don't talk about churches," said Captain C.; "if you do, you will drive me out of this country." I said he was profane, very; and yet he was made a trophy of grace, and became one of the humblest and most devoted Christians I ever knew. How? The case was this. I was preaching a sermon from these words, "Tekel, thou art weighed in the balances, and art found wanting." When I came to weigh profane swearers, amongst other things, I remarked: "An old writer has said,

'The devil sometimes turns fisherman; when he fishes for ordinary sinners, he is willing to go to some expense; he baits his hook with the riches of the world, the honours of the world, and the pleasures of the world; but when he fishes for profane swearers, he throws them the naked hook, and they bite at the naked hook;—cheap in the devil's account.'" This was carried like an arrow to his heart. He was deeply convicted, and a few days after, was a happy convert. "Captain C.," said I, "what first set you to thinking?" "O, Mr. Baker," replied he, "the idea of the devil's catching me with a naked hook. I could not stand that, sir." I have already stated the remark he made about churches, "Don't talk to me about churches, or you will drive me out of this country." Now mark the change. Shortly after he found peace in believing, he was called off to some distance on Monday morning, and did not reach home until Wednesday afternoon. Riding up to his house, he saw a good many horses hitched near his premises. Not knowing that an appointment was made for preaching, upon inquiry, he was informed of the fact. "O, I am glad of it," said he, "I am so hungry for preaching; I have not heard a sermon since last Sunday!"

Here I may mention the case of Dr. B., a member of the Texan Congress, a Senator. Powerfully wrought upon, he, with some fifteen or twenty others, attended an inquiry meeting, held by brother Wilson and myself. One day, going from one of these meetings, he said to me, as I was riding at his side, "Mr. Baker, I wish to ask you one question, and I wish you to give me a plain answer. To-morrow there is to be a horse-race at such a place. I am a candidate for re-election to the Senate, and I am expected to be there to make a political speech. Would it be wrong for me to go?" "Dr. B.," replied I, "you are now under the strivings of the Spirit; if you go, I believe it will cost you your soul; and what," added I, "is a man profited if he shall gain the whole world, and lose his own soul?" "Sir," said he, "I don't care about being elected, but I don't like the idea of being defeated." "Very well, Dr. B.," said I, "I have nothing more to say; if you do go I believe it will cost you your soul." The next day, instead of going to the race-ground, he was at church. I think he will bless God for ever that he did so; for whilst I am writing these lines, I do believe his ransomed soul is bending before the eternal throne. Some eight or ten years after his hopeful conversion, I met with him at G. He was then a much esteemed elder of the Cumberland Presbyterian church. We were engaged in very pleasant conversation, when a gentleman stepped in hastily, and said, "Dr. B., the Indians have killed two young men near your house."* "Is it possible!" said he. Alas! some five days after, he himself fell by the hands of the cruel savages.

It was in the spring of 1840 that this meeting took place, at Independence and the Chrisman settlement; and this was the date of the organization of the Brazos Presbytery, April 3d, 1840. The brethren met at Chrisman's school-house, and or-

* Dr. B. resided in the country, about fifteen miles from G.

ganized the first Old-school Presbytery in the then Republic of Texas, viz.—

The Rev. Hugh Wilson, of the Presbytery of South Alabama. Rev. John McCullough, of Newton Presbytery, New Jersey. Rev. William Y. Allen, of the Presbytery of Western District, Tennessee. Ruling elder, Mr. John McFarland, Independence church.

The Presbytery, having organized, drew up and adopted its views of faith and doctrine, which were in exact accordance with the standards of our Church; but a question of ecclesiastical connection was started which occasioned much debate: Shall this Presbytery be connected with the General Assembly of the Presbyterian Church in the United States, or shall it assume an independent character? As it was under a foreign government, and as there seemed to be scarcely any possibility of carrying up the records or any appeal to any higher ecclesiastical court in "The States," it was finally determined to remain disconnected with the General Assembly, until some new light should be thrown upon the subject.

Monday, April 6th. The Presbytery met according to adjournment, in a log out-house, near the dwelling of Mr. L. I was present, and invited to sit as a corresponding member from Tuskaloosa Presbytery, Alabama. The matter of ecclesiastical connection was mentioned to me, and my opinion was asked. I approved of the action of Presbytery, and, accordingly, no connection was sought with the Synod of Mississippi, or General Assembly. This gave great offence, and caused the Board of Missions to withdraw the commission and pecuniary aid previously given to the Rev. Hugh Wilson, who, for several years, had been in the employment of the Board. This proved a serious affair to this worthy brother, who was, with his family, in straitened circumstances, and who was thus suddenly cut off from his principal means of support. It excited my sympathy, and upon my return to the States, I wrote a letter of remonstrance, couched in strong language, addressed to the Corresponding Secretary.

When the brethren were together at the Chrisman settlement, we had some talk about establishing a Presbyterian College in Texas. The spot was even selected. It was a high and commanding eminence, some three or four hundred yards from brother Wilson's residence. Standing on the spot, the scene around was most beautiful. On the one hand were wide prairies, green and pleasant to the eye; on the other, we saw the extensive Yegua forests, stretching far away, in all the loveliness of the original and unbroken grandeur. I made an attempt at obtaining subscriptions. Calling upon Captain P., who married the sister of S. F. Austin, he was much pleased with the idea when stated, and promised to make a donation of fifteen hundred acres of land, embracing, I think, the very spot which we had selected as a site for our college.

At this time Dr. Baker kept, in a small memorandum book, a journal of daily events. From its little pages we continue the narrative.

Washington County, Texas, Tuesday, 21st April, 1840. Visited this morning. Found Dr. H., who formerly could not remain during the whole of a sermon on account of his habit of smoking, evidently under very serious impressions. During prayer with the family the Doctor wept. Rode to Chrisman's settlement, and preached at night to a full house. Had a deeply solemn and interesting season; perhaps there was not a single careless person present. Brother Allen had preached several sermons since I left.

Wednesday, 22*d*. Preached to pretty much the same congregation at 11 o'clock. After sermon requested the serious, and those who had obtained a hope, to go into another room, whilst Christians remained for prayer. It appears that the seriousness is very general throughout the settlement. The following persons have professed conversion, embracing most of the substantial members of the community: * * * Mr. G., when under conviction, was so much wrought upon that he got off his horse one day going to meeting, and begged a Christian friend to pray for him. At night preached again, but had not my accustomed liberty. Congregation large, and in a peculiarly interesting state; but I was completely thrown out of the harness by a fly drawn into my throat, and by a mother who was rocking her child in her lap, and keeping up a certain noise with her foot during nearly the whole service. What a poor creature am I!

Thursday, 23*d*. Visited several families, and rode in company with brother Wilson, who is a most excellent brother, and is much pleased to see the seed which he has been sowing now springing up. It is right that they that sow and they that reap should rejoice together. At night, preached at Independence to a very attentive congregation. Several here have recently professed conversion, and others are under awakening influences.

Friday, 24*th*. Spent the day in reading, visiting, &c. At night, preached to a large and very attentive congregation on the supreme divinity of Christ. One gentleman was present, I am told, who had not heard a single sermon for twenty years!—and his wife is a professor of religion! Wonder if his wife has adorned the doctrine!

Saturday, 25*th*. Addressed children at half-past nine, and at eleven o'clock preached from Rev. xii. 7, 8. Had much liberty, and at the close was completely melted down; and whilst tears were rolling down my cheeks, I was enabled, with unusual earnestness and power, to urge sinners in the name of a beseeching God, to abandon the black banner of Apollyon, and range themselves under the white banner of the Prince of Peace. In the afternoon brother Allen and myself both exhorted, and then I addressed mothers. This meeting will long be remembered; hope much good was done. At night brother Allen preached, and I closed with an exhortation; reminding the sinner that there was only one person in the universe to whom his salvation was necessary, that is, himself, and pressing upon him the language of the Apostle, "Do thyself no harm."

Sabbath, 26*th*. Sacramental Sabbath. Preached in the morning from Mark xv. 34. Had something of an unction. At the close of the sermon there was almost universal weeping. Brother McCalla being present, administered the sacrament of the Lord's Supper. Twelve persons were admitted by the Session, all new converts save one, who was received from the Campbellite church after examination. Four of the young converts were baptized. During the recess called in the blacks, (who had been lingering about the doors and windows,) and preached a sermon to them from these words, "O, taste and see that the Lord is good." Brother Allen, with much earnestness, preached in the afternoon, and I closed with an exhortation. At night I preached my last sermon. At the close there was much tender feeling; there seemed to be weeping all over the house. After returning to brother Wilson's house, conversed with his daughters, who appeared to be under very deep conviction. Brother Wilson attempted to lead in family prayer, but his feelings overcame him, and I had to close the prayer. The Lord's name be praised for what was seen and heard and felt this day!

Monday, 27th. Took an affectionate leave of brother Wilson and family, and in company with brother Allen and Mr. Holcomb and wife, who yesterday had come on horseback eighteen miles to preaching. On the road fell in company with a young man, Mr. Henderson, who resides in Columbia, but had just come from Austin. Mr. H. says he had to swim four creeks, and in one had well nigh been drowned. How providential I did not go to Austin, as I originally intended. Indeed, I find that ever since leaving home, I have had reason to mark the hand of a wise and gracious Providence. I made great efforts to get to Texas at an earlier period, but was held in check by a very remarkable train of providences; and yet it appears I reached Texas just at the right time. Had I come sooner, the season would have been unfavourable for missionary operations; had I come later, I would not have had sufficient time before the setting in of warm weather. The Bible says, "The steps of a good man are ordered by the Lord." I do not say that I am a good man, but the promise I have claimed and acted upon.

Brother Allen and myself reached San Félipe a little after sunset (forty miles.) We sent around notice, and preached to about twenty-five persons. Brother Allen led in the exercises, and I followed. I do not recollect that I ever spoke with more ease and fluency in all my life. Mr. K., our landlord, remarked that the people would have been willing to remain until midnight. I am promised a large congregation here if I will only preach on the Sabbath.

Tuesday, 28*th*. Reached Mrs. P's (thirty miles) early in the afternoon, and proposed preaching in her house at night. Mrs. P. cordially consented, and accordingly at night I preached to a congregation of about sixteen, consisting of the family, some carpenters who were employed in building her a splendid house, and a few travellers. After sermon had quite an argument with two ladies just from New Orleans, hearers of Mr. C., a Universalist preacher. They insisted upon it that it was perfectly right for members of the church to attend balls, &c., and that certainly it was right for the pastor to go where his people went! At length I brought forward an argu ment which completely silenced them.

Thursday 30th. Preached at Mr. F's, in Columbia, at eleven o'clock, to more than I had anticipated. In the afternoon brother Allen preached, and I fol lowed. At night, was astonished at the number of persons present. I preached a long sermon; at the close, much feeling.

Friday, May 1st. Rode to East Columbia, and preached at eleven o'clock in a vacant store; about seventy-five present; great attention and some weeping. Brother Allen preached in the afternoon; after which I had much liberty in exhortation. At night, preached at Mr. F's, in West Columbia; had a large congregation and very solemn meeting. After services, spent a few moments in speaking to blacks, who seemed to be much interested.

Saturday, 2d. Preached in the morning with much freedom; in the afternoon held an inquiry meeting at the house of Mrs. Bell; some ten or twelve present. Two more have obtained a hope; some were powerfully wrought upon, who had been very irreligious. At night preached again.

Sabbath, 3d. Rode to Brazoria, and preached in the room occupied as a court-house. The room was crowded, and many were out in the piazza. The sermon was long, but none seemed impatient. Preached in the afternoon, and also at night. Think a very deep impression was made, particularly at night. Found an opportunity to preach a short sermon to the blacks also.

Monday, 4th. Preached in the morning to about forty persons, chiefly females. At the close, conversed with several, who appeared to be under deep exercises. In the afternoon brother Allen preached a short sermon. At night I preached my last sermon to a full house, from these words: "Be not righteous overmuch." Toward the close, when I urged the necessity of being righteous enough, there was great solemnity and much feeling; one young lady in particular wept aloud. Her mother, an aged woman, was at her side; not converted, but apparently very serious. Dr. C. informed me that Colonel H. directed him to say, that if I would come to Texas to live, he would make me a present of some four or five hundred acres of land. This gentlemen, it seems, was pungently convicted under one of my sermons a few days since, and was one of those who attended the inquiry meeting on Saturday last.

Tuesday, 5*th*. Rode with brother Allen five miles, to Mr. H's, where we breakfasted, and had a friendly conversation with Mr. H. and his lady, on some doctrinal points. After breakfast, rode three miles further, to Major C's, who had invited me to visit him, and preach at his house; accordingly I preached a sermon to about fifteen white persons, and a goodly number of blacks were in the back piazza. Two or three white persons wept; and I noticed one man in particular whose countenance indicated deep thoughtfulness and anxiety. They listened with great interest for some twenty minutes; and when I closed my remarks, they still seemed unwilling to retire. Believe some good was done.

Wednesday, 6*th*. Rode with brother Allen to Mr. W's, where there was an appointment for preaching. Brother Allen preached, and I followed. Mr. W.

and lady had attended the meeting in Columbia, (perhaps fifteen miles distant,) and had been much wrought upon, but not converted. In the afternoon, brother Allen and myself taking an affectionate leave of each other, I rode to the house of Mr. P.

Thursday, *7th.* According to appointment preached this morning at the house of Mr. P. It rained, and yet some fifteen white persons were present and listened with great attention.

Friday, *8th.* Had a lonely ride to Y's. Reached there about sunset, and being much jaded and somewhat unwell, I threw myself upon a bed to rest. While lying down, I was told that a Mr. W. had about an hour before set out for the landing on Matagorda Bay, about three miles distant, whence a boat was to start for Matagorda, and that if I would ride fast I might get to the landing before the boat would start. Accordingly I rose, and hastening on, I reached the boat, leaving my horse with Mr. Y., who promised to make no charge. The boat proved leaky, and we had a terrible time of it.

Saturday, *9th.* What a night, what a night! All exposed on the bay in an open boat, and a fresh north wind blowing all night. I had a blanket, but it was soon made soaking wet by the leaking of the boat. It was, however, my only bed; and ever and anon, finding the water invading my couch, I had to rise and bail the boat, or get some one else to do it. The sun rising next morning in a clear sky was some comfort, but the breeze was too strong to permit our sailing; so we remained in the same position until about noon, when the wind slackening a little, we weighed anchor, and set sail for Matagorda, which place we reached about eight o'clock at night. I had neither breakfast, dinner, nor supper on board of the boat, save one biscuit and a small piece of beef, and had come off without supper the night before. One might suppose I would have had a ravenous appetite, but no such thing; I felt jaded and almost worn out. My feet had been wet for some fifteen hours, and I longed to get into a comfortable bed. Finding a very indifferent house of entertainment, and partaking sparingly of a very indifferent supper, I was put into a very indifferent bed—no, I must not call it a bed—on a broken cot, with a straw pillow, I spent another wretched night.

Sabbath, 10th. Rose unrefreshed; felt badly all day. At eleven o'clock heard Mr. I., the Episcopal minister (an interesting man, and the only resident minister) preach in the Masonic Hall, the only preaching place in town. At night I preached to a very full house on the evidences of Christianity. Very good attention was given, and although my sermon was an hour long, there was not the slightest indication of impatience.

Monday, 11th. Felt badly; yet, after breakfast, took a view of the town. In the afternoon I had a chill, and at night felt quite feverish and lightheaded; nevertheless, I preached; had a crowded house; some went away, not being able to procure seats. Never, perhaps, in all my life, spoke with more freedom and power; was much favoured with devotional and heavenly feelings; do hope that some deep impressions were made. Although Matagorda is considered a very hard place, the people attend church, I am told, very well; but there are not more, from what I can learn, than ten converted persons in all the town; and not a single soul, it seems, has ever yet been converted in this place. When in Columbia, I heard it stated that, some months since, there were only three professors in town—one was a Presbyterian, another a Methodist, and the third a Baptist; and the three uniting, formed themselves into an Episcopal church!

Tuesday, 12*th*. Spent a very restless night; had a fever, and a slight pain in my head, nearly all night. Towards morning had a profuse perspiration, and felt rather better; during the day hardly knew what to do; could neither read nor write, nor lie down, nor take exercise with any satisfaction, until towards evening, when, the weather clearing off, I began to feel much better. At night preached, but had no liberty at all; the house, however, was quite full, and the congregation, as usual, very attentive.

Wednesday, 13*th*. Felt very well in the morning. Visited, and held a meeting for mothers; but, in the afternoon had a return of the chills, which were succeeded by a hot fever, which, after I had suffered much, went off in a profuse perspiration. Whilst lying restless in my bed, the thought occurred that it was possible I might die in Matagorda. I can truly say my desire was that the Lord's will might be done. There were two things, however, which made death rather undesirable at this time; one was, that I was among strangers—I had rather, if it please God, die in the bosom of my family; the other was, should I die in Texas, it might discourage some ministers from coming to this new Republic. With regard to my prospects for another world, thank the Lord, they are pleasing. If I know the state of my own mind, I am willing to go at any time; nay, sometimes I think I can say even with the apostle, "I have a desire to depart, and be with Christ, which is far better."

"Lord, 'tis an infinite delight
To see thy lovely face;
To dwell whole ages in thy sight,
And feel thy vital rays."

Thursday, 14*th*. This morning felt much relieved; the doctor, however, advised me to keep my bed all day; accordingly, I scarcely left my room, and read as much as I conveniently could. I feel much debilitated, and greatly desire the arrival of the brig "Sam Houston," in which I expect to embark for New Orleans. Being indisposed all day, of course I did not preach at night.

Friday, 15*th*. Woke up this morning feeling rather enfeebled. Thought I saw the "Sam Houston" in the bay, but was sadly disappointed. About ten o'clock my fever returned, and continued about eight hours.

Saturday, 16*th*. Spent a very restless night; did not get any sleep until towards morning; woke up however in the morning feeling considerably better. Looked out upon the bay for the "Sam Houston," but she had not yet made her appearance. Kept my bed nearly the whole of the day; I was very sick. The Episcopal minister, in the kindness of his heart, called to see me, and upon his rising to leave, I requested him to pray. Accordingly, he opened his prayer-book, and read some two or three short prayers; but, I must confess, that I thought an extemporaneous prayer, prompted by the occasion, would have had a better effect upon my religious feelings. The doctor who attended me, and others, were very kind.

Sabbath, 17*th.* Although weak, was enabled to attend church, and hear Mr. I. preach. In the afternoon attended the Sabbath-school. Found it very small; only about twelve scholars present, and two or three teachers. I made a few remarks. At night I preached to a crowded house. During the day I looked forward with special interest to the occasion, and thought I should be able to speak with peculiar tenderness and solemnity; but so soon as I began to speak, I found that I had not that physical strength nor command of voice which I hoped. A little attack of sickness, how it pulls one down!

Monday, 18*th.* Felt much prostrated, and could do little more than read, and wait the time to preach at night. Understand that a very unusual impression was made last night. The sermon, it seems, has started much inquiry, and given rise to much conversation this day. Some were much pleased; but others thought I bore down rather hard. At four o'clock I addressed about twenty children, and at night preached with some freedom to a congregation even larger, perhaps, than it was last night. It was a crowd indeed.

Tuesday, 19*th.* Last night had a kind of giant pain in my back. Never had such a peculiar kind of pain in all my life. In the afternoon, I preached a short sermon on the subject of experimental religion, according to notice previously given; after which the ladies present remained to form some plan to procure the occasional preaching of some Presbyterian in this place. At night we had a very large congregation, and I was enabled to speak with some considerable tenderness and energy. Many tears were shed, and I think that, by the grace of God, the impression this night was decidedly happy. As there was a prospect of my embarking to-morrow, I endeavoured, after the sermon, to set before the congregation, in a clear and succinct way, the mode of the sinner's acceptance with God.

Wednesday, 20*th*. Health much improved. Very impatient to spread the wing for the States. The captain of the "Sam Houston" had said he would sail this day; but upon inquiry, found that he would not sail until to-morrow. As the people seemed very anxious that I should preach for them again, in the evening the bell was rung, and I preached to a congregation nearly as large as usual. In this sermon, I spoke with considerable energy, but lacked tenderness.

Thursday, 21*st*. How tantalizing! The captain says he does not think he can sail until to-morrow. Could do little else than lie down and read. Feel that my whole system has been prostrated.

Friday, 22*d*. Not to-day, but probably *to-morrow*, again. What a trial of one's patience! Went down to the landing, to see if I could not go in some boat to the head of Matagorda Bay, where I had left my horse. In that case, my plan was to go to Velasco, and embark there, or at Galveston; but about an hour by sun, the captain called, and said he was going. All in haste, I hurried on, and in the captain's yawl we reached the brig, lying off Dog Island, a little after dark. Was very glad to find myself on board the brig; but soon found that the captain and most of the passengers were profane. Told my story of "pot-hooks and hangers," which had a happy effect.*

Saturday, 23*d*. Had to wait for a lighter, bringing a load of cotton; so we did not set sail until after eleven o'clock. About four o'clock reached Pass Cavallo. Cast anchor, and went to catching fish with a seine; caught some, but were not very successful. Made arrangements for preaching on board the brig in the morning, and at Mr. D's in the afternoon, in case we should be wind-bound.

Sabbath, 24*th*. Light breezes, but favourable, so the captain made a signal for a pilot, and by twelve o'clock we had got through the Pass, and soon found ourselves out of sight of land—"*Undique pontus, et pontus undique.*" Had no good opportunity to preach, some being sea-sick, and others asleep in their berths. Breezes fresh, but from wrong quarter, so we were swept too far to the south.

Monday, 25*th*. Breezes from the right point, but very light; made very little headway—what a school for patience!

Tuesday, 26*th*. Calm nearly all night; in the

* The story alluded to was to the effect, that a certain minister was once travelling in a stage-coach, in which another passenger, who was very talkative and profane, was interlarding his conversation every now and then with an oath. When at length he became silent, the minister, in turn, began to tell his story, somewhat in this way: "I was once in a certain place—pot-hooks and hangers!—where I met with such a person—pot-hooks and hangers!—who said to me—pot-hooks and hangers!" &c. The gentleman, rather surprised, interrupted him by asking what he meant by his singular interjections. "Why," said the minister, "you have your way of telling a story, and I have mine; and of the two, I think mine is the best."

morning fresh breeze, but not favourable. Hold religious conversation occasionally with the captain and fellow-passengers; but, somehow or other, felt unusual backwardness—had more satisfaction in my own private meditations. Had a chill, followed by a fever, which lasted nearly all night.

Wednesday, 27*th*. Spent a wretched night. There being much of a calm, the rolling of the vessel, the flapping of the sails, and the creaking of the ropes, annoyed me much; but not half so much as the gambling, which was kept up until three o'clock in the morning. The card-table being near my berth, I was under the necessity of listening to all that passed. What a hell it must be to be linked to such characters! O, gracious God, gather not my soul with sinners! The game played was *Faro*, and I calculated that, during this one sitting, one of the players repeated this form of expression, "Five loses—ten wins—ace loses—Jack wins," about two thousand times! It was horrible! Out of respect to me they did not swear much, but occasionally an oath would slip out. On one such occasion I said, "Captain, don't you like new ideas?—I have just got a bran-span new one. You know," continued I, "that many Universalists swear they will be damned, &c. Now, if all are going to heaven, how can they thus swear that they will be damned?" I believe he did not like this new idea much, for he answered not a word. Head winds still! Well, it is the Lord that holds the winds in his fist, and the waters in the hollow of his hand; and let his will be done.

Thursday, 28*th*. Wind still unfavourable; if it were not for interesting books, we should hardly know what to do. Our card-players are inveterate gamblers; night and day they do little else than play. In the afternoon my chills returned, and then a fever, which lasted nearly all night. Slept on deck.

Saturday, 30*th*. No change; wind still from the north-east; dead ahead. The Lord reigneth; all is well. Missed my chills—thank the Lord!

Sabbath, 31*st*. An awning was spread on deck, and, with permission, I preached a short sermon to all on board. The vessel rocked too much for me to stand, so I sat. The wind still ahead, but the weather pleasant; no storms; pleasant breezes ever since we sailed. Although the voyage is long and tedious, yet I thank the Lord I have had some sweet seasons in meditation and prayer; have been thinking a good deal about the vanity of the world, and the immense importance of having an interest in a Saviour's love. The thoughts of heaven are very sweet to me, and I am ready to say,

"Let heavenly love prepare my soul,
And call her to the skies;
Where years of long salvation roll,
And glory never dies!"

Monday, *June* 1*st*. Pleasant breezes, but still unfavourable. As I have now been absent from my dear family nearly seven months, and have not received a single letter for some eight or nine weeks, it is natural that I should desire to reach home as soon as possible. But let patience have her perfect work.

Tuesday, 2*d*. Taking the usual observations at

twelve o'clock this day, found that we were about thirty miles from Ship Island, and about one hundred and twenty from the mouth of the Mississippi; wind pretty much from same quarter still—how remarkable!

Wednesday, 3*d*. Head-wind; so much swearing on board, and so much card-playing, make the voyage disagreeable, but we have uniformly pleasant breezes and fair weather; wind getting more favourable. On a fair and pleasant morning, however, I came up upon deck; every thing was beautiful, every thing was cheering; the wind was fair, the air was balmy. At a distance, but in sight, was the light-house, tall and white, at the mouth of the river. There also were ships at anchor; some, with white spreading sails, going in, and some going out. This, to my eye, was a scene of rare beauty. To crown the matter, up came a powerful steamboat, and coming near, a rope was thrown on board of our brig. Thus grappled, we went on with wonderful speed; I was affected; and seeing the ocean behind me, and the broad river leading to the desired port opening before me, I thought of the moment when the Christian, finishing his warfare on earth, is about to enter with joy the haven of eternal rest! I wept! Overcome with delightful emotions, I hastened to the bow, from whence all had retired, and there I wept aloud! My soul was full of joy and triumph! So, thinks I, as this powerful steamboat takes this vessel on—so, perhaps, will some strong angel, at last, be sent to conduct me to the haven of eternal rest!—my long-desired, my sweet, my eternal home!

CHAPTER X.

LABOURS AS AN EVANGELIST—PASTORATE AT HOLLY SPRINGS.

DR. BAKER'S autobiography proceeds:

Reaching New Orleans in safety, I got on board the first steamboat, and soon exchanging that for a horse and gig, I hurried on to Mr. C's residence; where my family boarded. And now a scene was presented which I shall not soon forget. My little daughter, a dear child, (Agnes Elizabeth,) was in the yard in front of the house, playing with her cousins, Rowena and Mary C. She saw me in the distance, and recognizing her father, ran to meet me, screaming for joy, "Pa is come! pa is come!" My horse knew not what to make of it, and began to prick up his ears, and was about to run. Jumping out of the gig, I had to hold him fast. "Don't scream so, my daughter," said I, "you will frighten pa's horse." Dear child, in her great joy she did not think about that; but like a bird she flew to meet me, and when I stooped down to kiss her, she in a paroxysm of joy threw her arms around my neck, and I might say, almost smothered me with her kisses. Dear child, I shall never see her running to meet me any more! I shall never hear that sweet voice any more! Those dear arms will never be thrown around my neck any more! She sleeps in death now! That sweet voice is hushed. That lovely form reposes under the clods of the valley. The grass has long been green upon her grave. She was my youngest child, and very dear was she to her father's heart.

She was about ten years of age when she was taken from her affectionate parents. But, thank God, there was hope in her death. She had been a Sabbath-scholar in early life; when not four years old, her mother took her to the Sabbath-school; she was delighted. When I came home from preaching, she came up to me with eyes sparkling with joy, and said, "Pa, ma took me to Sunday-school this morning, and said I might go next Sunday, and Sunday after too."

On her bed of death she suffered much. "O, my pain!" said she, on a certain occasion. "Where is your pain, my dear?" asker her mother. "All over," replied the dear little sufferer. At first she seemed alarmed, and begged her mother to pray for her; afterwards all fears were removed—a heavenly peace seemed to take possession of her soul. Waking up one day out of a sweet sleep, she looked at her mother, and said: "The harp! What did you bring me away for, mamma?" "What did you say, my dear?" replied her mother. "The harp!" said she again, "What did you bring me away for?" Dear child! she thought that she had been in heaven, hearing "the voice of harpers, harping with their harps."

On one Sunday night, the last with her on earth, she called a servant girl, to whom she was much attached. "Melissa," said she, "I love you; come lie down by my side." The servant obeyed. "Melissa," added she, "didn't you know that I am going to die to-night?" "O, well," said the girl, "if you die to-night, the blessed Jesus will take you right up to heaven." "Well!" said she; and that was the last word my dear Agnes Elizabeth ever uttered on earth. The next morning the struggle was over. Her body was slumbering in the arms of death; her ransomed spirit reposing, as I trust, in the bosom of her blessed Saviour.

I was not present when my little daughter died; I was in Gainesville, where I had engaged to supply the pulpit for a short time. I received a letter from my son W., stating that his sister was very sick; but at the bottom there was a line written by Dr. O., stating in substance that no danger was apprehended. By the next mail I was informed that my daughter was dead. The news was so unexpected that I was stunned; I shed not a tear; I was as one bewildered. I returned to my chamber, read the letter over again, and then could not refrain from weeping aloud; for I loved her much. O, thought I, if I could only have been with her in her last moments! But there is a providence, and God does all things well. My idol taken from me, the very earth seemed darkened. But I trust I was enabled to say, with holy Job, "The Lord gave; the Lord hath taken away. Blessed be the name of the Lord!"

It was about this period that Dr. Baker wrote as follows:

"MARION, *June* 18*th*, 1840.

"DEAR BROTHER GALLOWAY—I have been to Texas. I have just returned; and so well pleased am I with what I have seen and heard in that new Republic, that I think I shall make it my home. The lands in general are very rich, and some parts of the country are extremely beautiful. But what is more important, the people set a very great value upon a preached gospel, and come out wonderfully. I have often said, on week evenings as well as on Sabbath-days, Where do all these people come from? I think the associations of early life must have some influence in this matter; a mother's tears and a mother's prayers are not forgotten. Moreover, there seems to be a disposition to roll away the reproach cast upon them, that they are a set of outlaws and demi-savages; and, besides, you know that what is scarce is much prized.

"The population of Texas may amount to one hundred thousand souls, and there are comparatively very few preachers amongst them. The Methodists have some twelve or fourteen, the Presbyterians only four or five. How many there are of the Baptist communion I know not; not many, I think; and of the Episcopal Church I have heard of not more than two or three. I have preached in places where no gospel sermon had ever been preached before; and I have seen adults who had not heard a single discourse, some for eight, some for twelve, and some for twenty years. I saw a lady and gentleman who, on a Sunday morning, rode eighteen miles to church, without having any certain information that there would be preaching that day. You may judge how much they were delighted to find that it was a communion season, and that there was a blessed revival of religion going on. Having both of them been professors of religion in the old States, I trust they received spiritual benefit that day. I will not now enter into particulars; suffice it to say, I had the pleasure of witnessing several precious seasons of refreshing in Texas, and had the satisfaction of seeing some of Austin's colony happily brought in. *Laus Deo!*

"With Christian salutations, your brother in Christ,

DANIEL BAKER."

"GAINESVILLE, *August 2d*, 1840.

"MY BELOVED DAUGHTER—I think it likely that you were much disappointed that I did not go to Tuskaloosa at the time expected. I was sadly disappointed myself; but so it was, I could not conveniently go. You know I told you that I am like a 'Portuguese man-of-war,' a curious kind of fish, that spreads its sails to the breezes of heaven, and floats about over the ocean, wherever the winds and the waves may waft it. So have I been since my return from Texas. I look up to heaven for direction, and go whithersoever the winds and the waves of Providence conduct me.

"I stayed at Dayton longer than I had expected. We had a delightful time, a sweet season of refreshing. On Wednesday, after the services had commenced, there were some sixty or seventy in the inquiry meeting; one of them a political partizan from Demopolis, Major T., who, with some others, had come to Dayton, not to seek the salvation of their souls, but to aid in the election of General Harrison. Stop! I have made a little mistake; it was on the Sabbath, the very next day after he had addressed the people. This I think quite remarkable. On Thursday afternoon, as I was informed, all the stores and shops were shut up, a case without precedent there, even on the Sabbath. Brother C. puts down the number of converts at fifteen. Blessed be God! On my way to Marion, I preached some six or eight sermons in Woodville, and think that a very good impression was then made. On my return to Marion I received a letter from Dr. C., of Texas, one of the most interesting and encouraging I ever received in all my life. He was pleased to say, "The people of Texas will bless God that a Baker was sent to Texas;" and adds that not one of the converts had faltered.

"Excuse me, Theodora; are you not my own much loved daughter? I hope my own child will not charge her father with boasting; but the matter is so pleasing to me, it wakes up, as I trust, so much gratitude in my bosom, I thought I would record it. The fact will encourage me in time to come. On reaching —— from Dayton, I also received a communication from the church and congregation inviting me to this place; and here I expect to remain until I start for Texas, which, I suppose, will be about the 10th of October next. May God's richest blessings rest upon you, my beloved child. Farewell.

"Your affectionate father,

DANIEL BAKER."

"LA GRANGE, *Jan.* 13*th*, 1841.

"MY BELOVED DAUGHTER—I have written a goodly number of letters to you and your mother within a short time past. If I have given you a surfeit, you can just fold up this letter, and lay it aside until your surfeit is over.

"I am now in La Grange, in the midst of a protracted meeting, which is becoming more and more interesting every day. The meeting will probably come to a close next Monday. I then expect to visit brother Williamson's charge at Somerville, and then return to Holly Springs, at which place I hope to receive letters from you, which will have an influence upon my subsequent movements. I came to this place from Hernando, a new village, about fifty miles distant, where we had a precious work of grace; no great revival, to be sure, but several persons were hopefully converted, all men; amongst whom are numbered Colonel H., General T., and Dr. B., all men of the very first respectability. The latter gentleman, in particular, is said to be a man of the first order of talent, and a ripe scholar. I had the pleasure of baptizing him last week; and, as you may well suppose, it was a season of no common interest. The Doctor was powerfully wrought upon himself, and there was much weeping throughout the house; I think some would have shouted aloud, if they had not been afraid of Presbyterians.

"I hope, my daughter, your health is good. Take care of it, my child, for your old father's sake. You are now my only rose. Your sister, your precious little sister, has been snatched from my sight, and I must see her no more until I go to heaven. There I hope to see her crowned, and in her Saviour's bosom. O, my beloved Agnes, your father still weeps at the remembrance of thee! But it is all right; still will I say, 'The Lord gave; the Lord hath taken away; and blessed be the name of the Lord.'—'Melissa, didn't you know that I am going to die to-night?' 'O, well, my dear, if you die to-night, the blessed Jesus will take you right straight to heaven.' 'Well!'—This I have thought upon a great many times; it has given me great consolation. Has Melissa been rewarded for mentioning the sweet name of Jesus to my dying child? At any rate, do get a silver dollar, and give her for me, with my thanks. Be sure to comfort your dear afflicted mother, and tell her to cast all her burdens upon the Lord.

"Your ever affectionate father,

DANIEL BAKER."

No one who has read thus far, and certainly no one who knew Dr. Baker personally, can have failed to see that he was a man of the warmest attachments. Toward no human being did he cherish unkind feelings; and in regard to all men it was his habit, formed by principle and long practice into a second nature, to put the most charitable construction on their conduct, and to say either the best that could be said of them, or nothing at all. Wherever he discerned—and he had a quick perception—any excellence of character, there his heart fastened itself. For each child of God he had that ardent love which the Apostle gives as a leading proof that the person loving has passed from death to life. His error was that he had too great faith in men, especially in professing Christians; believed all they said to him, hoped all they promised him; that disposition, in fact, which is commonly known as simplicity of character. Even when made aware of some gross imposition practised upon him, his feeling toward the individual was all pity, with scarce an emotion of anger. With all this, he never hesitated to express himself decidedly, where principle was concerned, whoever was smitten thereby; but this was generally in a manner so conciliatory and manifestly sincere, as rarely or never to give offence. Toward his own family he cherished so strong an attachment as to lead him rather to overrate them; and this made his estimate of all whom he loved, in or out of his own household, an unreliable one for others. All could not look through his eyes; too hopeful, too charitable, too glowing.

His ardent and happy temperament gave him the glow of perpetual youth, and, till his death, it was frequently his playful remark, "I do believe now I am younger than any of my children." So full was he of playful feeling, so heartily did he enter into the joys and sorrows of youth, that he was always their most welcome and beloved companion. In his own home, and elsewhere, he was careful not to weary them with too frequent religious conversation, or family worship at unseasonable hours, and unduly prolonged. In his study he permitted no interruption, studying whatever related to his profession, and the Bible above all; writing with the utmost care, often re-writing again and again whatever was to come before the public; but out of his study, he would relax completely, and was never more happy than when working with his children in the garden; an occupation in which he took great delight.

Many of his missionary tours were made with a son riding in the gig beside him. The writer well remembers accompanying him on such a tour when a boy; the more distinctly because of the little hymns his father then taught him as they journeyed along the solitudes of Florida and Georgia, through deep sand, and the waving of great forests. Nor does he forget how often his father, absorbed in some meditation, riding with the forgotten rein of his horse in his listless hand, was rudely wakened to the realities of life by the upsetting of his gig. As the writer, three times in succession, found himself lying on the ground with his father upon him, he very naturally inferred that the upsetting obstacle was upon the side of the road which came more under his father's watch than his.

And here the question will arise, To what degree can a father who is a minister, permit himself to be occupied by public duties, to the comparative neglect of the close, and personal, and perpetual oversight and education of his own children? It was a frequent saying with Dr. Baker, "Duties never clash." No head of a family ever loved those of his own house more than the subject of this Memoir; yet, necessarily, a very large part of his time was spent from home; consequently, the duties of a father were given up by him to the mother, or delegated to teachers; and yet no parent could love, or make more careful provision for his household than he did. It is impossible to say that he neglected the duty of husband and father for that of preacher of the gospel; his motive was too sacred and self-sacrificing, the blessing of God on his labours was too manifest.

The autobiography proceeds:

When about leaving Texas, I was urged to return

and make it my home; and to induce me so to do, several persons offered to make me a present of land amounting to about two thousand acres in all. But I was unwilling to leave "the States" at this time; and after fulfilling my engagement at Gainesville, I went to various places where I had been invited to hold protracted meetings.

From the pages of a little memorandum book we copy the following rapid journal, kept by Dr. Baker at the time of the meetings spoken of above.

Tuesday Morning, February 13th, 1844. Left Holly Springs in the stage; reached Lexington on Wednesday afternoon, and preached to a large congregation at night. Reached Vicksburg on Friday, 16th; attended prayer-meeting at night. Remained in Vicksburg until Wednesday, 28th, during which period preached fifteen sermons; made various addresses; congregations large; some cases of awakening; nothing very special. On the evening of the 28th, preached to a small audience at Raymond; short notice; some interest. 29th, addressed Mr. N's school; about fifty children and young ladies present. At the close, addressed adults; a goodly number present. In the afternoon, called to see Mr. W. and lady; conversed on the subject of religion; neither is a professor; seemed interested. At night, preached to a large and very attentive audience.

Friday, March 1st. Reached Jackson before sunset. The bell was rung for preaching, but just as we were about starting it began to rain very hard; the pastor thought it not worth while to go.

Saturday, 2d. Rainy day, streets muddy; yet

preached at night in the old State-house; rather small congregation.

Sabbath, 3*d*. Preached in the morning in same place; full house. In the afternoon preached in the Methodist church; some feeling. At night preached in the old State-house; very full house—hard rock.

Monday, 4*th*. Prayer-meeting at ten o'clock. At night preached in the Methodist church; goodly number out—Governor B. and lady.

Tuesday, 5*th*. In the morning, meeting for mothers; well attended; much tenderness. At night preached; congregation as usual.

Wednesday, 6*th*. In the morning preached on the subject of experimental religion; good meeting. Afternoon had inquiry meeting; some five or six present besides professors. At night preached to young men; good meeting.

Thursday, 7*th*. Preached in the morning and at night.

Friday, 8*th*. No preaching until night; spent the day in visiting.

Saturday, 9*th*. Preached morning, afternoon, and night. In the morning, much feeling.

Sabbath, 10*th*. Attended sunrise prayer-meeting, as for four preceding mornings, and preached five times this day; at nine o'clock in penitentiary, at eleven in church. In the afternoon, two sermons; one to whites; immediately after to blacks, and again to whites at night; large congregations, particularly in the morning and at night; sacrament.

Monday, 11*th*. Rainy day.

Tuesday, 12*th*. Went to Raymond, and preached at night.

Wednesday, 13*th*. Attended the mothers' meeting in the morning, and preached at night; very rainy; about twenty persons present; spoke to Mr. N. about his devoting himself to the ministry, and found he was much inclined that way.

Thursday, 14*th*. Preached in the afternoon; one lady in particular very much wrought upon. Preached at night; hope some good was done.

Friday, 15*th*. Reached Brandon, and preached at night to a pretty large congregation.

Saturday, 16*th*. Preached in the morning. In the afternoon addressed children, and at night preached again.

Sabbath, 17*th*. Preached to crowded house in the morning; long sermon; good impression. Preached in the afternoon; then addressed coloured people. At night preached again; much feeling.

Monday, 18*th*. Preached in the morning and at night; interest increasing. In the afternoon had a mothers' meeting, one of the best of the kind I had ever attended.

Tuesday, 19*th*. Preached three times, and invited the anxious to remain; had a melting time; four or five persons professed conversion. This afternoon at the close of service, took a vote whether the meeting should be continued another day; nearly all in the house arose, and very promptly.

Wednesday, 20*th*. Spent the morning in visiting, and preached in the afternoon and at night; two or three cases of hopeful conversion this day. At night took a vote for continuing the meeting another day longer; same result.

Thursday, 21*st*. Preached in the afternoon, and

held an inquiry meeting. Preached at night, and invited the serious to remain; about thirty-five awakened, of whom some ten or twelve were hopefully converted. Blessed be God!

Friday, 22*d.* Rode to Canton, and preached at night to a small congregation.

Saturday, 23*d.* Preached morning, afternoon, and night; some interest.

Sabbath, 24*th.* Attended prayer-meeting at nine o'clock, and made an address at the commencement. Preached in the afternoon and at night; solemn time.

Monday, 25*th.* Preached on experimental religion in the morning; in the afternoon addressed mothers; great many present; much tender feeling. Preached again at night.

Tuesday, 26*th.* Addressed children in the afternoon, and preached at night; think a deep impression was made.

Wednesday, 27*th.* Attended inquiry meeting; thin; had been heavy rain, yet four or five present. Supposed I had preached my last sermon last night, but was encouraged to make appointment for this evening. At night, preached to a larger audience than was expected; great solemnity.

Thursday, 28*th.* Preached at S. to perhaps one hundred and forty hearers; believe good impression was made. Preached also at night; had a thunder storm.

Friday, 29*th.* Reached Camden; weather very unfavourable; cold, yet preached twice.

Saturday, 30*th.* Preached in the morning at church, and at night at Mr. M's.

Sabbath, 31*st*. Preached; large audience. Talked to blacks. Preached again at church, and at night.

April, 1*st*. Preached two sermons at church; several persons anxious. Preached also at night.

Tuesday, 2*d*. Preached in the morning to a good congregation; in afternoon, addressed children and mothers; at night preached at the house of Mrs. F.; two or three converts. Richland—preached.

Friday, 5*th*. Reached Franklin, and left on Tuesday, 9th. Preached fourteen sermons, and made several exhortations; it was hoped that much good was done, although not more than three or four professed conversion.

Wednesday, 10*th*. Preached at Benton at night; people much interested; greatly desirous that I should return.

Thursday, 11*th*. Preached at Yazoo City at night to a pretty good congregation; had little or no liberty in consequence of echo.

Friday, 12*th*. Preached in the morning to a handful; in afternoon addressed professors; had large congregation. At night, preached again.

Saturday, 13*th*. Preached three times; congregation increasing in size and interest.

Sabbath, 14*th*. Brother McInnis was installed; brother Smiley preached the installation sermon; brother Gray gave charges.

The narrative proceeds:

My support was precarious; and feeling it very unpleasant to be absent so much from my family, I longed to "cast anchor." I wanted a HOME! In about six months after my return from Texas, I received an invitation to the church at Holly Springs,

Mississippi, at that time very small; so small, indeed, that, as a certain uneducated man remarked, "it required a telescope to see it." I accepted of the invitation; brought my family there; and, purchasing a very humble establishment in the town for, I think, four hundred dollars, I took possession of my log-cabin with devout feelings of gratitude and joy. I had a home, at last; and, humble as it was, it was to me like a little palace. My labours were blessed as a pastor, and enjoying the affections, as I believed, of the people of my charge, I was a happy man. I remained in Holly Springs some nine years, preaching, at different times, with varied success. As the church found it difficult to raise the full amount of my salary, (one thousand dollars,) I was permitted to have a certain portion of my time to dispose of as suited me; and, in accordance with my habits and peculiar turn of mind, I held numerous protracted meetings, which were uniformly more or less blessed. One was in Dr. Edgar's church, Nashville; another in Denmark, Tennessee.

One who was at this time an elder in Dr. Edgar's church, thus speaks, after the death of Dr. Baker, in regard to the meeting alluded to.

"According to the almost general custom at the West, a four days' meeting was held by this church at its communion services; and it was also customary, if practicable, to obtain the aid of other preachers beside the pastor. On the occasion of which we now speak, Rev. Mr. Baker, who at the time had charge of a church at Holly Springs, Mississippi, accepted our invitation to assist Dr. Edgar. After Mr. Baker's second sermon, a great degree of solemnity was apparent through the congregation; and it was dismissed under a trembling hope of many of the church that God was about to send forth his Holy Spirit among the people. From this time there was no diminution of interest during the entire period of his visit, which lasted about a fortnight. In that time he preached twenty-seven times, besides giving exhortations, and conversing with those who attended the inquiry meetings.

"Day as well as night meetings were appointed, and were well attended. Business men so arranged their affairs as to attend in numbers; females, for a time, threw aside the thoughts of other matters; and the salvation of the soul seemed the great absorbing subject of all classes. Mr. Baker exercised his peculiar faculty for arousing the dormant feelings of Christians, and bringing conviction to the hearts of the unconverted, and it was not long ere numbers were inquiring as to what they should do to be saved. Quiet solemnity pervaded all the meetings, and the most fastidious could make no objection on the score of over-wrought feeling or religious fanaticism. The young and the old, the fashionable and unfashionable, the wealthy and the poor, were merged in one common cause, and engaged in one common devotion, until a large number of true penitents had presented themselves as candidates for admission to the sealing ordinances of the church.

"In two weeks after the first communion, it was adjudged expedient and proper by the pastor and session to hold another; when about forty were admitted. Among them were many quite young, and an old gentleman who had imbibed infidel principles in youth, and now, at seventy years of age, still held them. He was directed by an unseen hand and power, to attend for the first time in his life a prayer-meeting, and was soon brought to acknowledge as his Saviour that Jesus whom he had despised. Although the special meetings were suspended soon after Mr. Baker's return to his charge, the good spirit that was enkindled seemed to remain in the church, and at the next communion another large number was added; making a total, if my memory serves me right, of nearly one hundred, who were brought into the church as the fruit of this man's faithful labours. Deeply is the remembrance of these scenes engraven on my own heart, and often does it animate my soul as I engage in social or other prayer for the revival of God's work now. The great glory of this work of grace was its genuineness and permanent effects on the church. I have no hesitancy in saying, that its influence is felt to this day, not only in the First Church in Nashville, but also through all that city. Many of its subjects have been ever since, and are now among the faithful labourers in that portion of God's vineyard. In a conversation with Dr. Edgar, some years after, we naturally recurred to this happy period to both of us, and in reply to a question on my part, as to the subsequent lives of those who had then professed their love to Christ, he answered, that they were such as to draw out his thanksgiving to God; he had never known a body of professors more faithful; and while many might have lost, in a degree, the power of their first love, he could not remember one who had been made a subject of the discipline of the church.

"Were this revival of God's work the only instance of the success of this faithful man, as an instrument of good to the church and the world, it would be of itself a trophy for which angels might contend; but, as is well known, it is but one of a multitude; and all that he was enabled by his great Master to accomplish, ought to inspire profound gratitude in every part of the Zion of God, and be the means of awaking a desire and determination on the part of every minister of the word to follow his noble example, and reap the same precious reward.

"Daniel Baker is no longer among us, but the same light that followed his footsteps while upon earth will illumine his memory to the latest period of the church militant, and be merged in one still more glorious in the church triumphant."

The following letters cast light on this period.

(TO HIS WIFE.)

"PULASKI, *May 5th*, 1842.

"MY DEAR ELIZA—Our meeting in Tuscumbia was closed on Sunday night last. It was a good meeting; some thirteen or fourteen persons professed conversion, nearly all of whom were married ladies and heads of families. There was only one young unmarried person among the converts—he a youth about W's age. O, that W. would follow his example. I reached this place in time to preach on Tuesday evening. The people turn out here extremely well, and we anticipate a divine blessing, and, of course, good times.

"I trust I shall be the honoured instrument of leading many souls to Christ during my tour; and what is more, I hope some of them will in due time be made heralds of the cross. I think it quite likely that this will be the case with two of the converts in Florence—one the son of brother S., who died last summer, and the other a cousin of his. This plan of visiting the churches, and holding protracted meetings, I think a very good one, and with the divine blessing, must, I think, lead to very happy and very important results. But I confess it makes me feel rather unpleasantly sometimes, to be absent from my family and the people of my charge so long. Do tell the elders to be sure to have preaching as often as possible, and by all means to keep up the weekly prayer-meeting.

"I must tell you a little incident of my travels. Tuesday last was a very rainy day, and as we were travelling heavily through the mud and mire, we saw an old woman trudging along the road, without shoes or stockings, with a large bundle under her arm. Astonished to see so old a person out in such weather, and travelling in such style, I got out of the carriage, and became a sort of fellow foot-traveller of hers. I asked her how old she was. 'Eighty-four years,' said she. 'And how many miles have you to go this bad weather?' 'Eighteen,' replied she. 'But,' said I, 'you are too old to be travelling in this way; you will get sick. Why don't you make your sons help you on?' 'Why,' said she, 'I never had but one son, and that was a *gal!*' Giving her fifty cents, I advised her to stop at the first house, and wait for better weather. She seemed very thankful, and stopped accordingly.

"Your affectionate husband,

DANIEL BAKER."

"PULASKI, *May 12th*, 1842.

"MY DEAR SON—I have preached fifteen sermons in this place already; I preach in the morning and at night. The people come out in crowds. I think I never saw people turn out better in any place where I have been; and I am happy to say, we have the prospect of a very great and blessed work of grace here. There is a very general awakening, and some ten or twelve persons have already professed conversion. We hope this number will be considerably increased within a few days. How strange! Your father is made the instrument of the conversion of many abroad, and there is a dear son at home yet unconverted. O, my dear son, how happy would I be to be made your spiritual father, even as I am your own father in a natural sense. My dear boy, do not neglect your precious soul.

"God bless you, my son; and may you be happy in time, and through all eternity.

"Your ever affectionate father,

DANIEL BAKER."

"HOLLY SPRINGS, *August 15th*, 1842.

"DEAR BROTHER GALLOWAY—When absent from home last spring, I attended several protracted meetings, in nearly all of which we had pleasing proofs of the divine presence. The converts, however, were not numerous, only about some fifty or sixty in all; but when we think of the value of the soul, even this is a great matter. Two or three of those hopefully converted will, I trust, devote themselves to the gospel ministry. One is a son of our lamented brother S., and the other a nephew. I have been invited to assist at a protracted meeting, to be held in a town called Denmark, some sixty or seventy miles from this place. I trust we shall have a blessing; and I am more encouraged from the fact that the Lord has recently poured out his Spirit in various places in the region round about. O, for more zeal in our Master's cause! O, for a holy enthusiasm! for such an enthusiasm as animated the Apostle Paul, when he exclaimed, 'The love of Christ constraineth us.' I do think, my dear brother, that many of us Presbyterian ministers might be vastly more useful than we are, if we could only be brought to go the whole amount, and lay out our full strength in the cause of God. Do, my brother, pray for me. I expect to attend several protracted meetings this fall; and I do hope that the Master will crown them every one with his blessing. I preached once to your people when at Springfield, and from what I could see and hear, I think you have much reason to thank God and take courage.

"Yours sincerely,

DANIEL BAKER."

Narrative continued.

One of the meetings was in St. Charles, and another in St. Louis, Missouri, in both of which places strong encouragements were held out to me to make a settlement. In one case, the matter proceeded so far, that I actually gave notice of my intention to resign my charge, and requested the congregation forthwith to unite with me in a petition to the Presbytery to dissolve the pastoral connection. A vote was taken, and a reluctant consent was given. Immediately I entered upon preparations for leaving, when, lo! before the next Sabbath arrived, the people changed their mind, and utterly refused to let me go. So the idea of going to St. Charles was given up, much to the dissatisfaction of the people there.

Frequent and important were the moves which Dr. Baker made in life; and even the least was not made until after an earnest seeking of wisdom from God. To this, when looking back upon his long and varied life from near its close, he ascribed the fact that he had never made a move which he had afterwards cause to regret. When any important step was before him, he would always spend a day, solemnly set apart for the purpose, in fasting and prayer for divine guidance. And so, not a journey was entered upon, however unimportant, no business was transacted, no important letter written, or visit paid, or conversation held, but was preceded by special prayer for wisdom from above.

At the close of a protracted meeting in a certain place, he expressed one night to the pastor, with whom he was staying, some doubt as to whither he should on the morrow bend his steps. "Never mind," said he, "I will know what to do when the moment for decision arrives." Next morning, at breakfast, he remarked, "Last night I lacked just ten dollars of money enough to reach a point I desired to visit next; but I committed the matter to God, and this morning I was met, in a walk I took, by a stranger, who stopped me, and pressed ten dollars on my acceptance. To my inquiry what I was to do with it, 'O,' he said, 'anything you please,' and so left me. Now I can go to that point." This is only one of many similar providences. Whatever darkness rested on his path, he never suffered it to trouble him in the least, so serene was his faith in God. "What is the use of having such precious promises in Scripture, like jewels in a casket," he would say, "if we never take them out and *use* them?" His habitual custom was to endeavour to fall asleep at night with prayerful thoughts in his mind; to wake in the morning, his first breath prayer: "Divine Master, what wilt thou have me to do this day?" was the spirit, and often form of his first waking thoughts.

Those who have followed this man of God as he led the way to the Throne of Grace, will remember that he trod as along a path familiar to his feet. He greatly disliked making public prayer a mode of exhortation, or statement of any kind, or of decorating it with flowers and figures of speech. He regarded prayer as addressed to God, and in no sense to the people; and he endeavoured to clothe his addresses at the mercy-seat in words left by the Spirit on the page of Scripture. The fulness, scriptural richness, heartfelt simplicity, and sincerity of his public prayers, no one who knew him can ever forget. In the prayer-meeting, at the family altar, in the sick-room, at the meetings of church judicatories, his prayers were always adapted to the peculiar circumstances. Whenever he led in worship, he stood as if with his foot upon the step of the Throne—as if with his hand grasping the priestly robe of the great High Priest—not familiar or irreverent in the least degree, yet coming boldly to the Throne of Grace—with him the alone source of all blessing—for this express and only purpose, that he might obtain mercy, and find grace to help in that special time of need.

Family worship was the most invariable part of the household routine, with the exceptions already alluded to. As to private devotions, his uniform practice was to spend the first hour of the day in his study, in these. The hour of sunset was his favourite time for evening prayer; and he would endeavour to have the time fixed for family worship at night as soon as possible after supper, before even the youngest became sleepy. In all his travels a well-worn Testament was his inseparable companion; and as he often had to pass the night, with many others, in the one room of some cabin by the roadside, the early dawn of morning and the starry shades of night would find him in some secluded spot of field or grove, holding that communion with God more essential to his happiness than aught else. He disliked any thing which prevented him from going direct from his closet into the pulpit; never permitted any thing to prevent this when he could help it. He had also made it, by use, a second nature to engage in ejaculatory prayer; frequent, but silent and brief prayer during the rapid business of the day. None but one as familiarly associated with him as the writer of these lines would have known this, for there was nothing of the Pharisee in his devotions; no moment at which he did not seem to be in his usual genial and accessible mood, ready for any good word or work. But here was the secret of all that he was, and of all that he accomplished;

> "When one that holds communion with the skies,
> Has filled his urn where those pure waters rise,
> And once more mingles with us meaner things,
> 'Tis e'en as if an angel shook his wings.
> Immortal fragrance fills the circuit wide,
> That tells us whence his treasures are supplied.
> So, when a ship, well-freighted with the stores
> The sun matures on India's spicy shores,
> Has dropped her anchor and her canvass furled
> In some safe haven of our western world,
> 'Twere vain inquiry to what port she went;—
> The gale informs us, laden with the scent."

All his springs were in God, and he abode near those springs as at the one oasis in a desert world. If this branch bore much fruit, it was solely and only because it abode in the vine. If God the Holy Ghost wrought in and by him, it was because such was his unceasing petition at the Throne of Grace; and to what child of God is not this throne equally accessible through Jesus Christ! If all ministers of the gospel were, by close communion with God, channels thus of the descent of the Holy Spirit upon others through them, how great, how overwhelming would be the presence of this divine agent upon the church and the world!

We resume the autobiography.

On one occasion a singular proposition was made to me, which, however, I accepted. The Rev. Angus

Johnson, a co-presbyter, and a very zealous brother, wishing me to visit certain very destitute places in Mississippi, offered to give me one hundred dollars for one month, if I would go along with him and do all the preaching he might require. His proposition was acceded to, and away we went, through cane-brakes and regions of country where scarcely the form of any preacher had been seen before. Brother Johnson was a pretty hard master, but as I had myself some liking for the service exacted, I did not fly from my contract. I preached many sermons, and I hope many precious souls were converted. But my hire—did I get that? Yes; the full amount stipulated was promptly paid.

During the period of my connection with the church in Holly Springs we were favoured with several seasons of refreshing; one was under my own ministry, one when I was aided by the Rev. Mr. Vancourt, of Denmark, and another under the ministerial labours of the Rev. Mr. M., of Canton. The one most remarkable took place during the visit of Mr. V. Many of the most prominent citizens of the town were brought in; among the rest, Mr. M., who, at a subsequent period, became a leading man in the eldership.

At this time Dr. Baker writes as follows:

"HOLLY SPRINGS, *December* 21*st*, 1842.

"DEAR BROTHER GALLOWAY—I have some very pleasing intelligence to communicate. We have had a blessed and powerful work of grace in my church. We had a protracted meeting in September last, and about seventy precious souls were made, as I hope, to bow at the feet of our blessed Redeemer! Protracted meetings were held nearly about the same time in all the other churches; and the result of the whole is, the hopeful conversion of more than two hundred souls in our town! To God be all the glory! Amongst the converts in my church, I am peculiarly happy to say is my youngest son, who has already turned his attention to the sacred office. Once he was deeply tinctured with the principles of infidelity, and was a great admirer of Byron; but, after his conversion, when asked whether he was willing to be a preacher, he replied, with much emotion, 'Pa, I would be willing to be a ditcher, for Christ's sake.' I have sent him to Princeton to prepare, if it be the Divine will, to preach the glorious gospel of the blessed God. I have another son, who was last week taken under the care of our Presbytery as a candidate for the gospel ministry. How greatly have I been blessed! Bless the Lord, O my soul!

"In pursuance of an arrangement made with my people, that I should have a certain portion of my time, I have lately returned from a missionary tour of five weeks. During that period I preached about seventy times, and it pleased God to bless my labours to the hopeful conversion of more than eighty souls. Many of them are persons of standing and influence, and a goodly number are young men of considerable promise; three or four of whom have already announced their purpose to devote themselves to the service of God in the gospel ministry. I do think, my dear brother, that pastors may do much good by occasionally going on missionary ex cursions. The very great pressure of the times has made it impossible for my people fully to support me, and this has led me out into other fields, and the result has been happy. What I shall do the next year I know not; but I believe the Lord will direct. I have lately received an invitation from the Presbytery of Louisville to ride as a missionary in their bounds, with a salary of one thousand dollars, and the promise of more if required. I may accept, and I may not. I have committed the matter to the Lord. Time will make known all things.

"Wishing you and your dear family every blessing, temporal and spiritual, I subscribe myself,

"As formerly, as ever,

"Yours in a precious Saviour,

DANIEL BAKER."

The narrative proceeds:

It was at this time that one of my sons professed conversion. He had, when very young, with his brother D., been brought under very strong religious exercises, at the Institute, near Marion; but those early impressions had, it seems, passed away; and now, about sixteen years of age, and reading law, he seems to have become quite forgetful of his soul's eternal interests; nay, more, he seems to have become spiced with scepticism, and once told me plainly, that he could never believe in that religion which would send such a man as Byron to hell. I reasoned with him, and finally wound up with this remark: "Well, my son, I hope you will be converted yet; aye, and become a preacher, too." As I made this remark, the native enmity of the human heart began to work, and said he, with strong emotion, "Pa, I had rather be a ditcher than a preacher!" It was, I think, only some four weeks after this that he was numbered with the anxious. His convictions were apparently very deep, and he was brought near the borders of despair.

On one occasion, I remember it well, he went from the inquiry meeting directly up to his chamber. After remaining there a time, engaged in prayer, he came into the dining-room, where his mother and myself were. Standing before me, with a sad countenance, he said, "Papa, I don't think I will go to the inquiry meeting any more." "Why, my son?" "Pa, I can't be converted." "O yes, my son, you can." "No, pa, my heart is so hard I can't be converted." "Why, my son, the blessed Jesus is able and willing to do every thing for you." It seems to have been a new thought. The way of salvation was made plain, and he was enabled to receive Christ as offered in the gospel. In a few moments a sweet smile came over his countenance. I suspected what had taken place, and my arms were around the young convert, and his mother's too. And there, in that same dining-room, a scene was presented worth an angel's visit from the skies. After we were all more composed, said I to him, "My son, are you not willing to be a preacher now?" With much emotion, he replied, "Pa, I would be willing to be a ditcher for Christ's sake." That was music to my ears. Soon after this, he gave up the idea of the legal profession, and in a few weeks, even in the depth of winter, he set out for Princeton, via New Orleans and New York.

Here, for the sake of historical connection, I may mention a circumstance which occurred several years after. W. had finished his classical course. He had graduated in Nassau Hall College, with one of the honours of the institution. He had returned to the home of his parents, and the time had nearly arrived when he wished to go on again to Princeton, to join his brother, who was already in the Theological Seminary. It was his wish to go; it was mine, also. But it was necessary to get one hundred dollars. I told him I had not the amount, but would get it, if I had to mortgage some little property which I had in the State of Ohio. I called upon a warm friend of mine, who was usually flush. I mentioned the case, and requested him to lend me the amount for a short time. He said that really he had not it. Disappointed when I was confident of success, and finding that my son was anxious to go on in few days, I felt that I was in a close place; but my rule during almost my whole life has been, when in trouble, to lay all such matters before God in prayer; and now an old disciple, I can put to my seal that the precious promises, yea, all the promises of God recorded in Scripture, are true, and may be relied upon.

Now, what a remarkable providence was connected with this matter. Being invited to administer the sacrament of the Lord's Supper in a small country church, some forty miles distant, I preached from these words, "Alleluia, for the Lord God omnipotent reigneth!" I had some liberty in speaking. There was an elder present who had had some peculiar domestic trials. At the close of the services, he invited me to go home with him; and when we were alone in one of his rooms, he said to me, "Mr. Baker, your sermon this morning has done me more good than any sermon I have heard for ten years. Mr. Baker," added he, "what do you intend to do with your son W.?" "He has the ministry in view," said I, "and I intend to send him to Princeton." "Will you have any difficulty in getting the means?" This was a hard question, just at that time. I replied, "I don't know, sir; but I intend to send him to Princeton, if I have to mortgage some property I have, to get the means." "Well, Mr. Baker," said he, in a very kind way, "I will give W. one hundred dollars this year, and one hundred dollars the next; and I am willing to do something for your son D., too." Suffice it to say, before I left his house, he placed a one hundred dollar note in my hand. This providence, so remarkable, touched my heart. I was eager to get home, to tell my son how good the Lord had been to us. I reached home at night. The next morning I placed the note under W's plate; and when he saw it, to make a good and lasting impression upon him, I said to him, "My son, remember this saying of your father, which I have borrowed, 'They that notice kind providences shall have kind providences to notice.'"

During almost the whole of Dr. Baker's residence in Holly Springs, two of his sons were at Princeton, prosecuting their studies for the ministry. He had never made an effort, or even cherished a desire to accumulate money, so that it seemed absolutely impossible for him to give his sons a collegiate education. But when they had professed religion, and expressed a desire to enter the ministry, the thing assumed altogether a new light in his eyes. "You are already educated enough for the service of the world," said he to one of his sons, when that son had united with the church; "but now that you have become the child of God, I will educate you thoroughly for his service, if I have to live on a crust of bread." The sacredness of domestic life must not be violated; but if the veil were lifted, it would reveal sacrifices and struggles, to accomplish the preparation of his sons for the service of the Master he loved so well, continued through many long years.

The following letters, addressed chiefly to his sons at College and Seminary, need no introduction.

"KNOXVILLE, Tenn., *May 3d*, 1843.

"MY DEAR SON—I reached this place a few days since, and am to labour as a missionary in this region for some two or three months. May the Lord grant his blessing. Remember, my dear son, you must take exercise, and do it regularly; and it must be of the right kind. When I was at College, I was very studious; and not bearing the idea of losing any time, my plan was to unite study and exercise. My custom or practice was, for some time, to walk three miles every day; that is, a mile morning, noon, and evening. My walks were solitary, and I employed the time generally in committing to memory some lesson or speech, or something of the kind. The result was, I would frequently return to my room in a state of great exhaustion, such exercise being to me rather an injury than a benefit. For exercise to be profitable, the mind must be recreated as well as the body. Ball-playing and gymnastic exercises are the very thing. I hope, my dear son, that you will not neglect your health. See to it, that soul and body both enjoy daily and vigorous health. I think it would be well for your reading and writing, as a general thing, to have some bearing upon the grand object of pursuit which you have in view. You recollect the language of Paul to Timothy: 'Study to show thyself approved unto God, a workman that needeth not to be ashamed.' You may think this counsel not quite so appropriate just now; but the suggestion, even at this period, I think can do no harm. You must not expect either frequent or long letters from me for some months to come; you know your father's manner of doing things when out on a preaching tour—preaching incessantly. I find little time to write to any one: and, besides, I have rarely any conveniences for writing. Another thing, my hand becomes unsteady by reason of much speaking. Yesterday I preached three times, and this morning —only see my scrawl! Last night I had a crowded house, galleries and all. I hope the Lord has something for me to do in this place, and the region round about.

"Be sure to write to me soon, at this place, and communicate every thing which you may deem interesting. Tell me all your wants, and be free in writing on any and every subject. You know, my son, that your father loves you very tenderly; and nothing interesting to you can be uninteresting to him. While I think of it, I must tell you, that on Friday last I heard of another young man, a Mr. M., who had been converted some years ago under my ministry, becoming a herald of the cross. He was once very far from religion, but grace proved triumphant. To God be all the glory! Such intelligence is very pleasing to me, and, thank the Lord, I have it every now and then. I have reason to believe that some thirty or thirty-five of my spiritual children have already entered the ministry. Bless the Lord, O my soul!

"Your ever affectionate father,

DANIEL BAKER."

(TO HIS WIFE.)

"KNOXVILLE, *May 18th*, 1843.

"MY DEAR ELIZA—Upon my return from Baker's Creek, twenty-six miles distant, I received your interesting and very welcome letter of the 8th inst., and am happy to learn that you are all coming on so pleasantly, and the garden too. I confess I feel very much as if I were in a state of exile, and shall be not a little pleased at the time appointed to return to my family and my charge. It certainly was a great undertaking to come so far, and be absent so long; and I am free to say, that I am strongly inclined to think it will be the last time I shall enter upon a tour of such a kind. I know not which makes me feel worse, to be absent from my family or my charge. Every now and then I feel rather unpleasantly upon the subject; but I quiet myself by considering that my present enterprise was entered upon after prayer and reflection; and, moreover, that certain circumstances seemed to render it almost necessary. I think, however, it is the last tour of the kind I will ever take. Things in this region of country are in a sad state; I mean in relation to church matters.

"I have reason to believe my visit to East Tennessee will be useful, not only, as I trust, in bringing sinners to Christ, but in calming down feelings, and in giving encouragement to Old-school Presbyterians, who are here in the minority. Old-school ministers are very scarce, and the coming of one into their midst is like a pleasant breeze in a hot day, or a little shower of rain in a time of drought. In this respect, I think my tour will prove an important one; but I hope it will prove a blessing in all other respects also. * * * The meeting was interesting. Some were brought under deep conviction, and one or two perhaps converted; but the chief good in all probability consisted in the church being brought into a better state.

"The meeting at Baker's Creek, from which I have just returned, was a blessed one. Great feeling was manifested, and I believe, much good done. On the last day of the meeting, (Tuesday,) when the anxious were called for, there was quite a rush, and all the adult non-professors of religion in the house, except some two or three, came forward to be prayed for. Six professed conversion, but I think the number must be greater than that. Amongst those who professed was a Mr. M., whose wife is a sister of General Houston, of Texas. Yesterday I passed through Maryville, the nest of Hopkinsianism. I saw Dr. A.; he invited me to come and see him, and spend a night at his house, and even invited me to preach for him. Amongst other things, he has abolished the use of wine at the sacrament, and uses raisin water. O, the poor Church of Christ! how it has been troubled by some of its professed friends! I think heaven must be a very sweet place; for there are no troubles there.

"I think about you all, my dear E., very frequently, and right glad shall I be when the time comes to set my face towards Holly Springs. I wish to see myself in my own house, in the bosom of my own family once more; and I also wish to be in my own pulpit, and amongst the people whom I love, once more; but I must not be impatient, for I have a work to do in this region; and having put my hand to the plough, I must not look back until my work is done. The people in these parts take great interest in preaching, and come to hear me in crowds, although the season is not favourable; the evenings too short for meetings in town, and in the country this is a very busy time with farmers. I have preached several times in Knoxville, and a considerable impression has been made. This evening we are to commence a protracted meeting. The weather, however, is very unfavourable; it is raining now, and there is a prospect of a long spell of wet weather. The clouds, however, are in good hands, and you know my rule is, Be careful for nothing. Love to all.

"In great haste, your affectionate husband,

DANIEL BAKER."

(TO A SON IN HOLLY SPRINGS.)

"KNOXVILLE, *July 7th*, 1843.

"MY DEAR SON—If you will take the map of Tennessee, and look at the north-east corner, you will see Leesburg. This has been my '*Ultima Thule;*' and it is remarkable that the most remote house I visited, the one farthest from home, was the house of the postmaster, a son of whom professed conversion; and the father himself was powerfully wrought upon, and I hope, by this time, may be rejoicing in Christ. It seems as if the Master had said to the servant—Go as far as that house; give the inmates of that house a call to repent, and then you may return. My labours have been very considerably blessed, and it has pleased the Lord to give me some stars in every place. The converts in all may be something like ninety or a hundred.

"My dear son, remember you too have a soul to be saved. It is a jewel of price unknown. It is too precious to be lost. Let me advise you to take good care of it. When you shall have entered the ark, then will your dear parents have the sweet hope of finally meeting every child of theirs in heaven. O how delightful this would be!

"At the very earnest request of brother McMullen, his elders, deacons, and the young converts, I am to spend the next Sabbath in this place. The Sabbath after, I shall probably be in Kingston, the Sabbath after that at Columbia, and after that I shall hurry home with all practical dispatch. I hope to reach home by the first or second Sabbath in August, I presume not sooner. I suspect I wish to be at home as much as any of my congregation can possibly desire; but you know my disposition; when I undertake a thing I like to go the whole amount. I do say the undertaking was a great one; but I think I shall not enter upon such another shortly.

Home, sweet home, will henceforth have more attractions for me than ever.

"Your far distant but ever affectionate father,

DANIEL BAKER."

(TO A SON IN PRINCETON.)

"HOLLY SPRINGS, *August 9th*, 1843.

"MY DEAR SON—Last Friday evening I reached home, after a very laborious tour of missionary labour of nearly four months. My preaching when in the field was at the rate of something like seventy sermons per month. We had many interesting meetings and some hopeful converts in nearly every place; but circumstances were in some respects very unfavourable. In consequence of the backwardness of the spring, planters were very busy; and in consequence of the season of the year, the evenings were, of course, very short. The Lord, however, was pleased to bless your father's labours to the hopeful conversion of about ninety or one hundred precious souls; amongst them were about fifteen young men engaged in classical studies; some of whom, I trust, will devote themselves to the sacred office. And here I may remark, that when I was preaching in the neighbourhood of Washington College, I was urged to accept of the Presidency of that institution, (the edifice is a very good one, and the students numbered sixty-eight,) but I declined. I do not feel myself qualified for an office of that kind; and moreover, I think I can be more useful as a preacher.

"I think your cousin John has not made any profession of religion. Endeavour, my son, to do what you can to win him to Christ. Wherever you are, always be aiming at doing some good. Be willing to do good on a small scale, on a large scale, on any scale; and wherever you may be, and however employed, never neglect the devotions of the closet. I wish you, my dear son, to have a high standard of piety and usefulness. I wish you would read Baxter's Saints' Rest. I have been reading it, I may say, with unabated interest for thirty years, and I think it has done me much good.

"Your affectionate father,

DANIEL BAKER."

(TO HIS SONS IN PRINCETON.)

"HOLLY SPRINGS, *June 1st*, 1844.

"MY DEAR SONS—Your joint letter, bearing several dates, the last being 9th May, came to hand only a few days since, and was particularly welcome, as we had not received one for a long time. You both enjoy good health—what a blessing; and every thing seems to smile upon you—how thankful should you be; and we, your parents too; for whatever affects your happiness, of course affects ours. When you rejoice, we rejoice also; and when you weep, we also are disposed to weep. At this time I think we may all say, 'The lines have fallen to us in pleasant places, and we have a goodly heritage.' And O, may each have a heart to respond, 'Bless the Lord, O my soul, and all that is within me bless his holy name.' * * * Of course, however, you will not understand me to be very favourable to 'the credit system.' The 'cash system' is now, and has for several months past, been your father's system at home; and I hope, in all ordinary cases, it will be acted upon by my sons, not only while at College, but through all subsequent life.

"Are you the author of the '*Fragmen Comediæ nondum perfectæ?*' If so, let me tell you I think its latinity is better than its Christianity. I do wish it were possible to banish all Pagan Classics out of our schools and colleges, and instead of Cæsar, Ovid, Horace, Homer, &c., substitute Latin and Greek writers of a Christian stamp. Heathen mythology, and the system of divine truth we have in the Bible, are as widely different as winter and spring; or rather as night and day. But while I am upon the subject, if you or your brother should have any of your pieces published in your periodical, let us know your signature, and then you need have no pencil marks, which may be considered rather a violation of the Post-Office law. I wish you, my sons, to be conscientious in small as well as in great matters; conscientious at all times and in all things—for the Bible says, 'He that is faithful in that which is least, is faithful also in much; and he that is unjust in the least, is unjust also in much.' Let nothing interfere with your religious duties and religious enjoyments.

"Our garden, under the auspices of your brother, is still flourishing. We have two little watermelons formed upon the vines; one cucumber. Our crop of cherries amounted to just exactly two. Two what? —two bushels?—two pecks?—two quarts? No; two cherries! But you are not to think this a specimen of our garden. O no; for we have had peas, and radishes, and strawberries, and raspberries, &c. in sufficient abundance. Moreover, we have two bee-nives; and at this time the bees are very industrious, gathering honey for their master and mistress. Industrious creatures!—is it right to rob them? But I suppose they were made for the use of man. Our Saviour took a piece of a broiled fish, and of a honey-comb, and did eat. Let every thing have a Bible warrant.

"Your mother, sister, and brother, unite in cordial love. The Lord bless you both, my dear sons, and make each of you a burning and a shining light

"Your ever affectionate father,

DANIEL BAKER."

(TO A SON AT PRINCETON.)

"HOLLY SPRINGS, 16*th December*, 1843.

"MY DEAR SON—Your very welcome but long looked-for letters have been received—I cannot, however, add, in due course of mail, for your letter from Philadelphia was about twenty days on the road; and yours from Princeton, dated the 20th and 27th of November, was not received until last night. I assure you, in both cases, our patience was tried very severely. Mail night after mail night your brother H. would return empty-handed from the office. 'Any letters, H.?' 'No letters; but here are two *Expresses* and one *Presbyterian*.' 'Theodora,' says I, 'just look at your mother!—see what a long face she has got!' 'Well,' says she, 'I believe it is not worth while to look for a letter any more.' 'O, yes,' your father would say—who, you know, always looks upon the bright side—'O, yes; we'll be sure to get a letter the next time.' The next time comes, but still no letter! What can be the matter? 'Why,' says

I, 'they are so busy, I suppose, at the commencement of the session, they cannot find time to write.' 'And, pa,' says your sister, 'you know the mails, of late, are very irregular.' Amid this chit-chat and family scene, the old lady in the rocking-chair in the corner, with a sad and woe-begone look, would not say much, but she would think the more. She would not tell us how many dismal images were before her mind about the broken bones of one darling son, and the sick-bed of another, lest we should laugh at her; but we could plainly see that the over-anxiety of a mother's love had set her imagination to roving, not in flowery fields, but in some ugly places. Last night, however, for the second time, a long chapter of disappointments came to an end. H. came in, and threw down a letter upon my table, post-marked Princeton; and then came the contention who should read it. I began, but as your father's eyes are not the best in the world at night, and he would make mistakes, the letter was handed to your sister, who read it very fluently; but, according to an ugly fashion of hers, she would be stopping every few lines to make some remark—'O, T.,' her impatient mother would say, 'read on,' &c.

"Your affectionate father,

DANIEL BAKER."

(TO A SON AT PRINCETON.)

"HOLLY SPRINGS, *May 5th*, 1845.

"MY DEAR W.—Yesterday I administered the sacrament of the Lord's Supper at Hudsonville, and although the day was very rainy, we had a crowded house, and I hope some good was done. O, my son, our blessed Redeemer has done great things for us, and we must never cease to remember his dying love. Let him ever occupy the throne of our hearts. I hope your meditations of him are frequently very sweet. How often do you and your brother take the sacrament of the Lord's Supper? I hope you find communion seasons to be precious seasons. May God bless you, my dear son, and make you not only truly pious, but deeply pious. Aim at high attainments in the divine life.

"When I was in Princeton I enjoyed religion much, and I think I was made an instrument in the hand of God in doing some good in College. Indeed I think, without boasting, I can say that the glorious revival which took place in College when I was in my senior year, was owing in some degree to my instrumentality. I proposed the prayer-meeting, which was held weekly for nearly six months, to pray expressly for an outpouring of the Spirit on the College. For some time before the revival commenced, I was in the habit of having special conversations with certain students on the subject of religion; and on the day of the national fast, I proposed to my room-mate that we should go from room to room, and endeavour to 'break the bands of wickedness.' After some demurring he complied, and we spent much of the day in conversing with our fellow-students on the subject of religion, making our address direct and pointed. Six or eight of the stndents were awakened that very day, and this was the commencement of the revival in which some fifty students were hopefully converted. I kept a diary at the time; I regret that I have lost it, as it con tained a record of many things which might have been both interesting and useful to yourself and brother.

"I hope you will understand my motive in mentioning what I have done—not to speak my own praise, for I well know that I have been sadly deficient in duty, but to encourage you and your brother to begin the blessed work of winning souls to Christ whilst you are yet in College. And here let me request you both to commit to memory this passage, found in the book of Daniel: 'They that be wise shall shine as the brightness of the firmament, and they that turn many to righteousness, as the stars for ever and ever.' Read Baxter's Saint's Rest, and the lives of Payson and James Brainerd Taylor. You have done it already, you say—suppose you do it again. I think I recommended Smith's Lectures on the Sacred Office. Have you yet read the book? If so, how do you like it?

"Our garden is very flourishing; the strawberries are ripe, and as many perhaps as three quarts could this morning be gathered from the vines. If you and your brother were here, you should have strawberries and milk—yes, and cream and sugar too—that you should. Cherries are just turning; our raspberries will be abundant. Your mother this morning came out of the garden, and standing at the window of my study, showed me some which she had gathered, being the first that had ripened. Some of our plum-trees are loaded, the plums being about as large as your thumb, but still green. I have corn up about a foot high, and it looks better than I have yet seen any where. As for English peas, we have had them on our table for some time past.

"Affectionately, your father,

DANIEL BAKER."

(TO THE SAME.)

HOLLY SPRINGS, *July 22d*, 1845.

"MY DEAR SON—Did you know you are in circumstances of temptation? Selected as a speaker to represent your Society, and chosen as one of the editors of the ——, you have reason to be on your guard, lest these honours and distinctions draw off your mind from that which is more important. Whilst I wish you to excel in whatsoever things are lovely and of good report among men on earth, I wish you also in all things to have a wise reference to a dying hour and a judgment-day. Be sure you never omit the devotions of the closet, nor suffer yourself to pass them over in a formal and hurried manner. See to it, my son, that you enjoy religion, and enjoy it every day. On the very ground where you now are, your father had much religious enjoyment nearly thirty years ago; and you know how it was with James Brainerd Taylor since that time. O, that you and your brother might both catch the spirit of him who has already (fully ripe for heaven) entered into his rest.

"Speaking of entering into rest, I am reminded of the case of Mrs. C., one of the converts in our revival in Holly Springs, when you were brought in. She, you may recollect, joined the Episcopal church. During her illness, which lasted several weeks, I called upon her some eight or ten times. She was sometimes calm and pleasant in her feelings, but she had not those clear views of Christ which she had at the commencement of her religious career. She confessed that she had not kept up a close walk with God, as she ought to have done. She had lived too much in the spirit of the world; and sometimes she was fearful that she had mistaken the matter, and really had no religion. I myself had but little doubt of her piety; I believed her to be *a Christian under a cloud.* She was not exactly willing to die, because her evidences were not as clear as she desired. During my last visit, I prayed that all clouds might be scattered, and that she might have clear views of her Saviour. Upon my return from a camp-meeting which I attended a few days after, I saw a new-made grave. 'Whose grave is this?' I was told it was Mrs. C's. 'How did she die?' 'O, quite happy —in the full hope of heaven.' It seems, that not long before she breathed her last her countenance brightened; she looked up with joy, and exclaimed 'The long expected One is come at last! Blessed Jesus, I am willing to go now!' O, my son, never lose sight of death. 'I die daily,' says Paul. There is an habitual, and there is also an actual preparation for death. We should always bear in mind not only that we must die, but that we may die soon, may die unexpectedly. O, to be always ready, that whether death come in the morning, or in the evening, or at the midnight hour, we may be found as servants waiting the coming of their Lord.

"Would you believe it, last Saturday I received another letter from St. Charles, renewing the invitation for me to come. I wonder if some young man from the Seminary could not go there? We want more ministers of our persuasion—that we do; we want them here; we want them there; we want them in Texas; we want them in China; we want them everywhere. Only think, the Emperor of China giving encouragement to the introduction of the Christian religion into his dominions! What a magnificent field for missionary operations! The Sandwich Islands affair upon a large scale. Surely, the millennium must be near at hand.

"Your account of the Commencement, and the day which preceded it, was very interesting to us all. When you marched up in your silk gown, and took your seat upon the stage with your associates, amid music and the applause of your fellow-students, I suppose you had quite a new set of feelings. In writing home, do not be afraid of mentioning small matters. Every thing which relates to yourself and brother, you may be sure is read with interest by all in your father's house. You see how unstarched I am—writing about every thing, just as things occur to my mind. I write extemporaneous letters, and such I like to receive. I hope you and your brother have had a pleasant vacation, and that in health and spirits you are prepared for the labours of another session. God bless you, my son. Love as usual.

"Your ever affectionate father,

DANIEL BAKER."

(TO THE SAME.)

HOLLY SPRINGS, *October 14th*, 1845

"MY DEAR SON—In regard to the matter upon which your mother gave you and your brother some sage advice, and which, it seems, occasioned you both some little amusement, I would only add a remark or so. The hearts of the young are sometimes very susceptible, and therefore you both would do well to be upon your guard. Do not be in too great a hurry; avoid 'entangling alliances.' If you see one fancied to be the loveliest and the best in all creation, remember you have not yet ranged over the face of all creation; and there are as good fish in the sea as any that have ever been taken out of it. A word to the wise, you know, is sufficient; and certainly, being serious, you may be put among the wise. But, to be a little plainer and more serious—be prudent; remember your high calling, and let nothing cripple your future usefulness. Seek divine direction, and seek it before your affections are engaged. Some, in early life, are too hasty and inconsiderate; therefore be prudent and discreet. This is your father's advice. If it please God, I hope each of you may be blessed with a companion of the right stamp; but all in good time.

"Can you sing? I hope you can and do sing. This is a matter of very considerable importance for one who has the ministry in view. I wish you to cultivate your musical talent, if you have any; this will contribute much to your usefulness when you go out as a herald of the cross. As flowers in a garden, so is music in the ministerial life.

"You wish to know my sentiments on the subject of Papal baptism. I side with the General Assembly fully and strongly. When I read the article in the *Princeton Review*, I confess I thought it very ingenious and very able; nay, more, I confess it staggered me. Although I believed the position taken to be false, yet for some time I knew not exactly how to meet the arguments; but upon examination, I think I can detect some fallacies now, and others I think I shall yet detect. It is urged that Papists use water—the element divinely appointed. Yes; but do they not add other things? Peter said, Who can forbid water?—but the Papists say, Who can forbid water, and salt, and oil, and spittle? Now, if thirsty, you ask for water, and I give you this compound affair, would you not reject it? Here is a cup of coffee; I hand it to you, and take not a particle of it away, but only add a little arsenic—would not the element be materially, essentially changed? It is affirmed that Papists hold all essential truth, such as the supreme divinity of Christ, the doctrine of the Trinity, the atonement, &c. Be it so; but what is admitted in one place, is virtually denied in another. They say that Christ is God, and the next moment show me a wafer, and tell me *that* is Christ! They admit the atonement of Christ, and yet talk about the merits of saints, and works of supererogation. How preposterous! But I have neither time nor space to argue the matter. Let me give you a short-metre view. We Protestants contend that the Church of Rome is the 'Mother of Harlots.' Now, I opine that no harlot has the right to administer baptism; least of all, the mother of harlots.

"Your own father,

DANIEL BAKER."

(TO THE SAME.)

"HOLLY SPRINGS, *Sept.* 3*d*, 1847.

"MY VERY DEAR SON—Your last letter to me came to hand this morning, and I am free to say, it has given me more pleasure than any you ever wrote. The statement made in relation to your religious experience and increasing desire for the gospel ministry, was particularly gratifying to me; for I wish above all things that you may ever have spiritual health, and that your standard of personal piety may be much higher than, I fear, is too common. Your usefulness and happiness in life will both depend, in a great measure, upon the warmth of your zeal and the devotion of your heart to the cause of your Redeemer; and I pray God that the sweet love of Christ may always be richly shed abroad in your soul. God grant, my dear son, that you may (avoiding what in me is evil) go very, very far beyond me in whatever is good and right. This I will say, my ardour of soul and determination of purpose have, I do believe, increased my usefulness greatly; and these things also have added much to my personal happiness. It is good to be zealously affected always in a good thing. My son, do remember this, and remember one of your father's old sayings: 'We should be willing to do good on a large scale, on a small scale, on any scale.' And be sure every morning to have that disposition which might prompt you to say, 'Divine Master, hast thou any work for me to do to-day?' I hope, my son, that you will cause your influence to be happily felt in the Seminary, and wherever you may be; and I hope you will begin early to 'cast about' how you may most usefully employ your next vacation. Do not consult your personal ease or private inclinations, but the glory of God and the good of souls. God grant that you may have a bright crown when you enter heaven, and there bathe in a full tide of glory, as in the full, broad sunlight of heaven.

"Last Friday evening I returned from a missionary tour in the 'Western District,' which lasted five weeks. It was laborious, but delightful. Besides numerous exhortations and many 'some more last remarks,' I preached fifty-nine long sermons. The result was, that in addition to the reviving of many of God's people, about sixty persons were hopefully converted; and perhaps twice sixty were brought under awakening influences. Bless the Lord! I received very pressing invitations to preach in several places where I could not, and smiles and kindness were showered down upon me wherever I went. To crown the matter, on a certain day, one gentleman, a convert, brought forward a child to be baptized, and named him Daniel Baker! When the name was uttered by the pastor, it took me entirely by surprise. So I have now two little namesakes in that region of country. May they put tenfold more honour upon the name than I have done. And then the satisfaction of thinking that I have, in the hands of God, been made instrumental, as I hope, in the sound conversion of some sixty precious souls, or more! I tell you, my son, if the minister of Christ has to pass through a wilderness, there are are some green spots in that wilderness; if his pathway is sometimes rough and thorny, it is also sometimes smooth and strewed with flowers. Lights and shadows, joy and sorrow, hope and fear, these things fill up his days on earth; and then, all light and no shadows, all joy and no sorrow, and the full fruition of hope, in a world where fear finds no entrance: yea, glory; a crown of glory; a throne of glory; an exceeding and eternal weight of glory. O, who would not be a Christian, and especially a Christian minister! My son, you have made a good choice. The Lord make you a chosen vessel. The Lord make you valiant for the truth; a good soldier of Jesus Christ; a workman which needeth not to be ashamed.

DANIEL BAKER."

(TO THE SAME.)

"HOLLY SPRINGS, *December 8th*, 1847.

"MY DEAR SON—Two letters enclosed in one envelope, one from yourself, and the other from your brother, came to hand a few days ago, and gave us a great treat. My son, I am rejoiced to learn that 'the ordinances have been richly blessed' to you; and I will tell you that what you have said in relation to 'scholasticism' and intellectual piety, &c., has given me more pleasure than I can express. I feared at one time that you had a spice of 'transcendentalism' in you, and that your piety would be more refined than deep; but God has now given you, I trust, better views, and better feelings, and better aspirations. Yes, my son, let the blessed Saviour be upon the throne of your heart, and for the love of him be willing to 'give your reputation to the winds.' Have the cross and great eternity continually before you, and think more of the honour which cometh from God than of that which cometh from man only. Whilst reading some two or three of your last letters, and noticing certain things which you said, in relation to your change of views and feelings, I could not refrain from weeping for joy, and exclaiming frequently, as I read on—Bless the Lord! O, my dear son, I wish you, and your dear brother too, to have a warm, heartfelt piety. I wish the love of Christ to be the ruling passion of you both; and God grant that each of you may have the spirit of an apostle, and the spirit of a martyr.

"A few weeks since, I attended a protracted meeting in Somerville which lasted eight days, during which time I preached something like twenty sermons. We had much unfavourable weather, and yet we had a precious season. When we were about to close the meeting, on Tuesday evening, I received a note signed by forty-one young men, mostly non-professors, urging me to continue the meeting a few days longer. I complied, and preached on until Thursday night. On Thursday morning, the young men held a sunrise prayer-meeting; and although the morning was very cold and cloudy, eighteen were present. Among the converts were several interesting young men, and one lady of much gaiety and fashion. On returning from Somerville, my horse started, and threw me upon the frozen ground with great violence; but thanks to a kind Providence, I was not much hurt. Two of my doctrinal sermons are about to be published in Memphis. The gentleman who started the idea insisted upon my taking ten dollars for the manuscripts.

"Your ever affectionate father,

DANIEL BAKER."

"HOLLY SPRINGS, *March 29th*, 1848.

"DEAR BROTHER GALLOWAY—Your welcome, most welcome letter, dated the 17th inst., has been duly received. I thank you, sincerely thank you, for your kind and affectionate remembrance of me. Most cordially can I reciprocate your expressions of Christian love and fraternal regard, and the thought of meeting you, and others like you in heaven, is very pleasant to my soul. From the period of my first becoming acquainted with you, and sharing in your kind hospitality, I have not ceased to think frequently and affectionately of you as a friend and brother peculiarly beloved in the Lord. How I would like to have you as a neighbouring minister! and how pleasant it would be sometimes to labour together, and occasionally to exchange pulpits with each other.

"As good news from a far country is like cold water to a thirsty soul, so has your letter been to me. I rejoice, my dear brother, I rejoice exceedingly to learn that the Lord is with you, blessing so abundantly your labours of love. Thank God, the promise is true, that they that sow in tears shall reap in joy; and that he that goeth forth weeping, bearing precious seed, shall doubtless come again with rejoicing, bringing his sheaves with him. O for a stronger and more simple faith in God's blessed word! for want of this we oftentimes lose much. 'One of your dear boys,' you tell me, 'has shared in the blessings recently vouchsafed to the people of your charge, and another much exercised.' How good has the Lord been to you! 'I have no greater joy,' says the beloved disciple, 'than to hear that my children walk in the truth.' This joy, I hope, will be fulfilled in you. Tell the first ever to lean upon the Saviour, and ever to be firm as a rock; and tell the other he must never rest until he has found the 'one pearl of great price.' God grant that in due time all of your children may be given to you in the Lord, and that your whole family may not only be united on earth, but unbroken in heaven.

"I returned from a missionary tour in Arkansas only a few days ago. This tour lasted eight weeks, and proved a very laborious, and I hope I may add, useful one. I preached about one hundred times, chiefly in the towns of Little Rock, Van Buren, Fort Smith, Clarksville, Norristown, and Batesville. The meetings in each place were crowned with a blessing; Christians were refreshed; feeble churches were strengthened; many sinners were awakened; and about sixty persons were hopefully converted, in all. Some were hard cases; some peculiarly interesting; but no case more pleasing than that of Dr. L., a physician, and son of my old friend, Dr. L., of Washington City. He was awakened under my preaching at Little Rock, but did not profess conversion until a few days after I left. Both he and his bride brought in!—and perhaps not more than one week after their marriage! In Batesville, our meeting was a particularly delightful one. Several of the gayest of the gay were then brought in. Arkansas is a rough State, behind all others in almost every thing. It has been strangely neglected, particularly by our denomination; for in the whole State, it seems, there are not more than some four or five efficient Presbyterian preachers.

"My health is uniformly good; O what a mercy! All the members of my family are in the enjoyment of their wonted health also. Please present our kindest regards to Mrs. G., and all the members of your dear family.

"Yours, in a precious Saviour,

DANIEL BAKER."

CHAPTER XI.

SECOND MISSION TO TEXAS.

THE autobiography continues:

It was in June, 1848, perceiving, as I supposed, that my preaching in Holly Springs was not doing much good, I became restless and unhappy, and wished another field, where I might be more useful. I had not been in this state of mind many months, when one day going to the post-office, I found a letter there for me, a crowded sheet, from the Rev. S. F. Cocke, of Lavaca, giving a glowing account of Texas, as presenting a great and most promising field for missionary enterprise. This excellent brother and myself had some acquaintance many years ago, but we had lost the history of each other; and in his letter he stated, that although he did not exactly know my residence, yet at a venture he would address me at Holly Springs. This seemed to me very remarkable, and after much reflection and prayer, I thought I must at least visit Texas once more. Accordingly I resigned my pastoral charge, and left my family in Holly Springs.

At this time Dr. Baker began a journal, from the pages of which we quote.

Journal.—Texas Mission, 1848. On steamboat.

June 12*th*. Having preached my farewell sermon yesterday morning to a very crowded house, I left Holly Springs in the stage this morning for Memphis, which place I reached about four o'clock, P. M. After transacting some business, took up my lodging on board of Shaw's wharf-boat, waiting for a steamer for New Orleans.

June 13*th*. Spent the day chiefly in reading "Every Man's Book," a poor concern. About eleven o'clock at night got on board the Savanna, secured a good berth, and "turned in."

June 14*th*. Distributed religious tracts, and had some conversation with a profane swearer. Saw on board a man who had been dreadfully scalded last Saturday night, on board the Grey Eagle, which had been run into by the Sultana; conversed with him about the goodness of God in sparing his life, when, by his own confession, he was not prepared to die. Circulated for him a subscription paper, and raised twelve dollars and thirty cents; cautioned him against buying whiskey. Continued reading "Every Man's Book;" wanted to know what Universalists have to say.

Thursday, 15*th*. The tracts put upon the tables having been all taken up, this morning brought forth a new supply. Read the life of Boos, a very interesting memoir of a Roman Catholic with Protestant principles. A gentleman, Mr. A., one of the passengers, took me aside, and said he wished to take counsel with me. He said there was a man on board, who, it was believed, had kidnapped a coloured woman and her three children, passing them off as his, when they were free. It was affirmed that he, B., had given a man two hundred dollars to get them on board at Memphis. The woman, upon being questioned, stated that her former master, Mr. T., had emancipated her about eight years ago; that he was now dead, but had two brothers living at Baton Rouge, who knew all about the matter. Under these circumstances, it was thought most advisable that a letter should be handed to these brothers immediately on the boat reaching Baton Rouge, which would be to-morrow afternoon. Got acquainted with a Roman Catholic priest on board; had an argument with him, but find that I can make no great impression on him, no more than he can on me. He read the life of Boos, and I a Defence of Catholicism; we have become quite intimate, and talk very freely.

Friday, 16*th*. A young man came up to me, and asked if my name was Baker, and whether I was not one of the ministers who held a protracted meeting in Darien some eighteen years since. Replying in the affirmative, he observed, that his father and mother had both been converted under my preaching; that he had heard them talk a great deal about me, and he must have a copy of my sermons to send to his mother. The Roman priest and myself continue our friendly discussions; I propounded some "difficulties," which he met very lamely. This afternoon, a little before sunset, reached the landing at Baton Rouge. The letter already mentioned was immediately sent off to Mr. T., who lives five miles from town. Just as the boat was leaving the wharf, Mr. T. stepped on board, and told the captain that there was a free coloured woman on board whom he wished to see. He went forward to the bow, and seeing her, said, "Lydia, is this you?" The poor creature, overjoyed, exclaimed, "O, Mr. T., I'm mighty glad to see you!" and rushing forward in a transport of joy, caught his hand in both of hers, and seemed ready to devour it with her kisses. Poor creature, how precious was this deliverer to her! I immediately thought of the sinner received by the great Redeemer, when in trouble worse than that of this poor kidnapped woman. At a late hour of the night Mr. B. was taken into custody by an officer of the law, and the woman and her children were in the mean time put ashore by the captain, and taken care of by her protector, Mr. T. Mr. B. stated that the woman's former master owed him, and had no right to emancipate her. I suspect this will prove a bad business for B. The way of transgressors is hard.

Saturday, 17*th*. B. and his train gone, and there is much talking on board in relation to the matter. Reached the wharf about half-past nine o'clock, P. M., and stayed on board of the boat; by reason of musquitoes, it proved a *tristis nox*—sad night.

Sabbath, 18*th*. Visited Dr. Scott's Sabbath-school, and made some remarks to teachers; about two hundred scholars. Visited brother Stanton's Sabbath-school; addressed the scholars—about eighty. At eleven o'clock went to hear brother Stanton. Dined with him; in the afternoon preached for him; the congregation very small. Being invited by my good friend, Mr. C., to make his house my home, I accepted the invitation, and tarried with him.

Monday, 19*th*. First thing, I inquired for a conveyance to Texas; found a schooner, to sail in the evening; took my passage. Conversed with I. C., son of my host, who has had the ministry in view for several years, but who had become discouraged; hope my remarks had a happy influence. Went to Mr. M's store, and got a supply of tracts.

Tuesday, 20*th*. Schooner did not start last evening; disappointed; returned to Mr. C's, and had some further conversation with I., hope it may please God yet to lead him into the ministry. Left the wharf finally about ten o'clock at night; schooner full of freight, and crowded with passengers, chiefly foreigners, bound for Texas.

Sabbath, 25*th*. After a pretty good run, reached Pass Cavallo this morning about nine o'clock. The captain, having anchored off Decora's Point, chartered a shallop, and sent the passengers to Port Lavaca, about twenty-seven miles; reached there about half-past three in the afternoon. Cordially welcomed by Mrs. Cocke, her husband being absent. At her request, authorized notice to be sent around that I would preach at night. House full, and many standing without, at the door and windows; audience profoundly attentive; hope some good was done.

Monday, 26*th*. Wrote a long letter to my wife, and brought up my journal. Fanned by Texas breezes. Preached at night. Wareroom pretty well filled.

The following are extracts from letters written at this time.

'PORT LAVACA, (Monday,) *June 26th*, 1848.

"MY DEAR E.—Well, here I am in Texas, at Port Lavaca, sure enough; and in fine health and spirits too. I took my passage in New Orleans, on board of the schooner European, on Monday morning last, and expected to leave that evening, but, owing to some cause or other, the vessel did not start until the next evening at ten o'clock. The schooner was a small one, deeply laden, deck all littered up with barrels and other freight; and we had passengers enough, I assure you—something like thirty! It was very unpleasant to be so crowded, but I comforted myself with the thought, that if in the stage, I should probably be more crowded still, and moreover the voyage will not be long. Indeed, I was glad to have any mode of conveyance, for the Government needed some two hundred vessels to bring our soldiers back from Mexico. One captain was offered, as I was told, thirty thousand dollars a month for the use of his vessel!—a steamer, I suppose. But, to proceed: we had pleasant weather and a fine run, reaching Pass Cavallo yesterday morning about nine o'clock. The captain anchored, and as he wished to go to Matagorda first, he kindly chartered a large sailing boat, or sloop, to take the passengers to this port, distant about twenty-eight miles. Getting on board, we left the European at her anchorage about noon, and, with a fine Texan breeze, we reached Lavaca about half-past three o'clock, passing smoothly and swiftly over the gently rolling waves of this beautiful bay, called Matagorda Bay. The town of Lavaca was soon seen in the distance; drawing nearer, we had presently a more distinct view of it, pleasantly situated upon a bluff about ten or twelve feet high. As we were sailing up, I observed a house, a neat dwelling with an open piazza (here called a gallery,) overlooking the bay. Thinks I to myself, perhaps that is brother Cocke's residence; and sure enough, so it was! I went in, and met a most cordial reception from your cousin, Mrs. C., her husband not being at home. Sitting in the piazza, overlooking the broad and beautiful bay, fanned by the fresh breezes of Texas, we chatted awhile, but soon found it desirable to retreat into the parlour, as the breeze was rather too strong and too fresh to be agreeable. O, what a waving of window-curtains, and rattling of sashes, and slamming of doors! Verily, if these breezes are zephyrs, they cannot be called gentle zephyrs, for they are not gentle at all.

"About sunset we were called to supper in the back piazza—'gallery,' I should say—and if in the front piazza I had a wide bay before me, now my eyes rested upon a broad prairie; each a kind of ocean, swept by the ever fresh breezes of this promised land. Brother C. not being at home, as I have said, his good lady, your cousin, asked me if I would preach at night. I consented, with pleasure, of course; and in a little time, every family in town was notified. As I was going to church—no, it was a little before we started—I asked, 'Do you think we shall have thirty persons present?' 'Yes, a hundred,' was the prompt reply; and sure enough, so it was. The house was full, every seat occupied; and I know not how many standing at the door, smoking cigars. O, it is pleasant to preach to a people who seem to be so eager to hear the word of life. It rouses me delightfully, and I feel as if I was in my own native element; or, as the saying is, like a fish in water. I do believe I was cut out for a missionary—no mistake. Addressing a new and hungry congregation, I seem to have new life infused into my soul. I do hope my Master has something important for me to do in Texas. The people seem very anxious that I should preach again to-night; indeed, I am told that I might make an appointment for any time, and they would come. * * * O, I must not forget to tell you, that on arriving at brother C's yesterday afternoon, I asked for water to wash my face and hands. I was soon taken into a room, and there was a bowl nearly filled to the brim; a pleasant sight to one sadly sunburnt—but lo, and behold, it was salt water!—and this morning, for my ablutions, a bowl of salt water again! How I do miss the cool fresh water out of my own well; how I feel the loss of it; what a luxury you have that I have not. Who will give me to drink of the well of Bethlehem? said David. Who will give me to drink of my own well in Holly Springs? said I. But we have fine watermelons here, and that, you know, will slake thirst very well.

DANIEL BAKER."

(TO HIS SON W.)

"PORT LAVACA, *July 18th*, 1848.

"MY DEAR SON—This, my sixth letter since leaving home, is addressed to you. I still think Texas is the very place for me, and perhaps for you also. It presents a new, wide, and very promising field for missionary enterprise. Yesterday I finished a meeting at Indian Point, some eight or nine miles distant from this, on the bay. It is a flourishing village, that has come into notice chiefly within the last twelve months; formerly being a place for German emigrants who were in a state of transition into the interior. Six months ago there were not, I suppose, twenty Americans in the place; now, one hundred or more. Recently, lots have been sold to the amount of four thousand dollars; and within six or eight weeks past, persons have come in to settle there whose property is valued at two hundred and fifty thousand dollars. Well, in this new place, I have lately preached some fifteen sermons; and I am happy to say my efforts to do good have been greatly blessed. Six or eight persons hopefully converted, the first who ever professed conversion in the place; one of whom I baptized, the first adult ever baptized in the place. Moreover, I administered the sacrament of the Lord's Supper; the first time this sacrament also was ever administered in the place. About twenty persons of different communions sat down at the table. On Monday, took the requisite steps for organizing a Presbyterian church of eleven members; the first church organized of any denomination.

"I ought to have mentioned that I succeeded in

forming a Sabbath-school here, embracing eight teachers and forty-four scholars. Astonishing! No one ever dreamed of half that number. Two of the converts, so called, were brought in at the right time, one to be Vice-Superintendent, and the other Librarian. I have many sacrifices to make, and hardships to encounter. I have full employment, and am just as happy as the days are long.

DANIEL BAKER."

(TO HIS WIFE.)

"TEXAS, 1848.

"MY DEAR E.—I have entered upon a most important mission; pray for me. Do you feel as if you were left alone? You are in the midst of your own children, and, what is better still, I trust the God of heaven is with you. Cheer up, my E., cheer up! Cast your burden upon the Lord—he will sustain you. Take every thing quietly. Do not indulge in any anxious care, or depressing anxieties. Have faith in God and his promises. Take pleasure in dwelling upon the thought that God reigns—that a wise and merciful Providence extends to all things, especially to every thing which concerns the happiness of his children, his elect, whom he hath loved with an everlasting love. Think much about heaven and its enduring joys, and may God give us both

'A calm and heavenly frame;
A light to shine upon the road
That leads us to the Lamb.

"I hope to see you again in three months, it may be in less time; and even if we should never meet again on earth, have we not the same home in the skies? Tell H. to be sure to dig deep and lay a good foundation. God grant we may all finally land in heaven. Once again, I say, cheer up, and forget not to pray for your husband,

DANIEL BAKER."

Journal continued—1848.

Tuesday, 27th. Brother Cocke not returned yet; felt crippled, and scarcely knew what to do. Spent much of the day in reading, and preached at night. Congregation much the same as last night, but rather more solemn. At the close of the services addressed the coloured people standing about the door on the outside.

Wednesday, 28th. Procured some religious tracts, and spent a good part of the forenoon in visiting and distributing them. Brother C. came home about two o'clock; preached at night.

Thursday, 29th. Preached at night, and spent the day in reading and visiting. Several prominent men of the place seem to be getting much interested in religious matters.

Friday, 30th. Preached in the morning. Some considerable tenderness, especially a certain gentleman, whose wife had been brought in under my preaching when I was in Texas, about eight years since. A lady of great energy of character and influence, but hitherto no professor, appears to be getting very much interested. As a proof of her energy of character, I was told that some years ago, when President Houston ordered the archives to be removed from Austin to Houston, she opposed the order; and when the men appointed by the President were about removing them by force, she had a cannon loaded and properly stationed, and having a match in her hand, she declared she would fire upon any person who attempted to touch the archives; and did actually, for the time, prevent the removal. Preached at night; congregation larger than usual.

Saturday, July 1st. Attended prayer-meeting at nine o'clock, and preached at eleven, and also at night.

Sabbath, 2d. I preached in the morning; brother C. administered the sacrament of the Lord's Supper. I baptized Mrs. B., who I trust is a truly converted person. In the afternoon I addressed the children, many parents and others being present; much good done. Preached at night; crowded house; many out in the piazza.

Monday, 3d. Addressed mothers in the morning, and preached at night; amongst others, a lady of fashion, Mrs. S., was much wrought upon. To-morrow there is to be a Fourth of July celebration in the morning and a fair at night.

Tuesday, 4th. Attended the celebration; was called upon to offer the prayer, after which a young lawyer, Mr. L., delivered an oration, which was really splendid. At night, took two or three turns in the room where the fair was held, and without taking supper returned to my lodgings at brother C's. Had some conversation with two comparatively young men, who, although professors elsewhere of the Presbyterian church, have not connected themselves with the church here. They started some difficulties which I hope to be able to remove.

Wednesday, 5th. In the afternoon passed over to

Indian Point, some eight or ten miles distant, and preached at night in the school-room, which was excessively crowded, many also standing without. This town, a year ago, had not more perhaps than three or four American families; now I suppose some forty or fifty.

Thursday, 6th. Preached in the morning and at night to nearly the whole population, in a fine room that had been fitted up for the occasion; all very attentive, and some much wrought upon.

Friday, 7th. Preached in the morning, and after preaching ascertained that the people generally were desirous of having a Sabbath-school. Having brought with me a supply of books, I mentioned the fact. In a few hours, more than a sufficient amount was subscribed to purchase a library, &c. At night brother C. preached a very good sermon from these words, "How long halt ye between two opinions?" I followed with an exhortation; some good was done, it is hoped. Made an appointment to administer the sacrament of the Lord's Supper next Sabbath-week, preaching to commence on Thursday evening.

Saturday, 8th. Returned to Port Lavaca, and preached at night; congregation not so large as usual.

Sabbath, 9th. Preached in the morning to a full house, and also at night. In the afternoon preached to the blacks; some wept. After the sermon, came out, and so to speak, preached another sermon at the door.

Wednesday, 12th. Went out with brother C. and wife, to visit Mr. P. and wife, some two miles in the country. Found them both sick; prayed with them before I left. At night, attended a meeting of the citizens, to talk about the propriety of forming a Temperance Society; made a speech, and submitted the form of a constitution, which was adopted. The meeting proved more interesting than was expected. Brother C. seemed to think that it was worth while for me to have come from Mississippi, if I had done nothing else.

Thursday, 13*th*. Went again to Indian Point to preach a few days, and administer the Sacrament next Sabbath. When we went last week, at the pressing invitation of Mr. W., the proprietor of the village, we were left to bear our own expenses; and although he had provided a room for our accommodation, when we retired, after preaching, found that there was no chair, table, or bed in the room. At that late hour we had to seek accommodations elsewhere. Hope a bed will be provided this time. Stayed with Mr. B's family, who lived in the attic story; slept on a mattrass in the ware-room, amid hogsheads of sugar, &c.

Monday, 17*th*. Returned to Port Lavaca this afternoon, after preaching eight sermons at Indian Point. Had a blessed meeting; seven or eight hopefully converted; several more left under serious impressions. Administered the sacrament of the Lord's Supper to some twenty communicants of different denominations. Proposed to organize a Presbyterian church; received the names of eleven persons, five males and six females; five of whom were received on examination, and six from other churches. As four of those who joined were members of other churches, and were not furnished with letters of dismission, and the male converts were too recently converted to be elected elders, I thought it advisable to postpone for a few weeks the regular organization of the church. On Saturday afternoon, addressed parents and children, and formed a Sunday-school auxiliary to the American Sunday-school Union; eight teachers, and forty-four scholars—astonishing! Only a few months ago there were not more than four or five American families in the place. Baptized Mrs. E., the first person ever baptized at the place; those converted the first ever converted at the Point; and the sacrament of the Lord's Supper had never been administered there before. This meeting has proved, in every respect, a most interesting and delightful one. The meeting at Port Lavaca might have been equally blessed had it not been for three things, the Fourth of July, the Ladies' fair, and a ball, all in immediate prospect.

Within six or eight weeks past lots have been sold at Indian Point to the amount of four thousand dollars, and persons have come to reside whose property is estimated to be worth two hundred and fifty thousand dollars; likely to be an important place before long. At night, attended a meeting of the Temperance Society in Port Lavaca; made a speech; fourteen new names added.

Tuesday, 18*th*. Spent the day in writing to my son W., reading, visiting, &c.

Wednesday, 19*th*. Made arrangements for starting, after an early breakfast this morning, for Victoria, *via* the Rev. Mr. B's, but the horse I was to ride had been sent for water, and did not return at the time expected. Finally concluded to wait until to-morrow morning, and go in the stage. Spent the day in reading Kirwan's Letters, &c. Attended prayer-meeting at night.

Thursday, 20*th*. About half-past nine set out for Victoria. Dined at Mr. M's pleasant place. Gaius, mine host, charged nothing for dinner; wanted me to preach in that neighbourhood. In the afternoon was overtaken in a very severe thunder-storm. Stage so indifferent, got very wet. Stopped at a house which proved to be Dr. C's. Gave me a cordial reception.

Friday, 21*st*. Dr. C. having borrowed a horse and buggy, took me to Victoria in the morning, and lodged me with Mr. C., an elder, and the only male member of the Presbyterian church in the place. Preached at night. Things in a sad state here; no church fit to preach in, and, although the population may be eight hundred, only about eight male professors of all Protestant denominations.

Saturday, 22*d*. Preached in the morning; addressed professors of religion in the afternoon; and preached again at night. Congregation increasing. We occupied the brick school-house, the old church being only fit for lizards and snakes.

Sabbath, 23*d*. Had prayer-meeting at half-past eight; some tenderness. Preached to an overflowin house; some twenty or thirty without. In the afternoon preached a Calvinistic sermon. Well received. At night, an overflowing house and great solemnity.

Monday, 24*th*. Could not attend prayer-meeting in the morning by reason of an inflamed eye. Putting a green patch on my eye, preached in the morning and at night. In the afternoon, addressed children. Three or four persons under awakenings; one professed conversion; was told there was at night as many persons without as within. At night service, made another appointment to preach to-morrow night, if my eye would permit. Made inquiries, and found the people very ready to do something for the support of the gospel; could raise, perhaps, two hundred dollars. Mr. P. and Dr. C., who had been members in the old States, but not enrolled here, signified their wish to be enrolled; and also Mrs. H., who had been a member of the Episcopal Church elsewhere. Made arrangements for a camp, or protracted meeting, to be held on Diamond Hill, on the 10th of August next.

Tuesday, 25*th*. My eye much inflamed; called in a physician; cupped and blistered; was confined all day to my bed; of course, did not preach at night. The people just in the spirit of attending upon preaching—mysterious providence!

Sabbath, August 13*th*. Have had, so to speak, a long nightmare; for nearly three full weeks in almost total darkness. This day one Mr. A. called to see me. Having reason to believe he had been touched under my preaching, although my eyes were still bandaged so that I could not see him, I exhorted him to attend without delay to the great concern.

Tuesday, 15*th*. Mr. A. called in the evening in his carry-all, and invited me to go out and spend the night with him in the country, about two miles. Hardly thought it prudent to go, by reason of the state of my eyes; but as he seemed very anxious, I went with him. Immediately after family worship,

I made some remarks of a religious nature, when, to my astonishment and most agreeable surprise, he told me that he had found peace in believing, as he trusted, that morning. It seems my remarks to him last Sunday, when on my bed, had great effect. Having no rest in his mind, on Monday afternoon he sent for his brother-in-law, Dr. P., who was a professor; told him his distress, and asked what he must do to be saved. Could not sleep all that night; but early on Tuesday morning found peace. This relation of his experience produced great effect upon all present; appeared like a revival on a small scale. After much conversation and singing, Mr. A. went out and exhorted his servants, who had gathered about the door to hear what was going on; exhorted them to seek the salvation of their souls, until a late hour. Blessed be God!

During his long imprisonment in his chamber, Dr. Baker's chief sorrow was that he was thus stayed from his efforts to do good. With an active spirit that knew no rest, he employed much of his time in dictating letters—letters breathing the very spirit of resignation to the will of God. Cessation from labour was to him a heavy affliction of itself. This reminds the writer, that being with him once during one of his missionary tours, on which he was accustomed to preach at least once every day, he complained one Monday morning of having so "dissipated a feeling—nothing to do." He had preached twice the day before, and was to preach at least once on the day after; but something prevented his preaching that day. During his temporary blindness, he manifested a care to give as little trouble as possible, and a gratitude for the attentions shown him, characteristic of the man. "It matters not," said he, when it seemed most probable he would never see again, "it matters not; I shall nevertheless see the King in his beauty." The eyes of his kind host filled with tears when, years after, he related this incident to the writer.

Sabbath, 20*th*. Ventured to preach this morning. In the afternoon, Dr. C. and wife were received as members.

Monday, 21*st*. Fear I have sustained some injury to my eyes by preaching yesterday, but hope not much.

Tuesday, 22*d*. Expected to start this morning for brother B's neighbourhood, but was prevented by the weather and the state of my eyes.

Friday, 25*th*. Set out for Cuero. Reached Mr. James S's, (elder.)

Sabbath, 27*th*. Rode ten miles, and preached with difficulty on account of my eyes. In the afternoon, spoke with more ease. Made an appointment for next day, same place. Went home with Mr. ——, and next day was pleased to find nearly as many present as on the Sabbath. Preached and addressed parents and children two hours. In the afternoon, went home with Mr. T., and spent the next day at Dr. P's.

Wednesday, 30*th*. Called upon Mr. B., and spent the night with him on my way to the "Colletts." Was told that Dr. P. intended to build a church on his land; and said he would give one hundred dollars a year to any preacher who could instruct him.

Thursday, 31*st*. Preached in the morning and afternoon at the house of Mr. P. About twenty persons present; all unconverted except one.

Friday, *September*, 1*st*. Preached at the house of Mr. C. to eighteen adults, nearly every one unconverted. Some impression was made.

Saturday, 2*d*. Preached at the house of Elder S. to about thirty; some feeling.

Sabbath, 3*d*. Preached twice in the open air without goggles, to, it may be, seventy—great impression.

Monday, 4*th*. Preached to about forty; much tenderness. One professed conversion, and nearly all much wrought upon.

Tuesday, 5*th*. Set off for Victoria.

Wednesday, 6*th*. Preached at Mr. A's.

Thursday, 7*th*. Commenced protracted meeting at Victoria; brothers C., B., and C. present.

Tuesday, 12*th* Closed the meeting. Preached nine sermons, besides addresses, &c. Good meeting. Perhaps twelve or fifteen hopefully converted. During the meeting, baptized two adults, Mr. A. and Mrs. B., and ordained two elders, Mr. P. and Dr. C.

Thursday, 14*th*. In the evening had a meeting exclusively for the unconverted; good attendance, and I believe much good was done.

It shows the playful disposition of the subject of this Memoir, that in the course of a long letter to his family, dated Victoria, September 6th, 1848, he thus writes: "While I think of it, I will mention an incident told me by one whom everybody respects, and loves, and calls 'Uncle Jimmy,' an elder of the church here. This good man went to church one day to hear a preacher named S. On that occasion, for some reason or other, the congregation was rather small, the preacher having no hearers except Mr. Smith, (my informant,) a Mr D., and two children, four in all. Notwithstanding the smallness of the congregation, the preacher, having sung and prayed, rose and was about to take his text, when Mr. D., with whom the preacher had stayed the night before, addressed him thus: 'Mr. S., as I am a sort of Roman Catholic, I would like to confess as I go. I was drunk last night.' 'Why,' replied, Mr. S., 'you treated me very well, sir.' 'Yes,' said he, 'but I was drunk, *very* drunk; and Mr. S.,' continued he, 'if *you* were ever drunk, you must know how bad a man feels when he is getting sober. So I will lie down upon this bench, Mr. S., and as I don't wish to disturb the congregation, I hope, Mr. Smith,' he said, turning to uncle Jimmy, 'I hope if I should snore you will wake me; for I dont wish to disturb the congregation.' Saying this, he stretched himself upon the bench, and was soon fast asleep, sure enough; and beginning to snore, he awoke, and making a move for the door, 'Mr. S.,' he said to the preacher, 'as I don't wish to disturb the congregation, I believe I will go and sleep under the shade of that live-oak yonder.' So off he went, and the congregation was reduced to Uncle Jimmy and the two children; and as the preacher occupied about an hour and a half, and the children went out and in, eating grapes, Uncle Jimmy composed the entire congregation which Mr. D. was so anxious not to disturb."

The autobiography resumed.

After preaching some time to full and very attentive audiences in Victoria, I took a tour higher up into the country. I went to Cuero and preached, and there formed the acquaintance of Mr. S., clerk of the court, which was held in a log-house not more than twelve feet square. I also called upon Dr. P., whose wife had been a member of the Presbyterian church in "the States." Among other places visited by me was Clinton, where I preached to some twenty persons, not one of whom, save the elder who was with me, made any profession of religion; no, not one, male or female. This, however, in that region of country, I found to be no uncommon thing. I preached also at what is termed the "Colletts." It was in a private house, that of a man who, as I found out afterwards, was very profane. Here I took occasion to repeat the remark of the old writer, about the devil turning fisherman, and catching profane swearers with the *naked hook.* Like Captain C., of whom I have made mention, the remark struck him very forcibly; and a few days after, he told me that a circumstance had lately happened to him which made the impression upon his feelings peculiarly lively. It was this: Walking in his piazza one day, he came in contact with a line having a *naked hook* hanging down. Coming against it with some force, it caught him by the ear; and so completely fastened was the hook in his ear, that he had to break the hook before it could be removed. Whether the impression made upon him was as good in its results as in the case of Captain C., I know not; but one thing was encouraging, some few days afterwards he came about thirty miles to hear me preach.

After leaving Victoria, I preached one sermon to a small company in brother B's bounds, and then in company with him I passed on to Goliad, where I preached three times on the Sabbath, and twice on the day following, to congregations which increased in number and interest every time. Goliad is the county seat of Goliad county. At the time I visited it, the population numbered four hundred and fifty; three years before, there were only two American families in the whole county. At Goliad, I saw two of the old military stations—one on each side of the Guadaloupe river—the walls cracked, and the whole establishment in a dilapidated state; but being upon elevated positions, they could be seen over the wide surrounding prairies at a great distance; and when seen, especially at the rising or setting of the sun, they presented an appearance both romantic and grand. I walked through the building on the west side of the river, and with melancholy interest looked into the room where Fannin had been confined as a prisoner; and coming out, the fatal spot was pointed out to me where he and his brave men, some three hundred in number, were so cruelly and treacherously murdered in cold blood.

Here I saw and conversed with Judge Hunter, one of the very few who escaped that dreadful massacre. He told me that he was led out with his companions to be shot; and when, at the firing, some two hundred and ninety fell dead, he, although not touched, fell upon his face as dead also. After remaining motionless for a time, a Mexican came, and standing over him, drove a bayonet into his body. This was not all; the soldier then struck him on his head several times with the butt-end of his musket. To crown the matter, an attempt was made to cut his throat. The knife, however, being dull, no serious injury was done in that way. As Judge Hunter narrated these things, he removed his stock, and showed me the scar upon his neck. The whole account which he gave of the matter was indeed a thrilling one.

After returning and preaching one more sermon in brother Blair's bounds, midway between Victoria and Lavaca, I hurried on to fulfil an appointment for a two days' meeting in Dr. P's neighbourhood. There was some considerable interest awakened, and the people coming in from all quarters, greatly desired that the meeting should be continued; but the thing could not be, as I was confined to my chamber the next day by rheumatic pains in my head, occasioned by exposure the day previous. Leaving that neighbourhood, I went to San Antonio, taking Gonzales, Seguin, and New Braunfels in my route.

At this time the Indians were very troublesome in all that region, and my life was in much danger; but protected by a kind Providence, I reached San Antonio in safety, where I preached several days in a church built by the praiseworthy exertions of brother McCullough. The people came out in crowds, and behaved extremely well. Here I found Mr. A., the former disciple of Fanny Wright, who had been brought in under my preaching in Florida, a long time ago. I was much rejoiced to find him steadfast in the faith.

Every day whilst I was in San Antonio, I heard of the Indians committing murder and depredations all around. Purposing, however, to go to Austin, I borrowed a gun, but finding it to me an awkward weapon, I returned it; and it was well, for had trouble come, in all probability I would have shot at the stars just as soon as at the Indians. Understanding, however, that the stage would leave San Antonio for Austin on Monday morning, with several gentlemen on horseback for mutual protection, I thought I would avail myself of this opportunity, and accordingly made arrangements to go along with them. Taking time, however, by the forelock, I started a little earlier than the hour fixed upon, and permitting my horse to walk on slowly, I passed by the Alamo, and soon found myself out of sight of the town, on the road solitary and alone. I did not like it much, but, looking back frequently, I expected every moment to see my company coming on; but no; Mr. T., the contractor, having been married that morning, occasioned a delay of more than an hour. By this time I had reached the Salado, where the Indians had been prowling a few days before. I looked with some timidity, I confess, on this side and that, knowing that I was in some peril. As I was slowly ascending the sloping hill on the east side of the Salado, I met a young man on horseback, heavily armed. Stopping to talk a little on the road, he pointed to a place on my left, about three-quarters of a mile distant, and said, "There are some Indians now!" With their blankets wrapped around them, they were partly concealed by the musquit bushes and the grass. Becoming very social in my feelings, rather than have no company at all, I concluded to go back with this young man. After a short time, however, I fell in with my company, and with them took a fresh start for Austin. That night we camped out where the Indians had been committing depredations the very night before.

About this time and place a report got abroad that I was murdered by the Indians. The men, it seems, reported that they saw me going back to San Antonio, and when asked why I was going back, I told them that I had seen Indians; and when they rallied me and pronounced me a greenhorn, who in my fright took something else for Indians—they said I could not stand that, and to show them my courage, I just brushed up and went on ahead, and they saw no more of me until they saw my scalp on the road, and a part of my black coat! Whether this was the true origin of the report of my death, I know not; but it was soon spread abroad in all the papers, and generally believed too, that I was dead—cruelly murdered in cold blood! My wife's sister, hearing the intelligence, put on mourning. My own brother kindly wrote a letter of condolence to my wife, beginning with these words, "My dear sister—what shall I say?" &c.; and Dr. Laurie, of Washington City, wrote me that he had prepared to preach my funeral sermon—had actually risen to his feet, and announced his text, when some one handed him a note in the pulpit, stating that it was a mistake. Dr. L., in his letter to me, winds up with this remark: "I was glad to have the report corrected, but certainly it spoiled my sermon." This affair gave me the rare privilege of reading my own obituary.

In proceeding with the narrative, we would remark that what follows was written immediately on his return home from Texas.

In due time I arrived safely at Austin, the capital of Texas; and here, besides preaching some fifteen sermons to promiscuous assemblies in that city, I made special addresses to heads of families, to young men, to young ladies, and to children, not forgetting the children of Ham. Our meetings were chiefly at night, and were invariably well attended by all classes, even the most prominent members of government. Moreover, we had some interesting inquiry meetings; some fifteen individuals or more were numbered with the anxious, of whom several gave evidence of a blessed spiritual change, and would no doubt have connected themselves with the Presbyterian church, had one been in existence there. I did hope to have the pleasure of organizing one, but the grand difficulty here, as in many other places, was to get suitable persons to fill the office of ruling elders. I think that a devoted and talented minister of our communion might be very useful here. I say talented, because there is an unusual amount of intelligence in this city; and, I may add, encased infidelity—all profess to believe the Bible, and yet many take a marvellous pleasure in repeating cavils and objections of every kind. Permit me here to repeat a remark made in my former report, "Let inferior preachers be retained in the East; let talented ones be sent to the West." It is easier to keep a house, already built, from falling, than to erect one when the materials are yet in the forest; and I will add, as a general remark, that I do think the standard of ministerial excellence should be higher than it now is. In Texas, the people will not come out on week-days, and not very well on Sabbath-days, unless they think the preacher is "worth hearing."

There is a very flourishing and admirably conducted Sabbath-school in Austin. The superintendent and teachers are of high character, and deserve great credit. They have a certain spice of enthusiasm, which all must have in every pursuit, if they would be greatly successful. The meeting in Austin was a good one, and I suppose would have been more so, had it not been for a feverish state of excitement amongst the people, occasioned by frequent accounts of Indian murders and depredations.

Leaving the beautiful town of Austin, I turned my face towards Victoria, where I hoped, on the first Sabbath in November, to have the pleasure of meeting brother Cocke, of Lavaca, and other brethren on their way to Presbytery. After receiving some touching proofs of the kind regards of the good people of Austin, on Monday I rode to Webber's Prairie, on the Colorado, sixteen miles distant; and sending out runners to give due notice, I preached that night in the house of a friend. I thought we might have about twenty persons present, when, lo! there were some fifty or sixty. O, when souls are hungry for the bread of life, how they will flock to a place where a table is spread! That night, I think, much good was done. Here I was told by "mine host" of an incident illustrative of the heroism of Texan females, which occurred near this place not many years ago.

A party of one hundred Indians had killed two men working in a field, and put a third to flight. In these circumstances, a young woman, scarcely sixteen years of age, undertook to protect her family. Putting on a captain's uniform, with a cocked hat, she courageously walked out of her house, and beckoned to the Indians to come on, at the same time making signs to those within the house (only some women and children, and an old man) to repress their ardour and keep still. The Indians, supposing that the brave captain's company were within, eager to charge, thought it best to withdraw from so dangerous a post, and they accordingly fled! Certainly the Texan Congress should have granted her a captain's commission and pay for life.

From Webber's Prairie I went to Bastrop, a pleasant town on the Colorado, of four hundred inhabitants, famous for its neighbouring pine forests and saw-mills. Here I was cordially received and kindly entertained by a Christian brother, who had been an elder in the Presbyterian Church, but now of the Cumberland order, because no church of our communion existed there. This brother very industriously circulated a notice that I would preach at night; I did so. The church was well filled; a more attentive audience I could not wish to see; and I think a good impression was made, for I was earnestly requested to remain and preach until over the Sabbath. This not falling in with my arrangements, I declined; and the next day, riding forty miles, I reached Lagrange, in time to send runners around, and preached at night. Here I was kindly entertained by Dr. Townsend, who had been a ruling elder of our church in one of the blessed old States. He insisted upon my spending the Sabbath in this town (rather larger and more flourishing than Bastrop); I consented, and preached in the court-house some eight or ten sermons, chiefly at night. Much interest was manifested here, and I was told that they had scarcely ever seen such full houses in that town before; and it may not be amiss to mention that one gentleman went, as I was informed, to every tippling house in the place, and offered each rum-seller a dollar for every evening he would close his shop and go to church.

Understanding that the distinctive doctrines of our communion were sadly misapprehended in this region, I preached, by appointment, a long doctrinal sermon to a large and deeply attentive audience, and have good reason to believe that many prejudices were happily removed, and that much good was here done in various ways. I organized a church here—consisting, it is true, of only five members—but there is an encouraging prospect for a considerable increase, particularly if the Board could, at some early period, send them a man of the right stamp; for such a one, it was thought that four hundred dollars could be raised in Lagrange alone.

Leaving town on Tuesday morning, I set out for Col. Turner's settlement on the Navidad. A gentleman of wealth, and supposed to be rather an infidel in his sentiments, residing here, had heard me preach at Indian Point some three months before, and was so much interested that he requested me, in a peculiarly earnest manner, to visit his neighbourhood. Whilst wending my way to the residence of this gentleman, about eight miles from his house I fell in with a farmer in good circumstances, who was going home, and lived not so far distant. Learning from me that I was a missionary in the service of our Board, he told me that he was a Presbyterian himself, but had not heard a Presbyterian for *eighteen years.* As the day was far spent, I proposed preaching at his house that night. He was greatly delighted; and although he had just walked ten miles, he went off the road, to this house and that, inviting the neighbours all around. Late at night they came in; and, after a very solemn meeting, a gentleman and his lady tarried one full hour for religious conversation. They seemed to be thorough-going Christians and Presbyterians, both in feeling and sentiment, and greatly desired that kind of preaching to which they had been accustomed in days gone by. When informed that I had just organized a church in Lagrange, they seemed to be much pleased, and spoke of having their names enrolled, although thirty miles distant.

The next day I reached the residence of the gentleman who had invited me into this region of country, and very cordial was the reception which both he and his lady gave me, and almost incredible were the efforts made by him to circulate the appointment for preaching at night. When the time arrived, the room was nearly filled with men, whilst many of Africa's sable sons and daughters were gathered about the door. Seed was sown that night, which, I verily believe, will yield good fruit, sooner or later.

Judging from a scene which took place next morning in the house of my friend, I hope to meet both himself and lady in heaven. Before parting, he told me that he would subscribe liberally for the support of a Presbyterian preacher in his neighbourhood; and when I finally gave him my hand, and bade him adieu, he was almost convulsed. His wife also, not a professor, seemed to be as painfully wrought upon as her husband. How rejoiced was I, that I was permitted to preach at least one sermon in that destitute region, and to have one precious opportunity for religious conversation and prayer with that interesting family.

Journeying on towards Victoria, I preached the next night at a little village called Petersburg. As it was raining when I reached the place, I had no idea of preaching there or anywhere else that night; but stopping at a store to inquire about a person who lived a few miles distant, I was recognized, and earnestly requested to tarry and preach there that night. Of course I consented; and, dark and rainy as it was, I had the pleasure of preaching to nearly all the people in the place. We had even two or three Roman Catholics present, and a priest! And equally strange to tell, the individual who was most active in "getting up" the meeting, and who *clerked* it for me, was, I am sorry to say, in the habit of dealing out death by the half-pint! But he has a pious mother, if I mistake not, and his conscience was evidently not at rest.

On Friday evening I reached the house of a friend near Victoria, and scarcely was I safely housed, when there came up a regular *Norther*, such as I had never known before; the wind blew with great violence. It rained also, and in thirty minutes I suppose the thermometer fell thirty degrees. These northers are, I believe, peculiar to Texas. They usually last from one to three days. When coming on, the cattle in the prairies seem terrified, and hasten into the timbered bottoms, where they find a safe retreat. The northers, however, that are violent, are not frequent, and when over, we have the clear blue sky, and every thing is as pleasant as spring.

On the morning after the norther just mentioned, the banks of the Guadaloupe were strewed with *pecan nuts*, and many persons, male and female, old and young, went out to gather them. For the novelty of the thing, I went myself, and in a few hours gathered two pecks or more. Some dear little children whom I had addressed when in Victoria were eager to fill my sack. The pecan crop, once in three years, is a great affair in Texas. It is considered equal to the cotton crop, for one hand can gather from one to three bushels a day, and the picking season lasts from six to eight weeks. It is estimated that this year fifty thousand bushels of pecans will be exported from the Guadaloupe alone. So then, if the heavens do not rain manna in Texas, many of the trees of the forest shower down nuts which bring more than a dollar a bushel on the spot —certainly a kind provision, at least for the poor. On the next day, being the Sabbath, I preached three times in Victoria, to comparatively small congregations, as the notice was very limited, and many of the people were out *pecanning*.

Sadly disappointed in not meeting the brethren of

the Presbytery here, with whom I greatly desired to confer in relation to the spiritual affairs of this young and growing State, I left Victoria on Monday for Texana, a small town on the La Baca, and preached there that night to every person in the village, as I was told, except two or three, who were not well. I was urged to remain and preach several days, but thought it best to pass on, wending my way towards Wharton, on the Colorado, and Columbia, on the Brazos.

As I was passing through a wide, wild, and trackless prairie, I lost my landmarks, and night coming on, I had, unarmed, to camp out, solitary and alone, on the edge of a strip of timber fringing Jones' Creek. Kindling a fire at the foot of a tree, and, taking my saddle-blanket for my bed, my saddle for my pillow, and my umbrella for my pavilion, I quietly laid me down, and thought about Jacob at Bethel, when, journeying to Padan-Aram, he laid himself down to sleep, and dreamed about the ladder set upon the earth, and whose top reached unto heaven. Jacob slept, and dreamed a pleasant dream; but there was no sleep, nor pleasant dream for me—for just as I was endeavouring to compose myself to sleep, suddenly the wolves and panthers began a serenade, which grated horribly upon my ear. Seizing a firebrand, and now wide awake, I rushed towards the place whence these unwelcome sounds proceeded, and making all manner of outrageous noises, I did what I could to drive my uninvited serenaders far away. In this I partially succeeded; but did not think it prudent to sleep, as the howling of the wolf and the cry of the panther were heard at intervals during the whole livelong night; and there was danger, particularly of the panthers springing upon me when defenceless and unprotected upon the ground.

Truly that was a long and dismal night to me; especially as towards morning it began to cloud up and threaten to rain. A few drops fell, but happily for me, with the shades of the night passed away also the clouds from the face of the sky; and the next morning, early enough, the supperless missionary, taking down his pavilion, and rising from his couch, resumed his cheerless and lonely way; and now came a dark, dark time indeed. True, the sun was shining brightly, and many deer, as yet unacquainted with man, were bounding merrily and gracefully on every hand; but bewildered in the wild and trackless prairie, I was lost, *lost*, LOST!

After wandering about in every direction, myself and horse without water for some thirty hours, I began seriously to think that I should at last have to lie down and die in this untravelled wilderness, far away from my family and the habitation of man, without a friend to close my eyes, or dig my grave! The idea of dying in this lonely place, and then being devoured by wolves and panthers, I confess was very dismal to me. But, God be thanked, whilst I was thus bewildered and lost, and knew not what to do—whilst despair was every moment deepening its gloom around me—having turned in another direction, and nearly the opposite of that in which I was going, I saw in the distance a white flag waving upon a pole, to mark the entrance of a foot-path into the timbered bottoms of the Colorado. O, that flag!—

that beautiful white flag! I thought it was the prettiest thing I had ever seen in all my life. My heart leaped for joy, and I was ready to exclaim aloud, Blessings upon the man who put it there! It made me think very sweetly about the Star of Bethlehem; that blessed and only star of hope to a dying world. Certainly I shall not forget this matter, when, in the sacred desk, I shall speak of the cross of Christ, which marks out to sinners, bewildered and lost, their only pathway to heaven.

Having at last found the much desired way to the place of my destination, and having gone four miles through the heavily-timbered and vine-clad bottoms of the Colorado, I came to the river, but there was no ferry there. After calling and waiting a long time, a man finally appeared on the other side, and pointed to a certain place where the river, though deep, might be forded. Plunging into the stream, I passed safely over, but not without becoming very wet.

On reaching Wharton I changed my clothes, and got some refreshment. I would then gladly have preached, but the only place in which an audience could be assembled was already engaged for a dancing party.

In the course of his labours among all classes of persons, in all sections of the land, incidents would often occur not at all common in the even life of the city pastor. On one occasion, while describing, in the course of a sermon, the exceeding sinfulness of the impenitent, a backwoods hearer arose and withdrew, with a long, shrill whistle of utter incredulity.

In the midst of a sermon on another occasion, the fixed and solemn attention of the congregation was broken by a yawn so long and loud as to make the rafters ring. Promptly and severely was the yawner rebuked by the speaker. He proved to be a preacher of another denomination settled in the place, who took this method of showing *his* opinion of the preacher.

Coming down from the pulpit, after an earnest address to professors of religion, in another place, a white haired man pressed forward and shook him long and cordially by the hand. "You trust that you are a Christian?" said Dr. Baker—but, as he spoke, an unmistakeable odour from the lips of the man himself answered the question in the negative. "*Trust* that I am a Christian?" replied the man—"*trust*, sir?—I KNOW that I am."

It illustrates, too, the diversified experience of the subject of this volume, that once on a Sabbath morning, standing in his pulpit as pastor of a church, he felt compelled by conscience to enter his solemn protest as a minister of the gospel against a certain measure to which the dominant political party of the State stood pledged, many of whom were members of the church seated before him at the moment. The protest was made on purely moral grounds, and so satisfied were all with the sincere conviction of the speaker, that, so far as is known, no one was alienated from the pastor, nor scarce a murmur uttered.

Very rarely indeed did he ever come in collision with any one—upon not more than one or two occasions in his whole life. He had perhaps almost too great a care, and even anxiety, to be on terms of peace, and more than peace, with those whose wrong-headed stubbornness and malignant disposition were well calculated to provoke the most patient beyond endurance. Only after every possible manner of conciliation was exhausted, would he desist from the effort to be "at peace with all men," even such as these. On one such occasion, when, in hatred to his doctrinal belief as a minister of the Presbyterian Church, a grievous wrong was done him, in vain were retaliatory measures urged upon him. After employing every mode of settling the matter, unruffled from first to last, he was forced to yield a manifest right, saying as he did so to his exasperated friends, "Never mind; only let us carefully do what is right, and leave results to God. Mark my word, he will sooner or later vindicate us in the matter." Not many months had passed before his words were most remarkably made good.

It is not known that any one ever accused him, in thought even, of a desire to domineer, or to force through any measure against the wishes of others. At the same time, when satisfied of the importance of a measure, he embarked himself in it heart and soul, "*suaviter in modo, fortiter in re.*" When any church court met in his own church, he invited those brethren to preach, and those only, whose labours he thought would be attended with good to the people. In Synod and Presbytery, he strongly reprobated sacrificing the good of the people to the personal feelings of any minister; he even obtained the passage of a resolution in one Synod, directing the minister of any church in which the judicatory was to be held, to write beforehand to such brethren, among those who were to be present, as the pastor thought best adapted to do good, informing them of the fact, and urging them to come to the place of meeting specially prepared for what he regarded as—especially in a frontier field—the most important part of a ministerial convocation, namely, the religious services.

It was the habitual practice of Dr. Baker to urge the salvation of the soul upon men wherever and whenever it was possible. He was peculiarly happy in never doing this in such a way, or at such a time, as to defeat his object; yet in the parlour and along the roadside, no one, white or black, male or female, young or old, ever gave him the least opportunity to say a word on the subject of religion that he did not improve; and in such a manner as never to offend, but often to do good.

Riding in a stage with a young man who was very profane, he rebuked him for his sin. The stage arrived at its destination, Baltimore, and the passengers dispersed over the city. A night or two after, walking along the streets, Dr. Baker and the young man came suddenly face to face upon each other, under a street lamp. Instantly seizing his hand, the young man thanked him for the reproof; told him of a pious mother, whose prayers and entreaties he had hitherto neglected, and solemnly promised never again to utter an oath. Are not Christians guilty in not, at least, attempting to do good wherever they may be, and even where the prospects of success are discouraging.

Once, when in a town far west of the Mississippi river, Dr. Baker mingled with a crowd of persons pressing around the desk of a stage agent to obtain seats in the stage. In his turn he announced his name, extending his hand at the same time with the money for his seat. But his arm is grasped from behind—"No sir, no sir," exclaims a voice, "I must pay that bill;" and it was paid by a strange gentleman, who then led Dr. Baker aside. "More than twenty years ago, at a meeting in ——, you were made the means," said the stranger, with tears in his eyes, "of leading me to Christ. The paying that bill for you is the least I can do to show my feelings towards you."

Events similar to this were of continual occurrence. Travel where he would, he was rejoiced not only by the present blessing of God upon his labours, but also by new assurances of that blessing having attended his labours in days long gone by. A youth sent to guide him to the place of worship, accidentally meeting the writer forty years after, told him of the urgency with which Dr. Baker had entreated him to attend to the greatest of all concerns. The very child that nestled for an instant on his knee, the maid-servant entering his room with a pitcher of water, the hostler who held his stirrup as he mounted his horse, in receiving other tokens of his interest, never failed also to hear a word in season in regard to that great salvation which occupied all his soul, and which he yearned to make known to every human being.

It need not be added that he never declined to preach on a single occasion where it was in the bounds of possibility to do so; and he would rebuke affectionately any brother whom he saw decline, or even hesitate, to preach, when an opportunity presented. It was his invariable custom in travelling to preach every night wherever he might happen to stop, if even the smallest congregation could be got together; or, if this was impossible, he would hold family worship at least, adapting the services to impress the minds of all who took part.

In arriving toward night at a village in which there was no Presbyterian church, and in which he had no acquaintance, he would obtain the use of whatever public building was in the place, and hire some one to go around with the information that there would be preaching there that night. Where no one could be obtained to do this, he would do it himself; the weariness of a long day's ride was forgotten in the hope of leading some sinner to his Saviour, or of reviving the piety of some child of God. If it was necessary, he would himself purchase candles, and light the place of worship; even hammer upon the triangle, often used in frontier towns as a bell, or pull the rope by which the court-house or school-house bell was rung. As the sounds of the triangle or bell were heard, the people would flock to the place, some from curiosity to hear the preacher, but most of the congregation entirely ignorant, until the services were actually begun, whether the person who stood before them was a lecturer upon phrenology, animal magnetism, mesmerism, temperance, or a candidate about to make a stump speech; or if a preacher, whether he was evangelical, Universalist, Campbellite, or Mormon. The first service, however, never failed to bring forth, often to the astonishment of the whole village, before ignorant of the fact, some latent Presbyterian, or Christian of some other denomination, or a friend, at least, of religion. From some such beginnings interesting meetings would often result. The preacher would enter the place unknown; he would leave it to be remembered, perhaps, by every person in the community, with esteem, and, mostly, with veneration and love, to the end of their days. On one such occasion he had gathered a congregation in the little log-cabin which was erected in the centre of the square, and served for every public use. The room was crowded with hearers, and more continually coming. In the opening of his discourse, the preacher perceives that many are collecting outside, unable to enter. The clapboard door can be only partly opened—but all must hear—shall hear! Pausing in his discourse, he requests "some gentleman present to remove the door from its hinges." There is a moment's hesitation, and the request is repeated, with the reason for it. Six or eight of the strongest spring forward, lift the ponderous door from its hinges, lay it out of the way outside, and the services are resumed with redoubled interest on the part of the preacher and of the audience within and without.

Arriving, in the course of his missionary labours, at an intelligent and flourishing village in the West, by invitation he began a series of meetings in the court-house, used in common as a place of worship for all denominations. Many attended from a considerable distance, for in this, as in every place visited by him, there were some who had known him, or heard of him, who had made his arrival widely known. At one of the hours appointed for wor ship, a minister of another denomination insisted on preaching to the congregation assembled to hear Dr. Baker. From first to last the sermon was a violent attack upon a doctrine held dear to all branches of the Church of Christ, save the Ishmaelitish one to which the intruding minister belonged. Upon this doctrine he exhausted his whole stock—a large one—of ridicule and abuse. At the close of his sermon, the speaker, breathless from exertion, waves his hand to Dr. Baker to lead in prayer, who declines. Nothing daunted, the speaker offers prayer himself; then coolly gives notice that *he* will preach in the same place at the next hour of worship. Dr. Baker rises, not in the least embarrassed, and remarks that he is under the impression that the congregation which crowds the room would prefer that *he* should preach at the hour specified. It is perfectly easy, however, he remarks, for the congregation to correct him if he is mistaken, and settle the question on the spot. "All present," he exclaims, "who prefer that *I* should preach at the hour specified, will please rise." Instantly, the whole congregation, apparently, were upon their feet. Requesting them to be seated, he then says, "All who prefer that this brother should preach, will please to rise." But one or two persons, ardent zealots of the peculiar views of the other preacher, arose. "Very well," says Dr. Baker, "we have decided this matter in a way which is always final with Americans. Providence permitting, I will preach in this place at the time mentioned. Receive the benediction." And so the congregation was dismissed.

In this connection it is well to remark, that Dr.

Baker had what are called "peculiarities." These were only the carrying out, in daily life, of certain principles which were occasionally uttered by him as maxims, or rather as axioms. Thus he would often say, "Nothing is disgraceful but sin." He gave this as his sufficient reason when, on returning to his residence one evening while pastor of a city church, he found lying near his door, upon the sidewalk, an intoxicated countryman, and assisted his servant in carrying him into the house, rather than have him sleep all night upon the stones. The intoxicated man spent the night on a pallet made for him, but was up and gone before morning, carrying with him from the minister's house a sermon, so to speak, which he would never forget.

If in his walks along the streets he saw any thing which he desired for himself or family, on purchasing it he would bring it home himself if possible, having none of that little pride which is so common in such matters. The writer has seen him returning home bearing in his hands a huge house-broom; or, riding up to the door on horseback, with a large rocking-chair on the saddle before him, which he had bought, as a present to a member of his family, and, as usual, was impatient to bestow. Nothing pleased him more than to lay off his coat, and labour in his garden or field, whenever his duties would permit.

Not long before his death, when President of Austin College, and residing in Huntsville, where this institution is located, it struck him as being very desirable to have a sidewalk made from the town square to the College building, which is upon an eminence some half a mile off. Drawing up a subscription-paper, and subscribing liberally himself, he ceased not until he had obtained the amount needed. The next thing was to obtain a contractor to do the work; but owing to the nature of the soil, the task was an almost impossible one, and no contractor could readily be obtained. Nothing daunted, he took the job himself, employed hands, and superintended the work, with his coat off, until it was thoroughly completed. To bridge a wet chasm, two full length trees were required; the person who was to have them on the spot at an appointed time, failing to be prompt, Dr. Baker instantly procured the necessary team of oxen, repaired with help to the forest, and soon had the ponderous logs in their place. While hard at work with hoe and axe—labouring, as he did with all his might, in whatsoever his hands found to do, at all times—a brother minister passing by, reined in his horse, with feelings greatly shocked at seeing the Doctor of Divinity and President of the College so occupied. "My dear sir," he exclaimed, "I beg you will let the servants do that." "They do not know how," answered Dr. Baker. "But many persons do not like to see you thus employed; they do not think it proper." "Very well," replied the busy workman, never pausing from his toil, "you tell them, my dear brother, to mind their business, and I will attend to mine." In all things, without the least departure from the inherent dignity of character which was inseparable from the man, he acted out his belief that nothing but sin disgraces one.

"Do good on a large scale, on a small scale, on

any scale." This was a maxim frequently on his lips, and repeated often in his letters to his children; and he himself endeavoured to practise it, as every other precept inculcated by him. If an obstacle lay in his path as he walked, he would stop and remove it, for the benefit of the next comer. Even in driving his vehicle along the road, after safely passing over some limb fallen from a tree, or rock in the way, if his time and strength would permit, he would alight and roll the obstruction aside. To glorify God by being useful to his fellow creatures was the one desire and object of his life; and he gave himself up to preaching the gospel, because he could, called as he was to this work, be thus most useful to men—never neglecting, at the same time, any lesser ways of serving them as opportunity offered. The whole doctrine and practice of religion with him was summed up in this, that he habitually endeavoured to be, "not slothful in business, fervent in spirit, serving the Lord." He would express himself even strongly in regard to those whose excellence seemed to consist merely in an indolent amiability.

"A grain of common sense is an excellent thing." It was in accordance with this maxim that he was always careful to prevent, as far as he could, every thing calculated to distract the attention of a congregation. Smoking pulpit lamps, rattling windows; seats so constructed that no one could sit at ease upon them; the place of worship so near a public highway as to be liable to distracting sights and sounds; a disagreeable echo in the place of worship; an unnecessary turning over of leaves, and making whispered arrangements in the pulpit after the congregation had assembled; arranging the elements of the communion after the services had begun; appointing the time of worship at an hour inconvenient to the hearers; protracting services so as to weary those present—things of this nature, which, by an exercise of common sense could be obviated, he would regard as almost a device of Satan himself to prevent good being done. On the same principle he never, in his own house, would protract the services of family worship to an undue length, especially in the morning; and it was his rule to omit them altogether on those nights when there was public worship. Any thing which would necessarily disgust, or weary, or lessen the attention of one in a religious exercise, he was careful to avoid.

A brother in the ministry, relating the following in regard to his acquaintance with Dr. Baker, illustrates another maxim which was often upon his lips:

"The pastor of one of our churches had heard of his labours, and of his wonderful success in his Master's work. Quick as thought, he resolved to get his assistance for a week or two in his own church, if possible. An effort was made, and the time appointed; but when the day set apart for a beginning arrived, the rain was falling in torrents. True to his appointment, however, the good man was seen driving up to the pastor's dwelling. A little disheartened, his first remark to Dr. B. was, 'I am truly sorry, sir, that we have such bad weather for the beginning of our meeting. I am fearful as to the result.' With a tranquil smile, which I shall never forget, he replied, as he laid his hand on my shoulder, 'My dear brother, the clouds are in good hands; let the clouds alone.' How much of the spirit of heaven was in that expression! Right sure am I that it will be remembered as long as I am permitted to preach the gospel. Rarely does a cloudy Sabbath appear, and never does it rain on the Lord's day, without my thinking of this well-timed and wise remark. Almost always do I enter the pulpit with a cheerful heart, whether it rains or shines. The clouds were in good hands, (adds this brother,) for some forty persons were brought in during the meeting that followed, notwithstanding the rain."

It need scarcely be remarked here, that his belief was clear and constant that the finger of God was in every event, from the greatest down to the very least. This was the secret of his unbroken cheerfulness under the most mysterious and otherwise discouraging providences. "The Lord reigns!" was the sovereign explanation of every event, and perfect cure of every ill.

We resume the narrative.

On Friday, November 10th, I reached Old or West Columbia, a town near the Brazos, once of some importance, but now almost entirely deserted; and in the vicinity, at the house of Mrs. Bell, (a mother in Israel), I met a cordial reception. There was the house where our lamented brother Hunter boarded—there the room in which he slept—there the books he was wont to read—and there the table upon which he was wont to write his eloquent and masterly sermons. Even his inkstand was there, and every thing left untouched, as if the beloved pastor had only stepped out, and would return in a short time. How mysterious, that one so talented and so highly esteemed, and so lately installed, should be so suddenly snatched away. But methinks a voice comes to this mourning people from on high, and it is this: "Be still, and know that I am God!"

On Sabbath morning I preached in brother Hunter's church in Old or West Columbia, and in the afternoon and night in the Methodist church in New or East Columbia. Considering the shortness of the notice, and the state of the roads and weather, the congregation each time was larger than could have reasonably been expected. And here I would remark, that it was peculiarly acceptable to the Presbyterian church here that I should pay them a visit just at this time. It was soothing to their feelings, as manifesting a kind sympathy with them in their recent and sad bereavement.

New or East Columbia is a shipping port, and a somewhat flourishing town on the Brazos, and may number about four hundred souls. On Monday I rode to Brazoria, twelve miles distant, the county town of Brazoria county, and would have preached there at night, but as the weather was unfavourable, and I saw no one who seemed willing to put himself to much trouble to circulate the notice, I thought it best to return to Mrs. Bell's, and preach to her servants at night, which I did; and much pleased was I that this idea occurred to me, for the meeting proved a highly interesting one; and I think the occasion will be long and gratefully remembered by these children of Ham.

On Tuesday I set out on my return to Victoria,

my radiating point, by the way of Egypt, a settlement famous for corn, sugar, and good people. Rain, rain, rain, all the week rain; nevertheless, I reached Egypt, about eighty miles distant, in time to preach once on Saturday, and three times on the Sabbath. On Saturday few were present, as few knew any thing about the appointment; but on the Sabbath the house was crowded, although the day was far from being favourable—the notice short and the sugar mills in full blast. Not that these good people desecrated the Sabbath—O no! to their praise be it spoken, they were always careful to have their fires quenched before twelve o'clock on Saturday night, and not kindled again until the Sabbath was fully past; and they have lost nothing by it; for, if I am correctly informed, all came there poor, and all are now in good circumstances. It would be well if some sugar-planters in other places would profit by their example.

Certainly Texas is destined to be a great State; and I could wish that the ministers of our denomination, and especially our young men who are preparing for the ministry, would think more about Texas than they do. True, there are not many "feathered nests" there yet, but there are what should be vastly more inviting, wide fields of usefulness. The destitutions in that young and growing State are many and great. O that the churches of our beloved Zion would think upon these things, and remember, that in Texas and other frontier States, many precious souls are hungering for the bread of life; and also remember, that the night cometh when no man can work. Methinks one on reading this says—"Well, I will give five dollars to the cause of domestic missions; I can give this amount and not feel it." Suppose, my Christian brother, you give *twenty, and feel it.* Your Saviour *felt what he did for you.* A remark of this kind once heard from the pulpit thrilled through my whole soul, and made me do more than empty my purse. I borrowed from a friend. The idea of *feeling what I gave* was delightful.

I reached Victoria at the time expected, and would have preached at night, but the weather was unfavourable, and the people still out *pecanning.* Although I did not preach, I had a conference with some choice daughters of Zion here, who were resolved that the church edifice in this town should remain in an unfinished state no longer. Heaven speed them in their holy purpose! One of these ladies was brought in under my preaching a few months before. Of woman it was said,

> "Last at his cross, and earliest at his grave;"

and I do believe, if piety should take her departure from earth, her last resting-place would be a woman's heart. Just before leaving Victoria for Lavaca, I was informed that one of the young converts here died the last week, and, God be thanked, died having "a good hope through grace."

On Wednesday, the 22d of November, I reached Port Lavaca, and was cordially greeted by the people generally. I would have preached in Lavaca, but the church was remote, not glazed, and the weather bad. Particularly anxious to preach one sermon more at Indian Point, I got on board of a sailing boat early in the afternoon, but being becalmed on the bay, I did not reach the town until nine o'clock at night; I was cordially welcomed to the house of one of the newly-ordained elders. The next morning I called upon a few Christian friends, and was much pleased to learn that the Sabbath-school which I had organized still flourished, and the young converts are all doing well; that the church has been regularly organized by brother Cocke; and that two of those who had professed religion during my preaching in the place, had been duly elected and installed ruling elders. To crown my satisfaction, and fill up the cup of my happiness, a highly respectable gentleman, a physician, who had been awakened at the meeting referred to, was on this occasion enabled, as I hope, cordially to embrace the Redeemer, whilst I was reading to him the words of Christ to Nicodemus, as recorded in John, 3d chapter, from the 14th to 19th verse inclusive. Yes, whilst this blessed portion of Scripture was laid before him, and briefly commented on, his countenance began to brighten, and the way of salvation opening with divine clearness and beauty to his soul, he exclaimed, "O, I never had such views of my Saviour before!" Immediately he hurried into another room where his wife was, and with a glad heart told her what the Lord had done for his soul. This case, and that of the gentleman on the Navidad, have forcibly reminded me of the words of the poet,

"Though seed lie buried long in dust,
It sha'n't deceive our hope;
The precious grain shall ne'er be lost,
For grace insures the crop."

Taking my passage on board of the steamer Yacht, I hoped to reach Galveston at least early on the morning of the Lord's day; but, in consequence of a strong head-wind, we did not reach that city until one o'clock in the afternoon of that day. Going directly to the residence of the pastor, brother Henderson, he gave me a most cordial reception, and at his request, I preached in his church, both in the afternoon and at night. The congregation, however, was not large on either occasion, as curiosity had carried many to the Roman Catholic Cathedral, which, amid many pompous rites and "imposing" ceremonies, had been consecrated that day. How any one, in the shape of a human being, can be taken with such things, I cannot tell! Even a little child present, not five years of age, after observing the marches and counter-marches, and changing of dresses, and tall candles, and little bells, and genuflections, &c. &c., remarked to her mother, "Ma, I am tired; let's go; I don't like this kind of circus!" Infatuated ones! when will they come back to the simplicity of the gospel, and the good sense of primitive times?

As the first steamer which was to leave Galveston for New Orleans was to start on the Sabbath, and as I was earnestly requested by brother H. and others to remain and wait the next boat, which was to leave on the Friday following, I consented; but, as the weather for the most part proved very unfavourable, I did not preach as often as I desired. Some of our meetings, however, were crowded and deeply solemn, and although not more than one or two professed conversion, a goodly number were evidently much wrought upon; moreover, the people of God were much revived, and the pastor thinks that much good was done in various ways. When the period approached for me to leave, I received touching proofs of the kind regards of the people generally, and was urged by the much-esteemed pastor and others to remain a month, or at least a week longer.

It may not be improper for me to state, that here, as well as in several other places, I endeavoured to present the distinctive doctrines of our Church, with clearness, in all their beauty, and power, and heavenly charms; and such was the effect produced, that I was requested to have one sermon in particular published without delay; and to secure this, one of the most prominent members of the church handed me a piece of gold, and insisted upon paying me in advance for twenty copies. Almost overwhelmed with the kindness of the good people of Galveston, I left this beautiful city in the packet steamer, for New Orleans, on the 8th December.

Galveston is indeed a beautiful city; having broad streets, and many handsome houses, connected with which are gardens adorned with shrubbery, and laid off with great taste. Every thing looks clean and neat, and I noticed a vast improvement since the year 1840, the period of my first visit to that place. Besides the great Roman Catholic Cathedral, which I have mentioned, the Methodists, Baptists, Presbyterians, and Episcopalians, have each a neat church edifice, and so also have the German Methodists. The population, at the present time, numbers about five thousand; and although the city, in its commerce, has been injured by annexation, its prospects are still good. Brother H. has been pastor of the Presbyterian church in Galveston for about seven years; his labours have been faithful, and greatly blessed; and, having lately received and accepted a call to the church in Jackson, Mississippi, he will leave behind him many friends, and a name which will be as "ointment poured forth." Galveston, then, as well as Columbia, now calls for a new pastor. O that God would increase the number of our ministers a hundred-fold! The steamer in which I had embarked at Galveston having been detained off the Balize several hours by a dense fog, I did not reach the Crescent City until late on Sabbath afternoon. I preached one sermon on the boat, however; and on Monday evening I took another boat for Memphis, and arrived there in time to preach for brother Coons, of the First Church, on Sabbath morning. The next day, being the 18th, I had the happiness of returning to the bosom of my family, and receiving the affectionate greetings of the beloved people of my late charge.

Before leaving Texas I went, as before remarked, to Galveston, and preached several sermons, and would have preached more, but was prevented by the unfavourableness of the weather, and a slight indisposition. At this time, as I have said, brother Henderson, pastor of the church, was about leaving, having received an invitation to the church in Jackson, Mississippi. I advised brother Henderson to recommend the Rev. S. F. Cocke, of Lavaca, to succeed him. I returned to Holly Springs, intending to wind up my affairs, and have my commission renewed as a missionary in Texas. In a few weeks, however, I received an invitation to the church in Galveston, for one year. I accepted, and leaving my family in Holly Springs, I went on to Galveston in the winter of 1848, expecting my family to come on in the following spring; which, I think, was early in April of 1849.

It was at this period that Dr. Baker received a letter from Lafayette College, Easton, Pennsylvania, announcing to him that the degree of D. D. had been conferred upon him by that Institution. All his life he had great scruples in regard to being "called Rabbi" in any form. Yet it occurred to him that there might be as much ostentation in refusing the title as in adopting it. He pursued a middle course; took no step whatever in the matter. That he was grateful to the friends showing him this token of their kindness, was a matter of course; but it is not known that he, by letter, accepted, or in any other way assumed the title thus conferred.

Here it may be remarked for the information of those who did not know Dr. Baker personally, that he possessed a dignity of manner, and a refinement of bearing, such as are not popularly ascribed to a missionary toiling upon the frontier. The fact that he had passed his life—a large part of it at least—in the most intelligent and refined society in the land, is itself a guaranty of this, even if dignity and refinement of manner had not flowed inevitably from the depths of his piety. Those in whose houses he was a guest, will remember his scrupulous observance of all the proprieties of life, in the chamber as well as in the drawing-room. He was very impatient of any breach of even the minor courtesies of life on the part of ministers; and if the minister thus guilty was young, he failed not, if opportunity offered, to remonstrate gently with him, knowing that his usefulness might be greatly lessened by such things. A young brother who, absorbed in eating, permitted himself to forget the courtesies of the table, he gravely rebuked when alone with him. He may himself have failed in possessing what may be regarded as one of the accomplishments of life—being a good listener. If the topic was one in which he took no interest, he may have, at times, turned the subject of conversation too suddenly. His mind would occasionally travel off into some other path of thought, while being in the attitude of attention; he would occasionally interrupt; he would not unfrequently help out, with words of his own, some one whose thoughts or words did not flow as rapidly as his. His manner manifested somewhat of the hurry of one upon whom is devolved a large business; if this is thought excusable in a millionaire, may it not have been excusable in him? The extreme courtesy of his bearing, especially toward ladies, partook of the old-school stateliness, so rapidly vanishing away.

Possessed of a fund of information and anecdote, Dr. Baker was a most acceptable guest at the dinner table; and those who have been most with him, can hardly say whether he has caused them to weep or laugh most. The wonderful happiness of the man made his very presence as sunshine wherever he went. There was vigour, hope, joy, in his very eye; and all manifestly from the same divine source. Jesting, punning, anecdote merely for anecdote's sake, he greatly disliked; and irreverent quotations of Scripture, or any thing like jesting upon sacred themes, he regarded with abhorrence.

CHAPTER XII.

FOUNDING OF AUSTIN COLLEGE—LABOURS AS AN EVANGELIST, AND AS AN AGENT OF THE COLLEGE.

THE autobiography continued.

My labours in Galveston were not entirely in vain, for in a few months there was a very encouraging addition to the membership of the church. At the Fall meeting of the Presbytery, held, I think, in Washington, the subject of establishing a Presbyterian College in Texas was brought up. Something had been done, but not efficiently. The Rev. Mr. McCullough had, about two years before, been sent on to the North as Agent, and had obtained a considerable number of books, and money to the amount of about five hundred dollars. But Goliad having been the place fixed upon, and this location not having been much approved of, the matter was permitted to remain without any further action. I made a speech in Presbytery in favour of our making a renewed effort, and proposed that a committee of three should be appointed to fix upon some eligible place in middle Texas. The motion prevailed, and Messrs. Blair, Miller, and myself were appointed that committee. About this time I was urged by the Board of Missions to become their general missionary in Texas.

It is sometimes feared of evangelists that they will not "wear well" as settled pastors. A letter now lies before the writer, in which this fear was expressed of Dr. Baker, before he had entered upon his first pastoral charge. The reader of this volume need hardly be told, that in every church of which Dr. Baker was pastor, his influence in the community and the interest in his preaching knew nothing but steady increase, until the hour when some providence called him away from a reluctant people. The secret of this lay in his heart as well as his intellect; the one glowing with ever increasing emotions, the other ever expanding with unceasing study and reflection. It was the remark of one of the most intellectual men of the day in regard to this man of God, "Grace works in him like genius in other men." His sole wish and aim was to make perfectly clear to his hearers one truth; but that truth is an inexhaustible one, ever the most interesting of all truths here on earth; a theme which will be ever fresh throughout eternity. If he never decreased in interest, the merit lay in his theme, not in himself; hence he retained, from the time he first appeared in their pulpit to the day of his death, the heartfelt esteem and love of all the churches of which he was in turn pastor. Each of these churches followed him, in all his wanderings, with their prayers.

"Although Dr. Baker has been long absent from us," writes an elder of the Frankfort church, "yet are his faithful and self-denying labours for our spiritual good remembered by those who enjoyed the privilege of hearing the divine message from his lips, with a tender and sincere affection rarely seen in this world of change." This brings us to an incident of this period of his life, furnished by the same elder.

"In 1848, nearly twelve years after Dr. Baker had left this charge, we learned from the religious journals that he had engaged as a missionary of the Domestic Board, to travel in Texas. At the suggestion of the Superintendent of the Sabbath-school of our church, the school resolved to adopt him as their missionary, and do what they could towards his support. The fact was communicated to him by the agent of that Board, when he immediately addressed the following letter to the school, which was printed, and each scholar furnished with a copy.

"GALVESTON, Texas, *July 20th*, 1849.

"To the Sabbath-school Children of the Frankfort Presbyterian Church.

"MY DEAR YOUNG FRIENDS—Some time ago I received a very pretty letter from the Rev. Mr. Sturdevant, who visited your school, I presume, not long before. He was much pleased, and said some things to me in his letter which touched my heart, and made me love the people of Frankfort, and especially your Sunday-school, more than ever. Would you like to know what he said? Well, I will tell you: He said that when he visited your school, he found many Sabbath-school teachers who had been in that school when I was pastor of the church, and that they had not forgotten me, but 'still cherished my memory with great affection, and were making my name as familiar among the children as that of St. Patrick in Ireland!' This remark made me smile, and yet pleased me very much. Why I smiled, you can guess very well; and why I was pleased I need not tell you, for you know we all love to have our friends, whom we love, to think and talk kindly of us, especially when we are far away, and have not seen each other for a long time. God bless them, every one; and if we never see each other again on earth, may we meet in heaven! But Mr. Sturdevant, in his letter, said something else, which touched my heart more than all, and I could scarcely keep from shedding tears when I read it. He said that your school had agreed to adopt me as their missionary in Texas, and had given him a pledge to bring in a monthly contribution for my support. This was very kind indeed. It showed a kind regard for me, and, what is better still, a great love for the cause of Christ, and for poor perishing sinners too. And Mr. Sturdevant also mentioned that when, a little after they heard that I was killed by the Indians—which made them all very sad—they did still give a considerable sum to the missionary cause. Children, when I read this letter my heart was quite melted within me, and I felt as I had not for a long time. May heaven richly reward your beloved Sabbath-school teachers, and yourselves, for every kind thing done and said for me, for Texas, and for the cause of Domestic Missions!

"The sad account of my having been killed and scalped by the savages, was not true, as every body now knows; but many persons did believe it at the time. It was all a mistake: God protected me. But, dear children, I was in danger, for I was near where the Indians were; and I got an arrow, all stained with blood, which had been taken out of the body of a white man who had been killed near the place where I was. If I can, I will send it to you, and when you see it, all stained with blood, it will make you think of the one who had been chosen as your missionary; and I hope will also make you think how good your Heavenly Father was to me, for there were twenty persons killed by the Indians, and I was not far off, and I might have been killed too. But although I did not fall by the Indian arrow, I was in great danger more than once, in crossing swollen streams; and, children, once I was LOST, and began to think I would have at last to lie down in the lonely prairie and die, far away from house and home, without a friend to close my eyes, or dig my grave! One night I camped out alone, and did not dare to sleep a wink, because the wolves and panthers were around me, howling and making ugly noises, almost all night long; but God protected me again, and I think I ought to be very thankful, especially as I heard, soon after, of a man upon whom a panther sprang; and of another, who being lost, like myself, had to lie down and die, and was not found until he had been dead several days.

"But kindly preserved through all these dangers and difficulties, now I am in Galveston, a beautiful city, on an island, having water all around. We have a fine beach on the sea-shore, and while I am writing, I hear the roaring of the surf. I have a nice church, and a flourishing Sunday-school; we have more than one hundred scholars, and they all seem very glad when Sunday comes, that they may go to Sunday-school. We have a little box, and the children come up and drop in their dimes and half dimes on the first Sabbath in every month, and it seems to please them very much; and well it may, for who knows but what they give to the missionary cause may be the means of leading some grown persons, and some dear children too, to heaven. I am going to be a missionary again, and in this same Texas. O, children, you do not know how much we need Presbyterian preachers in this State. We want fifty or sixty, and we have not more than ten. I wrote a long letter some time ago, and it was printed in a great many papers. I begged our young preachers to come to Texas, for they were needed very much here—more, perhaps, than in any place in the world. But it seems I cannot get any to come; so I thought, old man as I am, I would leave Galveston, and go out into the wilderness, and woods, and prairies of Texas, and try to get the people, who do not see our preachers often, to think about their souls, and break off from their sins, and love the sweet and blessed Saviour, who died for us all. Children, are you not sorry for those in Texas who have nobody to preach to them, and nobody to gather their poor dear children into Sunday-schools? Well, I hope you will do something for them.

"As I am still alive, and wish to go as a preacher up and down through this much neglected State of Texas, if you still would like to adopt me as your missionary, or if you wish to help the Board who wish me to be their missionary, you must get your Superintendent to write to Mr. Sturdevant, and tell him what you are willing to do. I think this will please him very much, and the Board too, and, what is a thousand times better than all, I think it will please your Heavenly Father, and may be the means of saving many precious souls, who, in heaven, will love you much for thinking so kindly of, and caring for them. And remember, dear children, if you wish to try to get some of the people in Texas to go to heaven, you must be sure to try to get to heaven yourselves. O, it is a sweet place, a blessed place; and if you get there you will be as angels, with your crowns so bright, and your robes so white. I do believe that there are a great many children there already, and many others are on their way to that happy world now. A little girl, only thirteen years of age, joined my church last Sabbath; she was permitted by the Session to sit down at the table of the Lord, and take the sacrament. She seemed very happy, and I do believe she is a real Christian. Would you not like to be real Christians too, and go to heaven when you die? Then you must pray to God to give you a new heart, and make you good children. I used to live in Frankfort; I used to preach in your church, and talk to your school; but I don't know that I shall ever be in Frankfort again. Many of you, I suppose, never saw me. No matter; if we get to heaven, we will see and love each other there; and there we will see our blessed Saviour, and the holy angels, and all our pious friends, and be so happy for ever and ever! God bless you all, my dear children, and bless your dear parents, and your beloved Sabbath-school teachers too. Amen! and Amen!

"Your very sincere friend,

DANIEL BAKER."

Autobiography continued.

I accepted of the appointment before mentioned, and entered upon the labours of a general missionary, with the view of also carrying out the wishes of the Presbytery touching the selection of a proper location for our contemplated College. During this tour I visited numerous places, preaching as I had opportunity, and holding protracted meetings where such were desired. Amongst the meetings held was one at Palestine, East Texas, in company with brother Becton. This meeting proved a delightful one. Some twenty persons were hopefully converted. Upon the close of the meeting, we organized a church consisting of about eighteen members. Three elders were chosen and set apart to their office; one of whom was Judge T., one of the recent converts. Two days after his professed conversion, he was made a ruling elder. This may seem to have been rather hasty, but in his piety and fitness for the office, there was but one opinion; and his subsequent course has proved that the choice was a good one.

I had as yet never been in Huntsville, Middle Texas; but having heard a favourable account of the place, I went there, and held a protracted meeting, which lasted a few days. This meeting was blessed to the hopeful conversion of a few souls, of whom one, Major W. H., was subsequently made an elder.

As the meeting drew to a close, I mentioned to some of the prominent citizens of the place that the Presbytery of Brazos had resolved to take measures for the establishment of a Presbyterian College somewhere in Middle Texas. I told them I was pleased with Huntsville, and wished to know if the citizens desired the College to be established there. A town meeting was immediately called. Colonel Y., Mr. W., and other gentlemen made speeches in favour of the enterprise. Subscription papers were then put into circulation, and in a few days some eight thousand dollars were subscribed, to be paid in five equal annual instalments, "for the erection and support of a College by the Presbyterian Church, at or within a mile of Huntsville, Texas; to be called Baker College." I was told of the unexpectedly large amount subscribed, but for several weeks I could not get a sight of the paper, nor did I ever dream of such a name being given to it. When the secret was at last made known to me, I instantly, but in a respectful way, declined the honour.

The letter which follows was addressed at this time to his son in Galveston.

"HUNTSVILLE, *August 10th*, 1849.

"MY DEAR SON—Did you ever!—rain, rain, rain! Streams swollen—bridges gone—the whole land flooded! I have had to 'rough it' indeed. With great difficulty I managed to reach this place on Sunday morning in time to preach, after riding until near nine o'clock the preceding night, and fourteen or fifteen miles in the morning. Many had given me out; yet we had a very large congregation, and I never saw persons more eager for preaching. Weather and walking for the most part exceedingly bad; almost ashamed to think of calling the people out; and yet the congregations surprisingly large. I hope much good will be done here. Broached the idea of our locating a College here. People wonderfully in favour of it; will subscribe, as I am told, liberally. One gentleman of standing says he thinks ten thousand acres of land can be obtained, and a large amount in money; and General Houston, I am told, says that it would be a greater advantage to the place to have a Presbyterian College located here, than to have the place made the seat of government. My mission is truly an important one. God grant I may be enabled to give a new and great impulse both to the cause of religion and education.

"Huntsville is a pleasant place, and the country around very beautiful—rolling and picturesque—water good and abundant—many mill seats—country healthy, &c. The very place, I think, for our College. Monday, 13th. Had an immense crowd yesterday; very general seriousness; many awakened; some few, I hope, converted; prospects encouraging. My mission is a great one, a glorious one. I am likely to do ten times more good in the country than in Galveston. I hope the Lord will cause my influence to be felt most extensively and happily throughout the whole State.

"Your affectionate father,

DANIEL BAKER."

(TO HIS DAUGHTER.)

"MONTGOMERY, Texas, *September 1st*, 1849.

"MY DEAR AND ONLY DAUGHTER—I have not written a single line since I left Galveston; and lest you should become a little jealous, I must rob your mother of another letter intended for her, and address this to you. The month of August has been a busy one to me. I rode two hundred miles; preached fifty times; baptized two adults; ordained three elders; received several to the communion; paved the way for organizing one church, and wrote some dozen letters or more. This, I think, will do for 'a venerable father going down the steeps of old age,' especially in the month of August! And another thing—during the same month I broached the idea of locating a Presbyterian College at Huntsville, and had a subscription to the amount of seven thousand eight hundred dollars placed in my hand, and the assurance of another subscription of one hundred thousand acres of land! If every month in the year I can do as much as this in the wilds of Texas, neither I, nor anybody else can regret that I exchanged the pleasant life of a pastor for the laborious one of a missionary.

"My health is still good, only I confess I feel a little jaded; and to tell you the truth, I could, just at this time, enjoy very well a week's repose in the bosom of my family, hearing you and your mother sing, 'Home, sweet home;' and I do think if I had a pair of wings I would have paid you a flying visit before this time. But here I am in the midst of a glorious missionary field, far away from my family, but doing some good I hope; and I must say, that of late I have thought more frequently than usual upon these words of our Saviour—'I must work the work of Him that sent me, while it is day, for the night cometh when no man can work.' And I will add, that sometimes, like the hireling spoken of by the man of Uz, I am ready to long for the shades of evening, that I may enter upon my rest. Indeed, the other day, my feelings were almost overwhelming, while I heard some sweet voices singing these beautiful lines:

'See the kind angels at the gates,
Inviting us to come,
There, Jesus, the forerunner waits,
To welcome travellers home.'

"This is the principle upon which we should act in all things. The bright side! The bright side! Always look upon the bright side! Love to your mother—to all.

"Yours affectionately,

DANIEL BAKER."

Autobiography continued.

At my request, Col. Yoakum drew up the charter of the College, making such alterations as I suggested. Availing myself of the earliest opportunity, I laid the charter before brothers Wilson and Miller, preparatory to its being submitted for the action of the Presbytery. Fearing that Judge G., of Grimes county, an influential member of the Senate, would oppose the charter on account of its denominational character, I called upon him, spent a night with him, and made such statements and explanations as entirely satisfied him; and from being, as was supposed, a decided opponent, he became a warm friend and advocate of the charter. At the next meeting of the Presbytery, which was held at Independence, in the study of brother Wilson, the charter was submitted, and every section and feature carefully scanned. An attempt was made to postpone the final action of the Presbytery on the subject, on the ground that the brethren of the West were not present. "Does not courtesy to our brethren of the West require this postponement?" said one brother. "No, Moderator," said I, "a postponement will be a death-blow, for the Legislature meets biennially, and if we do not get a charter at the coming session of the Legislature, we cannot get it for two years, and this will discourage those who have so liberally subscribed."

Whilst discussing, afterwards, some point in the charter upon which there was some diversity of opinion, another member of the Presbytery arose and remarked, "Had we not better, Moderator, not decide just now, but write on to some of the Colleges at the North, and see what their charters are?" Much excited at such a motion, which, if carried, would ruin the whole affair, I arose and said, "Moderator, we have understanding enough to frame our own charter; and I tell you again, any such postponement will be equivalent to a complete relinquishment of the enterprise." Happily, all objections were overruled, and a committee was appointed to secure the needful charter.

When the naming of the Institution was called up, I found that there was a communication from the original subscribers, requesting the Presbytery to sanction the name originally given. I was asked if I would consent. I again declined the honour proposed to be done me. Retiring, that the Presbytery might not be trammelled by my presence, the matter was discussed, and when I came in again, I found that the Institution was named AUSTIN COLLEGE, in honour of Stephen F. Austin, the great Texas pioneer.

Soon after the meeting of Presbytery, Dr. Baker wrote as follows to his son at Galveston.

"WASHINGTON, Texas, *October* 16*th*, 1849.

"MY DEAR SON—We had a harmonious meeting of Presbytery. Brothers Miller, Wilson, Becton, F., and myself present, and four ruling elders. All things went off very well. We have fixed upon Huntsville as the seat of our literary institution, and have named it Austin College—certainly a much better name than the one originally intended. I am for prompt action, and my motto is, 'Strike, while the iron is hot.' Some things were started in Presbytery, such as waiting to have a fuller meeting of Presbytery, and waiting until we could get the form of what was called a Constitution from some of the northern seminaries; but these things were promptly met and put down. We had a constitutional meeting of Presbytery, and if other brethren did not come, we regret it, but we had power to act without them; and how did we know that we should have a larger meeting on the 22d of next month? How did we know that we should then even have a quorum?

I like 'delicacy,' and 'courtesy,' and all that, but, in a noble enterprise, I like prompt action and success more.

"I do think that God is with us, and, in due time, glorious results will crown this noble enterprise. Mr. —— seems to think that I am a little too sanguine, a little too headlong; but I mature matters a little more carefully than he supposes. If he knew the process of reasoning by which I came to my conclusions, he would rather say '*Euge!*' than 'Don't go so fast;' and the fact is, I have seen so many wretched failures, purely from want of zeal, determination, and prompt action, that my mind is perhaps more braced up than otherwise it would be. Only think! the scheme of a College started nearly ten years ago, and even the foundation not yet laid! And the tract of land offered to me by Mr. Perry, for the College, suffered to pass out of our hands!—which tract of land has since been sold, as I have been informed, for two thousand dollars! O, procrastination! thou art not only 'the thief of time,' but the conqueror of all good purposes! My son, receive your father's counsel—Never put off till to-morrow what ought to be done to-day.

"I have cold water thrown upon me on all sides; but I am resolved to feel it no more than the marble statue, upon which pours a perpetual shower, at the Fairmount water-works, near Philadelphia. I shall endeavour to have a good reason for every thing I do and say, and then go ahead. A long time ago, Mrs. Hoge remarked, 'Daniel Baker is always blundering; but somehow or other, he always blunders right.' The secret of the thing is this—I endeavour to look at things in all their bearings; and if I seem to step from one hill to another, it is not because I have not walked over every inch of the intervening ground, but because I do not think it necessary to point out every foot-print which I have made. Another thing is this: there are promises in the Bible, such as, 'Acknowledge the Lord in all thy ways, and he shall direct thy paths;' and, 'If any man lack wisdom,' &c. What is the use of having promises, if we do not make use of them? No more than having land or money, and making no use of it.

"I wish you—mother, sister, brother, and all—to be void of care, and just as happy as possible; even as happy as I am, when I think I am serving my Master, and doing good. I have been appointed by Presbytery to visit the old States, to solicit contributions.

"Should any Princeton student come, be sure to remember my 'letter.' If sister N. should come, your mother would find some way to accommodate her; aye, and even Dr. O., should he come along with her. If your father can sleep upon the ground, when engaged in the cause of Christ, I am sure that any son of mine, or even my only daughter, to accomplish a good object, would be willing for a night or two to sleep upon a pallet.

"Your almost too affectionate father,

DANIEL BAKER."

With a heart pained at the destitution he had witnessed in his journeying through Texas, he addressed a letter to the students of Princeton Seminary, dated Galveston, March 2d, 1849, which was published in the *New Orleans Presbyterian.* After detailing the necessities of the State, he adds:

"Let it not be forgotten, that he who comes to this State must be no drone, nor speculator in lands. He must be a man of God, indeed; a man of intelligence and zeal; a man, like Barnabas, full of faith and the Holy Ghost; and, like Paul, 'in labours more abundant.' Come then, dear young brethren," exclaims this venerable pioneer for Christ, who invited them into no path in which he had not trodden before himself—"come on the wings of love; come in the exercise of faith and prayer; come prepared to do the work of an Evangelist, and make full proof of your ministry. Come in this spirit, and you need fear nothing. I tell you plainly, we have no beds of roses here; but we have wide fields of usefulness. We have no California gold here; but we have many precious souls, which, as jewels, may be safely casketted for eternity."

At the meeting of the Presbytery of Brazos, then the only Presbytery in the State, in July of the same year he obtained the appointment of a committee to address a call for aid, to the ministers and members of the Church in the old States, in behalf of Texas; and, as chairman of that committee, addressed to them, through the papers, a thrilling appeal.

These appeals did not have the effect in full which he greatly desired; for, writing to the Secretary of the Board of Domestic Missions, December 12th, 1851, he says: "The tide of immigration is flowing upon us surprisingly, but scarcely any ministers of our communion coming in upon this tide. What are we to do? We call, but they will not come. Brother Jones, I have lately had a new idea. Despairing of efficient aid from the old States, I think we must raise up preachers amongst ourselves. The other day this idea flashed upon me with great force; and now, when I see a promising young man in the Lord, I make it a practice to tap him upon the shoulder and say, 'Young man, are you sure it is not your duty to preach the gospel?' I am happy to say there are now some four or five in the circle of my acquaintance in Texas who have the ministry in view. The Lord increase the number of such an hundred-fold. Our College enterprise is still in a prosperous state; I trust it will be a great blessing to Texas and our Church."

Yes, let it be for ever remembered by the Church in Texas—let it be distinctly impressed upon the minds of the Trustees and Faculty of Austin College in all succeeding generations—the one idea of its founders, that for which they wept, and prayed, and toiled, and gave of their means, was that it might be an institution wherein there might be raised up for Texas, generation after generation, a native ministry. For all generations to come, then, palsied be the hand which shall ever cast a ballot to alienate the institution in any way from this, the main purpose of its existence—that sacred purpose which prompted its aged servant to travel and to beg as he did; and which was one motive, at least, which prompted the free contributions of many thousand Christian givers over the land—givers whose eyes will ever rest upon the institution, watching for the fruits therein of their giving. So long as Austin

College shall number one learner within its walls, withered be the tongue of any teacher therein who shall utter a syllable which has a tendency to prevent, in the case of a single student, the accomplishment of this, the chief and holy object for which, above all others, the College was conceived, born, and reared.

At the time Dr. Baker prepared these last pages of his narrative, his mind was so much occupied with unfolding the earliest history of the College—the history of an institution for which his brethren and himself hoped so much—that he entirely forgot to make any allusion to an excursion of a more purely missionary character than any he had ever made before. From the hour he was a student in College, he had laboured here and there over almost every county, not to say State, in the Domestic Missionary field. He is now permitted the, to him, rare privilege and pleasure of walking and working along its outmost boundary line; even of crossing that line into the darkness beyond. In this way.

About December, 1849, he returned to Galveston from his missionary travels in the interior of the State. Arriving in Galveston at the close of the day, he takes his seat at the supper-table of his son, then in temporary charge of the church there, wearied with his journeyings. At the table, the conversation is turned upon the destitute region along the Rio Grande, unvisited then, so far as was known, by ministers of any denomination. The weariness of the travel-stained missionary is forgotten as he converses; the ruling passion of his soul is aroused. How delightful to preach Christ in these "regions beyond!" When he is rested, he really must seek some means, if possible, of visiting that dividing line of Protestantism and Popery. The opportunities of visiting that region are few, and the mode of travel exceedingly inconvenient and unpleasant. "What matters it," says the man of God, "shall any one be able to find his way there for *any* purpose, and not the preacher of the gospel?" The son then casually mentions, that in passing along the wharves that day he had seen a small vessel which was to sail for the mouth of the Rio Grande. "When?" asks the father. "To-morrow," is the answer. "I will go in her," is the immediate and characteristic reply.

Early next morning the writer accompanied his father to the wharves. There lies the little sailing vessel; so very small, so heaped with rigging, and barrels, and boxes, there seemed to be no room even to sit. The passenger makes a place for himself, valise in hand, upon the narrow deck; the lines are loosed; the little barque drifts off; then its sails are raised, and, leaning perilously to one side, it glides rapidly away; the white hair of the aged missionary can be seen no more; and even the gleam of the white canvass is soon lost in the blue horizon. As the writer watched the outward flight of the tiny barque bearing its precious freight, he almost blamed himself for letting his father know of the vessel, even though his own heart could not but glow, if it were only from sympathy, in the object to be accomplished. The following lines, in pencil, a few days afterward, relieved him of any apprehension of the safety of the missionary so far.

"MOUTH OF RIO GRANDE, *December* 23*d*, 1849.

"MY DEAR SON—This morning, Sabbath, I preached to almost the whole population of this place, about fifty; the first sermon ever preached here. Not a single professor of religion present, I believe, save the pious sailor who hands you this. Only think, about fifty accountable creatures, and only one who makes, I believe, any pretension to religion! Is not a missionary needed?

"After the service was over, a person at the door held out his hat, and, to my perfect surprise, the amount thrown in, four dollars and forty cents, was placed in my hands. I expressed my surprise, and mentioned that I desired nothing. But, no—I must take what was so freely offered. I am sure it was a free-will offering, for some gentlemen who had retired before the hat was held out, came in and insisted upon giving something, saying that they were much pleased with the sermon, &c. I am to preach again in the afternoon, and at night. May the Master bless my labours here. Excuse this scrawl; no ink at hand.

"Your affectionate father,

DANIEL BAKER."

It need hardly be remarked, that in all cases of donation as above, the sums given were accounted for to the Board of Missions as deducting that much from the salary due him from it.

Beginning at the mouth of the Rio Grande, he visited and preached at every inhabited hamlet up this river. In Brownsville, the largest place on the American side, he made some stay, preaching with considerable success. From this place he thus writes to his daughter.

"BROWNSVILLE, *December*, 26*th* 1849.

"MY DEAR DAUGHTER—Well, here I am in Brownsville! Yes, in the far-famed town of Brownsville, on the Rio Grande! But I must tell you all about matters and things. Last Sabbath I preached at the 'Mouth' three sermons. Every person in the place came out to hear me, I was informed, except two or three; and a right solemn meeting we had, particularly at night. On Monday morning I was anxious to push on for Brownsville, about thirty miles distant. A steamer was expected in a day or two, but as there was some uncertainty about the thing, and I was impatient to go on, in connection with two or three other gentlemen, as anxious to get on as myself, I chartered a—horse and cart! and came rattling on over a fine road in great style! You never saw such a country in all your life! Not a single forest tree between this and the 'Mouth,' nor for hundreds of miles around, except what is called the mesquit, the ebony, and the marmosa, which in general are about the size of ordinary peach-trees—and no houses—not even log-cabins! Here and there, at great distances, you find a ranche, a kind of shanty or hovel, made of cane, and thatched with a kind of grass, or rush; a miserable shelter. These wretched hovels are filled with lazy Mexicans, who lounge about from one year's end to another, doing almost literally nothing at all, except gambling. On Monday last, our chariot, (*alias* cart,) about one o'clock stopped at one of these ranches, where we fed our horse, and feasted on some cheese and pilot-bread which we had along with us. To make our dinner more sumptuous, I bought a *pollonci;* and I must say I never enjoyed a snack more in all my life.

"While tarrying at this ranche, several Mexicans were playing cards—gambling. The quarter of a dollar paid for horse-feed was gambled off before we resumed our journey. Our driver, or charioteer, not being a Son of Temperance, but one of John Barleycorn's children, found it a little difficult to plumb the road, but, drunkard fashion, went, as it were, reeling along; and he was particularly unskilful on this occasion, as he was very wrathful with one of his cronies at the 'Mouth,' with whom he had intended to fight a duel that morning! O, what foolish talk, and what an amount of it; and by reason of his wrath and liquor he took a wrong road, and for some considerable time was going right away from Brownsville! I regretted this very much, as it prevented my reaching there in time to preach that night. About sun-set, however, I reached the wharf-boat, used as a tavern or hotel here, where I purposed to tarry that night; but as I had no opportunity of preaching, and there, in full view on the opposite side of the river, was Matamoras, I thought I would pass over and spend the night in that town, especially as Captain P. had kindly invited me to make his house my home.

"Leaving my trunk on the wharf-boat, that the Mexican custom-house officers might not be fingering my clothing, I went over in a ferry-boat to the other side of the river, for which I paid only six-and-a-quarter cents. I took a hack that was at hand, and had a pleasant ride into the heart of the city, about one mile distant, for which I paid only twelve-and-a-half cents. As the coachman and myself, in the matter of language, were barbarians to each other, I felt myself in a curious predicament. All I could say was 'Captain P., Captain P.,' but he knew not where he lived, and I was 'in a fix.' Set down on one corner of the plaza, I wandered along, and finally lighted upon a Frenchman, who, in broken English, gave me to understand where Captain P. lived. There I was cordially welcomed; and much pleased was I to find that Captain P's bride and her sister were Sabbath-school teachers, and members of the Presbyterian church. After supper the Captain took me to see the American Consul, whose lady is also a member of the Presbyterian church, the Consul being nominally a Presbyterian also. They gave me a most cordial welcome to Matamoras, and invited me to dine with them the next day; and also very kindly invited 'Doctor Baker' to make their house his home.

"That night, you will observe, was Christmas eve; and leaving the house of Mr. S., the American Consul, I went out with Captain P. by moonlight, to see the town, and the 'carryings on' in this part of the dominions of the 'Man of Sin.' We went down one street, and up another, seeing nothing worthy of observation, until we came to the market-house, and here was a crowd. Tables were spread, and stands were seen, upon which were placed cakes and fruits of various kinds; and another set of tables, around which were gathered a great many persons of the lower class, gambling; all standing, save the owner of the table, who was seated, handling the cards, and uttering words which, of course, I understood not. Whilst I was in company with Captain P., sauntering about, there came up a man, a priest! This man was also a gambler, and profane—but not a regular one—who was introduced to me, and very graciously invited the Captain and myself to go into a drinking establishment hard by, and *take a drink!* Declining the invitation, I agreed to wait until the Captain returned. Whilst waiting, three Mexicans came up to me, and seemed to be examining my person rather more curiously than I desired; but fortunately at that moment the Captain returned, and we went back to his house, and talked until it was time to go and see the cathedral, at twelve o'clock at night. I did not like much to mingle with such a crowd of Mexicans at that time of night, but went in. Soon the music struck up, and the ceremonies commenced. All at once they began to kneel; and thinking that I might get into a scrape, I made haste and went out. You will recollect that there are no seats in the cathedral, no roof, no floor! It is little better than an open enclosure, walled around; the altar being at one end, under a kind of tent. I suppose about one thousand or fifteen hundred persons were seen kneeling, literally upon the ground, within the walls of this great cathedral, the moon and stars having full permission to shine upon them.

"It was about half-past twelve when I returned with my kind friend, and upon a cot I sought repose; but there was no repose for me, there was such an outrageous noise! Besides the ringing of bells, and beating of drums, and shall I say, 'the sound of the cornet, flutes, harp, psaltery, sackbut, dulcimer, and all kinds of music'—besides all such sort of things, there was one thing of all others the most abominable, the voice of some three or four sentinels, placed on the top of some houses, singing out, every ten minutes, 'On the alert,' in Spanish, in a voice and with tones the most dismal and hideous that ever I heard in all my life. It was something like the caterwauling of cats, but vastly more unpleasant to the ear. And only think, I had to lie in my cot, and listen to this every ten minutes! I suppose, during the live-long night I did not sleep one half an hour. But I ought to have told you, that before the midnight ceremonies spoken of, the soldiers in the garrison had a grand supper. Seated at a long table, they were served by their officers, and every now and then there were '*vivas!*' given, which made the welkin ring again. As the establishment was adjoining Captain P's premises, we looked through a hole in the wall, and saw their capers; but not having as clear and extensive a view as we desired, we got a ladder, and getting upon the roof of Captain P's house, we had a full view. O, that night! how many curious sights and things were crowded into that Christmas-eve night!

"The next day I dined with the Consul, and taking a hack, came over to Brownsville, where I preached at night to a great crowd. So many persons came in, that additional benches had to be sent for. This was not expected. As there were so many fandangoes, &c., in town that night, it was thought we should not have very many. In the crowd were several of the officers of the army, of the highest grade, and their families. I must say, it is a long time since I had more pleasure in preaching. It was in Brownsville, and to a crowded and most attentive audience, who hung upon my lips, eager, it seemed, to catch every word. My sermon occupied one full hour; but there was no indication of restlessness. Indeed, it was remarked by a gentleman (and he not usually a church-going man) that he could have remained and listened three hours longer. I am the first regular Protestant preacher of any denomination that has ever preached in Brownsville. I feel much delighted that God has sent me here, and I hope he will bless abundantly my labours of love. I hope to have a good meeting to-night also.

"Rio Grande City and Roma, the only other towns of any importance on the left bank of the Rio Grande, are some three hundred miles higher up. I do not know, but I think it likely that I shall visit them before my return, which, I suppose, may be in some five or six weeks from this time.

DANIEL BAKER."

At every neighborhood visited by him he preached as often as possible, searched out such professors of religion as were to be found, and organized Sabbath-schools. He seems to have been treated with much respect as the "American Padre." At one place he rang the bell to assemble the people into the *jacal*, which was used for public meetings. Just as he entered upon the services he was entreated to be as brief as possible, as the place was wanted for a *fandango* the moment he was done.

It is believed that he was the first preacher of the

gospel whose voice was ever heard upon the Rio Grande. He would often speak of this excursion, remarking, in his playful manner, that it was the first time in his life that he had known a Presbyterian minister to be ahead of the Methodists! If he was indeed the first preacher there, as is believed, then should his name be recorded for ever as that soldier in the army of Emmanuel, who, in the inevitable westward march of that army, was permitted to stand in advance of all the rest upon this farthest border line. According to the eternal purpose and promise of God, the day shall dawn whose meridian sun shall sparkle upon the white folds of the banner of the cross, floating full and free over Mexico. When that day comes—and its coming already streaks the east with light—as the hearts of Christians swell with delight, gazing, from abroad and beneath it, upon that banner of peace and good-will, then let them not forget the name of him whom God so honoured as to permit, even in old age, to be the first to plant that banner upon the walls, at least, of the conquered realm.

(TO HIS WIFE.)

"RIO GRANDE CITY, *January* 11*th*, 1850.

"Here I am, high up on the Rio Grande. It seems to me to be, so to speak, almost out of the world. Only think! some three hundred and fifty miles from the mouth of the river, and, perhaps, nearly four hundred west of San Antonio. I reached this place about noon this day, and can write you but a very short letter, as the steamboat which takes the letter will start in a little while. This is a small, but apparently flourishing little town, and I expect to form a Sabbath-school here, and will probably remain and preach until some time next week, when it is my present purpose to go on to Roma, a similar town some fifteen miles higher up the river, and shall, I suppose, spend one Sabbath there, and then I expect to turn my face homeward, and shall hurry on to Galveston with all possible speed. But, I do assure you, it is very uncertain when I shall be able to get a passage from the Mouth. Only think, this is January 11th, and I have not seen the President's Message yet! . . . . . . God bless you, my dear wife, and all the members of our little circle.

"In haste, affectionately,

DANIEL BAKER.

"A prince from Germany is in the room in which I am writing. He has just shaken hands with me in a very cordial way."

In, perhaps, all the places at which he held meetings, he was urged to send ministers out to settle and organize churches, and most liberal promises were made of aid in erecting churches and in supporting ministers who should come. After his return to Galveston, he received from the same region most urgent letters to the same effect. The founders of new towns in the West, often reckless and irreligious men, even infidels, are perfectly aware that a school and a church are essential to the existence, not to say respectability and prosperity, of their new "city." Hence their first step, after laying out the town, toward the covering their lots with houses and their streets with citizens, is to obtain by liberal inducements a resident teacher and preacher. It is a resident preacher that is desired. In all new towns on our frontier, a minister of the gospel, it is universally acknowledged, effects far more for the cause of religion and morality out of the pulpit than in it. His Christian life, conversation, presence—if he be indeed a man of God—does more, during his six day's genial intermingling with the people, than all he can possibly say or do upon the Sabbath. Presbyterian ministers in new fields have a strong tendency to "settle down" in one spot; this diminishes the extent, but greatly increases the local strength of their influence. Thus, in the providence of God, the zealous circuit-preacher of other denominations, worthy as he is of all praise, and the quieter Presbyterian preacher, work together successfully, each doing a work for which he is better qualified than the other.

No one had a higher esteem than Dr. Baker for those noble servants of Christ, of other evangelical denominations, whose feet are so active to follow the backwoodsman with the gospel, wherever he goes, even into the very lair of the wolf and lurking place of the Indian. All honour to such men. He who has lived on the frontier well knows, that along the vast line of westward emigration, no neighbourhood of a half-dozen cabins, no family even in the narrow home of an emigrant wagon, is ever ahead of the preacher of the gospel of some evangelical denomination. Scarcely have the flying hoofs of the startled wild horse died in the distance, before the preacher is seen, Bible in hand, under the spreading live-oak. During the six days, the ring of the emigrant's axe, for the first time since creation, fills the woods with the sound of falling trees; but on the first day of the first week, the same woods are almost sure to awake to the homely but powerful voice of the circuit-rider, making the forests ring with the accents of salvation; and the new settlers will assemble for worship; and nowhere can be found a manlier or more shrewd audience, even though their eyes and ears are alert during the sermon, for the swaying bush and cat-like tread which betrays the approach of the Camanche.

"As I was riding last week across the prairie to an appointment," said a preacher to the writer, "I saw a Camanche, feathered and painted, coming right down upon me, fast as his horse could travel, lance in rest. I had nothing but an old umbrella; so I committed my soul to God, and rode steadily on, looking right in his face. He came full speed down upon me; but just as his lance was at my breast, he turned it aside and rode on, without drawing rein. I never looked behind, but blessed the Lord, and rode on to my appointment."

How near the subject of this Memoir came to a bloody death by these sons of Shem, driven back before the children of Japhet, we have already seen.

But to resume our narrative.

Arriving at the mouth of the Rio Grande, having effected all in his power as a missionary in that region, Dr. Baker was kindly offered a free passage in a vessel bound to Galveston. But it was not to sail for several days, and being impatient, in this crisis in the history of the College, to return at the speediest moment, he embarks on a small sailing craft, manned by a captain and one man, himself the only passenger. The captain assures him that in three days he will land him at Galveston. They set sail, when suddenly a *Norther* springs up, and the frail bark is driven near two hundred miles southward before it. After a week's tossing on the short, sudden billows of the Gulf Stream, in conflict with the fierce wind, the vessel again nears the coast at Aransas Bay, to be again driven southward. A week more passes. The wind abates; soon the land is in sight, near the mouth of the Sabine, far east of their destination. It is almost possible to throw a biscuit ashore. Again the Norther sweeps down upon them, and this time the fragile shallop and its three voyagers is driven helplessly southward, far from land, among billows upon which the vessel tosses like a nut-shell. Meanwhile, the provisions intended for a three days' run have almost given out, and the water too, though both these have been doled out with the utmost care, in quantities barely sufficient to support life.

To add to the trouble, the captain finds that the only man he has shipped as his crew, pretended to be a sailor only to secure a passage to Galveston, knows nothing whatever about even handling a rope, much less holding the helm. Frantic with rage from the first, the captain curses and beats his man during all hours of the day. As the passenger can render no assistance, he remains under deck, in the miserable little berth. The deck is but a few inches over his face as he lies, and during the raging of the storm, he hears the furious cursing of the captain, and the heavy blows which he inflicts upon his only assistant. In the morning, as he stands upon the careened and slippery deck, he sees it spattered with the blood of the beaten man. The storm rages more and more. At last the captain announces to his passenger that they must go down; and falling on his knees, with his arm around the straining mast, the man calls loudly upon the Virgin for help, vowing the largest candles for her altar, if once he is permitted to land. Dr. Baker remarks to the man, that giving up his profanity and ferocity would be far more acceptable to the God of the storm; and then descends, lies in his berth, and calmly resigns himself to the will of God. "Never, in all my life," he afterwards remarked to the writer, "did I feel more perfectly calm than when I expected each plunge of the vessel would be to the bottom. I was enabled by prayer to acquiesce entirely in the will of God. Was I not in the path of duty?"

But God has work still for his aged servant. Many hundreds of souls are at that moment far from the Saviour, whom he is to be made the instrument of leading to Christ; and not yet is the College in that condition to dispense with the labours of this man of God. Again the storm subsides at the divine command, and after an almost unparalleled tempest of three weeks upon the raging gulf, in a bark almost too frail for use on a peaceful lake, reduced to their last atom of food and drop of water, the passenger is permitted to land once more, but north of the Sabine, far from his port. A few days more, and he arrives safely in the bosom of his family, in his usual health and spirits, all the more ready from gratitude to God for whatever duties lie before him. He had purchased in Matamoras, among other Mexican curiosities, a few *polonces*, sugar cones wrapped in shucks of corn, for his family, and these he brought with him safely; even hunger could not force him to use them; it was characteristic.

It should be added, that the captain, though rough in his manners, like most men of his profession, was nevertheless both kind and respectful to his passenger, whose very aspect awed and restrained even the rudest. After landing, he draughted and presented to his passenger a chart of the tortuous course they had sailed. In memory of those perilous hours, Dr. Baker caused this chart to be handsomely copied and hung upon the walls of his study, where it still remains, both a curiosity and a precious memento of him whose life's voyage is now ended, and whose sails are for ever furled in the haven of eternal rest.

Autobiography continued.

The charter was signed by Gov. Wood on the 22d day of November, 1849, and the first meeting of the Trustees was held in Huntsville on the 5th of April, 1850. "Present: Daniel Baker, R. Smither, J. Hume, G. C. Reed. H. Yoakum, J. Branch, Sam Houston, by his proxy H. Yoakum, H. Wilson, and J. C. Smith, by his proxy S. R. Smith." On motion, I was appointed President *pro tem.* The next day, A. J. Burke and J. W. Miller appeared, and also took their seats as members. The Rev. S. McKinney, whom I had urged to come to Texas from Holly Springs, and for whom I had obtained the situation of teacher in the Male Institute in Huntsville, was present, and was elected President of the College. At this meeting of the Board, the site for the college building was fixed upon. Two places had been offered—Capitol Hill, on the south, and Cotton-Gin Hill, on the north of the town. I had, in my own mind, fixed upon the latter place; and supposing there might be a few votes against it, and wishing the vote in favour to be recorded as unanimous, I rose up and made a speech, stating how important was unanimity in the case before us, and expressing a desire that when the will of the majority was ascertained, the minority would yield with a good grace. Col. H. and Dr. B. were the only ones that I supposed would vote for Capitol Hill. They sat in front of me; and when I expressed an earnest hope that the minority, upon the will of the majority being ascertained, would yield, I thought Col. H. and Dr. B. looked as though that would be a bitter pill for them to swallow. Well, the vote was taken, and lo and behold, Capitol Hill carried the day by an overwhelming majority! I was left nearly solitary and alone in my vote. Immediately there was a roar of laughter, and every eye was turned upon me, to see how I would take the pill intended for others. Without a wry face, however, I complied with my own prescription, and swallowed it down. "Gentlemen," said I, "I am an American, every inch of me. Let the majority rule. You have seen proper to make choice of Capitol Hill. Be it so; I yield. Let Capitol Hill be the site of our College."

On the 6th of April, 1850, I was appointed Permanent General Agent, with a salary of one thousand dollars per annum. Shortly after my appointment, I received first a verbal, and some weeks after, a written communication from the Rev. B. Chase, of Natchez, Mississippi, stating that he had some lands in Texas, which he was willing to donate to Austin College. This was as the rising of the morning star upon our noble enterprise; it cheered us greatly. A few days after my appointment, I set out upon my first tour, and was absent from home some seven or eight months.

During this, as during all his absences, Dr. Baker seized every opportunity to write to his family, extracts from which letters are inserted in their order. On the shaking table of the steamer, at the hotel, at the roadside cabin, by the fireside of a friend, at every chance interval of rapid travel—at any moment when, glowing from the street, the parlour, or the pulpit, he could get the opportunity, he would dash off a running account of passing events. His letters teem with a thousand various plans, and hopes, and brilliant expectations in regard to the College. What if many of these came to nought—blossoms blooming their moment, then falling to the ground, bearing in their wilted bosom their abortive promise of fruit?—faster than they perished, other plans, hopes, and expectations arose in his rapid career, blotting out even the memory of disappointments. Every letter fairly overflows with his own happy and sparkling spirit. Unless absolutely necessary, unpleasant things he never mentioned—why should he? The manifold disagreeable incidents inseparable from such an agency as his, are thrown into the shade completely, as fast as they occur, by the pleasing incidents which sprang incessantly from under his active hand like sparks from under the hammer of the smith. A letter from him was eagerly opened, with a confident feeling of pleasure as to the unknown contents; much as one breaks from off a box of precious ointment a seal bearing a well-known and approved stamp—the exhilarating contents could be certainly counted upon—the spirit of almost rapturous piety as a matter of course.

It was intended to prepare a list of the places visited by Dr. Baker while travelling as agent for Austin College; but this was found impossible; the points are too numerous, and his movements were too rapid. During his long career from his entrance into the ministry, as an evangelist, missionary, pastor, and agent, he held meetings in hundreds of places over all portions of the Union, of which there is little or no mention made in this volume. Throughout this work, it has been the care of the compiler to condense into as small a compass as possible this narrative of the life and labours of his father. Will he be pardoned if he says, that there is such a warmth, and depth, and ever-fluctuating, ever-sparkling ocean-swell in the history of such a man, as to make the keeping that history within due bounds the most difficult part of his whole undertaking.

The letters from which extracts are made below are used with reluctance, and only because they furnish almost the only history of the work of grace under his preaching. Apart from the instrument used by God, and leaving him out of consideration entirely, the work of the Holy Spirit, as nar rated in these letters, is worthy of record for its own sake, and to His glory. And let the reader bear in mind, that these were letters written by a husband and father, in the unreserved confidence of a warm heart—never intended for the eyes of any but the beloved ones to whom they were addressed. A large part of each letter has necessarily to be suppressed, for family and other reasons. This must account for and excuse the mutilated appearance of the extracts.

Early one spring morning, the stage drove to his door at Huntsville. The writer assisted him into it, shook hands with him, and was about to close the stage-door, no longer to detain the impatient driver, and still more impatient horses. But, again grasping the hand of his son, the father drew him toward him, and said, in subdued and rapid tones, "My son, my dear son, I may never return; if so, remember you are a servant of Christ. Be sure you give your whole heart to the work—good-by:" and the stage rolled rapidly away, bearing him off as agent of the College, upon his first tour.

"NEW ORLEANS, *May 6th*, 1850.

"MY DEAR SUSAN—I am just on the wing for Cincinnati. I am happy to inform you that I meet with smiles on every hand. The College enterprise is considered a noble one. Some persons subscribe for the sake of learning and Texas, and some because of their friendship for me, and the remembrance of days gone by. I could mention some very touching things; but suffice it to say, I did not know that the poor old Texan missionary had so many warm friends in other places. Really, I meet with so many marks of respect and affection, that I can scarcely realize I am the same person who wandered in the prairies and wilds of Texas. But the best of it is, to have my spiritual children, of whom I had previously no knowledge, taking me by the hand, and expressing their overflowing gratitude for benefits received, by my instrumentality, so many years ago. God be thanked! God be thanked, that I ever was permitted to preach to dying sinners the unspeakable riches of Christ!

"I have succeeded in my agency far beyond my most sanguine expectations. Besides remitting three hundred and seventy-seven dollars, there are good subscriptions for something like five or six hundred dollars more. The bell of the steamboat is about to ring, so, with much love to all, I subscribe myself,

"Yours, most affectionately,

DANIEL BAKER."

Dr. Baker proceeded to Brooklyn, where he supplied for a time the pulpit of Dr. Jacobus, then in Europe for his health. A gentleman, in whose amiable family he was a guest at this time, thus speaks, among other remarks, in a letter to the compiler of this volume:

"It was in the year 1850 your father became an inmate of my family, for the short period of three or four weeks, at which time we saw much of that Christian character which so adorned his whole life. While far away from his home it could not be said he was among strangers, for his bearing was such, that a very short acquaintance made him a friend among friends. What made him so especially dear to us, was that cheerful Christian spirit which was so manifest in all his walk and conversation. Few could help being drawn towards him; even the child, to whom he became as a child. His prayers were those of a man of God, sincere and earnest, and, I think, were not uttered in vain for those who had the privilege of enjoying them. Well may it be said—for him to live was Christ. With every member of my family an attachment was formed which is cherished to this day, and the little mementoes he left with them are more prized than jewels."

Yes, with a sweeter influence, and clearer evidence, and stronger logic than is found in even his ablest sermon, his daily life was a beautiful and perpetual recommendation of the religion he preached. In the circles in which he was most intimately known, was he most frequently and triumphantly quoted as a living and irresistible proof of the truth and efficacy of religion! Himself a daily illustration of, and running commentary upon, the gospel, he effected as much for his great Exemplar by his life as by his labours. Often have men of the world exclaimed of him when disgusted by the inconsistencies of other professors, "Well, here, at least, is *one* man who *is* a Christian."

He thus writes to his wife:

"BROOKLYN, N. Y., *September 27th*, 1850.

" * * * Jenny Lind is gone to Boston, where great preparations are made to receive her. I must tell you a thing or two. The room at Castle-Garden, where she has been giving her concerts, is said to be the most spacious in the United States; and yet every night, it is supposed that nearly nine thousand persons were present, besides a great crowd around the house, and how many on the house, I cannot tell!

"She sings admirably, but after all, I suspect the angels can beat her! and if you compare her concerts in Castle-Garden with the concert of saints and angels as recorded in the fifth chapter of the book of Revelation, you will perceive that earth cannot compete with heaven. O, heaven! sweet heaven! how bright and resplendent will be thy scenes of glory! and how unutterable and thrilling thy never-ending joys! Here we are astonished at looking at a mass of eight thousand persons assembled in one concert-room; but how far does this fall short of those assembled around the throne in heaven! A great company of the redeemed which no man can number, and besides these, only think how many angels—ten thousand times ten thousand and thousands of thousands!—all robed and crowned! all singing the praises of God and the Lamb, with voices loud as thunder, and each voice even incomparably sweeter than that of Jenny Lind! O, who would not be a Christian! Who would not wish to go to heaven!"

It may be added here, that Dr. Baker sent, at this time, a volume of his "Sermons" handsomely bound to the Queen of Song, accompanied by a note. The letter written to him by her in reply, is a beautiful one, and indicative of a pious heart.

Writing to a son, he says:

"PHILADELPHIA, *October* 19*th*, 1850.

"I am at last on the wing, and thus far on my way home. A gentleman in Brooklyn, rich and liberal, who would not give me a cent for Austin College, nevertheless subscribed one thousand dollars for the building of a church in Huntsville, on condition that Texas pays her bonds to him for money advanced. This subscription he gave me when Texas was likely to go off at a tangent. After the action of Congress touching the ten million affair, I went to this gentleman and remarked, 'Mr. L., I have a laugh upon you, sir; you subscribed one thousand dollars, I suspect, under the influence of despair, but General Houston says that the money which you advanced to the Texan Government will certainly be repaid. And, sir,' continued I, 'you will have to fork over your thousand.' 'Very well,' said he, 'I am ready, on the condition stipulated; and Dr. Baker, let me see your paper again.' I handed it to him, and he wrote as follows: 'And also, now the Congress of the United States has placed the means in the hands of the State to enable her to pay those bonds, *another thousand dollars* for the same purpose, on the same conditions, either to be added to the former, or to be applied to building another Presbyterian church in Texas, as the Presbyterian Synod or Presbytery may deem best, both sums to be paid as soon as I shall obtain payment of the bonds.'

"On Wednesday evening last we had a grand meeting in the Central Presbyterian church in this city, designed to wake up a new interest in the cause of Domestic Missions. Drs. Jones, Plumer, and myself were the selected speakers. We had a crowded house. I was somewhat intimidated, but had much more freedom than I expected. I will tell you how I commenced, and then you may guess what I said. 'This is an interesting scene; this is an interesting occasion; it is worth an angel's visit from the skies; and, as Paul once said, that it was not expedient for him doubtless to glory, but he would come to visions and revelations of the Lord; so would I say this evening—it is not expedient for me doubtless to make a speech, for that is out of my line; I choose rather, in a plain and simple way, to tell you of what I have seen and heard in waste places and frontier lands. Permit me, then, to take you by the hand, so to speak, and lead you along with me in some of my missionary tours.' I then laid before my audience some of the most interesting and heart-stirring events which had fallen under my own observation. I had some freedom; the people smiled, and the people wept; and I think a very happy impression was made. Dr. Jones made a very beautiful address. I wish we had a few Plumers in Texas, and also a pretty smart sprinkling of men of the stamp of my own countryman, Charles Colcock Jones. Heaven multiply and bless such men!

"Remember me kindly to all—Your ever affectionate father."

The noble donation of two thousand dollars alluded to was in due time paid as promised; one thousand went toward erecting the present beautiful church in Huntsville; the other thousand—Mr. Lamar consenting—by a unanimous vote of the Synod of Texas, at its first meeting, which was held in Austin, 1851, was devoted to the church there. The name of the munificent donor will live for ever in the religious as well as political annals of Texas.

Dr. Baker thus writes to his wife:

"WILMINGTON, N. C., *Nov. 7th*, 1850.

"There are some ugly things connected with my agency; for the work of *begging* has in itself no charms; and when I meet with repulses and rebuffs, and sometimes almost insults, I might be tempted to give up almost in disgust. At any rate, I might make myself very unhappy. But no; I am determined to be happy in my employment, and happy I am. Indeed, notwithstanding many undesirable things, I believe I scarcely ever was happier in all my life, especially now, as home begins to loom up before my eyes. I have been urged to remain and preach here all this week, and was told that if I did, one hundred dollars would be given for Austin College. I have consented, and I am happy to say we have at this time very pleasing indications of the divine presence—every prospect of a blessed work of grace."

DANIEL BAKER."

Speaking, in a letter to his son at Austin, of the trials of ministers in Texas on account of inadequate support, he proceeds:

"SAVANNAH, *Nov. 18th*, 1850.

"Paul, you know, describes Christ as one 'who, though he was rich, for our sakes became poor, that we through his poverty might be rich.' And how touchingly does our blessed Saviour allude to this very thing: 'The foxes have holes, and the birds of the air have nests, but the Son of Man hath not where to lay his head.' And John, referring to a certain occasion, says: 'Every man went unto his own house, but Jesus went to the Mount of Olives.' Blessed Jesus! The poorest in the great crowd of his hearers had *some* house; but Jesus had none. So, when every man went unto his own house, Jesus went to the Mount of Olives. Methinks this gives a charm to poverty; at least, it may well serve to reconcile ministers to 'limited circumstances.' You recollect my remark—'We have no feathered nests in Texas, but we have fields of usefulness.' Some persons show much love with their tongue, but when the hour of trial comes, their hearts fail. Like certain characters, wonderfully patriotic—willing to shed the last drop of blood in their veins; but when the occasion offers, are found not willing to shed the first.

"I have set my heart upon making Huntsville, as far as I have influence, the Athens of Texas, in building up there a College of high character, one that shall be a credit to Texas, and an honour to the Presbyterian name. Yesterday I preached three times, and I am to preach again to-night. I spent two Sabbaths in Wilmington, preached some seventeen sermons, and I am happy to say that it pleased God to bless my labours. Some twelve or fifteen persons were hopefully converted, and a wave of happy influences seemed to be spreading on every hand. Without making scarcely an effort, I received there one hundred and seventeen dollars for Austin

College, besides making a good impression. My paper is full. God bless you, my son and daughter.

DANIEL BAKER."

"SAVANNAH, *November 26th*, 1850.

"MY OWN DAUGHTER—You cannot imagine what a cordial reception I have met with in Savannah. I have been here about ten days, and I was almost overwhelmed with kindness. Not in Savannah only, but wherever I go, I meet with warm hearts and smiling countenances. Why, really, I am led to think, or at least I am tempted to think, I am 'somebody.' But I know too well my unworthiness in the sight of God, to be lifted up. No, no, the dust is my place, and the plea of the Publican is my plea. People here come out in crowds. Last night, I am told, more than a hundred had to go away, not being able to procure a seat. I do think good and deep impressions have been made; and if a protracted meeting were now held, the results would be great, would be glorious.

"I wish you all to be just as happy as the days are long, particularly when I am absent. I wish you all, in some way or other, to be compensated for the absence of the head of the family. You may expect your old father to kiss you in about twelve days from this time. Love to all.

DANIEL BAKER."

Resuming his autobiography, we find the following summing up:

During this tour, amongst other places, I visited Houston, Galveston, New Orleans, Memphis, Cincinnati, Philadelphia, Wilkesbarre, Princeton, New

York, Albany, Easton, New Brunswick, Newark Brooklyn, Wilmington, Washington City, Baltimore, Georgetown, Savannah, Augusta, Freehold, and Mobile. On this tour I obtained books, maps, globes, and subscriptions in money to the amount of four thousand one hundred and sixty-five dollars. With regard to the land, I did this: I went to Natchez, saw brother Chase, and received from him a relinquishment of all the lands which he owned in Texas, amounting to nearly fifteen thousand acres. A large bundle of papers was placed in my hands; and as I was no lawyer, I confess it was a bundle of riddles to me. I looked over the papers, and for my life I could not tell whether the titles were good or not; but I thought if I had not legal knowledge enough to find out the value of the papers, I would borrow some. So, getting into a buggy with brother Chase, away we went to —— College, about eight miles from Natchez, the President of which had for many years been a lawyer in Texas, and was the very man who could tell us all about the affair. This gentleman, Mr. Green, was a friend of mine; and at my request he took the papers, and within an hour he handed them back, informing me that all was right, or nearly so; but certain things required prompt attention, or there might be some serious loss. I thanked him for his services—he would receive nothing more—and taking back the papers, I laid them aside in my trunk as a treasure.

Upon my return to Texas, I set about straightening matters, and, with the help of friends, succeeded in securing lands to the College valued at twenty-five thousand dollars. This has proved a great affair for us; for, when pressed, we have from time to time sold some, amounting in all to about three thousand dollars; and still the land remaining is worth, by reason of enhanced prices, as much as the whole originally was; nay, is now valued at thirty thousand dollars. I repeat it, this has been a great affair for us, enabling us in our policy to be bold, without being rash. We can give good salaries, and in case of pecuniary difficulty, we can fall back upon our landed treasure. God be thanked for raising up a friend at the outset, who has, by his liberality, placed us in circumstances so favourable to the success of our enterprise.

Leaving Huntsville in the spring of 1851, he goes out on a second tour to solicit aid for the College. The first letter written during this absence, from which we quote, is addressed to his wife, and dated

"WHARF-BOAT, Memphis, *May 13th*, 1851.

"MY DEAR ELIZA—Another scrawl. I have visited Vicksburg, Jackson, Yazoo City, and Memphis. Last Sabbath morning I preached for brother Coons. I am just waiting for a boat for St. Louis. Cholera has broken out in this place; I believe three or four persons died yesterday, and two last night—one a young man who eat his supper in good health—this morning a corpse! The sexton of the —— church rang the bell last night, and about three hours after the services closed, was in the arms of death. What poor creatures we all are!—how important to be ready to go at any moment. You need not be uneasy, my dear E., on my account; I am in the hands of a Being who is infinitely wise and good, and, as the saying is, 'I am immortal till my work is done.'

"Last Sabbath morning I preached from the words, 'As for me, I will behold thy face in righteousness; I shall be satisfied when I awake in thy likeness.' Had unusual freedom; many of the congregation were completely melted down; one lady was quite overcome, and shouted aloud. O what a blessed thing it is to be a Christian, and to have heaven in full view! My dear E., let us try to be more engaged—'O for a closer walk with God!'

"What a helter-skelter letter this is. When I am in more favourable circumstances I may do better; I thought a few scratches of your old husband's pen would be better than to hear those ugly words coming from the Post-Office—no letter. but I hear the puffing of a steamboat—love to all, all, all.

"Yours, affectionately,

DANIEL BAKER."

He writes again to a son:

"ST. LOUIS, Missouri, *May 27th,* 1851.

"MY DEAR SON—Our General Assembly closed its sessions last night. We have had a most delightful meeting—no judicial case of any importance, no unkind feeling, no harsh remark; every thing harmonious and pleasant. I think the impression made in families, in churches, and on the community, decidedly good. I preached five times, and made four Sabbath-school addresses. One was on occasion of what was called 'The Floral celebration;' nearly one thousand children were present, with many beautiful banners. It proved a very interesting occasion, and I hope some good was done. Dr. Humphrey preached the sermon on Domestic Missions; it was a masterly affair. Dr. Plumer preached the sermon on Popery; the sermon occupied about two hours in its delivery, and proved beyond all doubt the gross and palpable idolatry of the Papal Church. The argument was powerful, was triumphant! and, as the house was crowded to overflowing, I think the sermon will not soon be forgotten. There was, I am told, quite a 'smart sprinkling' of Papists present. The next sermon on Popery is to be preached by Dr. Alexander; and on Domestic Missions, by your father. The proposition for building a large Presbyterian church in Washington City was, to the perfect astonishment of many, indefinitely postponed.

"But what perhaps will interest and please you more than all, is this: the General Assembly has erected the Synod of Texas, and fixed upon Austin as the place of its first meeting, and the last Thursday in October as the time.

"You see what a scrawl this is! Positively, I can scarcely write at all; but certainly, as an affectionate son, you will excuse your old father.

DANIEL BAKER."

(TO THE SAME.)

"STEAMBOAT CRESCENT, near N. O., *August 15th*, 1851.

"MY DEAR SON—You see I am already upon my return to Texas. My tour has, upon the whole, been quite successful, say something more than two thousand dollars in money subscriptions. Besides this, the 'Texas Emigrating Land Company,' of

Louisville, Kentucky, have donated to Austin College one thousand dollars in a certain contingency, with the probability of that amount being trebled. Surely the Lord has been very good to me in giving me and the cause which I advocate favour in the eyes of the people, although I am so little qualified for the work in which I am engaged. Moreover, the providence of God appears to have been propitious in other respects. Last week I had some thought of stopping at Paducah to spend the Sabbath, when lo! there came on a most tremendous squall or tornado, which more or less injured some six or eight steamboats lying at the wharf; of which number some were completely wrecked, and some were sunk, carrying down to the bottom all on board. It is not known how many lives were lost, but thirty is supposed to be a low estimate. I saw the clouds rising. They really looked frightful, and I predicted that the destruction would be great somewhere. A little after this, I saw what might be called the careering of the storm. Its chariot of cloud or dust, I could not tell which, seemed to be rolling across the Mississippi, upon the very bosom of its waters, and not more than a mile distant. The wings of the tempest fanned us, and the roughened waters caused our boat to prance a little; but we were, providentially, out of the track of the sweeping wind, and were safe.

"I must tell you another thing. I had intended to leave the boat I was in at Memphis, and spend the Sabbath there; but the boat having been unexpectedly detained on the river, I found that I could not reach Memphis in time, and was strongly tempted to go on to New Orleans direct, without stopping, thinking that my original plan for observing the Sabbath being defeated, my mind would be relieved. But, it occurred to me, if I should build a church for the worship of God, and that church were consumed by lightning, would it be proper for me to say, I have built a house for God, that has been providentially destroyed, therefore I will do nothing more for my Maker in that way. I thought the case a parallel one, and determined to make another effort to show my respect for God's holy day. I will get the captain to put me out at some small place, where we might happen to be on Saturday night. The captain consented, and I was put ashore, about nine o'clock, at ——, a small town, occupied chiefly by Roman Catholics and Methodists. On Sabbath morning I went out very early to see if I could not have some opportunity to preach, when, much to my delight, I was told that one of the citizens, Mr. M., was a Presbyterian. Is it possible! I hastened to his house, and found him making preparations to go eight miles to a Methodist church in the country. He was very glad to see me. 'Why, Mr. B.,' says he, 'I know you, I have heard you preach!' 'Yes,' said his wife, 'I know Mr. B. too, I have never seen him before, but my brother was converted under his preaching, and he used to talk a great deal about Mr. B.' But, says Mr. M., 'there is another Presbyterian family living here!' 'Indeed! Well I would like to call upon that family.'

"The old lady, who had heard me preach in Virginia, and who, it was said, would be very glad to see me, was out of town, but it was soon arranged that she should be sent for. And she was sent for, and she came, and very glad she was to see me, for, 'a dear sister' of hers, who had been somewhat of an infidel, 'had been converted under my preaching.' Indeed! Is that so? Well, God be praised! Bless the Lord! O, thinks I, I am rewarded for turning aside here to rest on the Sabbath, according to the commandment. Not only have I cheered the hearts of some of our own stray sheep in a destitute place, but I have been told things which have made my own heart to rejoice and be glad. Bless the Lord! again, I say. Well, to make a long story short, I preached in the morning and at night to nearly the whole population—Methodists, Presbyterians, Roman Catholics and all! Yes, Roman Catholics too. They have a church edifice in the place, and once they had a priest, who, as it was supposed, was settled there for life—but he had left his people. 'They are not Roman Catholics,' said he, and away he went from those who had lived in the midst of Protestants long enough to learn that it was their privilege and right to do their own thinking! Well, I had a very pleasant Sabbath day; and next morning about three o'clock, comes along the Crescent, one of the pleasantest boats I ever was in, in all my life, and scarcely a profane swearer on board amongst either the passengers or crew! But, New Orleans is near at hand, so fare you well.

"Yesterday afternoon a man fell overboard from

this boat, and was drowned. This moment he is sleeping in his watery bed, and *they* know nothing of it—his family; for, poor man, he had left at home, I am told, a wife and six children! Surely, in the midst of life we are in death; and very precarious is the tenure by which we hold all our comforts here below. God bless you, my son.

DANIEL BAKER."

Resuming the autobiography, we find the results of this tour thus summed up:

I entered upon my second tour early in the year 1851, and, gleaning a little more in Houston, Galveston, New Orleans, Mobile, and some other places where I had been before, I visited in Mississippi—Vicksburg, Jackson, Yazoo City, Canton, Columbus; in Tennessee—Memphis, Somerville, Raleigh, Belmont, Bethany Church, Denmark, Zion Church, Nashville, Clarkesville; in Kentucky—Louisville, Frankfort, Lexington; in Missouri—St. Louis; in Maryland—Baltimore; in Texas—Centreville, Leona, St. Marks, San Antonio, Danville. The amount of subscriptions obtained this year, paid and not paid, exclusive of books, amounted to nearly four thousand dollars. Upon my return, and during the winter, I went twice to San Antonio.

CHAPTER XIII.

THIRD AND FOURTH TOURS AS AGENT OF AUSTIN COLLEGE

About February 1st, 1852, Dr. Baker left Texas on behalf of the College, upon his third tour. The historical interest attaching to the various meetings alluded to in the letters which follow, must be our excuse for quoting from them so freely.

"Mississippi River, on boat Atlantic, *Feb. 27th*, 1852.

"My beloved Wife—I wish I could see you, just now. I do not know how much I love you until I am absent. Then a thousand things start up, and exert a soft, sweet, melting power upon my heart. This morning, having occasion to play the tailor, I took out the implements which you had kindly prepared; and when I saw how nicely you had fixed matters, thinks I to myself, this is the work of my wife; she still loves me.

"Henceforth I will, I trust, be a better Christian. My locks are whitening, and eternity is coming on. O to be more gentle, and mild, and even-tempered, and heavenly-minded! In other words, O to feel more of the power, and taste more of the sweetness of the religion of our precious Saviour. Last Sabbath I preached from my old pulpit in Galveston, from these words: 'Gray hairs are here and there upon him, and he knoweth it not.' The drift of the sermon was to show the cause, proofs, and evil effects of spiritual declension. I had some liberty in speaking. I hope it did good to others. I trust it has done good to myself. Gray hairs! how much more easily seen upon the heads of others than upon our own! O, to see ourselves as God sees us! I think it would make us more humble, and less disposed to find fault with those around. I wish every sermon I preach might do me as much good as the sermon I preached last Sabbath morning.

"Farewell, my dear wife. God bless you. Amen!

"Your old husband,

DANIEL BAKER."

After visiting Canton, Columbus, Gainesville, a meeting of the Tuskaloosa Presbytery, and Eutaw, receiving donations for the College in each of these places, he reached Charleston, from which city he thus writes:

"CHARLESTON, *May 11th*, 1852.

"MY OWN DEAR WIFE—I reached this city on the 7th, and you may judge of the quickness with which I went to the post-office. I have been kindly invited by Dr. S. to make his house my home; but you may rest assured he gives me full employment in the way of preaching. Last Sabbath I preached for him twice—rather, in the morning, for Dr. P.; and I have been kept busy also preaching every night. I am happy to say that at this moment there is every prospect of a blessed work of grace. I shall remain and preach, and preach on till the meeting of the Assembly, if God spare my life.

"You know not, my dear wife, how cordially I am greeted in this place by some who were brought in under my preaching twenty years ago. It seems to me that God is already beginning to reward me for my poor services many, many years ago. The other evening, in the pulpit, Dr. S. was pleased to speak of me in a manner which proved his high regard for my person and past services; but which I thought was entirely too complimentary; and I confess I felt humbled, and was not a little disconcerted. Already my cup is full, and shall I, such a poor creature, have the smiles of God, and have such honour from man also? Not unto us, but unto God be all the glory!

"Last evening I was invited to take tea at the house of a lady who was brought in under my preaching many years ago, and her husband told me that their son, a promising youth, was awakened and converted, and also a young lady residing in their family, by the reading of my volume of *Revival Sermons.* The gentleman was in the habit of reading the sermons out in his family circle; and, in this way, God was pleased to bless them with the sweet hope of an endless life. When I see and hear certain things which touch my heart, it seems to me I have already almost reached heaven, my home, my sweet, sweet home. O what a good Master I have served, and how rich are his rewards, even in this world.

"Yours, with increasing affection,

DANIEL BAKER."

"EDISTO ISLAND, *June 5th*, 1852.

"MY DEAR ELIZA—I assure you it was no small gratification to me to see my son W. a member of the venerable General Assembly of the Presbyterian

Church. It seemed to mark a new era in the history of my life; and reminded me that I belonged to another generation, a generation which has now nearly passed away; and this feeling was deepened by seeing in the Assembly, M. D. Hoge, whose father was an unmarried young man well known to me in Hampden Sydney College. Indeed, I am continually meeting with persons and things which remind me that I am in the midst of posterity; that the shades of evening are gathering around me, and that my sun must soon go down. Well, be it so, if God will only grant that

'My sun may in smiles decline,
And bring a peaceful night.'

But it is time for me to stop—I don't wish to alarm you, but I must say, that although I am in good health, the sudden murmuring in my head has returned, and has become somewhat frequent of late. Nothing serious, however, I suppose. At any rate, God reigns, and both my life and soul are in the hands of Him who is infinitely wise and good. I am willing, I trust, to leave this present evil world just when it may please God to call me hence. 'Thanks be to God for his unspeakable gift!'

"I have just received a letter from the Hon. J. T., who was awakened under my preaching twenty years ago, containing two hundred dollars for Austin College, and fifty dollars to be given to Sabbath-schools in Texas. This is the very person who said he would go to hear me preach, and take an onion with him to rub his eyes, that he 'might cry at the right time;' and who, thank God, on that occasion, without any use of the onion, was brought to tears and to his knees also. Blessed be God!

"Farewell, my dear wife,

DANIEL BAKER."

(TO A SON.)

"SUMPTERVILLE, *June* 30*th*, 1852.

"MY DEAR SON—I am happy to inform you, that since we parted in Charleston, I have had much pleasant sunshine; I mean I have been much prospered in my agency, and personally have had many kindnesses shown me. First, I went to Edisto Island, where I had preached successfully many years ago, and was received almost as an angel of God. Without making any application, except from the pulpit, free-will offerings were in less than four days sent in to the amount of more than three hundred dollars. Going next to Columbia, I received subscriptions to the amount of four hundred and eighty-seven dollars and ninety-five cents. The President of the College, Dr. Thornwell, subscribed one hundred dollars, and the students two hundred and fifty-eight. Was not this noble! Passing on to Camden, there also, without making personal application to a single individual, I received in a few days one hundred and fifty-seven dollars and fifty cents. Thank God, almost wherever I go, I meet with those who were brought in under my ministry many years ago, several of whom are even ministers of the gospel, of whom I had never heard before. Even in the pulpit I am spoken of in a manner which almost overwhelms me. Only think, Dr. Thornwell made an announcement to the students of South Carolina College after this manner: 'In consequence of the tender relations which exist between many of your parents and the Rev. Dr. Baker, who has just addressed you, you are no doubt desirous to know his appointments; I will therefore state, &c. &c.' Heaven bless you and yours.

"Your ever affectionate father,

DANIEL BAKER."

"Personal friendship," he remarks, in a letter dated July 3d, 1852, "oils the wheels, and hence, without almost any effort on my part, they roll on delightfully. I scarcely hear a single excuse now. This is the more astonishing, as the churches in this region have contributed largely to Oglethorpe College, and at this time money is really very scarce. Wherever I go I am received with open arms. My spiritual children, especially, seem so glad to see me. Sometimes I feel almost overwhelmed! * * * The individual who gave this was, it seems, converted under my preaching; and I have found out that the person who sent the one hundred dollars was his brother-in-law, who was a rich man, and who rejoiced greatly at the conversion of one who was very dear to him. Bless the Lord, O how gracious has he been to me, blessing my labours, and surrounding me with friends wherever I go."

(TO HIS DAUGHTER.)

"BISHOPVILLLE, *July*, 10*th* 1852.

"MY DEAR MODEL DAUGHTER—* * * * Well, since that I have received cheering smiles, both from

God and man. During the last two weeks I have been preaching almost every day within the bounds of two churches in the neighbourhood of each other. It pleased God to bless my labours. Besides the reviving delightfully of old disciples, some twenty persons, chiefly men, have been hopefully converted, and quite as many more brought under awakening influences. This meeting was closed yesterday about noon, and a scene was witnessed which I am certain will not soon be forgotten. It was a melting time; the Master was with us, and of a truth we had 'a young heaven begun below, and glory in the bud.' I was presented, before leaving, with four hundred and fifteen dollars for the College. Was not this noble? And, remember, there had been no begging from a single individual; it was all a perfectly free-will offering.

"Did I not tell you, that if I had any friends in the world, they were in South Carolina? You cannot conceive, my child, how kind the people are to me, wherever I go. Their kindness is sometimes almost oppressive; I can scarcely stand it. To think that such an unworthy creature as I should receive such attentions, and that from all classes. The reason is, that not only some two or three thousand persons, perhaps, were brought in under my preaching, in days gone by, but it so happened that a goodly number of these were people of note, some of the favourite sons and brightest ornaments of the State. Surely, if any poor mortal man on earth has reason to thank God for his mercies, I have. And now, and evermore, I would say, to God be all the praise! O, for a more grateful heart; and, O, for grace to serve the

Lord with more zeal and fidelity than I have ever yet done!

"*July* 12. Since writing the above, I have preached a few sermons in this village, and am happy to say, there is every prospect of a pleasing work of grace in this place also. Nearly the whole congregation where I preached last, some ten miles distant, came here yesterday, with their pastor at their head; and, would you believe it, I am told that several persons came from Sumterville, twenty miles distant. I am told that I must preach, and others here would beg for the College. In this way I find I succeed best in my agency. If I were not to preach, or only preach a few sermons, and go about 'drawing teeth,' I would not get half as much for the College as I now do. And when teeth are drawn, are not the gums made sore? I expect in three days from this time to be in Columbia, where I hope to find letters from your dear mother and other loved ones.

"In haste, your old father,

DANIEL BAKER.

"P. S. I have heard of five or six more cases of hopeful conversion; say now about twenty-six in all, and perhaps as many as two-thirds of them young men. I mentioned at the outset, that we must have more ministers, and I think God has heard my prayer."

(TO ANOTHER DAUGHTER.)

"SUMTERVILLE, *July* 24*th*, 1852.

"MY BELOVED DAUGHTER—During the last three weeks, I have been preaching almost incessantly in the bounds of three neighbouring Presbyterian churches. Nearly the whole mass of the people in that region come out day after day. We held what are called 'basket meetings.' The people brought provisions along with them, and we would remain on the ground and have religious services, with proper intermissions, from ten o'clock in the morning to about four in the afternoon, having no service at night. Such meetings are well suited to country places, and I prefer them decidedly to camp-meetings. There was a general waking up, and the converts amounted to about thirty, and what is remarkable, about two-thirds of them may be called young men, the class to which my heart is particularly drawn. Some of these are of considerable promise, and I have reason to believe that four or five of them will devote themselves to the service of God in the gospel ministry. Blessed be God!

"I may here also just mention, that a little boy was baptized last Sabbath, and named—what do you think? Why, Daniel Baker! and I have lately heard of another little Carolinian who has to be known by the same homely name!—and, would you believe it, the day before yesterday, I had to sit for four daguerreotype likenesses! Surely, my dear daughter, your old father has much cause for gratitude and praise; for, of a truth, 'the lines are fallen to me in pleasant places, I have a goodly heritage.' O for grace to serve my Master more faithfully and zealously than ever! My time is very precious, and therefore, I must put you off with a short letter now; but, at some future time, I may send you a longer letter, a crowded sheet. * * * Heaven bless the little boy. I am quite willing that he should throw both pa and grandpa into the shade. But I must close. So, fare you well.

"Your affectionate father,

DANIEL BAKER."

It was an invariable custom with Dr. Baker, whenever a friend was afflicted, either to hasten to the house of mourning with words of consolation, or, when that was impossible, to write to that friend a letter of condolence. The following is the only one of the kind in this volume. It will be observed too, that the letter contains an account of the work of grace in Sumterville. It is addressed to a daughter recently afflicted.

"SUMTERVILLE, *August* 2*d*, 1852.

"MY LOVED CHILD—As it seems to cheer your dear heart so much, to receive even a line from your long absent father, I thought I would this morning send you a little brief note, to assure you of my continued health and continued love. The account which you give of your loneliness has touched my heart. At an early period your husband was taken from you, and then your infant, which you hoped would be your joy and consolation, was also snatched away, even before it could reward its mother with one sweet smile. This was truly a heavy blow! It was affliction indeed! But suppose my daughter, that your parents had also been taken? Suppose that they also were this moment sleeping in the same city of silence, side by side with your husband and dear little boy, would not this have been a yet deeper affliction? and would you not have been made to feel more lonely still? My daughter, you should think of your mercies, as well as your afflictions. So did Job—so should you. You recollect his language; how beautiful and how appropriate! 'Have we received good at the hand of the Lord, and shall we not receive evil? The Lord gave, the Lord hath taken away. Blessed be the name of the Lord.' Here we have the language and the very spirit of true piety. Let it be your own. Cheer up, my daughter; your Heavenly Father is upon the throne, and he does all things well. He has seen your tears. He has heard your sighs. He knows full well all the sorrows of your heart; and God, even your own God and Heavenly Father cares for you. Your sighs are recorded, your tears are in 'his bottle,' and rest assured, all things have been ordered in wisdom and in love. Yes, my child, He who notices the falling sparrow, certainly could not have permitted your loved husband and your dear little boy to sink into the grave without his notice and kind regard. Hark! He speaks to thee—'Be still, and know that I am God:' and again, methinks, He speaks to you, my daughter, in the softened, sweet tones of compassion and love, and says, 'Silence, my child, what I do thou knowest not now, but thou shalt know hereafter.' Therefore, cheer up, my beloved T., kiss the rod that smites you, and say, even in the language of the blessed Saviour himself, 'the cup which my Father giveth me, shall I not drink of it? Do this, say this from your heart, and all will be well! for, is it not written, 'all things work together for good to them that love God'? And what says the same apostle again? 'I reckon that the sufferings of this present time are not worthy to be compared with the glory which shall be revealed in us.' Yes, after sorrow, comes joy! After gloom comes glory! After the conflict of battle, the repose of victory! In short, after earth comes heaven, sweet heaven! even the visions of God, and the joys of a life which shall never end!

"Wednesday morning, August 4th. Last night, amid circumstances of very special interest and solemnity, our meeting in this place came to an end; and, truly, a most delightful, blessed meeting it has proved; a sweet, refreshing season indeed! Thirty cases of hopeful conversion, about two-thirds of whom may be called young men. I think I never saw a more interesting set of converts in all my life; as one has expressed it, 'They are the very pick of our town'—and another remarked, 'If it had been left to us to select, we could not have made a better selection.' To God be all the praise!

"The meeting embraced parts of three weeks. I will tell you how it was. I came here some six weeks ago, and, after preaching for a few nights, and begging as hard as I could for the College during the day, I obtained one hundred and twenty-five dollars. Perceiving that there was some religious excitement, I was urged to protract my visit, but I declined, and set out to visit what brother McQ. termed the 'model churches' on Black River. First I went to Zion Church, of which brother R. is pastor. I had been preaching there only about two days when an elder from Sumterville came to me with a letter from the elders of that church, stating that there was more religious interest in Sumterville than was supposed, and urged me to return for a few days longer. I told the brother I did not see how I could return to Sumterville, for my time was not my own, and, however pleasing it would be to me to preach in Sumterville, yet, as I had already reaped down that field, I did not think I could do any thing more there for Austin College. 'Well,' said Mr. K., 'if you will only return and preach for us a few sermons more, I will myself be responsible for fifty dollars.' 'Then I will go,' said I; and I did go, as soon as the revival which had already commenced in brother R's church allowed me to go—thirty being hopefully converted; about twenty of whom were young men. Resuming my labours, I preached to a people who very generally began to take up the inquiry, 'O, sirs, what must I do to be saved?' By Friday noon about twenty-two persons had professed conversion, and I had preached what was supposed to be my last sermon in the place. I had an appointment for Williamsburg, some forty miles off, for the next Sabbath; I was nearly ready to start, when in stepped a committee of gentlemen, appointed by a unanimous vote of the church, begging me to remain over the Sabbath, and, as an inducement to stay, I was told that I should have for the College fifty dollars more, and moreover that an express should be sent to Williamsburg church to tell them what had prevented my fulfilling my appointment. So I remained until Monday, at which time the converts numbered about thirty, embracing the very flower of the town; several young men, one or more of whom have the ministry in view.

"Now, in regard to my agency. Without saying another word, either in public or privately, they came forward nobly, and added, in subscriptions, two hundred and sixty-six dollars to what had already been given, making, in all, three hundred and eighty dollars! Thus was this field reaped down three times. Surely the Lord has been good to me, and I have at least been reminded of the language of the Apostle, uttering the outpourings of an admiring and grateful heart, 'Thanks be to God, who always causeth us to triumph in Christ, and maketh manifest the savour of his knowledge in every place!'

"I have received invitations to several other places, where, I trust, God will continue to prosper me, both as a minister and agent. How pleasant it is to follow the bent of my inclinations, and in this way not only do much good in winning souls to Christ, but in this way also more effectually promote the object of my agency. Had I been recreant to my ministerial vows, and lost the minister in the agent—had I just gone from place to place, and house to house with a pair of forceps, so to speak, 'pulling teeth,' I am satisfied I should not have succeeded one-fourth part as well. I thank God I have been taught a new and better way of begging for the College. Do good, and then try the power of a grateful heart. I have, besides paying travelling expenses, sent home in checks to the amount of nearly three thousand dollars; indeed, nearly four thousand dollars. God be thanked!—this will do very well. And how pleasant to have so many new spiritual children gathered around me! and to have so many touching and substantial proofs of being beloved by them!

"Your absent father,

DANIEL BAKER."

(TO A SON.)

"INDIAN TOWN CHURCH, *August 18th*, 1852.

"Well, my son, thank God I have some more good news to communicate. Invited to Williamsburg church—a country church—and taken there in a carriage some forty miles, I preached my first sermon there last Sabbath a week, and my last on the Sabbath afternoon following, closing with 'some more last words,' or familiar addresses on Monday morning. Fifty-two young converts were added to the church! and as, after making a public profession of their faith in Christ, they were requested to occupy the first table by themselves, the scene presented was beautiful. A long table, filled up with young disciples, and these the flower of the whole community; truly the scene was beautiful to parents and other pious friends who were looking on; it was indeed a scene of thrilling interest; it was worth an angel's visit from the skies. You may well suppose many cheeks were wet with tears, trickling tears of joy! And, no doubt, there were some Simeons present, who were ready to say, 'Lord, now lettest thou thy servant depart in peace, for mine eyes have seen thy salvation!' But this was not all. Our spiritual rose-bush, which had at that time many buds, appeared the next morning in fresh bloom; twelve more were found rejoicing in Christ. The whole number actually added to the church on profession, fifty-eight; the whole number hopefully converted, sixty-four; thirty-four males, chiefly of middle age, but some choice young men, who, it is thought, will certainly devote themselves to the gospel ministry. What hath God wrought!—to Him be all the praise! I preached not more than twenty sermons, and sixty-four precious souls converted! Again I say, to God be all, all the praise! Has not your father been greatly blessed and prospered? I think I can enter into the feelings of David, when, in the outpouring of a grateful heart, he exclaimed, 'Surely, this is not the manner of man, O Lord God!'

"My health is as usual, and so is my voice; but as I write so many letters, you may well be content if I am brief. How I should like to step in just now, and see how you are coming on; and I would like to see my little grandson—Heaven bless the dear boy, and his mother too.

"Affectionately yours in many bonds,

DANIEL BAKER.

"P. S. Three more hopefully converted since writing; all young men—whole number sixty-seven, yea, sixty-nine."

Others may be better able than the compiler of this volume, to estimate to what degree young men entering the church, and, afterward, the ministry, under such auspices as these, would form their idea and fix their standard of preaching thereby; to what degree the preacher would reproduce himself in ministers whom he was made the means of leading to Christ. If there be lines of likeness between father and child, will there be none between this father and those whom he so delighted to call his spiritual children? In estimating the usefulness of Dr. Baker, too, shall we count only those who actually made a profession of religion by the close of a meeting held by him? Must there be no count of those truly converted, but slower in making profession thereof? None of those whom God the Spirit then began to compel to come in, even though the actual entrance was not till, perhaps, years after? And let it ever be borne in mind, that faithful pastors, wherever he went, were the sowers—even where he was permitted to be the reaper. Nothing was more fully understood at each meeting, than this fact; and, at each meeting, without a particle of other feeling, he that sowed and he that reaped rejoiced together at the harvest of souls.

In a letter to his wife, referring to the meeting above mentioned, and especially to the communion scene, he says:

"INDIANTOWN CHURCH, *August 23d*, 1852.—Rainy day.

"You may well suppose many tears of delicious joy were shed. We had a little jubilee, a pentecostal season in miniature. To God be all, all the praise! But, to proceed. The very next day, last Tuesday morning, by invitation of the elders of the church, they have no pastor, I preached my first sermon in this place; and closed the meeting this day; and lo, the Head of the Church has been pleased to honour the labours of your husband here also, and yesterday morning twenty young converts came forward and made a good confession before many witnesses. Of these, twelve were men, nearly all young men, the remaining eight were chiefly young ladies. Is not this wonderful! Observe, the congregation here is not as large as at Williamsburg church, and in some respects the church here was not in a favourable state. Besides, the meeting embraced only one Sabbath. This has been to this people a time of sweet refreshing; the results far beyond what any individual, I suppose, had ever dreamed of. On closing the services this afternoon, there was much tender feeling; and almost every individual in the house came up to me to shake hands. I had been told that several ladies wished to shake hands with me, so I came down from the pulpit, and stood at the foot of the steps, and I believe that not only every lady, but every gentleman in the house, say two hundred, came up to bid me an affectionate farewell, and this they did with many tears. Their husbands, and fathers, and brothers, and sons, have undertaken to do something handsome for the College. I do not yet know the amount, but from what has been whispered in my ear, I suspect, considering the time I preached, it will be even more than has been given in any other place, Did I not tell you that the South Carolinians are some of the noblest people in the world! By their attentions, and overwhelming kindness they have touched, they have melted down my whole heart. God bless them, and reward them richly, both on earth and in heaven! But I must look upon my Heavenly Father as the great spring and source of all—for he has blessed my preaching to the conversion of so many; only think! on an average something more perhaps than two converts for every sermon! and these chiefly men, young men of promise, and middle aged men, prominent men, as prominent and influential as any in the whole community.

"And, my beloved wife, is it not remarkable, notwithstanding my incessant preaching for some eight or ten weeks past, my health is firm, and my voice is strong and clear as ever. It is said that the Lord blessed the latter end of Job more than the beginning. It really seems that this is true with regard to myself. Blessed be God, and for ever blessed be his holy name! By the favour of Heaven, I am now in the enjoyment of 'a green old age.' May I have the honour and happiness of bringing forth fruit as long as I live. One thing I know, I still love to preach Christ. The work is delightful; yea, I love it more and more. Thanks to Him who has implanted this feeling in my heart.

"You say that I must be 'a happy man.' Well, so I am. God has been pleased to honour me, and the people are continually giving me proofs of rare affection; and besides all, I have, as I trust, 'a good hope through grace.' So I can almost say with the Psalmist, 'Thou anointest my head with oil; my cup runneth over;' and I hope it is no presumption to add, 'Surely goodness and mercy shall follow me all the days of my life, and I will dwell in the house of the Lord for ever.'

"If the Trustees desire it, I am willing to return to this State again in due season; for, you must observe, I have as yet been to very few places which I originally intended to visit. Unexpected and pressing invitations have turned me off from my intended course. The incidents which occurred some twenty years ago seem not to have been forgotten; and as some of the favourite sons of Carolina were brought in under my preaching at that time, and have worn well, this has given me a notoriety which otherwise I would not have had; and this has inspired a confidence in me, which, on this tour, has helped me much. I could write a great deal more, but you see my sheet is full.

"Your absent, but not estranged husband,

DANIEL BAKER."

(TO A DAUGHTER.)

"MARS BLUFF, *September 8th*, 1852.

"MY DEAR SUSAN—You do not know how greatly the Lord has blessed my preaching, and how he has given Austin College and its Agent favour in the eyes of the people. Having invitations showered upon me, I have for several weeks past been going from one place to another, preaching Christ incessantly, say, on an average, two sermons every day; and, without a single exception, the Lord has remarkably blessed my labours wherever I have gone. The whole number who have professed conversion under my preaching, within eight or nine weeks past, is about one hundred and eighty, besides some twenty-five or thirty blacks. This, I confess, is marvellous in my eyes; and whilst I rejoice, I am led to exclaim, 'Even so, Father, for so it seemed good in thy sight.' To God be all the praise! So many cases of conversion, and the conversion of persons so prominent and respectable, must, of course, gladden many hearts; and as there is a very intimate connection between the heart and the purse, the converts and their friends, in their joy and gratitude, have poured out their 'free-will offerings' in a most surprising manner.

"Of course I am in good spirits. In the reception of so many kindnesses from God and man, it is right that I should be both grateful and happy. Sometimes, however, the attentions paid me seem to be almost going beyond the mark. Besides smiling faces, salutations, and compliments, suited to a better man than I am, I am sometimes amused when my friends in their kindness seem so desirous that I should have the best room, the best chair, the best coffee, the best bed. Who am I, and what is my father's house, that I should have so many roses strewed along my pathway through life!

"This day I preached my last sermon here, in a meeting which lasted five or six days; a blessed meeting, as usual. About a dozen professed conversion, and some thirty more were this morning at the inquiry meeting as anxious—the prospects for another powerful work of grace highly encouraging. Indeed, the pastor was entirely unwilling to close the meeting; and as I could not stay any longer, he sent off for some other ministers about forty miles or more distant. O how good has the Lord been to me, thus signally and in every place to honour my ministry! 'Even so, Father, for so it seemed good in thy sight.' Tell W. to give himself up wholly to the blessed work of the ministry, and God will bless him.

"I am writing on a trunk in the baggage-office on

the road; moreover, time is precious. So, fare you well. Your affectionate father,

DANIEL BAKER."

(TO HIS WIFE.)

"DARLINGTON C. H., *Sept.* 27*th*, 1852.

"MY DEAR ELIZA—Well, I can now say, at last, next week, God willing, I set out for home, sweet home. The Lord continues to bless my labours. The last meeting was a delightful one, some thirty-five, at least, brought in within six days; and at the meeting immediately preceding, the hopeful converts were put down at forty. Every meeting blessed, without one solitary exception. The whole number who have professed to find peace in believing, may, I think, safely be put down at two hundred and eighty; and the majority men—nearly one hundred young men. What hath God wrought? To God be all the praise! Tidings of these things have spread abroad, and has produced a great excitement in all this region of country, and crowds come out to hear me, wherever I go. In some respects this is all very pleasant, and I hope my heart overflows with gratitude to God for making me instrumental in doing so much good. But when I see such unusual crowds come out to hear me preach, and know that they have high expectations, too high for me to meet, I confess I feel as if I would like to go and preach where nobody had ever heard of me before. My bow has been bent for a long time; two sermons a day for twelve weeks. I am not broken down; my health and voice are still good; but I feel as if I wanted to 'turn aside, and rest awhile.' My time is precious, as you may well suppose. So, with affectionate salutations,

Your husband,

DANIEL BAKER."

(TO HIS DAUGHTER.)

"MARION C. H., *Oct. 2d*, 1852.

"MY BELOVED DAUGHTER—The joint letter, written by your mother and yourself, came to hand yesterday. You may well suppose I was pleased to receive it, when I tell you that, on breaking the seal, I read it over three times without stopping; and that, too, when my time was as precious as gold. Yesterday afternoon I closed a six days' meeting at Darlington Court-House. It was truly a delightful gathering. Crowds attended three times every day; and some came from a great distance. God was evidently in our midst. Christians were greatly revived, and about twenty-five or thirty persons hopefully converted; and, as usual, chiefly men, young men. All our meetings have been deeply interesting, and every one blessed; yes, thank God, every one. We have had nine protracted meetings, and each has presented all the heart-stirring scenes of a genuine work of grace. The converts average four for each day. This is wonderful indeed, particularly when it is remembered that a large majority are men, having a very considerable sprinkling of doctors, lawyers, and college students. No meeting was more delightful than the last. To God be all the praise! But the sweet notes of 'the church-going bell' are now falling upon my ear, so I must lay down my pen.

"Five o'clock. I have just returned from preaching my second sermon in this place. The prospects are encouraging. I expect to preach again to-night, and three times to-morrow. Some have already come from a distance, and more are expected.

"When I preached a few weeks since at Midway, it having rained much, the swamp was full. Some came to church literally through deep waters, and others, unwilling to venture, came round the swamp, some thirty miles. You say, these things must be pleasing; yes, but there are drawbacks. I know I cannot meet the expectation of all, for things have been coloured, and I have heard of many extravagant remarks. Indeed, there is with some persons such enthusiasm and wild talk in regard to my preaching and success, that I feel sometimes as if I cannot stand it, and must run away! I am smothered with roses; and although roses are very sweet things, the sensation of smothering is not the most agreeable in the world, and I rejoice that I am soon to spread my wings. This is Saturday, and I expect next Wednesday to set out for home, sweet home! And is it possible that I shall so soon be in the bosom of my own dear family! But stop—not so fast; I suppose I shall have to give Oglethorpe College a call, and must also tarry a few days in New Orleans.

"Monday morning. I preached three times yesterday. At night there was so much seriousness the anxious were requested to remain, and, much to our surprise and gratification, nine men came forward to the front seats. Blessed be God!

"Your affectionate father,

DANIEL BAKER."

"DARLINGTON COURT HOUSE, *October* 10:*h*, 1852.

"MY VERY DEAR SON—You recollect what I told you about myself when I was preparing for the ministry—that at one time I was very desponding. I thought that I would never be fit to preach to any white congregation, but was finally cheered by this thought suddenly flashing on my mind, that there were a great many negroes in our land, and perhaps I might able to preach to them. It is said of the Saviour, 'Having loved his own which were in the world, he loved them unto the end.' Even so, having seen fit to bless my labours at the very first, he has continued to bless them to the very last. I am to preach my last sermon here this evening.

"In haste, your ever affectionate father,

DANIEL BAKER."

The pastor of the Darlington church writes to a friend, October 14th, 1852: "Our most sanguine expectations as to visible results have been realized. The meeting commenced September 25th, and closed on the following Friday, after seven days continuance. Our spacious church was crowded day and night to its utmost capacity, to the close. People of all denominations flocked to hear the stranger from Texas; even some of the Jews came to hear him explain the Old Testament prophecies. On the third day, any who were seriously impressed were invited to meet in the session-room, when six persons were found earnestly seeking the way of life. Before the close of this meeting the pastor had the unspeakable pleasure of embracing his own son as a hopeful convert. From this time the meeting increased in interest and influence to the end. The largest number of inquirers, at one time, was about sixty. Twenty-seven are now cherishing the hope of having passed into the marvellous light of the gospel. There are others earnestly seeking the pearl of great price. The professed converts are chiefly, if not entirely, the children of pious parents, children of the covenant. A majority of them are young men, and promise much usefulness in the Church. The good Spirit seems to have paved the way for the earnest preaching of the stranger from Texas; they were a people prepared of the Lord. Dr. Baker's preaching is eminently Calvinistic. The doctrines of our Church—the divine sovereignty, election, total depravity, vicarious atonement, and efficacious grace, were prominently exhibited. The most melting, effective discourse, probably, was from the words, (John vi. 44,) 'No man can come to me, except the Father, which hath sent me, draw him.' Great stillness and solemnity characterized the large assemblies. It was truly an interesting spectacle to behold a sea of uplifted faces, with many streaming eyes, directed towards the speaker, as the words of eternal life fell from his lips. A community that will listen attentively to the truths so solemnly, simply, and earnestly delivered, must be greatly benefitted, though there be no immediate effect produced. The graces of old disciples have been rekindled. Were the same amount of pious zeal and individual faithfulness kept up to its full tension, as it might be, revivals of religion would be of frequent occurrence. Entire consecration to God, on the part of the membership of the church, doubtless, was the secret of the rapid spread of the gospel in primitive times. Dr. Baker's labours have been very abundant, averaging five or six hours of continuous speaking each day for a week together."

It may be mentioned here as a singular fact, that such Arminians as heard his doctrinal discourses heartily concurred in them as the gospel truth. "But he is a good Methodist, he does not preach the doctrines of his Church," they would triumphantly declare, until at last made aware that two of the sermons, to which they most cordially subscribed, were published by the Board of Publication as among their standards. The truth is, Dr. Baker presented these doctrines so clearly, both as to their foundation and inferences; proved them so from reason, revelation, and Christian experience, as to make it evident that they are indeed the gospel itself, in all its freeness and fulness, in all its sweetness and power. His whole aim was to do as Scripture does—exalt God, and humble man—place the almighty Sovereign and the offending subject in their actual relations to each other; and this, in order to show how infinite the love of God in stooping to save, and how absolutely essential the need, and certain the salvation of such a Saviour.

Another eye-witness of the meetings at this period—and these are but specimens of the meetings in which he engaged over a large part of the land, and during his whole life—thus speaks:

"The churches in Harmony Presbytery have been recently blessed with very unusual revivals of religion. In ten congregations where these revivals have occurred, more than three hundred and twenty persons have been added to the church; and it is remarkable that the most of these are men, of whom a considerable number are seriously pondering their duty in regard to the sacred ministry. This precious harvest consists, for the most part, of intelligent and educated men. Besides the addition of so large a number, and of such an important class, whose influence must materially affect the cause of religion, a gracious and profound awakening has pervaded this part of our State, reaching the most obdurate of the impenitent—either melting them to tears, or transfixing them with solemn thought. Very few, indeed, have escaped the powerful appeals and intricate searchings of the word of God.

"Dr. Baker, of Texas, the well known veteran—venerable, both for his silvered locks, and for the many signal instances, in years past, in which God has blessed his labours—has been among us, and has again witnessed the very marked seal of the Spirit upon his preaching. Vigorous, lively, indefatigable, with a soul fully charged with the divine message, his impassioned eloquence has been irresistible. He had commenced a tour through this part of our State on an agency for Austin College, but was completely borne away from his premeditated course by a sweeping tide. One importunate call after another drew him along from place to place, where his efforts have been signally owned in developing the fruit of good seed, that has been sowing for months and years in a good soil. All things, indeed, seem to have been in readiness for the development of these revivals. The ready and cordial response of the hearts of our people to the word of God, denotes that the soil was in readiness, the seed cast already germinating, and but awaited the shower from heaven to spring into life; and, like the shooting of the new plant into day, silent and imperceptible: when souls were awakened, the great Spirit composed the congregation into profound stillness, that he might speak to the conscience. Such was the characteristic order and stillness of our congregations, and so general the feeling, that the awakened and inquiring were not always easily distinguished from the multitude. To effect this, each pastor and session adopted the method most approved in his own congregation. No 'new measures' were resorted to in order to arouse the feelings. These were rendered unnecessary by the Spirit of God.

"It is especially gratifying to state that the distinctive points of our Old-school theology were clearly, fully, and faithfully preached. It has been imagined that these are calculated to check the progress of a revival, and have, therefore, been avoided on such occasions. But so far as my observation has extended, I am free to say that I think the religious movement among us is due mainly to the plain, frank, undisguised presentation of these great doctrines in their own solemn Scripture attire. The sovereign purpose of God in election, the vicarious atonement of Christ, the total inability of the sinner, the instantaneous work of regeneration, the perseverance of the saints; these, in all their glorious beauty and sweetness to the believer, in all their startling terror to the sinner, were set forth, without reserve, as the counsel of God. The singularly happy arguments and illustrations of the venerable Texan who was with us, and his peculiar skill in detecting where these great doctrines underlie the Christian's peace and joy, disarmed all gainsayings, and united the hearts of different denominations in perfect harmony. A beautiful and cordial union prevails; Presbyterians, Methodists, and Baptists, commingled their tears under the droppings of a sublime Calvinistic theology. The scene was novel and intensely engaging. Truly our great doctrines are all involved in the plan of redemption, and all true Christians feed upon them. May all our brethren be encouraged to lay aside a trembling delicacy, and, grasping the sharp tools of the word of God with a firm faith, as wise builders, build up the walls of our spiritual temple."

Resuming the autobiography, we find that the results of this, his third tour for the College, are thus summed up. Speaking of the meeting in Sumterville, already alluded to, he says:

This was the commencement of a series of revivals, chiefly in the Black River churches, in which, during the space of three months, about three hundred and fifty precious souls were brought in, the majority of whom were young men. This number, however, includes those brought in at Williamsburg, Darlington, Marion, Midway, and some other places not now recollected. Free-will offerings to the College poured in in a wonderful manner. Heavy remittances were sent home. It was one check after another; the whole amounting, I think, to nearly six thousand dollars. Besides these, "small tokens of affection" were pressed upon my acceptance. The complimentary notes accompanying these presents I laid aside very carefully, to be laid before the Trustees or Executive Committee of the College, that they might make such a disposition of the money as they might think proper. Crowned with most extraordinary success, both as agent of the College and herald of salvation, I was returning home in October in high spirits, and with a grateful heart, when I found the poet had but too much reason to say:

"We should suspect some danger nigh,
Where we possess delight."

On my way home I was robbed!

The circumstances of this robbery are detailed in the following letter to his wife:

"MONTGOMERY, Alabama, *Nov.* 10*th*, 1852.

"MY PRECIOUS WIFE—Here I am, fast anchored still; but I have not been lying upon my oars. I have visited West Point and Lafayette, at each of which places I have preached with some success, and have done something also for the College. * * * You would like a little history of the affair. Well, I will give it. The first time I saw the man, (Kean, Kane, or King,) was on the car the other side of Hamburg. A little incident marked our first acquaintance. It was a warm afternoon, and I was upon the sunny side. The car was pretty much crowded; but on the shady side, where was also a pleasant breeze, I saw this man and his wife, occupying a double seat, having another double seat so turned over as to furnish a resting-place for his lady's foot. Upon this double seat no person was sitting; and thinking that I needed the cool shade and the pleasant breeze more than the lady's foot or the carpet-bag which I saw there, I went and proposed to turn the double seat over, that it might be occupied by myself. In attempting to make this reasonable arrangement, he repelled me rudely. 'Sir,' said I, 'you have more than your share.' Saying this, I returned to my old seat on the warm and sunny side; but after a while, thinking that I might have appeared wanting in politeness to the lady, who was also concerned, I went back and made some slight apology. I ought to have done no such thing; but I could not think of being guilty of any rudeness, even in appearance, to a lady.

"When we reached the terminus, and were about to exchange the car for stages, the trunks of the passengers were put down upon the ground in an open space. I opened my trunk and took out some gold to pay my fare. Kean, it seems, was present when I opened my trunk, and noticed where my money was kept; and I believe, from that moment marked me for his victim. Arriving at Lagrange, he left his companion there, evidently that he might be more free to act.

"On getting into the cars at West Point, he took the seat immediately behind me, and became very gracious. He ascertained that I was going to Texas, and he gave me to understand that he was going to Mobile. So it was agreed that when we got on board the steamboat at Montgomery, we should occupy the same state-room. He must have first made the proposition, for I think I never could have done such a thing. On reaching Montgomery, as there was a boat about to start, I went immediately on board. He came immediately after, and had his name registered for the same state-room, taking the upper berth. Coming into the room about eleven o'clock on Tuesday night, October 12th, I observed: 'We have a very pleasant room.' 'I don't like it,' said he, 'for it is just over the boilers.' 'You can get another room, I presume, sir,' was my reply. But no; the fear of the boilers could not induce him to change his quarters. That very night, as it seems, he came in about midnight from the gaming-table, and perceiving that I was fast asleep, he took the keys out of my pocket, and quietly opening my trunk, his nimble fingers soon made their way to my money-box; and rifling it of its contents, gold and bank bills to the amount of about one thousand dollars, he then put every thing in good order, locked the trunk, and putting the keys where he had found them, got into his berth, and there remained until after I had arisen in the morning. He was then very impatient to get off; at eleven o'clock he did get off at Prairie Bluff. When the boat reached that place, my virtuous friend came to me in a state of much excitement, and said, 'Mr. Baker, I am going to take a ride with a friend;' and without bidding me good-by, he went away, being careful to have his trunk taken out by the back door.

"Some three or four hours after he had thus taken 'French leave' of me, I opened my trunk, when lo! to my astonishment and horror, I found that my money-box was light and empty. Calling a friend,

I made known to him the astounding fact. He called the captain, and soon the affair was made known to all on board. There was a consultation. A general search was proposed; but it was plain that no one could have taken the money but he who had occupied the same room with myself.

"The next thing was to get some efficient man to go in pursuit of him. One B. consented to enter upon the chase. He and myself, therefore, got on board of the first steamboat we met going up the river. We did not reach Prairie Bluff until after breakfast the next morning; so the thief had about twenty hours the start of us. Here, sending Mr. B. one way, it was thought advisable that I should take another. Whilst I was endeavouring to hire a horse for myself, which detained me one full hour, up drove Major H. in a buggy, having one spare seat. 'There,' said a friend, 'there goes the very man that will suit you. He is the ex-sheriff of this county, and understands such matters.' Although he was driving very rapidly, I ran after him and hailed him. Telling him my story he became much interested, and, although it was very inconvenient for him to undertake the pursuit, he consented. Jumping into his buggy, we rode about ten miles to the house of a friend, there got a fresh horse, and then, I assure you, Major H. was off, as the saying is, like a streak of lightning. As the well-trained hound chases the deer, nor easily misses the track, so it was with the ex-sheriff.

"We rode nearly all night, and, devious as were the windings of the thief, my friend did not, for one moment, lose the scent. Perceiving that the chase would be a long one, Major H. concluded to go to a town where there was a telegraph office. From this he sent a dispatch to the Marshal at Montgomery, whither he knew the thief was hastening. There the man was arrested—lightning struck! and there, to his utter astonishment, found lodgings provided for him, not in the hotel, but in the jail. Being searched, about six hundred and fifty dollars were found upon him in gold and South Carolina bills, agreeing most marvellously with what I had seen a few days before in my own strong box!

"I hurried to Montgomery, and paid my old room-mate a visit. As I entered the apartment where he was confined, he reached out his hand to me, saying, 'Mr. Baker, I know you!' Taking his hand, I replied, 'And I know you, sir!'—and added, 'Mr. Kean, you have put me to great inconvenience; I did not think you would have served me so!' 'Mr. Baker,' said he, 'I know your *person*, but I know nothing about your *affairs!*' If he should be convicted and sent to the penitentiary, some good will have been done; not so much, indeed, as if he had been convicted and converted by my instrumentality.

"The doctrine of a Divine Providence, as manifest in this whole affair, is a blessed doctrine; and, although this is not exactly the state of rewards and punishments, yet 'those who notice providences, shall have providences to notice.' I believe that, in some way or other, the hand of God is in it. He has, at any rate, permitted it. It must be so, for, if any event takes place without the divine permission, it must be either because God is not aware of it, or cannot prevent it. If he is not aware of it, he cannot be omniscient; if he cannot prevent it, he cannot be omnipotent.

"The morning after reaching Montgomery to attend this trial, I was reading Psalm 11th, and was struck with these words, 'The Lord loveth the righteous.' Poor sinner that I am, the Lord Jesus is made unto me 'righteousness,' and, therefore, in him I am righteous; and so I applied the passage to myself. I do believe that all will be overruled for good. Friends here are very kind. One of the proprietors of the most splendid hotel in the place, finding me there, although an utter stranger to me, kindly remarked, 'Mr. Baker, are you staying here? If, sir, you think proper to stay at this hotel, it shall cost you nothing.'

"Your affectionate husband,

DANIEL BAKER."

(TO A SON.)

"MONTGOMERY, Alabama, *Nov.* 12*th*, 1852.

"It is a fact, simple, Bible exhibitions of divine truth, are, of all others, the most effective, and no illustrations are so beautiful and touching as those drawn from God's blessed word. There is a sweetness and a charm about them truly wonderful; they fall pleasantly upon the ear; they come down with sweet and hallowed influence upon the heart; they please the rude and illiterate rustic, and also the man of literary taste and the finished scholar. For what was Apollos commended? Because he was 'mighty in the Scriptures.' And was not this the thing which gave a charm and a power seldom known to the preaching of Summerfield? My son, whilst others make a parade of learning, and boast of their knowledge of German literature, be it your praise that, in scriptural language, and with simplicity and power, you preach Christ and him crucified, as the world's last and only hope. This single sentence, 'It is a faithful saying, and worthy of all acceptation, that Christ Jesus came into the world to save sinners,' is worth a thousand of such sermons as are, in some places, most admired. I greatly desire that you should have your whole heart engaged in your Master's service. In this way you will find more pleasure in your ministerial work, and your labours will be more abundantly blessed. Remember what is written, 'Him that honoureth me I will honour, and he that despiseth me shall be lightly esteemed.' Never take your eye from the cross crimsoned with a Saviour's blood! Think much on the subject of eternity; think of its nearness, its reality, its grandeur; and, with quenchless and untiring zeal, work, my son, whilst the day lasts, remembering that soon the night cometh when no man can work. In your preaching, aim at being clear, convincing, powerful, and tender too; feel what you say."

(TO HIS DAUGHTER.)

"MONTGOMERY, *November* 22*d*, 1852.

"* * * Still here. If my patience is not made perfect, certainly it will not be for want of being sufficiently tried. Kean's case is postponed. My dear nephew here was mortally wounded the day before yesterday, by the discharge of a cannon, whilst the company to which he belonged was firing minute guns on the occasion of the death of Daniel Webster.

While he was ramming down the cartridge, the gun went off, and, sad to relate, your cousin had both arms completely shattered, and one eye seriously injured, besides receiving other wounds of a dangerous character. Poor fellow! he was taken to his house on a mattrass, in great agony, and presented a frightful sight; both of his hands blown off, and the bones of his arms not only shattered, but mashed as if they had been pounded by some heavy weight. The morning after, several of his fingers were picked up in the street, quite a handful of them. They were shown to me, wrapped up in a paper. Poor, dear Joseph! I had for several days been a most welcome guest of his. I was standing in the portico of the court-house, just opposite where the cannon was situated. I saw the flash, but little did I know what awful damage had been done. I was sent for, and was soon in the chamber of my poor, dear, suffering nephew. Seizing with eagerness every opportunity, I talked and prayed with him. It seemed to him, and his wife also, a remarkable and kind Providence, that had so ordered it that I should be with him at this hour of deep and overwhelming affliction; and I have reason to believe that I was made the humble and honoured instrument of leading him to Christ in his last hour. If so, is it not well that I was in Montgomery just at this time? Who knows but one reason why I was brought here, and detained here, was, that I might be instrumental in doing my nephew much good? This idea has cheered me not a little, and has almost reconciled me to my long and grievous detention.

"The trouble brought upon me by Kean has truly

been of a serious nature; but what is this to that which has come upon my nephew and his afflicted wife? Only the other day I was telling him of what had befallen me. Little did I then know that a ten-fold heavier calamity was hanging over him. Of a truth this is a vale of tears, a world of sorrow; and well has it been said, 'We know not what a day may bring forth.' Surely 'there is nothing true, there is nothing firm, there is nothing sweet, but heaven.' Happy he who can say,

God is mine all-sufficient good,
My portion and my choice;
In him my vast desires are filled,
And all my powers rejoice.'

"I need not send love; you all know my heart. Adieu.

DANIEL BAKER."

We resume the autobiography.

The amount stolen was about one thousand dollars, of which about six hundred and sixty-six was recovered. As I had been in the habit of making remittances with great promptness as money was collected for the College, the amount stolen was nearly all my own; and, in making out my account with the Treasurer, as may be seen by reference to the books, I charged myself with the whole amount, and the College lost nothing. This I could afford to do, inasmuch as by a formal and recorded vote of the Executive Committee I was permitted to retain what, as stated in the complimentary notes, was intended for myself personally. This affair of the robbery was a serious drawback to many pleasant things connected with this tour. But, upon the whole, it was a prosperous one; and, returning home, and finding no breach there, but every thing pleasant, and the College doing well, I thought that, after all, I had much reason for thankfulness and joy.

During February, 1853, Dr. Baker leaves Huntsville upon his fourth tour on behalf of the College. The following extracts are made from the many letters written home by him during this absence.

(TO HIS DAUGHTER.)

"SAVANNAH, *May 7th*, 1853.

"I have visited once more the scenes of my nativity. Of a truth, there is a power in association; and when I was lately amidst the scenes of my early childhood, this power of association waked up in my bosom feelings both pleasant and mournful to my soul; for,

'Is there a heart so cold, so dead,
That never to itself hath said,
This is my own, my native land?"

Having not been there for some twenty-two years, I really felt that I was 'a stranger in a strange land,' so many changes had taken place. I tried to find out the very spot where I first breathed the breath of life; but the house was gone, and the plough had passed over the place. All the shade-trees had disappeared, and not even a stump was left to mark my early romping-ground. The ditch, too, where with pin-hook and thread I was wont, in my childhood, to catch the perch and the bream, was filled up. Every thing was changed, and so changed, that I could scarcely recognize the place of my birth, sixty-two years ago. And although I had repeatedly visited Midway settlement since entering the ministry, and was there in the year 1831, still I was, as already said, 'a stranger in a strange land,' there were so many new faces.

"On Sabbath I cast my eyes over the congregation—every thing was new—so many strange faces; and even the few known before, had undergone surprising changes. Cheeks were furrowed which were smooth, and locks had become almost as white as snow which had been black as a raven. It really seemed that I belonged to the men of another generation, and had come back from the spirit-land! Truly, I felt as if I was 'in the midst of posterity.' I need not tell you that many faces smiled upon me, and that I was cordially welcomed every where. Moreover, it pleased God to bless my preaching to the conversion of some, I hope, and to the reviving of many more. Without making personal application to a single individual, the contributions to Austin College amounted to two hundred and forty-two dollars. O, how good has the Lord been to me in giving me so many friends, and in so remarkably blessing my labours almost in every place. To his great name be all the praise!

"Tell your mother that my pipe has been thrown away long time ago; I have not touched it since I left Huntsville, except to cast it from me, as an ugly thing which I wished to see no more. Was not this a good example?

"Your ever affectionate father,

DANIEL BAKER."

(TO HIS WIFE.)

"CHARLESTON, *May 20th*, 1853.

"I have received a good many letters, but only one from you, and that a short one. With regard to myself, I am getting along much in the old way; and that, I am happy to say, is very well, both as a preacher and agent. My labours have recently been blessed to the hopeful conversion of a goodly number, two of whom, I hope, will devote themselves to the gospel ministry. Last Sabbath night a young lady was struck under pungent conviction, at Beaufort. She was so much wrought upon that she threw her arms around her mother, in church, and wept aloud. On the day following, she was rejoicing in Christ. My agency has been prospered. On the 17th inst., only three days ago, I sent home a check for three hundred and fifty dollars; to-day I enclose another for one hundred and twenty-six dollars. This will be, in all, poured into the treasury, in cash, since I left Huntsville, sixteen hundred dollars. This is doing better than I expected. My visits both to Savannah and Midway were very pleasant. Many friends greeted me welcome. Surely goodness and mercy attend my steps wherever I go! O for a more thankful heart! This morning one of the merchant princes of this place sent to offer me the use of his carriage and servant for the day. What a genteel beggar I am!—riding about like a gentleman in a fine carriage! But I must close abruptly. Love to all.

"In haste, your affectionate husband,

DANIEL BAKER."

(TO HIS WIFE.)

"SALISBURY, North Carolina, *July 8th*, 1853.

"At last your letter has come to hand; it was dated the 14th of June—'better late than never.' And right glad I am to be able to inform you that all my labours of late have been remarkably blessed. One revival after another in quick succession! I believe I told you about my meetings in Wynnsboro' and Horeb church, South Carolina, in which twenty-four persons were permitted to cherish, as we trust, a good hope in Christ; six of whom were the sons of pastors and ruling elders! The meeting held at Charlotte was one of the most delightful I ever attended in all my life, forty-seven professed conversion, amongst whom were four lawyers, two physicians, six merchants, and a pretty large number of gay and fashionable young ladies.

"From Charlotte I went to Davidson College, some twenty miles distant. The meeting commenced on Thursday night, and closed on Wednesday morning following. We had overflowing congregations; for the most part three times a day. Nineteen of the students professed conversion; and besides these, some ten or twelve persons more, not connected with the College.

"At Wynsboro', where it was doubtful whether I could get one hundred dollars, I received more than two hundred! At Horeb, a small church in the country, where the amount anticipated was no more than some thirty or forty, it proved to be one round hundred. At Charlotte, where not much was expected, I received in subscriptions, paid and not paid nearly five hundred dollars! And at Davidson College, where the President said he thought I could not get more than thirty or forty dollars, I received nearly three hundred! In two places I had to tell them to—hold! I had enough; and I wished them to give no more.

"I stated the number of converts in Charlotte at forty-seven, but by a letter recently received from the pastor, the present number is fifty. How good has the Lord been to me, blessing my preaching to the conversion of so many souls! This reminds me of Paul's paradox, 'As poor, yet making many rich.' To God be all, all the praise!

"With affectionate salutations, your old husband,

DANIEL BAKER."

(TO THE SAME.)

"ROCKY RIVER CHURCH, Penicks, *July 28th*, 1853.

"Help me to bless the Lord for his goodness, and for his wonderful works to me, and to the people round about here! I thought the meeting in Charlotte was a glorious one, which lasted some ten or twelve days, and was blessed to the hopeful conversion of some fifty precious souls. I thought that the meeting at Davidson College, which was of scarcely seven days' continuance, and turned out more than thirty converts, of whom twenty-two were College students, was also a glorious meeting; but I must say, that the meeting at Rocky River church, which closed yesterday, seems to bear off the palm. Commencing on Thursday, it wound up on the following Wednesday; and, to our joy and astonishment, some seventy or eighty persons occupied the seats assigned to young converts! Of these, some forty-five or fifty were promising sons of pious parents. What a harvest reaped down in one week! To God be all the praise! How thankful should I be that my voice fails not, although I am made to do all the preaching.

"Now in relation to another matter—for the services of the last week I have received for the College nearly three hundred dollars! Surely the lines have fallen to me in pleasant places, and I have a goodly heritage. Blessed be God! Yesterday evening I received a letter from a pastor not far distant, who promises me three hundred dollars for the College if I will visit his church!

"Your affectionate husband,

DANIEL BAKER."

(TO ONE OF HIS SONS.)

"POPLAR TENT CHURCH, *August 6th*, 1853.

"Two of the very best meetings I ever attended in all my life, were held within the last two weeks, at two churches in the country; one called Rocky River church, and the other Philadelphia. Some eighty or more were brought in at the former, and nearly the same number at the latter; say about one hundred and fifty precious souls brought to Christ within two weeks! To God be all, all the praise! But indeed I have laboured very hard—every day speaking some four or five hours; and the churches being so near each other, has, I assure you, put me up to all I know touching the matter of giving new sermons; for you must observe, that although in almost every place we have a 'raft' of ministers present, yet in no single place can I get one of them to preach! no, not a solitary sermon. I have requested, I have urged them to preach, but they all with one consent make excuse! The crowds attending upon my preaching are immense. Tidings have gone forth that the Lord is blessing my labours in a remarkable manner, and the people pour in from all quarters. Really, I am oppressed. This warm weather, I can scarcely stand it! Last Sabbath I suppose that more than two thousand persons were present! I was obliged to preach in the open air; and being almost entirely overcome, I had actually to take my seat, and preach for a time sitting! Although it is cheering to know that of late the converts have averaged some four or five to each sermon, yet it seems sometimes that the labour, under the peculiar circumstances of the case, is more than I can stand; and I confess I look forward with pleasure to the time when, in obedience to the Trustees, I shall go on to New York to purchase the apparatus for the College. With regard to my success as agent, it has been far beyond my most sanguine expectations. Hearts opened—purses have been opened also; and in some cases (one in particular) the silvery stream flowing in, has been swollen to such an extent that I had to check it! I do not, at this time, know precisely how matters stand; but I think I have, since leaving Huntsville, (7th March last) added to the finances of the College some four thousand dollars in cash! How thankful should I be that the Lord has so abundantly blessed my labours of love; for if I had not been blessed in my preaching, I should never have been so successful in my agency. 'Bless the Lord, O my soul, and forget not all his benefits!'

"In haste your ever affectionate father,

DANIEL BAKER."

(TO HIS DAUGHTER.)

"PROVIDENCE CHURCH, *August 19th*, 1853.

"MY BELOVED DAUGHTER—I wrote to your mother not long since, and I have now nothing new to say, save that I still continue to preach incessantly—that I am still greatly prospered, and, wonderful to tell, my voice as clear as a bell! The meeting at Poplar Tent church closed last Wednesday week, holding on not quite six days. About sixty converts, and two hundred and sixty-five dollars given to the College. Last night, a week ago, our services commenced at Concord, and closed yesterday at noon. At the inquiry meeting yesterday morning, there were nearly two hundred present; of whom, perhaps as many as eighty were occupying the seats assigned to young converts! and remember, in all these cases, chiefly men! Indeed, nearly all the prominent men in Concord are now professedly on the Lord's side. As formerly in South Carolina, so now, in the old North State, I am almost 'smothered with roses;' and how thankful should I be, that my health continues strong, and my voice clear! Succeeding so well in this region of country, and having invitations upon invitations, I have concluded to remain awhile longer. For some five or six weeks past, I have had immense congregations; every Sabbath, in particular, from two to three thousand.

"It is really trying to my domestic feelings to be so long absent from my family; but I am, by the grace of God, doing so good a work—this reconciles me. Besides, home will be so much the sweeter when I get there. Love to all.

"Your affectionate father,

DANIEL BAKER."

(TO HIS WIFE.)

"STEEL CREEK CHURCH, *August*, 31*st*, 1853.

"MY BELOVED WIFE—Really, I am tired of talking so much of myself, my preaching, and my success; but you will excuse me this once more, especially as, the other day, there was some probability that my pen was laid aside for ever. Whilst I was speaking in the inquiry meeting, I was suddenly taken with a violent chill. A carriage was immediately brought to the door, and I was taken to the house of a kind friend, Colonel Greer, where I now am. On reaching his hospitable dwelling, I went to bed, and did not leave it for three days. The first day the fever which followed the chill was very high. The next morning I had another chill, followed by fever, but not so great as the day before; yet the doctor has since told me that there were some indications of congestion. For a time I was exceedingly weak—could scarcely walk across the room; and, without alarm, thought it likely that some kind friend here would write you a letter beginning thus, 'Dear Madam—Your husband has fallen asleep in Jesus;' and I pictured to my mind the scene which would then take place; and in the visions of my mind I beheld my daughter amongst the chief mourners.

"But enough of this fancy affair. God be thanked, on the third morning I missed my chill, and leaving my bed, I went to church on somewhat tottering limbs, and with somewhat salivated mouth, and with four red prints of mustard plasters upon my wrists and ancles. I preached what was equivalent to some two sermons or more. This morning I am getting pretty strong and fresh again, and hope to be able to do full service this day. But the doctors say I must not preach any more for some week or ten days. Accordingly, I have already countermanded the other appointments made, and expect to leave for the North in a few days. My last meeting was held at Providence church. It closed on last Thursday. It was greatly blessed. The pastor tells me that the number of converts is one hundred and three, and these, as usual, chiefly men. The contributions to the College amounted to about three hundred dollars.

"As the doctors have laid their commands upon me to stop preaching, and the providence of God also seems indeed to speak to me as Christ once did to his disciples, Turn aside and rest awhile, I may return home before the meeting of Synod. I shall, however, be better able to judge after reaching New York, from which place I purpose to write again. But I hear the sound of carriage wheels moving onward to the church, so I must abruptly close, or my letter will not be in time for the mail.

"Immense congregations attend upon my preaching—every Sabbath perhaps three thousand. People come from a great distance, and I am told there has not been such a glorious revival in North Carolina for the last fifty years. To God be all the glory!

DANIEL BAKER."

(TO HIS DAUGHTER.)

"STEEL CREEK CHURCH, *September* 1*st*, 1853.

"MY BELOVED DAUGHTER—Yesterday, with some intermissions, I was preaching, as usual, from ten to four o'clock. At the close we had quite a scene. I had pronounced my farewell benediction, when a gentleman of the first standing in this community came up to the stand, and lifting up his voice, wept aloud. Under the most pungent conviction, he called upon God to have mercy on his soul; and then said to me: 'Mr. B., you have made me feel as nobody ever made me feel before. Cannot you preach here one day more?' I consented, and accordingly made the appointment. But this day I leave, not for New York, as I gave your mother to understand, but for Statesville. There are some very remarkable providences about this matter, which I cannot now explain. Suffice it to say, a gentleman had come for me fifty miles, bringing a letter of invitation so pressing, and of such a peculiar nature, that I could not resist. I believe this thing proceedeth from the Lord; and I now expect to continue preaching in this State about three weeks longer, and then for the North. Let your next letter be addressed to me at New York; but be sure to write by return mail.

"It is nearly time to start for church, so, affectionately yours,

DANIEL BAKER.

"P. S. The fame of our meetings has gone abroad,

and hence, wherever I go, I have immense congregations; and many persons are curious to see the man that can preach so much."

(TO HIS WIFE.)

"MORGANTON, *Sept. 20th*, 1853.

"MY DEAR ELIZA—I am not in a writing trim; but as I am just on the wing for New York, I must drop you a line. Our last meeting was at Statesville, and like the rest, it was crowned with a rich blessing, and proved to be a glorious meeting. Sixty-six converts, and, as usual, more men than women. In regard to the place where I now am—it is small, not much material, but in many respects important; and the little church here greatly needed to be strengthened. The meeting has been interesting thus far, and some prominent persons brought in. * * * I am not sick, but weak; and when not preaching, I am almost all the time lying down. I am pressed to go to many places, but can undertake no other protracted meeting, at least this fall.

DANIEL BAKER."

(TO HIS SON.)

"WILMINGTON, N. C., *Sept. 27th*, 1853.

"MY DEAR SON—Thus far I am on my way to the North. The boat from Charleston was too late for the car, so I am to tarry here until to-morrow morning; but I do not much regret it, for I need one day's rest very much; and to secure it, I have done what I could to keep my friends in Wilmington from knowing that I am here. Yes, I do need rest, for I have been preaching a great deal of late; moreover,

I have been sick—three days confined to my bed—but I am doing pretty well at this time, though still somewhat weak. I was taken with the chills about three weeks since, and the doctor kept me in my chamber three days; but on the fourth morning, understanding that there was a great congregation assembled, and many having come from a distance, I ventured out, and being unable to stand, I preached sitting, to some eight hundred persons, in the grove. This meeting, as well as others, was crowned with a rich blessing. In the eleven protracted meetings which I have attended in North Carolina recently, something more than six hundred persons have been hopefully converted; of whom nearly three-fourths are males, from fourteen to seventy years of age. In some of these meetings, an unusually large number are heads of families; and I am happy to learn that the blessed work is going on, converts continuing to drop in after the special services were closed. 'Not unto us, not unto us, but unto thy name, O, Lord, be all the praise!'

"I could mention some very interesting incidents about the conversion of a lovely bride, and a young lady, whose mother did not wish her to go to a Presbyterian church; and about a man, of whose conversion no one ever dreamed; and of another, who had killed a man; and of another, who had been brought in emphatically at the eleventh hour; and of another, who was worth a quarter of a million of dollars; and of six youths, who were the sons of preachers and ruling elders. And I could tell you about the early and triumphant death of one of the converts, which served to make a powerful impression upon many.

But these things cannot be very well spread upon paper; it would take up too much time. I can better talk the matter over when I see you face to face, if Providence permit, at Galveston, in November next.

"With regard to the Presidency of the College, I have not accepted, and do not intend to accept, until I can know what duties will be required of me. My success as agent has continued to be far beyond my most sanguine expectations. I have sent home, or caused to be sent, more than four thousand four hundred dollars since leaving Huntsville the last time; and I have on hand more than fifteen hundred dollars! Surely the Lord has been very good to me!

"Must I not soon go the way of all the earth? I have had delightful views of Christ. During this whole tour I have preached him incessantly, and with positive love kindling and glowing in my heart; frequently with tears streaming down my cheeks! I think this has been one secret of the success: 'Him that honoureth me will I honour; but he that despiseth me shall be lightly esteemed.' Remember, my son, this saying of your father, that the sermon that does not distinctly present Christ in the beauty and glory of his mediatorial character, is no better than a cloud without water, a casket without a jewel, a shadow without the substance, or the body without the soul. Think of what Paul says, 'God forbid that I should glory, save in the cross of our Lord Jesus Christ'—and again, 'Christ is all and in all.' Think of it in your pulpit and in your study; when you lie down and when you rise up; when you go out and when you come in. Rest assured that there is no theme that has more power to melt the heart and subdue the soul. *Vale et vive.*

"Affectionately, your father,

DANIEL BAKER."

(TO HIS DAUGHTER.)

"NEW YORK, *October 6th*, 1853.

"MY DEAR CHILD—Last night I visited the Crystal Palace. Brilliantly illuminated with perhaps some twenty thousand lights, it presented a truly magnificent scene. After walking over a large portion of this immense and beautiful building, gazing with admiration upon the rare, rich, and endlessly diversified creations of art, almost ready to drop with fatigue, I sat down upon a seat in the gallery, or upper promenading place, from which point I had a commanding and beautiful view of the interior of the Palace, and the vast multitudes of ladies and gentlemen who were moving below and around me in every direction. These human forms winding their way amid statues and paintings, and silver and porcelain vessels, and rich tapestry, and ten thousand splendid things which I cannot name, presented a scene worthy of the pencil of the best artist. Not only was the eye feasted, but the ear also, for there was a band of music, which at intervals entertained the company with lively airs, the effect of which was peculiarly fine in this vast illuminated palace. But, my daughter, splendid and grand as this whole affair certainly is, in heaven we shall have what will throw all completely and for ever in the shade! The Crystal Palace, with all its gorgeous things, is the work of man—poor, dying man—but of the heavenly palace, God himself is the great and glorious Architect!

"Your ever affectionate father,

DANIEL BAKER."

He writes on his return home, to a student in the Seminary at Columbia, now the Rev. J. McDowell, of Sumter, South Carolina:

"HUNTSVILLE, *February* 14*th*, 1854.

"MY DEAR YOUNG BROTHER—I rejoice greatly that you have seen your way clear to devote yourself to the service of God in the gospel ministry. May God bless you, grant you the joys of his salvation, and make you a burning and a shining light in your day and generation. As for myself, I may say, with one of old, 'It is toward evening, and the day is far spent.' But as my sun is setting, it is cheering to see other suns rising. How pleasant to think, that when the present generation of ministers shall have passed away, another generation will be raised up to take their place; and then, how happy, how glorious will the final meeting be! The scenes presented in South Carolina some eighteen months ago were pleasant, but scenes still more wonderful, thank God, were beheld during the last summer in the 'Old North State.' God was pleased then and there to visit his churches in a remarkable manner. Hopeful converts were multiplied, may I not say, literally, as the morning dew. More than six hundred precious souls were, in a short time, made obedient to the faith, among whom were numbered, I suppose, at least three hundred young men! What a precious harvest! Who can tell how many may imitate your example, may join the army of the living God as soldiers of the cross and heralds of salvation!—and the final and blessed results who can tell! I should not be surprised if, before long, you shall have the pleasure of seeing some entering your seminary, for, before I left North Carolina, I heard of several young men of great promise who were seriously turning their attention to the sacred office. Well, let them come! I suppose you will receive them with open arms, and cordially greet them welcome! Let the number be multiplied! There is need, for 'the harvest is great, and the labourers are few.' May the Lord of the vineyard send forth more labourers into the harvest. What an honour to be an ambassador of Jesus Christ, and what high rewards and immortal honours in a future world await those who shall labour faithfully in their Master's service! What say the Scriptures? 'They that be wise, shall shine as the brightness of the firmanent, and they that turn many to righteousness, as the stars for ever and ever.' My young brother, give yourself wholly to the work before you. Take a pleasure in your new calling. Let your standard be high, not only in relation to mental improvement, but much more to spiritual attainments. For devotional exercises read 'Baxter's Saint's Rest,' 'Owen on Heavenly-mindedness,' and 'Smith's Lectures on the Sacred Office.' These books were greatly blessed to me. But, above all, the precious BIBLE; let that be indeed your *Vade Mecum*, your companion and counsellor by day and by night. But I must close.

"God seems to be indeed smiling upon our College, and we indulge the pleasing hope that this institution, founded in faith and prayer, will prove a rich blessing long after the founders thereof shall be numbered with the sheeted dead. Please present my best respects to the venerated Professors of your Seminary, and my kindest regards to your associates who may not have forgotten your old friend,

DANIEL BAKER."

CHAPTER XIV.

FIFTH AND SIXTH TOURS ABROAD, AND LABOURS IN TEXAS AS AGENT OF AUSTIN COLLEGE.

"HUNTSVILLE, *March 13th*, 1854.

"MY DEAR SON—With regard to our Education Convention, it seems to have excited more general and lively interest than I ever dreamed of. The Attorney-General says he will certainly be present; and by a letter recently received from Houston, I learn that they have appointed fifteen delegates, and these embracing some of the oldest and most respectable citizens of the place. May God's blessing be upon the Convention; for without that, nothing will or can prosper."

In 1853, while Dr. Baker was on a visit to Austin, it was determined by a number of gentlemen there at that time, to call an Education Convention, to meet at that place during the ensuing session of the Legislature, consisting of friends of education from all parts of the State. It assembled at the time appointed, and a second convention was held in Huntsville the next year after. It is to this that allusion is made in the letter. These conventions did much to increase and enlighten public sentiment in regard to education.

In this connection, while its object was a general one, it need hardly be said that Dr. Baker, to use a phrase of his own, "left no stone unturned" to advance the interests of the College of which he was agent. Never did he let any opportunity of advancing its interests remain an instant neglected. On one occasion, being in the lobby of the Legislature with the writer, the latter pointed out to him, near at hand, the President of a grand railway enterprise. Dr. Baker immediately sought and obtained an introduction to him, and began to call his attention to the cause of the College. "Say no more, sir, say no more," said the financier, "the company have already determined to donate one hundred thousand dollars in our stock to your institution." Somewhat astonished at the promptness, as well as magnitude of the donation, the Dr. asked if he would reduce his promise to writing. "Most certainly, sir," replied the railway king; and in a few moments Dr. Baker was in possession of a written document to that effect. "I do not think it will ever amount to any thing," he said to the writer, as they descended the steps of the capitol; "but it may; at least, it cost nothing to get it." It need not be added that the document is now valuable only as bearing the autograph of a very remarkable man. There were one or two other similar cases.

From the beginning of the College enterprise up to the hour of his death, Dr. Baker cherished the hope of obtaining aid for the College from the State, by some plan just and equitable toward all other *bona fide* institutions in Texas. He became ashamed, as he often remarked, of seeking aid for the institution abroad, while so little was done for it in Texas itself; a State so rich, too, in every sense of the word. Hence, session after session of the Legislature, he would visit Austin, armed with memorials. All that mortal man could honourably do, he did, in some form or other, to obtain this object. He was treated with great courtesy by the members in private, was invited to the floor of the Senate, was allowed the satisfaction of hearing his memorial read aloud out of its order on one or two occasions—even had the unexpected pleasure of seeing himself and his cause recommended to the Legislature in a message of the Governor—but all in vain. Each legislative session for years saw this great hope of his heart wax and wane.

The grounds of opposition to granting aid to a denominational institution were manifold. A few opposed the granting of State aid to such an institution out of sheer hatred to religion in every form; but these were few, very few. No State has fewer such legislators than Texas. Others were honestly opposed to granting aid to one College, lest the same should be demanded for a hundred other institutions in the State. Others acted from a vague horror of any thing like a union in the matter between Church and State. Others opposed from terror of "sectarianism," forgetful that a College, to be successfully managed, has to be in the hands of some body of men, and that, as an almost invariable rule, a denomination of Christians is the only body sufficiently united, interested, and energetic on principle, to conduct an institution with vigour and success; forgetful, too, that the field is open to all denominations alike—whose very competition is a guaranty of the dangerous pre-eminence of none, and the high order of all the Colleges under their care. But the mass conceived the duty of the State to education as performed, in the amount—over a million in lands and money—set apart by the State for common schools and a State University.

Though cherishing hope of aid for the College from the vast coffers of the commonwealth, and doing all that could be done to obtain this, yet never for a moment did he relax his exertions in other directions. About the beginning of 1854, it was determined to attempt obtaining twenty thousand dollars as an endowment for a "Baker Professorship of Mathematics." Henceforth Dr. Baker aimed steadily at this; and before his death it was accomplished, as will hereafter appear.

In April, 1854, he left Huntsville upon his fifth tour in behalf of the College.

"ROME, Georgia, *June 7th*, 1854.

"MY DEAR GOOD WIFE—I am preaching here every day, twice, and blessed be God, my labours are still being crowned with a blessing. Our meetings are crowded. I was told that Rome was a hard place, and there never was a revival here; but, blessed be God, the showers of heavenly grace are now descending. At Talladega there were about twenty precious souls hopefully converted. I trust we shall have more than that in Rome; and to God shall be all the praise. I have just returned from the church. We had, as I am told, a better attendance than usual, even on the Sabbath. The interest is evidently increasing. Besides my usual message, I had one from a young lady, who, within some two hundred yards, was very near her end. She said to me, 'Tell them I am dying, or I may be dead; but tell them to get religion, to come to Christ, and not to delay.' And then she exclaimed, 'O, sweet Jesus, sweet Jesus! Come, Jesus, come!' I assure you, that our meeting this morning was one of no common interest. Several will date this day as their starting-point in the race for glory, the commencement of a life which shall never end.

"Yours, as ever,

DANIEL BAKER."

(TO THE SAME.)

"DALTON, Georgia, *June 22d*, 1854.

"MY DEAR ELIZA—I have nothing special to say, but thought I would drop you a line, to let you know I am still alive, and preaching every day with some success, as usual. God be thanked, the meeting here has proved one of great interest; house crowded, and about eighteen persons cherishing, as I trust, 'a good hope through grace.' I have received so many and pressing invitations from churches in this region of country, that I find it difficult to reach Carolina. May the Lord lead me, as a father leads a child.

"The people give cheerfully, but not in large sums

Well, every little helps. But I think a lawyer, for the same amount of speaking, would get ten times as much as I do. But money collected is not the only fruit of my speaking. Some sixty persons, as I hope, have, by my humble instrumentality, been lately put in possession of the one pearl of great price. I am happy in my work; but, I confess, I get now and then a little homesick, and think that this must be my last tour.

"Last Sunday night I had, while preaching, one of my 'turns,' and came near falling in the pulpit; but it was owing, I suspect to the warmth of the evening, and the excessive crowd. Do not be uneasy; I am told that there are no symptoms of apoplexy, nothing but a common vertigo. Heaven bless you, one and all!

"From the man of silvery locks,

Your husband,

DANIEL BAKER."

(TO A SON.)

"CARTERSVILLE, Georgia, *July 3d*, 1854.

"I never did like stiff, starched, essayic letters. There is a power in association; and the mention, in your letters, of all little home matters, gives scope and liveliness to this exercise of the power of association; serves to place me in my own domicil, and surround me with all the nameless charms of domestic life. Why, the mention of the quantity of butter made, the quality of the peaches, and the number and size of the watermelons, would not be wanting in interest. 'Chit-chat, chit-chat,' that is what I like in home letters. This is a kind of substitute for a home visit, and gives an innocent and agreeable diversion to my thoughts, amid the graver scenes by which I am surrounded.

"While I think of it, I will mention something new, which I saw the other day—a cripple in a kind of chair, running, I think, on three wheels. Behind was a corpulent goat, 'fat as a butter-ball,' with his head pushing at the back of the chair. The goat seemed to be well trained, and performed his part to perfect admiration, pushing, and refraining to push, as his master gave command. I mean, when his master was sober; but sometimes he was not sober, and the goat, prompted by feelings of disgust, would upset the whole concern, and shell his master out. Well done, goat! DANIEL BAKER."

"ROME, Georgia, *August 2d*, 1854.

"MY ONLY WIFE—For two weeks I have had fever and ague; nevertheless, within the last three weeks we have had three blessed protracted meetings, a week each. Precious meetings indeed they were. Yesterday more than forty attended our inquiry meeting. At Sardis I came pretty near being killed—thrown from a buggy with great violence. God be thanked for all his mercies!

"In great haste, yours, as ever,

DANIEL BAKER."

(TO A DAUGHTER.)

"ANDERSON COURT HOUSE, *August 19th*, 1854.

"Our meeting at Good Hope lasted some five or six days. As usual, I did all the preaching. Very delightful the meeting proved. On inviting the young converts and anxious to go to another place there was quite a rush—some forty or more; and, strange to tell, nearly all men. Our meeting here is now in progress, and our prospects for the time as encouraging as in any other place. O how wonderful that God should bless my labours so! You cannot imagine how letters of invitation are showered upon me. One person told me he had come one hundred and sixty miles to hear me; and so many ministers too from churches all around. On my arrival, the other day, there were no less than some five ministers who came to the car to bid me welcome, and to invite me to visit their churches. I have heard of some four or five ministers who had been brought in under my preaching, of whom I knew nothing until within a few weeks past.

"I preach a great deal; my speaking, I suppose, will average from six to seven hours every day. When I am not in the pulpit I am upon the floor; and when I am not in the church with the great congregation, I am in the lecture-room with inquirers. Sometimes I feel a little jaded, but God seems to renew my strength day by day. I am so much occupied, and so frequently interrupted, that I have to write by snatches—so please tear up my letters, or throw them in the fire, when read. Again the church bell is ringing, and I must abruptly close.

"Your affectionate father,

DANIEL BAKER."

"GREENVILLE CHURCH, South Carolina, *September 4th*, 1854.

"MY DEAR SON—Since coming into this State, I have attended three protracted meetings, of about a week each. God be thanked, all have been blessed; Christians greatly revived, and some eighty or ninety souls hopefully converted. A large number are young men. Yesterday I preached to an immense congregation; prospects highly encouraging. Kiss Hartman for me—my only hope for posterity. The carriage is at the door to convey me to the church.

"Your affectionate father,

DANIEL BAKER."

"P. S. Just returned; had a delightful time; great congregation; much solemnity; very general feeling; some twelve or more hopefully converted. My speaking amounts to some three or four sermons a day; and this for some three or four months past. Many persons express their astonishment. 'Why, Mr. B., how can you stand it?—you can break down six preachers!' I confess it does seem a little strange, but so it is. When I finish one meeting, I begin another the very next morning; sometimes the very same evening! My Master sustains me; and, is it not written, 'They that wait upon the Lord shall renew their strength'? I feel just as strong and lively now as when I entered upon these meetings. Blessed be God! The people are beginning to give to the College. At two meetings, two hundred dollars each; one, one hundred and eighty dollars; another, one hundred and thirty dollars. I long to return to the bosom of my family. Pressing invitations are pouring upon me from all quarters; more than I can possibly comply with. If I had had such scenes before me when I was a young man! But I may say as the disciples said, 'It is toward evening, and the day is far spent.'"

(TO HIS WIFE.)

"LIBERTY SPRING CHURCH, *September 30th*, 1854.

"MY DEAR ELIZA—I wish to keep square with the whole world, and thus obey the Apostle's injunction, 'Owe no man any thing, but to love one another.' In relation to my ministry and my agency: I have of late been as successful as in my palmiest days in North Carolina last year. For some time past the converts will average thirty-five a week; and then, the converts are of so interesting a class, chiefly young men and young ladies. Our meetings for a few weeks past have been particularly interesting—one peculiarly so, at a church called Upper Long Cane. This was decidedly the very best we have yet had. There were jarrings before, but during the meeting the jarrings ceased, and there was most delightful harmonious feeling, to the great joy of the elders. O how it gladdened their hearts to see harmony restored, and some fifty converts rejoicing around them.

"The contributions in this church to the College for one week's labour amounted to upwards of three hundred dollars. The last meeting was at Newberry, where my labours had been greatly blessed some twenty-two years ago. I had so many invitations, I thought I could not hold a meeting there this time; but passing through, I preached two or three sermons; upon leaving, I received a written invitation, signed by forty-three young men, urging me not to pass them by. I concluded to accept their invitation. The meeting lasted one week, and closed last Thursday night. It was indeed a most delightful meeting—so many of the petitioners were brought in. The last day, when I proposed that all the young converts and inquirers should meet me in the lecture-room, some fifty or more hurried to the place. As Chancellor I. was an elder, he was invited to go in also. When he beheld the scene, his heart was melted. He attempted once to speak, and did say some touching things; but his feelings overcame him, and he wept aloud. One of his own sons was present, in the character of a young convert. He gave me one hundred dollars for Austin College. Was not this generous? but it was only after the example of Judge W., of Anderson, who had three sons brought in, and so, as a thank-offering, gave one hundred dollars. My dear E., is it not wonderful that the Lord should so greatly bless your old husband, whose scanty locks are becoming more and more silvered with age?

"To tell the truth, if encomiums give me pleasure, they give me pain also; for when I go to a new place, how can I meet expectations? One thing that comforts me is, I make no parade. I speak in a simple, conversational way, and my aim is, not to excite admiration, but to win souls to Christ.

"May the Lord bless the College, and protect it from all evil.

"Yours, with affection,

DANIEL BAKER."

From the same place, three days later, he writes to a son:

"If you ask why my preaching is so much blessed, I say again, 'Even so, Father, for so it seemed good in thy sight.' But if it will throw any light upon the subject, I will tell you that my plan is incessantly to preach Christ and him crucified; and this I do in an earnest, colloquial manner, and, not unfrequently, streaming tears attest the sincere and tender feelings of my own heart, aiming at the conversion of sinners. Being earnest and colloquial, I have the more fixed attention; and to understand the importance of this, take a burning-glass, and let the object, at the proper focal distance, remain in a fixed position, and it soon begins to smoke. So the mind, kept in contact with divine truth pouring upon it, soon begins to warm and kindle up. And with regard to the matter of feeling, you know, '*Si vis me flere, dolendum est primum ipse tibi.*' Now, preaching Christ so much, I keep upon my own mind a more distinct and lively impression of his wonderful love and compassion for our ruined race; and hence I present the matter with more feeling; and hence the effect upon the audience. God is a Sovereign, but he generally works by appropriate means.

(TO HIS WIFE.)

"GREENVILLE, *October 28th*, 1854.

"Our meetings are still crowned with a blessing—every meeting—every one! I have attended about twenty protracted meetings since I left home, and have preached every sermon save two—three sermons a day, on an average, for nearly four months past. The number of converts in all may be about five hundred and fifty, and so many men, and some cases so interesting! But the time would fail to tell one half. Sometimes when I get out of the pulpit, I feel jaded, and could almost wish that a brother would take my place; but when I get into the pulpit again, I feel perfectly fresh. But is not the remarkable success God is pleased to give, enough to impart new life and vigour to any man? I have now only some three or four more engagements, and then, home, sweet home!"

On the margin of the sheet he writes: "My hands are quite hard and rough. I *will* slap them together in the pulpit, notwithstanding the frequent remonstrances of my daughter."

(TO HIS DAUGHTER.)

"FAIRVIEW CHURCH, *Nov. 6th*, 1854.

"You wish me to write you a long letter once a week. What an unreasonable thing you are! Perhaps you do not preach as many sermons as I do. Matters are going on pretty much in the old way; only in almost every place more persons have been added to the church than were expected—proving that the work is genuine, and going on. To God be all the praise!"

In a note to a son from the same place, two days later, he says: "In one case a father and mother, and twelve children and grandchildren, were brought in. In this place, on Monday, fifteen attended the inquiry meeting; on Tuesday, thirty-two; and this morning, sixty-five."

In the course of all his labours it is not known that any one ever charged Dr. Baker, even in thought, with arrogating any thing to himself on account of the success God was pleased to give him. Nothing could be more clear to his mind at all times, than the simple fact, that he was the merest instrument in the hand of a Sovereign, who often uses the humblest "earthen vessels" to accomplish his noblest purposes: and for this express reason, that "the excellency of the power may be of God and not of us," though it is an Apostle who says it. That all his success was of God alone, was to him a *fact*, and a fact in which he rested all his joy and all his confidence during his labours. Even so far as human means are concerned, no one knew better than he how large a part of his success was owing to the labours of others before him. This has been already alluded to; and in a letter to the editor of a religious journal, dated Willington, South Carolina, November 22d, 1854, speaking of the brethren in whose churches his labours were so blessed, he says:

"I wish no credit to be given to me at the expense of pastors whom I so much respect and love. They are not only men of talents and piety, but efficient men, working men—pastors, in my opinion, of the right stamp, and whom, without an exception, their people love and delight to honour. If the voice of a stranger has wakened a new interest in their churches, this is no uncommon thing; for well do I recollect when I was a pastor myself, how the visit and preaching of another brother would, by the grace of God, exert a quickening influence upon myself and the people of my charge, when we ourselves were in a cold and slumbering state. There is something in a new voice, especially, when, for several days in succession, the great truths of Christianity are brought to bear upon the minds of men as the rays of the sun upon an object by the concentrating power of a burning-glass. If the meetings held recently in several of the Presbyterian churches in this region were 'remarkably blessed,' I ascribe it, under God, in a great measure to the fact, that much good seed had been sown in ground previously well prepared; and also to the cordial and efficient co-operation of pastor and people with the stranger from abroad. And, after all, the whole must be resolved into this—'Even so, Father, for so it seemed good in thy sight.' But if my preaching was crowned with a remarkable blessing, I believe one reason was this: Bearing in mind that the 'word of God,' and not the word of man, is quick and powerful, I was as a man of one book, and that book the Bible; and taking the hint from an inspired Apostle, I made Jesus Christ, and him crucified, my constant theme. This was certainly Paul's great doctrine; this was his sharpest sword, his chief battle-axe; and influenced by his example, I seized upon this heavenly-tempered weapon, and wielded it as well as I could.

"And here, my brother, permit me, as an old soldier of the cross, to say, that after long experience and close observation, I have come to the settled conclusion, that no doctrine has more power to soften the heart and subdue the soul than this. It is better than all the flowery and fine-spun theories in the world. Indeed, in my opinion, the sermon which does not present the blessed Saviour, is no better than a cloud without water, a shadow without the substance, a casket without the jewel, a body without the soul. Yes, it is Christ, and Christ crucified, which gives beauty and efficiency to every thing; and I think it would be well for every minister to remember these words, 'Him that honoureth me, will I honour; and he that despiseth me shall be lightly esteemed.' According to the Scriptures, in the economy of redemption, Christ is all in all. He is the hiding-place from the wind; and without him there is no covert from the tempest. He is the Saviour of the lost, and without him there is no salvation.

"I have been preaching Christ for nearly forty years, and in the contemplation of him I am more and more filled with wonder, admiration, and joy. Perhaps this may have given some new freshness, and power, and unction, and success to my preaching. 'O, that all but knew him!' In Christ there is a beauty that is unspeakable; there are wonders which human language cannot describe. If I may say so, in Christ there is an ocean of wonders. For, how wonderful, that he who was so rich, for our sakes became poor—so poor as to have no place to lay his head. How wonderful, that he who, in heaven, is the Saviour of all, should for our sakes, on earth, become a man of sorrows, and acquainted with grief! How wonderful, that he who is the final Judge, should himself, for our sakes, in the form of a man, stand condemned at Pilate's bar! How wonderful, that he who is the Lord of glory, should for our sakes be crucified! How wonderful, that he who is the Prince of Life, should for our sakes be brought under the power of death! And how wonderful, that he who fills immensity with his presence, should for our sakes, in the form of a man, be laid in Joseph's tomb! This has been the principal theme of all my sermons, and hence what some are pleased to call the 'remarkable success' which has crowned my preaching. And to God be all the praise!"

About this time a meeting was held in the place from which this last letter is dated—Willington, South Carolina. A member of the church, writing to a friend soon after, says:

"Twenty-two years ago, Dr. Baker held a meeting here. Many were made to rejoice in their Saviour during that meeting, and to this day testify to the goodness and mercy of God; but many are fallen asleep. When it was announced that the same Daniel Baker would again be with us, the news was hailed with rejoicing. Our prayers, that God would direct him to visit us, were answered; and, thanks to our Heavenly Father, the meeting was one of most thrilling interest. The last day, there were over seventy in the inquiry meeting, and about fifty of them professed a hope in Christ; and many enemies were made friends by his instrumentality. 'Blessed are the peace-makers.' It really seems as if the millennium has dawned upon us."

After his return home from this tour, he thus writes to a son in Austin:

"HUNTSVILLE, *January 3d*, 1855.

"MY DEAR SON—After more than eight months' absence, I found myself, at last, in the bosom of my family on the 26th ult., in fine health and spirits. Some three hundred young men, during this last tour, professed conversion under your father's preaching. I hope that many will be found seeking the sacred office. The revivals in Carolina were so extensive and glorious, that I see in the papers a proposition made that the Presbytery within whose bounds they occurred, should appoint a special day of thanksgiving. Since I came home, I received a letter, stating that forty-three had been received into the church, when the whole number supposed to be converted had been put down at thirty-five. I think, then, I do not exaggerate, when I estimate the number, during this last tour, 'made obedient to the faith,' at seven hundred. What a precious harvest this! It is certainly wonderful; but it is, 'Even so, Father, for so it seemed good in thy sight.' To God be all, all the praise!

"My sheet is crowded. God bless you all!

DANIEL BAKER."

It will interest the reader to know the sentiments entertained, in regard to the man and his labours, by those among whom he mingled during the meetings last spoken of.

One writes at this time:

"The Rev. Dr. Baker has just left us, after a series of meetings in our churches, whose great and unexpected results must for ever remain a memorial of the unfathomable goodness of God. The number of those who are serious and inquiring is upwards of seventy, while some forty of them are now rejoicing in hope of favour and reconciliation. Never has it been our privilege before to witness such a scene in the house of God—never, at least, one that gave so many unequivocal evidences of a genuine work. The congregations were most orderly and solemn; no shouting, not an outcry was heard that could possibly beget an artificial or mere sympathetic excitement; and no effort chiefly for such a purpose was once made. Nay, in proportion to the depth of feeling pervading the assembly, was the solemnity of its silence. It sometimes appeared as if the Spirit of God was actually brooding visibly upon the people, chastening and subduing their emotions, till almost a breath was audible. The visit and labours of Dr. Baker in our midst have also been greatly blessed in confirming and reanimating the people of God; for surely there is much that is eminently contagious in his warmth of love to the Saviour, gentleness of spirit, and comprehensive charity. All have been encouraged and strengthened, and many long at variance have met once more as brothers."

Another thus speaks:

"This devoted, indefatigable, and truly eloquent divine, is now conducting in our midst one of those deeply interesting meetings for which he is so justly famous. We had heard much of the Doctor even in boyhood, but not till recently were we favoured with the rare pleasure of witnessing ourselves his peculiar powers as a minister of the gospel. The half was not told us; he is truly an 'old man' *more* than 'eloquent;' and his strength consists in much that is infinitely better than the noblest command of language; yet even there, when fully warmed with his great Master's work, few living can surpass him. He is eloquent in a faith and an unction that seem to know no ebb; eloquent in a zeal and earnestness that beams in a face whose benignity once looked upon can never be forgotten; eloquent in a long life of energy and ripe experience that stands without a parallel in the present age, that is only comparable to that of Wesley or Whitefield, or the Apostles. What a relief it is—or to use one of his own favourite expressions, 'how delightful' it is to listen to such a man after sitting for years under the less animated and genial, the less practical and more purely argumentative sermonizing generally prevalent, and in many places sadly distorted from the simplicity of the Saviour, to the stiff, lofty intellectuality of the modern heroic school.

"Dr. Baker's powers are therefore evidently founded in a profound and discriminating knowledge of human nature, which leads him to adapt himself easily in every important particular to his audience. Do men love simplicity, especially in matters of great and lasting moment, such as the salvation of the soul?—he orders his style, his manner, and practical overwhelming logic, with a plainness and simplicity that is truthfully eloquent, while all is dressed in language whose purity and taste make it classic. Do they love zeal and earnestness of soul in one who would 'allure to brighter worlds and lead the way?'

his sincerity and devotion speak straight to the heart. Do they love gentleness and heartfelt sympathy in him who is commissioned to feed his Master's sheep, especially the lambs of the flock? the kindly emotions of a heart running over with love to his fellow men are manifest in every feature of his face, in every word he utters. In the mysterious providence of God, it is only in long and rare intervals that such men are given to the world, and they always seem to come just in time to re-illustrate the forgotten simplicity of truth, and its dignity as well; so came Socrates in the twilight of antiquity, to refute and expose the jargon of false philosophers; so came Butler in a later day, to vindicate the nature and truthfulness of a nobler philosophy. This is not fulsome praise, it is too true to be such; and it gives us unfeigned pleasure thus to honour a man whom God now honours eminently with his spiritual presence in the conversion of souls, and whose crown hereafter will sparkle with choice jewels."

Another thus speaks, looking back upon those meetings from an after period:

"No minister of our Church was more beloved by the brethren than this venerable servant of God. No one was more deserving of veneration. A few years since, he spent a few months labouring with the pastors of many of our churches—labouring as successfully in edifying ministers as in converting souls unto God. And who is there that can look back to the time of his sojourn among us without a feeling of regret that his face will no more be seen among us? His words, how much like the language of heaven!

One might almost have imagined that he was entertaining an angel unawares, during the intervals of public worship in the house of God. The most thoughtless could never avoid the conviction that he was listening to an ambassador for Christ, while seated in the public sanctuary; and the rude hand of time will never efface the many and salutary impressions which his visit has left behind. That was a favoured family who had the privilege of entertaining this man of God during these protracted meetings. How many little incidents which then occurred have been again and again related by one and another of the same household; and all tending to show the singleness of aim in this devoted servant of Christ."

Still another, relating an incident which occurred in the course of these meetings, remarks:

"Dr. Baker was often attacked in his travels by infidels and scoffers at religion. And no man was more successful than he in subduing such opponents, convincing them of the error of their ways, and leading them to Christ. Many who, when they first met with this great and good man, regarded the Bible as a false thing, invented by wicked men, and all who believe in its glorious and sublime doctrines as weak-minded, now give praise to God that he ever sent such a man to them, and blessed his earnest preaching and heart-touching conversation to their conversion.

"There is one instance in which he was the means of the instantaneous conviction, and we trust, the true conversion, of one who habitually and openly ridiculed the religion of Jesus and his people. Dr. Baker had been preaching at the place referred to for several days, and a revival of religion followed. This mocker of all that is holy went to the meeting on purpose to seek for something for which he might deride him, and those who were then led to see their danger, and to fly to the 'Rock of ages' for safety, under his powerful preaching. The services of the day had commenced when he entered the church. He took his seat in front of the pulpit. All was silence, save the voice of the preacher proclaiming the conditions of eternal life to that dying assembly, and the groans that would now and then escape from some agonizing penitent. It seemed that that was indeed the house of God, and that the Holy Spirit was there working in the hearts of the people. The engaging manner of Dr. Baker soon attracted and riveted his attention. The awful truths preached that day soon aroused his sleeping conscience, and convinced him of sin. His hard heart was softened, and the stern, the notorious scoffer, was subdued to tears. The man of God descended from the sacred desk, bringing the word of life with him, entered into conversation with the weeping man, and showed him that if he only would repent and come to Christ, he would forgive all his sins, and save him. He who had always before left the house of worship with a sneer of derision on his proud lips, on that day left, an humble penitent, weeping aloud as he rode away. He found peace in the wounds of a sacrificed Saviour—became a minister of the gospel in the Baptist denomination—led a consistent and useful Christian life; and from that day forward, found his greatest delight in the fellowship of those whom before he had despised."

"I have heard more finished orators"—remarks one, concerning his preaching at this time—"men whom it was more pleasant to hear; but I have seldom heard an orator who made his hearers understand him better, or who gave them less room, or less occasion, in fact, to dodge the conclusions to which he came. He is composed, and thoroughly in earnest. He seems himself to follow the track along which he leads you, to be practising his own precepts, and few are inclined to oppose a rebellious spirit to his teachings. It is the distinctive feature of his preaching, that he speaks not to a conception of his hearers, but to his hearers. Men have no time or opportunity to hand his admonitions over to their neighbours. Each is made to feel that he himself is the object, and that then and there, in view of the hopes of heaven and powers of hell alone, and upon his own responsibility, he must accept them or reject them."

The following letter to a son cannot fail to interest.

"HUNTSVILLE, *September 6th*, 1855.

MY DEAR SON W.—Although as yet I have received no answer to my last, yet will I write, especially as I have some pleasing intelligence to communicate. I have been on a mission to the Austin family, and my mission has been successful. They have agreed to endow a Professorship in Austin College, by deeding lands to the amount of twenty thousand—it may be, twenty-five thousand dollars. The Professorship is to be named after an only and beloved sister, Eliza Perry. I told the brothers that I left the amount to them, but the more princely the endowment, the greater would be the honour conferred on their sister. Moreover, the 'heirs' have turned over the claims of their uncle, Stephen F. Austin, on the late Republic of Texas, to our noble institution. I have conversed with a number of old Texans and others, and I find that the subject wakes up positive enthusiasm. So I think we shall certainly gain something by it.

"Another thing I must tell you is this: Mr. Guy Bryan has made the College a donation of a splendid painting, a fine likeness of Stephen F. Austin, large as life. It cost three hundred dollars. He had two painted by an English artist; one was designed for the Senate chamber, the other for the House of Representatives, at Austin: but one has been given to our College. A fine present this. It will be a fine and very appropriate adornment to our College chapel.

DANIEL BAKER."

After each absence from home, on his return he enjoyed greatly the quiet pleasures it afforded. For months he would enter with zest into its enjoyments. When not engaged in his study, he would be out in the field, the garden, the yard, with hoe and spade, hammer and saw, working with an energy which was his nature. No one could enjoy the familiar intercourse of the household more than he. Nevertheless, he had too long led an active life to rest contented at home. Like a mariner on shore, whose heart still heaves to the motion of the recent sea, whose blood still courses to the swift sailing, with favouring gales and over smooth seas, of the ship from which he has landed—so with the subject of this Memoir. Sooner or later he became restless in the narrower and lesser routine of life at home. In a few months after each return, the hand of his Master would lead him out again, a willing servant, to engage with fresh zeal in labours abroad.

The remark was often made in regard to Dr. Baker, how high he would have risen, had he gone from the outset into political life, instead of the pulpit. What a millionaire he would have become as a merchant. Let the truth be spoken. No, it is not so. It was the religion of Jesus Christ which, in almost every sense of the word, made him the man he was. We have seen that his childhood was moulded in a community peculiarly religious. We have seen, too, that while yet a boy, the Saviour passing by, had laid his hand upon his head, and bade him follow. In rising to follow this Master, he attained a larger manhood than he would ever otherwise have known. The knowledge of Christ elevated, expanded, and strengthened his intellect as nothing else could have done. It was the love for Christ, and the consequent love for his fellow-men, which enlarged, invigorated, and lent a swifter beat to his heart. Intellect, heart, even bodily frame, received from God the Holy Ghost a supernatural development and quickening. It was "the knowledge of the Son of God" which caused him to grow, so far as he did grow, "unto a perfect man, unto the measure of the stature of the fulness of Christ." Had he remained unregenerate, he would never, in any pursuit in life, have risen, as a man, to the rank of manhood he did attain as a servant of Christ. No other object whatever could have aroused him to the energy he displayed in striving for the salvation of souls. No conceivable motive could have "constrained" him as did "love of Christ." What duty was to Wellington, glory to Napoleon, love of country to Washington, the love of Christ was to him, as it was to Paul, and as it is to all servants of Christ, according to their measure of faith. This was the effectual antidote to him, against being in the least "puffed up" by the success of his preaching. He was not such a novice as to forget for an instant, that in whatever degree he excelled, it was solely and only the Spirit of God working in and by him; and this effectually cures any tendency on the part of those who loved and esteemed him most, to exalt him above measure. Place beside him the least successful minister in the Church—in whatever degree he excelled that minister, who can be so blind as not to know, that it was simply because a sovereign God had given to the one a larger measure of the Holy Spirit than to the other? Our wonder is not at the man, but at the wonderful working of the Holy Ghost in him and by him.

Wherever settled as a pastor, his studies were

pursued with characteristic ardour. He spared no pains in writing and re-writing his discourses. His familiar letters are the only papers from his hand upon which he did not bestow the most elaborate labour; and even these are singularly neat—never a blot, scarcely ever an interlineation even—for it had become a second nature to do his very best at whatever he put his hand. It need not be said, that in his study, the Bible was his chief book. While attaching the highest value to theological training, so far as that training made the word of God and human nature a subordinate study, he regarded it as an evil. Next to the Bible, he prized "Baxter's Saint's Rest," for devotional reading; but he was a rapid reader of whatever bore in any way upon his profession.

For all forms of metaphysics he had a positive aversion. As to studying the elaborate works of infidels against Christianity, he occasionally attempted it; but his patience would always fail. With him it was worse than as if he should stand at high noon, and, with the meridian splendour of the sun blazing full upon the page, read an argument proving that there is no sun. He was not philosophic enough for the task. Of religious poetry he was very fond. In regard to fiction, he was never known to read a novel in his life. Once a friend met him in the street, his arms filled with the novels of Sir Walter Scott, which he had borrowed, and was bearing home. In answer to some exclamation of surprise—"You know I preach against novel reading," he replied, "and really I ought to see for myself what they contain."

He never began the second chapter, however, of the first volume.

During the visit of Dickens to this country, his curiosity being excited by the enthusiasm aroused, he attempted to read "Oliver Twist;" it was a task, and an uncompleted one. By temperament fond of wonder and excitement, yet the wonders of romance were small with him in comparison to the awful and eternal realities upon which his mind so habitually dwelt; the "thrilling scenes" of the novelist, even had they been true, were tame to the scenes with which he was so conversant. The sister, weeping on the shoulder of the converted brother; the pious elder rejoicing in the conversion of a son, perhaps dissipated; the hoary-headed mother, clasping to her aged bosom her child who had long wandered from the household of faith; the pious husband exulting in the conversion of his wife, or she receiving the long-hoped fruit of many tears and prayers in the conversion of her husband; the inexpressible joy of the young convert in the first clear dawning upon the soul of the Sun of Righteousness; or the joy of a whole church, perhaps long distracted by feuds and barren of fruit, in the outpouring upon it of the Holy Ghost—frequent scenes such as these, made pale, to his eye, as the paper upon which it is printed, the most vivid fictions of the novelist.

As to the moral reformation of the world, written after so much of late by novelist, politician, and poet, his belief was a very plain and simple one, summed up in few words—first, "The heart is deceitful above all things, and desperately wicked," and, as such, doomed to eternal ruin; second, the one remedy for this is the blood of Christ, and the regenerating and sanctifying power of the Holy Spirit. There is no use of disguising the fact, he was a man of one book, the Bible; of one idea, the salvation of men by a crucified Saviour; of one occupation and object in life, the making known, as he was enabled of God, this salvation to men. And here was the secret of his enthusiasm in regard to the College, an enthusiasm which aroused more than the ardour and energy of youth in the man of three-score years. His leading object, thought, and hope, in regard to the College was, that thereby young men might be better qualified to serve God out of the ministry if not called, but especially in the ministry, if called of God. Young men of piety and promise had no peace, when in his reach, until they had prayerfully considered whether or not it was their duty to serve God as ministers of the gospel. To a father who sought his advice in regard to such a son, he replied, "I would give him the necessary education if I had to live upon corn bread and cold water three times a day!" Toward young ministers he had a warm feeling; and he was of opinion that such could greatly benefit themselves, as well as advance the cause of Christ, by spending, when practicable, the first years of their ministry upon the frontier; the domestic missionary work he regarded as an admirable school for the pastorate.

About the 1st of February, 1856, he left Huntsville upon his sixth tour on behalf of the College, and to attend the General Assembly. During this trip his labours were greatly blessed at various towns in Louisiana and Alabama. He writes during this tour as follows:

"TUSKEGEE, Alabama, *May 6th*, 1856.

"MY DEAR WIFE—No letter from home yet! But I hope to receive a large number a few days hence, for I shall probably reach Augusta to-morrow night or next morning, when I calculate on a feast, made more delightful by long abstinence.

"Well, I have been sick again; so sick, indeed, that I had to recall some of my appointments, and was in bed all day last Sabbath. Truly I have been labouring in the vineyard a long time; and as the hireling longs for the shadows of the evening that he may have repose, so it is with me. I think I can truly say, I desire to depart and be with Christ, which is far better. Last Sabbath, I think if the physician had said to me, 'It will soon be over,' I think I would have exclaimed, 'Good news!—good news!' But I confess, that if God please, I would rather breathe my last breath in the bosom of my dear family. I know I am a poor, imperfect creature, but I do not know that I shall ever be better prepared for my long home than I now am. But in relation both to the time and the manner of my death, I hope I shall always be able to say, The will of the Lord be done.

DANIEL BAKER."

"NEW YORK, *May 15th*, 1856.

"MY DEAR WIFE—This is the day for the meeting of the Assembly; the members are pouring in rapidly. I think, after this, the College must get another agent; I find that the object is by no means a popular one. More must be done at home. After the meeting of the Assembly I purpose to do what I can in New York and Philadelphia, and then try what I can do in Virginia.

"Affectionately,

DANIEL BAKER."

"NEW YORK, *May* 16*th*, 1856.

"MY OWN DAUGHTER—The Assembly convened yesterday. Two hundred and thirty-two members were enrolled the first day—the second, two hundred and fifty. A large Assembly, truly. Rev. Dr. Rice preached the opening sermon, from 2 Tim. iv. 1, 2. A very fine sermon it was. Dr. McFarland was elected Moderator. My name was nominated, but at my special request it was withdrawn.

"I am to preach for Dr. P. next Sabbath, and for Dr. A. the Sabbath after. I have received more invitations than I can attend to. Some of the salutations which I receive from ministers from various quarters are touching. I believe that many do love me. Well, my daughter, the Board have caught at the idea of publishing my Address to Children—title, 'Daniel Baker's Talk to Little Children.' It is going to be a pretty little book, with appropriate cuts. The new edition of my '*Revival Sermons*' is now in press. I never dreamed of such a demand. May God make the work a blessing to many, even when the hand which wrote the sermons shall be mouldering in the grave.

"Your own dear father,

DANIEL BAKER."

"New York, *May 31st*, 1856.

"My dear Son—We have had a most delightful meeting of the Assembly; every thing perfectly harmonious. On Saturday last, both Assemblies were treated to an excursion to Randal's and Blackwell's Islands, to see the benevolent Institutions located there. A very pleasant excursion it was; and on Monday afternoon we had another excursion (I mean those of our own Assembly) to Greenwood Cemetery. Some thirty carriages were kindly provided for our accommodation. Both excursions were made more interesting by speeches, singing, &c. I was called upon, but having a bad cold, declined. Dr. Lord has invited me to go to Buffalo, and I think I will go. With regard to my success as an agent, there has been nothing to boast of. The Legislature of Texas must render aid, or * * *

"From the old man of silvery locks,

Your father,

Daniel Baker."

After the adjournment of the Assembly, Dr. Baker held meetings in various places in New Jersey, Virginia, and North Carolina, with the usual blessing of God upon his labours. In his letters at this period, he speaks with peculiar feeling of meetings at which he had been present, in Hampden Sydney College, and in the University of North Carolina, at each of which institutions about twelve students made profession of religion. This gave him special pleasure; for, covetous for the increase of the cause of his beloved Master, with the eye of faith, he would reckon up the souls to be converted hereafter, by the labours of each educated youth—counting upon and rejoicing in the success of those labours in advance. It was a pleasure to witness his joy in the conversion of a youth of piety and promise—it was a joy, not only as over one sinner, but of multitudes of sinners saved—in anticipation—by their labours hereafter.

It is thus that he expresses himself, in a letter to Dr. C. C. Jones, during the meetings in South Carolina.

"You recollect, brother Jones, that in my sermon before the General Assembly last spring, I stated, in emphatic terms, that 'we must have more ministers,' and that my heart was towards the young men of our land, as Deborah said that her heart was towards the governors of Israel, who offered themselves willingly. Well, at the commencement of every protracted meeting which I held, I mentioned distinctly that the 'harvest was great and the labourers few,' and 'we must have more preachers.' And as we did not wish any one to enter the ministry unconverted, we must set our hearts upon the conversion of young men. And as for myself I was determined to make a dead-set upon this class in particular; and lo! already, God has granted the desire of our hearts. A little army of young men are already gathered around the standard of the cross; some of whom, I do hope, will soon be numbered amongst the heralds of salvation. Indeed, some, I am told, have already had their attention strongly turned that way. I trust we shall have at least one tithe.

"Nearly all who have professed converson have, by their respective pastors, been added to the communion of our church. Last Sabbath I beheld a beautiful sight—twenty young converts seated together at the table of the Lord; and the Sabbath before, a sight still more beautiful—one whole table filled up with young disciples, fifty in number! and amongst them so many prominent men, and lovely and promising young men! O, it was a scene of thrilling interest, well worth a journey of a hundred miles. Nay, more; well worth an angel's visit from the skies. To God be all, all the praise! Do, brother Jones, get many of our venerated and beloved pastors, evangelists, and missionaries, to say 'we must have more ministers.' Remember what I told you in Charleston, and what, of course, you knew before, that of seventy churches in the Synod of Alabama, thirty are not supplied; and that, in Texas, we have not more than about one minister of our communion to five counties. Our standard bearers are falling, and the number of candidates are decreasing. Only think of that! Something must be done. Do sound the tocsin of alarm, and let all who love our Zion come up to the help of the Lord, to the help of the Lord against the mighty. In other words, adopt some method of sending this saying, 'we must have more ministers,' through the churches, like thunder echoing among the mountains. I think that pastors and missionaries should take more interest in this matter. Pious and promising youth should be sought out and encouraged to enter the ministry.

"Do not misunderstand me. I am not for urging any young man, however talented, to enter upon the sacred office; but there is a certain kind of encouragement that might very properly be given, and ought to be given, to youths who bid fair to be useful in the ministry. And here I would simply make this remark—if I had not met with some encouragement (so far as I can see) I would never have entered upon the sacred office."

He was at all times eager, years after any successful meeting, to learn in regard to the firmness of the converts; and those who are familiar with the results of meetings at which he assisted, well know how very rarely he had cause for sorrow herein. But for the reason spoken of, in regard to young men brought in of God by his means, especially, he could say with the Apostle, "Now we live if ye stand fast in the Lord." Hence, and it is natural, his gratitude is most excited on hearing of ministers converted by his instrumentality. In this sense, with the utmost feeling of his mere instrumentality, he would rejoice to know of his "spiritual children," and even more still of his "spiritual grandchildren;" loving these, as is common in the earthly relation, with a love even purer and more tender than the others. Bear in mind the multitudes of men and women made by his labours, under God, so many separate centres—as citizens, friends, sisters, brothers, husbands, wives, fathers, mothers—of saving influences in their day, and down all after days. Then add to this the host of those brought in under his preaching, and afterward—as Professors in College and Seminary, as authors, as editors, as ministers in all branches of the Church—so blessed of God in their day, and down all generations after—who can calculate the power thus put forth by the Almighty, through the medium of even one individual, nothing in himself? There is in this the infinity as well as the glory and the bliss of eternity. Do not even Gabriel and Michael look up to such an office as this with holy envy? And what joy to wear in heaven a crown so sparkling with souls—a joy, not in the wearing the crown, but in the having such a crown to lift from the brow, and cast at the foot of the throne, exclaiming to him who fills it, "Thou art worthy, O Lord, to receive glory, and honour, and power!"

During this whole tour the health of Dr. Baker was not so strong as usual. Yet, if he did not now at all times mount up on wings as eagles, he nevertheless ran and was not weary, walked and was not faint. And now for the last time he crossed the Gulf for Texas. In the "Old States" his well-known face will be seen, his familiar voice will be heard no more!

It was a broad field, and for thirty-eight years had he toiled in it an ordained minister of Jesus Christ. East, West, North, South—over almost all parts of the United States—sowing the good seed along its furrows, on stony soil and good, summer and winter, seed time and harvest too, he had laboured in his Master's cause and in his Master's strength. His work therein is now done. Although he thinks not so, he leaves this field as the day-labourer withdraws toward his home at the close of the day. Some little work for Him he loves remains for his hands to do in Texas—but little more, and then—heaven. Taken quite sick on his arrival at Houston, in Texas, he stepped from the stage at his own door in Huntsville, during the first week of December, 1856, more wearied from his labours than ever before.

"I remained in office as President of the College," he says in his autobiography, "until January 7th, 1857, when I resigned the office of President, in order that I might give myself up wholly to the work of the agency, and"—such is the last line of his autobiography.

Turning to his letters home, it is found that from this period he toils for the College, with the same energy which had not faltered since his first conception of the institution for an instant; but now the field of his toil is narrowed down to Texas. The following letter is not only characteristic of the man, but shows how the Institution of his heart is appreciated in Texas, as well as in the older States.

"HUNTSVILLE, *May 30th*, 1857.

"MY DEAR SON—Last Saturday I returned from an agency tour of about five weeks in East Texas. I preached nearly sixty sermons. We had some precious meetings; about sixty persons awakened, of whom perhaps twenty or twenty-five were hopefully converted. I received about one hundred dollars in cash, and subscriptions to the endowment, something more than fifteen hundred dollars. Is not this doing pretty well for an old man operating in Texas; and that, too, just after Jack Frost had been committing such awful ravages in the field, the garden, and the forest?

"But I have still something better to mention,

and something which I think will surprise you. The Trustees of the College, at their meeting in January last, sold the remainder of the 'Wilberger tract,' to Messrs. J. C. and S. R. Smith, of this place, for five thousand dollars. After the deed was made out and every thing done in legal order, Mr. Sorley made me a proposition, in writing, to this effect, that if J. C. and S. R. Smith would cancel the engagement, he would give fifteen thousand dollars for the land. This astonished me. I immediately went to the Smiths, and without letting them know anything about the proposition made, I asked them if they were not willing to let us off. 'No.' 'Well, but,' said I, 'I will give you one thousand dollars to let us off.' 'No.' They were satisfied, and did not wish to give up the land. I then showed them Mr. Sorley's written proposition. They opened their eyes. They marvelled, and knew not what to say. I then made as powerful an appeal as I possibly could to their magnanimity. 'Now,' said I, 'gentlemen, by a kind Providence you have been placed in a situation in which you can virtually give ten thousand dollars to Austin College, without taking one dime from your capital. And what a reputation it will give you — a reputation most enviable, and founded upon a rock of granite. It would be better than if you had given us outright a check upon New York for ten thousand dollars. And only think how it would aid me in pleading with other men in behalf of Austin College! Moreover, gentlemen,' continued I, 'if I were not principled against dancing, it would make me dance for joy.' 'Well,' they replied, they would 'take the matter into consideration, and let me know their decision before long.' Day before yesterday I received a written communication from them, containing the following words: 'We agree to re-convey said land, provided the same can be sold for seven dollars and fifty cents per acre, as stated. In reconveying said land, we are well apprized that we surrender that which would result very profitably to us. At the same time, we cannot resist our great desire to see Austin College placed upon a permanent footing.'

"Is not this noble? I go next week to Galveston, Providence permitting, to consummate the affair. And now, we not only consider the 'Baker Professorship of Mathematics' endowed, but we shall have some two or three thousand dollars over and above, to go the endowment of a second Professorship! Surely we have special reason now 'to thank God and take courage.' Of course, my son, you will rejoice with me in the brightening prospects of our noble institution. Do send us some bright-eyed boys at the opening of the next session. Those that are dull you may send to the North. Let smart ones stay at home; let dunces go abroad.

DANIEL BAKER."

(TO HIS SON.)

"HUNTSVILLE, *July 1st*, 1857.

"I am happy to inform you that our endowment scheme goes on swimmingly. During my trip of some five weeks in East Texas, I obtained subscriptions to the amount of sixteen hundred dollars. During my more recent trip to Galveston, Columbia, &c., I obtained for the College, in notes and land, to the amount of some four thousand three hundred dollars. The whole amount, added to the resources of the College, since January last, is something like twenty-six thousand dollars!"

After a short stay at home, he revisited Eastern Texas; while there, he thus writes:

"HENDERSON, *July 13th*, 1857.

"MY DEAR WIFE—'Honour to whom honour is due. My first letter is for you. This is right, for I was acquainted with you before any other member of our family circle; even some forty-four years ago. O what changes since that time!

"I reached this place in time to preach on Saturday night, and three times yesterday (Sabbath.) The people came out in crowds to hear me. Something has awakened a special interest. They tell me of several of their relatives having been converted under my preaching; and I have been told something about some children, namesakes of mine!—all, till I came here, unknown to me. The people seem to hear with a strong hope of being benefitted. God grant that my labours may be greatly blessed. I think a very good impression was made yesterday morning, and particularly last night. No person has joined the Presbyterian church here on profession of faith for some two or three years past. On my coming on Saturday last, I am told a certain man of the world remarked, 'If Mr. B. will only convert twenty-five Henderson sinners, he shall have my riding horse, and he is worth two hundred and fifty dollars.' Well, although Mr. B. cannot convert a single sinner, yet the Lord can make him the means of converting more than twenty-five. A genuine revival of religion here is an event very greatly to be desired.

DANIEL BAKER."

(TO THE SAME.)

"MIDWAY, BETWEEN SHREVEPORT AND LINDEN, *Aug. 27th*, 1857.

"MY DEAR ELIZA—One meeting more, and then 'home, sweet home.' I have had pleasant times both in Shreveport and Linden; seasons of refreshing from the presence of the Lord. The meeting in the latter place was even better than in the former; and as to the matter of the endowment, I have succeeded beyond my expectation—about three thousand dollars! This will do for six weeks' labour. Besides, I have received nearly four hundred dollars in cash. But indeed I have laboured very hard—generally three services every day in the week. And only think how warm the weather has been! I confess I desire some repose, and that in the bosom of my family. Well, I purpose to return as soon as I possibly can; but I do dread the ride—two hundred miles on horseback in such warm weather, is almost too much for one who has reached the period of three-score and six. Last Monday I entered upon my sixty-seventh year—surely I am in 'the sere and yellow leaf.'"

"SHREVEPORT, 28*th*.

"Yes, your letter at last; and verily, one of your most interesting—quite playful. Well, I do like every thing in the form of sunshine and smiles. If, my dear wife, you were in better health, you would be more fond of the land of Beulah, where the sun is ever shining, and the birds are always singing.

DANIEL BAKER."

In the above, as in all his letters, Dr. Baker speaks of the remarkable liberality of the people in giving to Austin College. During his agency in behalf of the Institution, he obtained an amount nearly equal to one hundred thousand dollars, even throwing out of the calculation what has been promised, but not yet paid into the treasury. A large part of this amount was given as the result of meetings—as the reader is aware—during which God was pleased to pour out his Holy Spirit, reviving Christians, and converting sinners. What an illustration is this of the fact—for it is an invariable one—that *giving* is one of the graces wrought by the Spirit of God in the heart; and that the larger the measures of the Holy Spirit poured out, just so much the more do the recipients thereof "abound in this grace also."

CHAPTER XV.

CLOSING SCENES.

On September 9, 1857, Dr. Baker arrived in Huntsville from his journeying in behalf of the College in Eastern Texas. Nearly twenty years have passed since he first conceived the idea of building up in Texas an institution of learning of the highest grade. That idea grew within him through all those years into a fixed purpose; then was born into the world, at Huntsville, an enterprise which grew, under his untiring care and hard-earned sustenance and the prayers of all the brethren in Texas, into a robust childhood, full of fair promise for the future. From the outset, his interest in, and labours for the College, have known nothing but steady increase. So to speak, it was his Benjamin, the darling object of his old age. Enough has already been said in regard to the grand purpose of Dr. Baker and his brethren in establishing this Institution; one thing more must be added fully to explain his enthusiasm in the matter.

The feeling which Texans have for Texas is materially unlike that which even a Kentuckian or a Virginian has towards his own State. Owing to its comparative size and its past history, Texans do not regard Texas as a State merely, but rather, with a certain undefined feeling, as a nation in itself; and its peculiar present and prospective influence upon Mexico does not diminish this impression. No one in Texas partook more largely of this feeling than Dr. Baker; nor could the feeling but grow as he saw the population of the State increase from one hundred thousand, when he first stood upon its soil, to more than six hundred thousand, poured abroad over its vast area, and developing its immense resources.

The Institution of learning for which he laboured, being well located, and securely rooted in the love and pride of the Presbyterian Church, and of all the friends of education in the State, was regarded by him, as has been said, with ever increasing interest. More and more did he feel, that in labouring for this Institution, he was doing the utmost in his power for the cause of learning in Texas, and also for the cause of Presbyterianism; above all, for the welfare of the souls of men, and the glory of the Master he loved so well: and from the first lifting of his hand to the work, that Master had smiled his approval; that Master had given him success at home; had accompanied him wherever he journeyed, pouring out his Holy Spirit, and causing the soil to mellow and yield beneath the hand of his servant a rich harvest of donations for the College, and of souls for heaven.

Thoroughly satisfied he was, that in the whole matter, from first to last, he was in the path of duty. Disappointed and rebuffed very often in his efforts abroad, he was never once discouraged. Perils arose again and again inside of the College, threatening to heave its walls asunder—still his faith faltered not. It was his unalterable belief that God intended to establish the College, and make it an incalculable blessing to this vast territory, the name of whose pioneer it bears; a blessing, perhaps, to those regions beyond yet to be subdued beneath the feet of the Saviour. This was his belief and motive for exertion before the College was born; and never was this conviction stronger than when he was lying upon a bed of death at Austin. What was felt by him, was felt to an equal extent by all the brethren in Texas, save only that in the providence of God the work of carrying out their wishes was devolved more immediately upon him.

This confidence in the purpose and favour of God with respect to the College, meant, with him, only an assured confidence in the divine blessing upon all efforts in its behalf; and from the first he made every possible endeavour that was suggested to him by others, or conceived by himself. Were the lands of the College to be looked after—though in a remote part of the State?—At the earliest moment he was there, guiding his travel-worn horse through almost impenetrable cedar-brakes, searching for the confused corners and almost obliterated bearings; or, in the nearest surveyor's office, poring over musty and bewildered records, more difficult to trace on the paper page than upon the corrugated bark of live-oak and blackjack. Was anything to be accomplished by correspondence?—By the first mail went forth his letters, each written with an accurate precision, to obviate any possible misapprehension.

As to his efforts for the College during his six tours, we have seen how he toiled and how he succeeded. Six tours to beg for the College out of the State! He became more and more reluctant to beg in this way. It was very well when he first began; Texas was then smaller in population, and indefinitely deep in debt; but when that population so swiftly doubled itself, when that debt disappeared, leaving Texas with millions in its chest for present use, and incalculable resources for the future, with the steward in Scripture, it was his feeling, "to beg I am ashamed." Two resources were left him; one was a visit to England, Ireland, and Scotland; and he felt confident that if God led him east of the Atlantic, he would bless him, as he had so richly west of it. But he regarded this only as a last resort; his other resource, in which he had the strongest hope, was in aid from the State. How he hoped, and how he strove, session after session of the Legislature, to obtain this, has already been seen. On his return from Eastern Texas, he remained at home more than a month, making all possible arrangements to prosecute his plans at a meeting of the Legislature to take place at Austin in a few weeks.

Let us pause at this point in the history of this man of God. It is impossible to judge of men by their appearance in the pulpit and the parlour, when away from their own pulpit and home. A higher testimonial to Dr. Baker's character lies in this—that God blessed him fully as much in the pastoral relation as in that of Evangelist. Much as he was esteemed and loved in the churches in which his transient labours were so wonderfully blessed, he was even more esteemed and loved among the people of his own charge; and most by those among whom he lived longest. Yet, at least, it is not how he appeared in the pulpit, but what he was in private life; that is the true test of the man. These pages will be read by many in the various places in each of which for years he was pastor,—and I appeal to you, in so many cities and towns this land over, who knew him best, were his most intimate friends; you who, as ruling elders, sat with him so often in session; you, by whose fireside he has so often been seated in the unreserved intercourse of friendship, before whom he has come in and gone out in the perfect freedom of daily life for years; you who have known him under all the vicissitudes through which men pass in life—I appeal to you, if all that he seemed to be, under the most propitious circumstances, in public, was not confirmed, and more than confirmed, by all that he was in private? But a man may appear to his most intimate friends, and for years, other than he really is in the closer intimacy of his own family. Then, from within this sacred circle we say to you, as before God, that he was to our eyes, in every sense, all he seemed to those without. All? Far more! We knew his hourly spirit and converse; the outgush of his first feelings; his most unpremeditated words and deeds; his fastings and trials; his midnight wrestling, like Jacob, with God, when alone, as he supposed, with the Almighty. It is so—why should we not say it? Among all the names of men—even of patriarchs, prophets, apostles—there is no one whom we have ever venerated and loved in comparison with this man, whom we knew so well. Have we sinned herein? Pardon us, O Lord—the temptation was so great!

But, his defects of character—what were these? That the portrait may be lifelike and true, what are the shadows as well as lights? The biographer has pressed this question upon her, who should know above any one else; he has inquired as widely as possible of all who knew him; he has tasked his own memory to the utmost, and writes—what he has written. All that Dr. Baker seemed to be, he was—alway and everywhere—because he acted under eternal and invariable principles, even those of the religion he preached to others; and because he loved and feared, above all things, One whom he habitually felt to be at all times with him. He walked with God. So far as he was cleansed from sin, it was by the blood of Christ; so far as he was holy, it was by the power of the Holy Spirit, regenerating and sanctifying. He had nothing that he had not received. The glory of any excellence seen in him is, not to him *in* whom, but to Him *by* whom it was wrought. God forbid we should say too much of him, when even an apostle must exclaim, "O wretched man that I am, who shall deliver me from the body of this death?"

He has now attained his sixty-seventh year. The pen of the writer falters, and refuses to attempt to sum up what this servant of Christ has accomplished for his Master so far; it recoils from any effort to delineate farther the features of his character. It is not for a son to form an estimate of the life of a father; let the reader of this volume judge for himself. The facts are already in his hands, save a few remaining—alas, how few!

Deeply indeed must the spotless life, and abundant labours, and holy influence of this man of God have left their impress on the heart of Texas, when, on the first news of his death, the Legislature, in both of its branches, adjourned instantly. Though in the full career of a thronged and excited session, it refused to transact business in the shock of such a loss to the State, expressing in unanimous and heartfelt resolutions their sense of that loss.

"It becomes my painful duty," said a leading statesman upon the floor of the Legislature on that occasion, "to announce to this house the sudden and unexpected intelligence of the death of one of Texas' public benefactors; the Rev. DANIEL BAKER is no more! This sad intelligence burst upon us so suddenly and unexpectedly, that it has been difficult to realize the truth. I could not believe it until I visited the chamber where this great and good man, this venerable father in Israel, died. I have laid my hand on that cold and marble brow, have gazed on that face which I have so often seen lit up with animation and life, but now stamped with the cold impress of death. I have pressed that hand which I have so often grasped before in the warmth of friendship and affection, but now stiffened and cold. I know that he is dead. As a general thing, I am opposed to the obtrusion of our private griefs on this house to the interruption of business; but I consider the death of Dr. Baker a public calamity. He is justly entitled to the claim and rank of one of

Texas' benefactors. His exertions and usefulness were confined to no particular locality, no limited sphere. Possessed of a catholic spirit, of universal love and benevolence towards his fellow-men, he was prompted thereby to extend his sphere of usefulness as wide as possible. There has been scarcely a State in the Union but has heard his eloquent pleadings in behalf of religion and all the great moral interests of society. Twenty years ago I knew the deceased in Alabama. He was then the same devoted, enterprising, assiduous man and minister that he has been here; and since the scene of his usefulness has been transferred to this State, we all know with what untiring efforts he has exerted himself, not only in the cause of his Heavenly Master, but especially in the cause of education. He has left proud monuments in proof of these truths, and in honour to his memory. There stands not two hundred miles from this place, on the brow of a lofty summit, a beautiful edifice, surrounded by shady groves and academic walks. In it is opened a fountain of science, at which near one hundred youths daily drink. This edifice is Austin College, reared principally by the noble exertions of the lamented deceased, whose loss we are this day called to mourn. But, while these monuments stand, and I hope they may long continue so to do in honour of Dr. Baker, *he* is gone."

When the tidings of his death reached Huntsville, his own home, the editor of a paper there, himself not a professor of religion, thus expressed the result of a long acquaintance with him as a fellow-townsman:

"The news of the sudden death of Dr. Baker came like an earthquake on our citizens last Monday night. Hale and vigorous in our midst only a few short weeks ago, he is now at rest. Good and faithful servant, thou art gone! Hard-working Christian, thou hast found thy reward! Who is left to fill thy place here?—not one. Men like our venerable friend are only made once in an age. Alexander, Cæsar, Luther, Cromwell, Napoleon, Jackson—but one of each existed at one time; their places are never filled. So with Dr. Baker, in his sphere; his place cannot be filled. He died at his post. Truly a great man has fallen in Israel."

And these were but the sentiments of every inhabitant of the place. Immediately on hearing the news of his death, a town-meeting spontaneously assembled. By order of the College some time before, a portrait of Dr. Baker had been painted; this was displayed, while speaker after speaker rose from the throng to express, often interrupted with tears, the heart-felt affliction of all. It was determined to remove the remains from Austin, and deposit them in the College campus, to be crowned with a suitable monument, as a lasting memorial to the students, who generation after generation shall flock thither, of the founder and father of the Institution.

As the news of his death passed the boundaries of Texas, it was caught up by journals, secular and religious, and made known over the whole land with various yet unanimous comment. It was communicated by hundreds of pastors to their people from pulpit and in prayer-meeting, filling with sudden sadness houses of worship once overflowing, under his labours, with the gladness of revival. As the tidings spread more and more widely among the families that knew him, in cities, towns, villages, and scattered cabins along the farthest frontier, the exclamations of grief at the tables and firesides of ten thousand households—all these make up the impartial and unfeigned summary of, and comment upon, the Christian character, life, and labours of him who is gone. It is not necessary, it is not expedient, that a son should further speak where so much is said by others.

On the morning of October 22d, 1857, Dr. Baker took his usual affectionate leave of his family, little thinking, he or they, that never more on earth was he to see their faces. His wife followed him, as his horse was led to the block for him to mount. From the hour she had given herself to him, so many years before, to be his wife, she had as faithfully fulfilled the duties allotted to her, by their common Lord, as he had the duties allotted to him. And, as the wife and helpmeet of such a man, her duties were great, beyond what ordinarily devolves upon a minister's wife by far. As the wife of his bosom, as the mother of his children, yea, as her with whom he took, beyond the wont of most husbands, sweet counsel, and walked unto the house of God in company, their relationship to each other had been peculiarly happy; a closer or happier, earth never knew. He is as hale and strong as she is fragile, yet together they have trod the pilgrimage of life, together they approach its end. With anxiety she noticed the difficulty he had in seating himself upon the restive animal, and, with many charges to be careful, she bade him an affectionate adieu. For the first time in a long life, as she afterward remarked, she felt in parting with him, instead of the usual sense of pain, a singular sense of actual pleasure. Was it a premonition of their next meeting? Parting, thus, at the gate of their home, it was a separation of only a few months; they have met since within the gates of their eternal home, never to know parting more.

The Synod of Texas was to meet at Palestine, in Eastern Texas. Reaching this place in safety, he thus wrote to his son at Austin.

"*November 8th*, 1857.

"This is Sabbath evening. I have just returned from the church, where I preached, with some liberty, from the words, 'Come, and go with us.' I left the pastor conversing with several who have applied to be received into the communion of the church. We have had a full and a delightful meeting of the Synod. Every thing was perfectly harmonious. It has proved one of the most interesting meetings of Synod that I ever attended; I trust the results will be most happy. On Saturday night we adjourned, to have a final meeting to-morrow morning at half-past eight o'clock, for the purpose of fraternally mingling our devotions, and bidding each other an affectionate farewell. I set out to-morrow with brother W., and shall, as I suppose, spend the coming

Sabbath with him at Concord and Wheelock. The probability is I shall pass on immediately after the Sabbath to Austin.

"On Wednesday last my horse, frightened by the fluttering of my half-opened umbrella, ran away with me, and I was thrown with violence upon the ground, but, by a kind Providence, I received no serious injury. I intend to be more careful in the use of my umbrella in time to come. But I must not write any more to night, as I have, for a wonder, 'a shocking bad cold,' and writing by candle-light will do my weeping eyes no good."

It was his intention to have returned to Huntsville from Synod before going to Austin; he now determined to proceed to Austin immediately, as the letter shows. Eight years before this, the writer had gone to Austin, had organized a church there with five members, and had been permitted to see it grow steadily into a self-sustaining pastoral charge. For years it had been the wish of the church that Dr. Baker would attend a protracted meeting with them. Though he had occasionally visited Austin, circumstances had always prevented this. In view of this expected visit much prayer had been offered, and it was a matter of ardent desire and fervent prayer on the part of pastor and people that the visit would be attended with a blessing. But it was not to be; perhaps there was too much reliance on an arm of flesh.

Meanwhile the pastor of the church was taken seriously ill. As he lay in his chamber on the evening of Thursday, the 19th of November, 1857, a well-known foot-fall was heard upon the floor of the hall, and a well-known form entered his door. The more than fatherly sympathy with which he greeted the son, the cordial cheerfulness of his manner as he seated himself by the bedside, in the full glow of health, banished the atmosphere of sickness from the chamber as by a burst of sunshine. Embracing his daughter and grandchildren, he immediately recounted the manner in which he had been greeted by a group of members of the Legislature at the door of the livery stable, on alighting from his horse; how they had welcomed him to Austin, and assured him of their sympathy and assistance in obtaining aid from the State for the College—all in his usual lively vein, showing how greatly encouraged he was by the incident—it was but an incident—but encouragement was the atmosphere and element by which he was always surrounded. He complained somewhat of being fatigued, but was up early the next morning, and was engaged the rest of the week with his usual energy and hopefulness among the members of the Legislature, in his effort to obtain money or land for the College by legislative enactment. Upon this he had set his heart, and it was the absorbing theme of his thoughts and conversation to the hour of his death. It need hardly be added that he was treated by the members of the Legislature, and all others, with that marked respect and veneration accorded to him by every individual who knew him, or even met him without knowing who he was; such was the effect produced by his very aspect.

On Sabbath, November 22d, he preached morning

and night to large audiences, his son, the pastor of the church, being still confined to his bed. So great was the interest manifested at the night service, that it was afterward greatly regretted that notice had not been given, and preaching appointed for Monday night also. He had thought of giving such a notice on Sabbath night, he told the sick pastor afterward, but did not like to do so on account of not having previously consulted that pastor; so habitual was his delicacy of feeling in such matters, that he acted thus even when the pastor was his own son. During the ensuing week he laboured with his usual energy in behalf of the College, and all who met with him at this time will bear witness to the fact, that to attain his object he did all that man could. During this week he thus writes to his wife at Huntsville:

"AUSTIN, *November 28th*, 1857.

"I have now been in Austin more than a week, and expect to leave in a few days, on my return home—but not direct. I shall go by the way of Wheelock, where I expect to be in two weeks from this time.

"The boys, my grandchildren, have as much life as need be. H. is really a good boy, and D. is sweet and pretty, but has a high temper, and seems much inclined to teaze and lord it over his brother. Last night, after H. had got into bed, D. insisted upon his rising and coming to him. When H. complied, what did he wish next? That he should go into the closet; and when H. had complied with this whim, what next? He immediately closed the door upon him, and seemed to triumph in the thought that he had made his brother his prisoner. After H. was released, and had again got into bed, the little tyrant insisted upon going over the process again. The little boy is always upon the move, and has his own way of amusing himself. Last night, after putting on his night-shirt, he took a notion that he must equip himself and set out on a journey to another room. So, what does he do—gets his father's boots, puts on his grandpa's hat, which nearly swallowed up his whole head, and then, taking grandpa's walking cane, he must have the door thrown open before him, and away he goes. But, being told that he must say to all, Good-by, he made an attempt to take off his hat and bow to the company, when down he came.

"I have had a very bad cold lately—so hoarse I could not preach on thanksgiving day, as I was requested and expected to do. I hope I shall be able to preach to-morrow; and O that it may be with liberty and success! And so you were in our new church last Sabbath morning. God grant it may be the spiritual birth-place of many a precious soul.

"Our prospects for legislative aid for the College are brightening. Nearly all the members seem disposed to do something. The difficulty was the *basis* or plan; and now I think we have got it. To give one thousand dollars and one league of land for every ten thousand dollars obtained by private subscription or donation: the evidence to be furnished by the records of the College, attested by the Secretary or President of the Board of Trustees, under oath. This plan seems to be deemed by all most equitable and just, and I hope will prevail. In the

House I heard this morning some very complimentary remarks in relation to Austin College and myself; but a good substantial vote would please me much more. My time is very precious."

On the next Sabbath he not only preached morning and night, but made in the afternoon a special address to professing Christians, in accordance with his invariable rule, to speak as often as possible of that blessed Saviour, to preach whom was his delight and business in life. He was quite hoarse in the morning, more so at the afternoon service, and so much so at night that he could hardly speak. In rising to take his text at night, he remarked that he was *about to preach a sermon which, if he knew when he was to die, he would choose as his last;* and this because the sermon was full of Jesus Christ, to a degree unusual even in his preaching. It is Sermon III. in the First Series of his *Revival Sermons;* preached in accordance with a request of an elder of the Austin church, with which he gladly complied. He paused a moment after making the remark, as if considering what he had said, and then solemnly repeated the remark. And it was his last sermon!

Those then present will never forget the ardent though struggling words in which, for the last time on earth, he spoke from the pulpit of the excellency of Christ, the one Mediator between God and man. At the outset of his ministry, this Saviour had been his one theme. As we have seen, his first sermon was from Eph. ii. 8: "By grace are ye saved, through faith; and that not of yourselves: it is the gift of God." Forty years had he preached this

Jesus, wherever and whenever he could. Who can tell how often, or to how many? And who can tell the number of "sheep going astray," who, during these forty years of incessant preaching, were "returned," by his instrumentality, "unto the Shepherd and Bishop of souls?" Scarce a conjecture even can be made of the number. And now, as Jesus Christ was the beginning, so "the end of his conversation" too, was "Jesus Christ, the same yesterday, to-day, and for ever."

His son, being in the pulpit with him, having unbounded faith in the ability to preach, of a father whom he never knew to decline an opportunity of preaching, regarding the hoarseness as a slight and passing matter, and eager for a protracted meeting, such as had been so greatly blessed wherever he had held them, gave notice that his father would preach the next (Monday) night again. By Monday night, however, his hoarseness had so increased that this was impossible, to the disappointment, it may be said, of almost all professing Christians in the community. His affection of the throat did not prevent him from writing to the members of the Legislature as usual, and exerting himself in every way in behalf of the College. He was fully as cheerful as usual at the fireside and the table, glowing with life and hope, and full of pleasant remark and playful rejoinder.

During this week, he thus writes to a son at Huntsville:

"AUSTIN, *December 5th*, 1857.

"I really feel thankful to you and your mother for your joint letter. It is so pleasant to receive letters from home when one is absent; and especially when they enter into details. No home matters are uninteresting to him whose thoughts and affections cluster around his own domestic circle. I have been sick for something more than a week; first a very bad cold, and then a pain in my breast—something like what is called *angina pectoris.* I am going about now, but do not know that I shall be able to go to church to-morrow, to hear your brother William. I hope to be able, however, to start homeward on Tuesday next. I long to be at home, and when once there, I will not be disposed to take such another jaunt for a time, at least on horseback.

"The Legislature have so many things before them, that our College matter is like the hexameter verse, or wounded snake, it 'drags its slow length along.' We hope, however, that in due time something will be done. Rain, rain, rain! O, how much rain! The river is impassable here, even with ferry-boats. I wonder if I shall not have some trouble in getting home. W. crossed the river this morning with Dr. Taylor. It is night, and they have not returned; and to-morrow is the Sabbath, and I cannot preach; but, as it is raining still, it may continue to rain, so that nobody can go out. Well, it is all right. The will of the Lord be done."

His son, above referred to, however, managed to return, and preached morning and night. No language can express the anxiety of that son, that his father might yet be able to hold a protracted meeting in his church. The peculiar circumstances of the case made him even too desirous for this.

Nothing ever gave that father so much pleasure as such a meeting; and, of all places in the world, a meeting in the church of his own son, upon which the blessing of God should rest, no earthly thing could have given him greater pleasure. Yet, the perfect calmness of the father, so energetic, so ardent in every thing, contrasted strongly with the feverishness of the son. It was not that he did not desire the object as heartily, but his faith in God, whose providence prevented, was clear and complete. No language can express the perfect acquiescence of this servant of God, in the will of his Divine Master, in every thing, small and great. Labouring to the utmost of his power for the College and the cause of Christ, it was without fever, without the least perceptible perturbation of manner, or even of feeling, no matter what arose to cross and thwart. And it was a joyful acquiescence too; something almost awful in it; something of the serene repose of heaven, the calm beatitude of a saint in light.

The Sabbath dawned—his last on earth. As has been said, his son preached on that day in his church, which was in full view from the chamber to which his father was confined. Sitting by a table at the window of that chamber, he thus writes to the pastor whose church he had promised to visit on his way back to Huntsville. The entire letter is given—it was his last.

"AUSTIN, *December 6th*, (Sunday,) 1857.

"DEAR BROTHER WILSON—I have been sick, quite sick, for more than a week past. This day I looked out from my chamber upon William's church, and saw crowds wending their way, at the sound of the church-going bell, to the temple of God; but I could not go myself, even to hear my own son. These things being so, I thought I would drop you a line to let you know that it is quite possible that I may not be able to be with you at Concord next Sabbath. I hope, however, I shall; but really from my present state of health, I can say nothing positive even about Wheelock. But one thing I will say—I wish to come, and will, if not providentially prevented. Pray for me.

"Yours, fraternally,

DANIEL BAKER."

When his son returned from church, he told him how delightful it had been to him, to sit at his window looking at the church, thinking that he had a son then preaching therein the glorious gospel—"and I now feel willing to go," added this man of God.

On Monday, feeling somewhat better, he had made up his mind to leave for home, having accomplished all in his power for the College. Against this his son earnestly protested. But in vain was he urged to remain in order to preach more. Aware that his father acted promptly when his mind was once made up, the son resorted to one last device to detain him. As agent of the College, his father was engaged daily in obtaining subscriptions to the endowment of a Professorship, the coupon blank-book of which endowment lay upon the table while they conversed. When all other motives for remaining had been urged in vain, the son drew the book to him, and offered himself to subscribe one hundred dollars to the endowment, if his father would remain over another Sabbath. The father hesitated. As agent for the College, ought he to decline such an offer? He accepted the condition; the subscription was entered, and stands on the books of the College the *last* donation obtained by its agent! This matter being thus settled on Monday, in the afternoon of that day, the father accompanied his son along the streets of Austin for a walk. He walked quite slowly, however, leaning upon the arm of his son, and would often stop, complaining of shortness of breath; in every other respect he seemed the same as ever, as full of life and pleasant talk. Having lost the key of his watch, he called on one or two jewellers; they had none but of gold, and he would buy none but a steel one. "What is the use," he said, "of my spending anything upon myself, who am to be in this world for such a little while?—it will give me pleasure to get anything for *you.*" But this was only common with him; those things ever gave him most pleasure which he purchased for others. "I take vastly more pleasure in seeing you enjoy it than in using it myself," would be his remark.

After tea, on Monday night, feeling somewhat refreshed, he insisted upon going out again to call upon an influential member of the Legislature. In vain he was urged not to do so. "No, something important may be accomplished for the College," he said. It was not that he was rash or imprudent; so unaccustomed was he to sickness, or to failing to do at the moment whatever seemed to be possible to be done then, that he persisted in his intention.

Before he had reached the house of the member, often stopping upon the way to breathe, leaning heavily upon the arm of his son, he regretted having made the attempt. Having arrived at the house, and seated upon the sofa in conversation, though unable to rise when the gentleman first entered the room, he urged the claims of the College as earnestly and powerfully as ever before in his life. It was with great difficulty that he returned home. That night his son slept in the chamber with him, to anticipate every want; but more than once during the night he was wakened by his father walking across the room to wait on himself, rather, with his habitual unselfishness, than disturb his son's slumbers. Towards morning, however, he awoke his son; an idea had occurred to him in regard to the College, and to the College every thing must give way. He then detailed, one by one, ten "strong reasons," as he styled them, why the State should grant aid to the College. Next morning he was not content until they had been written out, printed, and arrangements made to place a copy upon the table of every member of the Legislature.

During Tuesday and Wednesday his feebleness seemed to increase. As usual with him, he was frequent in expressions of gratitude to Dr. M. A. Taylor, his skilful physician, who was also his host; and a great anxiety was manifested to give as little trouble as possible. The conversations had with his son and daughter at this time will never be forgotten by them. He did not seem to know whether he was dangerously ill or not, but with perfect calmness and quietness of spirit he made various remarks, "in case," he said, "I should die"—speaking of such an event with gravity, but perfect unconcern. At one time he alluded to the controversy then going on in regard to the Revision movement in the American Bible Society. Without expressing any opinion on the constitutional question involved, he spoke of his decided preference for Bibles without any headings at all to the chapters—the pure word of God, without even the least human admixture of any kind; and he repeated his often expressed dislike for Bibles having the Apocrypha, or even pictures in them. Speaking of the prospect that the State would not aid the College, he dwelt with pleasure upon his contemplated visit to England. He thought that he might be able to obtain something for the endowment, and that perhaps the same blessing in the conversion of souls might attend him there as elsewhere. This, however, like every thing else, he left serenely in the hands of God. "Every thing is perfectly dark before me," he often said, "but I walk like a child, with my hand in that of my Heavenly Father; he will lead me aright." Little did those who heard him thus speak, imagine how that Father was then drawing his toil-worn child to himself. "All my life I have walked as in a fog," he said: "I never could see far before me; but it always opened up clearly as I advanced."

On Wednesday night Dr. Baker sat until past ten o'clock in conversation with his children and grandchildren. It pleased God, that to the moment of his death he knew nothing of the decrepitude of old age either in body or mind. Never was he more animated in conversation than at this time. For some time, seated in his chair, making shadows with his hands upon the wall for his grandchildren, he shared fully in their merriment, and it was with reluctance that he retired at last to rest.

About midnight he was seized with great difficulty in breathing, arising from diseased action of the heart. His physician relieved him for a time, but before day he was taken with another and more violent paroxysm. This, however, was also relieved. During all this time he was as calm as in ordinary life. When, at his request, his son prayed by his bedside for his recovery, he gently but decidedly rebuked him on rising. "I asked you to pray for the presence of God with me, not for my recovery." Meanwhile he had arranged all his temporal matters, and expressed himself freely and frequently, yet with perfect calmness, in regard to the possibility of his dying. In regard to the College, he exercised only his usual faith when he remarked, that if God took him away, it was because the interest of that Institution would in some way be promoted thereby. In fact, there was no apprehension, no fear, no rapture, no excitement of any kind. His faith in God, his sense of acceptance in Christ, his anticipations of heaven—these were so much his habitual thought and experience in daily life for so many years, that the being brought to the verge of eternity caused him to think and feel in regard to them no more than he was already in the habit of doing; for near half a century his religion had been, literally, his life.

During Thursday morning he remained in bed, receiving, it need not be said, the unremitting care of those who regarded the privilege of so doing as among the most precious of their life. In the course of the morning a religious journal was brought in from the post-office; he read a portion of it, and the rest was read to him by his son, he making frequent and often playful comments. At one time while his daughter was attending on him, something occurred at which he even indulged in laughter. During the afternoon he requested his son to read from the Scriptures. Turning to the fifteenth chapter of first Corinthians, the writer read it to the end. At the conclusion, seeing his father lie still, and with closed eyes, he turned to another part of Scripture, and began to read, when his father motioned with his hand to stop; the tears streaming from his eyes, and the quivering of his lips as he attempted in vain to speak, showed, that in the passage already read, there was that which filled his mind—it could contain no more.

About half-past five o'clock on Thursday afternoon, December 10th—the same day that his son sat by his bed—in turning upon his left side, he was seized with the same difficulty of breathing. Calling others in, the son was absent a short time to summon the physician. Just before, in the course of conversation, his father had said to him, "William, my son, if I should die, I want this epitaph carved on my tomb—'Here lies Daniel Baker, Preacher of the Gospel. A Sinner Saved by Grace.' Remember," he added, "*A Sinner Saved by Grace.*" Even then that son could not believe his father's death so near. One so full of life—so overflowing with health—it was impossible. One so much needed, too, for the College, and in the Church of God! It was impossible! But when his son returned with the physician, the swift and sudden messenger from God was there before him. His father, seated upon the bedside, and labouring for breath, bore upon his face the ashen hue of death. "My son," he exclaimed, reaching out his arms to his son as he entered the door, "My son, my dear son, you are back in time to see your father die!" Seating himself beside him on the bed, and encircling his robust frame in his arms, that son could only agonize in such prayer as rarely rends the bosom of man with the fervour of its silent importunity, that a life so precious might be spared. But it was a nearer and dearer Relative who was taking him away from all earthly relationships to his own bosom. Seated there, in the full vigour of his remarkable general health, in the unclouded use of his intellect, more composedly even than in his usual addresses to the throne of grace, he lifted his eyes to heaven, and exclaimed, in the serene exercise of a perfect faith, "Lord Jesus, into thy hands I commend my spirit!" As the last word passed his lips, he closed his eyes on earth, to open them for ever on the face of that Saviour, whom, not having seen, he so loved.

Let the reader of the Life and Labours of this man of God draw for himself from these pages such lessons of wisdom as they afford. The Christian whom God has not called to the ministry, may derive hence, fresh impulse in the service of the same Master, whatever be the sphere of life in which that Master, for his own glorious purposes, has placed his blood-bought servant. And he who contemplates entering, or has already entered the ministry, let him, as he closes this volume, first kneeling in prayer for Divine assistance, arise and go out into the world with loins newly girded, resolved by the grace of God to equal, or if possible, excel him whose history is herein attempted to be portrayed. The same throne of grace whence he obtained all his power for good is equally open to all alike through Jesus Christ. "After he had served his own generation by the will of God, he fell on sleep," joining in heaven the multitudes of like-minded servants of God, who had gone before him in labour and in reward. "Wherefore, seeing we also are compassed about with so great a cloud of witnesses, let us lay aside every weight, and the sin which doth so easily beset us, and let us run with patience the race that is set before us, looking unto Jesus, the Author and Finisher of our faith."

THE END.

www.ingramcontent.com/pod-product-compliance
Lightning Source LLC
LaVergne TN
LVHW021239110826
845150LV00002B/359